Operational Business Intelligence im Kontext der Analyse und Steuerung von Geschäftsprozessen

Tom Hänel

Operational Business Intelligence im Kontext der Analyse und Steuerung von Geschäftsprozessen

🐎 **Springer** Gabler

Tom Hänel
Klingenberg, Deutschland

Die Arbeit wurde am 14.9.2016 von der Fakultät für Wirtschaftswissenschaften der Technischen Universität Bergakademie Freiberg als Dissertation angenommen

ISBN 978-3-658-16634-2   ISBN 978-3-658-16635-9   (eBook)
DOI 10.1007/978-3-658-16635-9

Die Deutsche Nationalbibliothek verzeichnet diese Publikation in der Deutschen National-bibliografie; detaillierte bibliografische Daten sind im Internet über http://dnb.d-nb.de abrufbar.

Gedruckt auf säurefreiem und chlorfrei gebleichtem Papier

Springer Gabler ist Teil von Springer Nature
Die eingetragene Gesellschaft ist Springer Fachmedien Wiesbaden GmbH
Die Anschrift der Gesellschaft ist: Abraham-Lincoln-Str. 46, 65189 Wiesbaden, Germany

VORWORT

„Drum grüß ich tausendmal mein Pretzschendorf im Tal"
(aus dem Pretzschendorfer Heimatwalzer)

Die vorliegende Dissertation ist im Rahmen meiner Tätigkeit als wissenschaftlicher Mitarbeiter am Institut für Wirtschaftsinformatik der TU Bergakademie Freiberg entstanden. Mein besonderer Dank richtet sich an erster Stelle an Herrn Univ.-Prof. Dr. Carsten Felden. Er hat die Arbeit von der Themenfindung bis hin zur Veröffentlichung betreut und mir stets die Freiheit gelassen, die ich für die Bearbeitung des Themas benötigte. Darüber hinaus war es ihm ein wichtiges Anliegen, dass die Ergebnisse international publiziert werden. So sind fast alle der Arbeit zugrunde liegenden Forschungsbeiträge unter seiner Koautorenschaft entstanden, der in jedem Fall eine inhaltliche und sprachliche Qualitätsverbesserung zu verdanken ist. Auch möchte ich mich für die mit den Publikationen verbundenen Konferenzteilnahmen bedanken, die es mir ermöglicht haben, neben der Arbeit an der Universität auch die Welt kennen zu lernen.

Bedanken möchte ich mich bei Prof. Dr. Hans-Georg Kemper für die Übernahme des Zweitgutachtens. Mein herzlicher Dank gilt weiterhin Prof. Dr. Andreas Horsch für den Vorsitz im Promotionsausschuss. Ebenso danke ich Prof. Dr. Jan C. Bongaerts und Prof. Dr. Rudolf Kawalla für die Mitwirkung in diesem Gremium und für ihre wohlwollende Unterstützung im Rahmen meiner Forschungstätigkeiten.

Allen Promovierenden des Instituts für Wirtschaftsinformatik danke ich für die zahlreichen Diskussionen inhaltlicher und methodischer Natur, die wir in monatlichen CC-Meetings sowie zur Summer und Winter School geführt haben. Ein besonderer Dank gilt an dieser Stelle Claudia Koschtial für die Organisation und die Einblicke in das wissenschaftliche Arbeiten. Auch allen anderen Kollegen am Institut sei der herzliche und offene Umgang untereinander gedankt, der es ebenso zuließ, ernste Worte untereinander auszusprechen. Marco Pospiech danke ich besonders für seine Kollegialität im gemeinsamen Büro und die vielen interessanten Gespräche quer über den Bürotisch. Ihm und ferner Michael Schulz, seinerzeit an der Phillips-Universität Marburg, danke ich auch als Mitautor für die erfolgreiche Zusammenarbeit.

Zu guter Letzt richtet sich mein Dank an Familie und Freunde für die Geduld und all die guten Wünsche. Anke Demmerling danke ich für die liebevollen Aufmunterungen und ganz besonders für die Rechtschreibkorrektur kurz vor Abgabe der Arbeit. Der größte Dank gebührt meinen lieben Eltern, die mich mit ihrer Weitsicht auf meinem gesamten Bildungsweg unterstützt haben. Anfängliche und von Zeit zu Zeit wiederkehrende Zweifel, vielleicht den falschen Weg eingeschlagen zu haben, konnten sie stets ausräumen und mich beständig, in humorvoller Art und Weise, dabei bekräftigen meinen Weg weiter zu gehen. Daher ist ihnen die Arbeit gewidmet.

Tom Hänel

ABSTRACT

Die Messung der Leistungsfähigkeit von Geschäftsprozessen ist ein elementarer Bestandteil des Geschäftsprozessmanagements. Soll-Ist-Vergleiche zwischen Leistungskenngrößen und Zielvorgaben ermöglichen eine kontinuierliche Verbesserung der Geschäftsprozesse eines Unternehmens. Als Datenquelle dienen operative IT-Systeme, die während der Prozessausführung zum Einsatz kommen. Für eine Leistungsbeurteilung von Geschäftsprozessen über ihren gesamten Prozessablauf hinweg müssen die dabei verteilt generierten Prozessdaten zusammengeführt und vereinheitlicht werden. In diesem Zusammenhang bietet Operational Business Intelligence (OpBI), aus der Perspektive der analytischen Informationssysteme (IS) heraus argumentierend, eine IT-basierte Unterstützung hinsichtlich der Integration, Aufbereitung und Präsentation von Prozessdaten. Dies ermöglicht eine automatisierte und standardisierte Bereitstellung von entscheidungsrelevanten Informationen bezüglich der Leistungsfähigkeit von Geschäftsprozessen. Um diese mithilfe von OpBI leistungsorientiert analysieren und steuern zu können, sind jedoch Technologien, Werkzeuge und Methoden aus dem Bereich der analytischen Informationssysteme mit den fachlichen Fragestellungen einer Analyse und Steuerung von Geschäftsprozessen in Einklang zu bringen. Diese Herausforderung wird in der vorliegenden Forschungsarbeit anhand von zwei Forschungszielen untersucht:

- Forschungsziel 1 besteht in der Schaffung eines IS-spezifischen Verständnisses von OpBI im Kontext der Analyse und Steuerung von Geschäftsprozessen.
- Forschungsziel 2 besteht in der Entwicklung IS-spezifischer Gestaltungsperspektiven für OpBI im Kontext der Analyse und Steuerung von Geschäftsprozessen.

Zur Erreichung der Forschungsziele wird in der Arbeit nach einem Mehrmethodenansatz vorgegangen, der wissenschaftliche Verfahren für einen analytischen und einen aktionalen Erkenntnisgewinn vereint. Im Ergebnis liegen eine Themenbegründung, eine begriffliche Abgrenzung, eine Anwendbarkeitsuntersuchung sowie Gestaltungsempfehlungen vor. Die Forschungsarbeit impliziert eine allgemeine Wissensbasis zum Verständnis der OpBI im Kontext der Analyse und Steuerung von Geschäftsprozessen. Im Rahmen einer fallspezifischen Wissensanwendung werden eine multidimensionale Datenmodellierung und eine CASE-basierte Systemgestaltung vorgeschlagen, um eine automatisierte Integration und eine standardisierte Analyse von Prozessdaten zu bewerkstelligen.

INHALTSVERZEICHNIS

ABBILDUNGSVERZEICHNIS

TABELLENVERZEICHNIS

ABKÜRZUNGSVERZEICHNIS

ADAPT	Application Design for Analytical Processing Technologies
APC	Advanced Process Control
BARC	Business Application Research Center
BI	Business Intelligence
BPI	Business Process Intelligence
BPM	Business Process Management
BPR	Business Process Reengineering
CASE	Computer Aided/Assisted Software Engineering
CPPS	Cyberphysisches Produktionssystem
ERP	Enterprise Resource Planning
ETL	Extract, Transform, Load
IS	Informationssystem
IT	Informationstechnologie
KVP	Kontinuierlicher Verbesserungsprozess
MES	Manufacturing Execution System
MI	Manufacturing Intelligence
OLAP	Online Analytical Processing
OpBI	Operational Business Intelligence
PDCA	Plan-Do-Check-Act
PDM	Produktdatenmanagement
PPM	Process Performance Management
SPC	Statistical Process Control
TCT	Total Cycle Time
TDWI	The Data Warehousing Institute
TQM	Total Quality Management

1 Einleitung

Die Analyse und Steuerung von Geschäftsprozessen charakterisiert organisatorische Fähigkeiten in Wettbewerb stehender Unternehmen. Derartige Kompetenzen sind aus Sicht des Geschäftsprozessmanagements notwendig, um betriebliche Abläufe zu beurteilen und darauf bezugnehmend Handlungserfordernisse zu koordinieren. (Bucher und Winter 2009) Eine verstärkte Durchdringung der Unternehmen mit Informationstechnologie (IT) und damit einhergehend eine steigende Vernetzung beeinflussen die Unternehmensprozesse sowie die Lieferanten- und Kundenbeziehungen (Laudon et al. 2010). Aus organisatorischer Sicht verstärkt diese Dynamik die Notwendigkeit auf verschiedene Einflussparameter flexibel zu reagieren und die Geschäftsprozesse immer wieder anzupassen (Becker und Kahn 2005). Derzeit herrscht ein vielfältiges Angebot an Konzepten vor, die den Unternehmen eine wirksame Entscheidungsunterstützung anbieten. In diesem Zusammenhang wurde mit Operational Business Intelligence (OpBI) ein IT-basierter Ansatz zur Diskussion gestellt (White 2005), der eine Analyse von tagesaktuellen Daten aus dem operativen Entscheidungsumfeld unterstützt (Eckerson 2007). Ein Ziel der analytischen Bemühungen von OpBI ist die Schaffung von Transparenz hinsichtlich Struktur und Leistungsfähigkeit von Geschäftsprozessen, um die Prozessflexibilität zu steigern (Ferguson 2008). OpBI unterstützt Fähigkeiten von Managern aus dem operativen Entscheidungsumfeld, um situationsbedingt in Prozesse einzugreifen und diese permanent zu verbessern (Davis et al. 2009). Die Relevanz des Themas bekräftigen aktuelle Managementstudien. Nach einer Untersuchung des TDWI (The Data Warehousing Institute) im April 2014 betrachten 53 Prozent der befragten Unternehmen operative Abläufe als wichtigstes Anwendungsfeld für analytische IT-Werkzeuge und BI-Techniken (Russom et al. 2014). Die BI-Studie der Unternehmensberatung BARC (Business Application Research Center) aus dem Jahr 2014 zeigt OpBI als einen der stärksten Trends im BI-Umfeld auf (BARC 2014). Gemäß dieser Befragung arbeiten 55 Prozent der Befragten an entsprechenden Vorhaben, während 23 Prozent eine Einführung von OpBI planen. Dies steht im Einklang mit den Ergebnissen einer im Jahr 2013 durchgeführten Studie im nordamerikanischen Raum. Demnach sind 67 Prozent von 248 befragten Unternehmen daran interessiert, analytische IT-Werkzeuge zur Verbesserung von Geschäftsprozessen einzusetzen (Henschen 2013).

Die Diskussion um OpBI verfolgt aus Sicht der Wirtschaftsinformatik eine Etablierung von analytischen Informationssystemen (IS) in das Management von Geschäftsprozessen (Gluchowski et al. 2009). Dabei sind vor einem IS-spezifischen Hintergrund technische, organisatorische und managementorientierte

Aspekte zu berücksichtigen (Heinrich et al. 2011). Eine derartige Differenzierung hinsichtlich des Einsatzes und der Entwicklung von Informationssystemen wird im Spannungsfeld der OpBI jedoch gemeinhin vernachlässigt. Der zunächst in der Managementliteratur (z. B. Davis et al. 2009; Arnett 2009; Eckerson 2007; White 2006) popularisierte Begriff ist überwiegend technisch geprägt. So stehen z. B. Erweiterungen von Soft- und Hardwarekomponenten im Vordergrund der Argumentation, um analytische Anwendungssysteme leistungsfähiger und zuverlässiger zu gestalten. Es fehlt jedoch an einer Auseinandersetzung, inwiefern die vielfältigen technischen Optionen mit den fachlichen Fragestellungen einer Analyse und Steuerung von Geschäftsprozessen in Einklang gebracht werden können. Neben diesem Mangel an Anwendungsorientierung existieren zusätzlich andere IT-basierte Konzepte im Kontext des Geschäftsprozessmanagements, die auf den ersten Blick eine weitreichende Ähnlichkeit zur OpBI aufweisen. Dies suggeriert eine scheinbare Austauschbarkeit der Konzepte, die in einer tiefergreifenden Auseinandersetzung zu einem Abgrenzungsproblem führt. Im Hinblick auf dieses Spannungsfeld besteht ein Forschungsbedarf hinsichtlich der Relevanz und IS-spezifischen Manifestierung der OpBI im Rahmen eines Managements von Geschäftsprozessen. Die damit verbundene Untersuchung wird anhand von zwei Forschungszielen geleitet:

- Forschungsziel 1 besteht in einer Klassifikation von OpBI in den Kontext der Analyse und Steuerung von Geschäftsprozessen, um ein IS-spezifisches Verständnis zu schaffen.

- Forschungsziel 2 besteht in einer Anwendung von OpBI im Kontext der Analyse und Steuerung von Geschäftsprozessen, um IS-spezifische Gestaltungsperspektiven zu entwickeln.

Die Forschungsziele adressieren eine Optimierung der Informationsversorgung für Fach- und Führungskräfte im Rahmen der Leistungsmessung und -beurteilung von Geschäftsprozessen. Dies setzt aus Sicht des Geschäftsprozessmanagements eine Gestaltung, Dokumentation und Implementierung der Prozesse voraus (Hammer 2015). Die Nutzung von analytischen Informationssystemen erfolgt zum Zweck des Prozesscontrollings und der Prozessoptimierung (Sesselmann und Schmelzer 2008). Dabei konzentriert sich die IT-Unterstützung auf den Betrieb von bereits vorhandenen Prozessen, um die Überwachung von Geschäftsprozessen anhand von prozessualen Kennzahlen voranzutreiben (Allweyer 2012). Die Grundlage einer kennzahlenbasierten Leistungsbewertung bilden im Prozessmanagement die Parameter Qualität, Zeit und Kosten (Gaitanidis et al. 1994). Dazu erforderliche Aktivitäten von Managern und Entscheidungsträgern werden in einer gegenwärtigen Diskussion mit IT-basierten Fähigkeiten für eine Sammlung, Verarbeitung und Analyse von Prozessdaten in Verbindung gebracht (Vukšić et al. 2013). Diese Verankerung von analytischen IT-Funktionalitäten spiegelt sich ebenso im Process Performance Management (PPM) wider (Allweyer 2012; Sesselmann und Schmelzer 2008). PPM ist jedoch nicht auf eine spezifische IT-

Unterstützung festgelegt (Blasini 2013), sodass eine konkrete Ausgestaltung von Informationssystemen konzeptionell nicht vorgesehen ist. Die Untersuchung der Vorteilhaftigkeit von OpBI bestimmt in diesem Zusammenhang den Fokus der Forschungsarbeit. Aufwand und nutzenspezifische Aspekte einer OpBI-basierten Entscheidungsunterstützung werden vor dem Hintergrund realer Anwendungsszenarien aus dem Produktions- und Dienstleistungsbereich betrachtet. Dabei wird ein Wissenstransfer zur Lösung spezifischer Praxisprobleme vollzogen.

In der Wirtschaftsinformatik grenzen die Gesichtspunkte Mensch, Aufgabe und IT in ihrem Zusammenwirken die zu betrachtenden Forschungsgegenstände ein (Heinrich et al. 2011; Gluchowski et al. 2008; Felden 2006). Diese IS-spezifischen Elemente sind für eine OpBI-basierte Entscheidungsunterstützung im Verlauf der Forschung zu präzisieren, um Gestaltungsmöglichkeiten für eine Integration und Analyse von Prozessdaten aus fachlicher und technischer Sicht abzuleiten. Der wissenschaftliche Beitrag der Arbeit liegt in der Erkenntnisgenerierung für ein Verständnis und eine Entwicklung von OpBI im Rahmen der Analyse und Steuerung von Geschäftsprozessen. Die Notwendigkeit dieser Betrachtungsweise ist Gegenstand der Diskussion in Kapitel 2. Im Anschluss daran stellt Kapitel 3 den Forschungsrahmen der Arbeit vor. Kapitel 4 beschreibt die Ergebnisse, die im Verlauf der Forschungsarbeit erzielt werden konnten. Dies erfolgt unter Bezugnahme auf bereits publizierte und sich im Publikationsprozess befindende Forschungsbeiträge. In Kapitel 5 werden die Forschungsergebnisse hinsichtlich Vollständigkeit, Generalisierbarkeit und Erreichung der Forschungsziele diskutiert. Abschließend zieht Kapitel 6 ein Fazit und zeigt Perspektiven für zukünftige Forschungsaktivitäten auf.

2 Notwendigkeit einer Operational Business Intelligence für eine Analyse und Steuerung von Geschäftsprozessen

Das Thema der Forschungsarbeit ist eine Untersuchung der OpBI im Kontext der Analyse und Steuerung von Geschäftsprozessen. In Abschnitt 2.1 erfolgen eine Beschreibung des Diskursbereichs und eine Auseinandersetzung mit den dazu in Beziehung stehenden Themengebieten. Im Anschluss an diese Diskussion wird in Abschnitt 2.2 der Beitrag der Forschungsarbeit aufgezeigt.

2.1 Diskursbereich der Forschungsarbeit

In den Diskursbereich fließen die Themengebiete der Entscheidungsunterstützung und des Geschäftsprozessmanagements gleichermaßen ein (siehe Abbildung 1). Der englischsprachige Begriff Business Process Management (BPM) wird synonym zum Geschäftsprozessmanagement verwendet.

Abbildung 1. Diskursbereich der Arbeit

Das Themenfeld der Entscheidungsunterstützung thematisiert eine adäquate Informationsversorgung von Entscheidungsträgern (Hansen und Neumann 2009, S. 999ff). Bereits Simon (1960) unterscheidet im Entscheidungsprozess verschiedene Phasen zur Erkennung von Entscheidungsproblemen sowie zur Generierung und zur Auswahl von Handlungsalternativen. Diese Phasen der Entscheidungsfindung sind fortbestehend Gegenstand der Diskussion geblieben und bilden den Ausgangspunkt für betriebswirtschaftliche Problemlösungen (Lassmann 2006, S. 414). In diesem Zusammenhang ist eine IT-Unterstützung zur Informationsversorgung von Entscheidungsträgern charakteristisch für analytische Informationssysteme (Chamoni und Gluchowski 2010). Die grundlegenden Betrachtungsperspektiven einer Entscheidungsunterstützung sind universell einsetzbare Informations- und Kommunikationstechniken, betriebliche Aufgabenstellungen sowie die Anwender und Benutzer von IT-Systemen, die eine Aufgabenerfüllung begleiten (Gluchowski et al. 2008, S. 2).

Das Konzept der Business Intelligence (BI) verfolgt vor diesem Hintergrund die Generierung von handlungsorientiertem Wissen infolge einer Transformation von verteilt vorgehaltenen Unternehmens- und Wettbewerbsdaten (Grothe und Gentsch 2000, S. 19). Um die erforderlichen Daten zu sammeln, zu speichern und zu analysieren, wird auf Anwendungen, Technologien und Prozesse der analytischen Informationssysteme zurückgegriffen, damit Fachanwender bessere Entscheidungen treffen können (Watson 2009). BI umfasst Technologien zur Integration, Analyse und Darstellung von Daten, wie z. B. Data Warehousing (Inmon 2005; Kimball und Ross 2002), Online Analytical Processing (OLAP) (Codd et al. 1993), Data Mining (Han und Kamber 2012), ETL (Sen und Sinha 2005) sowie Dashboards und Portale (Gluchowski et al. 2008, S. 16). Das BI-Konzept wird durch die begriffliche Erweiterung zu einer OpBI mit dem Geschäftsprozessmanagement in Verbindung gebracht (Gluchowski et al. 2009). Im Rahmen der Arbeit dient folgende Definition der begrifflichen Präzisierung der OpBI:

> *OpBI adressiert die IT-basierte Integration und Analyse von Prozessdaten, um Entscheidungsträgern die prozessuale Leistungsfähigkeit zu Gunsten einer kontinuierlichen Verbesserung der Gestaltung und Ausführung von Geschäftsprozessen transparent zu machen.*

Im Rahmen der OpBI-Definition werden die charakterisierenden Aspekte der BI hinsichtlich Entscheidungsunterstützung, Datensammlung, Datenaufbereitung, Informationsdarstellung und geschäftsrelevanter Informationen (Schrödl 2006, S. 12f) für eine Analyse und Steuerung von Geschäftsprozessen herangezogen. OpBI unterstützt damit die Sammlung und Aufbereitung von leistungsbezogenen Prozessdaten während der Prozessausführung. Die erhobenen Daten werden im Zuge einer Leistungsanalyse in handlungsorientiertes Prozesswissen transformiert. Dieses Wissen bildet die Grundlage für Entscheidungsträger, um die Prozessausführung durch Managementmaßnahmen zu beeinflussen. Gleichermaßen liefern die Analyseergebnisse Input für eine Beurteilung der Prozessgestaltung. Das dargelegte Verständnis von OpBI im Rahmen der Forschungsarbeit wird in Abbildung 2 veranschaulicht.

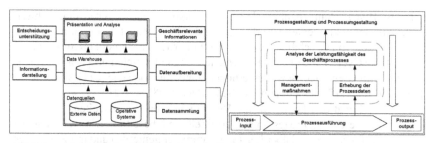

Abbildung 2. OpBI im Kontext der Analyse und Steuerung von Geschäftsprozessen

Abbildung 2 macht deutlich, dass OpBI eine Verknüpfung von Prozessgestaltung und Prozessausführung ermöglicht. Ein Prozess ist dabei zunächst einmal eine Abfolge von Arbeitsaktivitäten mit festgelegtem Anfang und festgelegtem Ende (Davenport 1993, S. 5). Es erfolgt eine Umwandlung von definierten Eingaben in spezifische Ergebnisse, die die Produkte eines Prozesses charakterisieren (ISO9000 2005, S. 23f). Geschäftsprozesse repräsentieren gebündelte Einzelprozesse, die sich funktional über ein gesamtes Unternehmen erstrecken und werthaltige Ergebnisse aus Sicht der Kunden produzieren (Hammer und Champy 1996, S. 52). Die Grundlage einer derartigen Geschäftsprozessorientierung bildet die Auffassung eines Unternehmens als Wertschöpfungskette (Value Chain) (Harmon 2014, S. 3).

Der Ansatz der Value Chain beschreibt im Rahmen der unternehmensbezogenen Leistungserbringung ein System von wertschaffenden und unterstützenden Prozessen, die untereinander in Beziehung stehen (Porter 1985, S. 36f). In den Prozessen der Wertschöpfungskette erfolgt die physische Tätigkeitsverrichtung sowie begleitend dazu eine Erfassung, Bearbeitung und Lenkung von prozessualen Daten, die zur Verrichtung der Tätigkeiten notwendig sind (Porter und Millar 1985). Eine Nutzung und eine Aufbereitung von Prozessdaten als Kenngrößen zur Bewertung der Leistungsfähigkeit von Geschäftsprozessen sind fortbestehend Gegenstand der Diskussion geblieben, um während einer kundenorientierten Wertschöpfung festgelegte Ziel- und Messgrößen einzuhalten (Dumas et al. 2013; Sesselmann und Schmelzer 2008, S. 65; Zairi 1997; Davenport und Beers 1995). Analytische Betrachtungen zur Überwachung, Steuerung und Verbesserung von Geschäftsprozessen sind demzufolge, zunächst einmal losgelöst von der Diskussion um OpBI, elementare und originäre Bestandteile des Geschäftsprozessmanagements (vgl. z.B. Hammer 2015, S. 5).

Das Geschäftsprozessmanagement vereint gegenwärtig die Konzepte des Business Process Reengineering (BPR) und der kontinuierlichen Prozessverbesserung (Hammer 2015; Reijers et al. 2010; Scheer et al. 2005). BPR betrachtet Prozesse ganzheitlich mit einem Fokus auf Kundenorientierung und macht die Leistungsfähigkeit von Prozessen von deren Gestaltung abhängig (Hammer und

Champy 1996). Demgegenüber legen qualitätsbezogene Ansätze den Schwerpunkt auf eine inkrementelle Verbesserung der Prozessausführung, um die Leistungsfähigkeit von Geschäftsprozessen kontinuierlich zu steigern (Neumann et al. 2005). Total Cycle Time (TCT), Kaizen oder Six Sigma bieten im Zusammenhang von evolutionären Prozessverbesserungen eine methodische Unterstützung an (Koch 2011, S. 117; Sesselmann und Schmelzer 2008, S. 372):

- TCT legt den Fokus auf die Verkürzung von Prozesszeiten. Es werden Barrieren im Prozessablauf ermittelt und beseitigt. Die Wirkung der Maßnahmen wird über Leistungsparameter gemessen und mit Zielgrößen verglichen. (Sesselmann und Schmelzer 2008, S. 383ff)

- Kaizen betont die Motivation und Befähigung von Führungskräften und Mitarbeitern hinsichtlich einer ständigen Verbesserung der Arbeitsprozesse und der Vorgänge im sozialen Umfeld (Imai 1992, S. 23). Im Vordergrund steht die Beseitigung von Verschwendungen jeglicher Art (Koch 2011, S. 127ff). Dazu stehen statistische Qualitäts- und Managementwerkzeuge sowie Verfahrensweisen und Checklisten zur Verfügung (Brunner 2014, S. 12ff).

- Six Sigma ist eine systematische Projektmanagement-Methode, die auf der Nutzung von Daten und statistischen Analysen basiert (Töpfer 2007, S. 45). Die Qualität der Prozesse wird anhand von Kennzahlen gemessen und verbessert (Toutenburg und Knöfel 2009, S. 20f). Das Ziel ist eine Gestaltung und Steuerung von Prozessen, sodass die Prozessergebnisse zu 99,99966 Prozent (6σ) fehlerfrei sind (Töpfer und Günther 2007, S. 3). Der Ursprung von Six Sigma liegt in der Betrachtung von industriellen Prozessen. Eine Anwendung der Verbesserungsmethode hat im Zeitverlauf auch administrative Prozesse und Dienstleistungsumgebungen erreicht (Koch 2011, S. 148f).

Die systematische Erfassung und Auswertung von Daten ist ein fundamentaler Bestandteil der vorgestellten Methoden, um einen kontinuierlichen Verbesserungsprozess (KVP) zu unterstützen. Insbesondere Kaizen wird dabei im deutschsprachigen Raum mit dem KVP gleichgesetzt (Kostka und Kostka 2013, S.12). Diesem Bestreben nach stetiger Weiterentwicklung der Prozesse liegt der Plan-Do-Check-Act-Zyklus (PDCA-Zyklus) zugrunde (Sesselmann und Schmelzer 2008, S. 376f). In einem Kreislauf werden Tätigkeiten zur Planung (Plan), Durchführung (Do) und Überprüfung (Check) von Prozessverbesserungen sowie zur Anpassung oder Standardisierung (Act) von Prozessen durchlaufen (Imai 1992, S. 86ff). Während eines Durchlaufs wird eine bestimmte Qualitätsstufe erreicht und über weitere Zyklen im Zeitverlauf gesteigert (Kostka und Kostka 2013, S. 15ff). Diese ständige Qualitätsverbesserung ist gleichermaßen kennzeichnend für das Total Quality Management (TQM) (Koch 2011, S. 198). Damit ist ein umfassendes Führungskonzept von Unternehmen verbunden, das die Ermittlung und Umsetzung von Qualitätsverbesserungen in allen Unternehmensbereichen in den Vordergrund stellt (Sesselmann und Schmelzer 2008, S. 17). Die Ausrichtung des Unternehmens an Geschäftsprozessen bildet neben der Mitarbeiter- und Kundenorientierung eine grundlegende Dimension des TQM (Koch 2011, S. 199ff).

Im Resümee sind prozessorientierte Verbesserungsmaßnahmen im Sinne des BPR fundamental auf die Gestaltung von Geschäftsprozessen oder, dem Paradigma der Qualitätsmanagementansätze folgend, inkrementell auf deren Ausführung gerichtet. Die datengetriebene Planung, Überwachung und Auswertung von Geschäftsprozessen zum Zweck der kontinuierlichen Verbesserung fällt dabei in den Aufgabenbereich des Prozesscontrollings (Allweyer 2012, S. 385; Kronz 2005). In diesem Teilbereich des Geschäftsprozessmanagements werden wiederkehrende Aktivitäten adressiert, um sich im laufenden Betrieb befindende Prozesse unter verschiedenen Gesichtspunkten zu analysieren und zu steuern. Aus operativer Sicht ist damit die stetige Messung und Kontrolle von Prozessleistungen auf Basis von Kennzahlen verbunden (Sesselmann und Schmelzer 2008, S. 256). Um Transparenz hinsichtlich der Prozessleistung zu schaffen, können die Parameter Kosten, Zeit und Qualität herangezogen werden, die wiederum den Ergebnisparameter Kundenzufriedenheit bilden (Gaitanidis et al. 1994, S. 15f). Für eine Erhebung der zugrunde liegenden Daten bestehen nach Allweyer (2012, S. 387f) folgende Möglichkeiten:

- manuelle Datenerhebung,
- Datenerhebung durch operative IT-Systeme sowie
- eine Aufzeichnung der Daten durch Workflow- oder BPM-Systeme.

Manuelle Erhebungen sind an Protokollierungsaktivitäten von Mitarbeitern eines Unternehmens gebunden. Mithilfe der erfassten Daten werden die Prozesskennzahlen per Hand berechnet. Die Datenerhebung kann mit Schätzungen einhergehen, um den damit einhergehenden Aufwand zu reduzieren. Die Eignung von rein manuellen Verfahren zur Datenerhebung im Rahmen einer kontinuierlichen Ermittlung von Prozesskennzahlen ist einzelfallabhängig und wird durch IT-Systeme ergänzt. (Allweyer 2012, S. 387)

Operative IT-Systeme werden eingesetzt, um die notwendigen Daten zur Verrichtung von prozessbezogenen Tätigkeiten vorzuhalten. In rein funktional ausgerichteten Systemen ist eine genaue Zuordnung von Daten zu bestimmten Prozessen nicht explizit vorgesehen (Allweyer 2012, S. 387). Geschäftsprozessorientierte Systeme, wie z. B. ERP-Systeme, arbeiten funktionsübergreifend. Die Systeme sind transaktional ausgerichtet und unterstützen die Bearbeitung von Prozessaufgaben ablaufgesteuert (Markus et al. 2000). Der Analysefokus liegt auf Abfragen z. B. hinsichtlich des Bearbeitungsstatus oder des Ressourcenverbrauchs. Eine multidimensionale Betrachtung von Effektivitäts- und Effizienzkenngrößen, wie sie für Steuerungsmechanismen im Geschäftsprozessmanagement angestrebt wird (Sesselmann und Schmelzer 2008, S. 11), ist per se nicht vorgesehen.

Workflow- oder BPM-Systeme ermöglichen eine Automatisierung und eine Parallelisierung von prozessbezogenen Bearbeitungsvorgängen (Seidlmeier 2002, S. 141). Das Ziel ist eine zeitliche und arbeitsplatzübergreifende Koordination der Prozessabläufe, während die Ausführung der zugrunde liegenden Aktivitäten weiterhin durch operative IT-Systeme unterstützt wird (van der Aalst und van Hee 2004, S. 146). Aus IT-Sicht repräsentieren Workflow- oder BPM-Systeme Softwarelösungen, die die Definition, die Ausführung und die Nachverfolgung von Geschäftsprozessen unterstützen (Grigori et al. 2004). Vor diesem Hintergrund werden Ereignisse, wie z. B. Prozessstart, Zeitpunkt der Fertigstellung, Eingabe- und Ausgabeparameter, beteiligte Ressourcen oder Störungen systemseitig aufgezeichnet. Diese Daten können zur Modellierung und Identifizierung von Prozessstrukturen im Kontext des Process Mining eingesetzt werden (van der Aalst 2011). Eine Kennzahlenbetrachtung zur Leistungsmessung ist innerhalb von Workflow- oder BPM-Systemen jedoch nicht vorgesehen (Allweyer 2012, S. 388; Kang et al. 2011).

Sowohl operative IT-Systeme als auch Workflow- oder BPM-Systeme zeigen Schwächen bei der Ermittlung und Auswertung von Kennzahlen im Rahmen der Leistungsanalyse von Prozessen. Zur Überwindung der beschriebenen Defizite wird die zu Beginn des Abschnitts 2.1 (Seite 23) aus der Perspektive der BI angesprochene Entscheidungsunterstützung in die Diskussion über Effizienz- und Effektivitätsbetrachtungen von Geschäftsprozessen eingebracht (Allweyer 2012, S. 390ff). Bereits Jost und Scheer (2002) weisen darauf hin, dass in diesem Kontext die Weiterentwicklung von bestehenden BI-Werkzeugen vorangetrieben werden sollte. Als Folgeerscheinung dieser Erweiterung der BI um geschäftsprozessorientierte Aspekte stehen eine Vielzahl von Begrifflichkeiten und Ansätzen zur Diskussion. Zunächst wurden Werkzeuge zur Leistungsmessung von Geschäftsprozessen mit dem Begriff Business Process Intelligence (BPI) etikettiert (Jost und Scheer 2002). Die Forderung nach einer zeitnahen Entscheidungsfindung im Rahmen des Geschäftsprozessmanagements hat sich durch die Wortverbindung Real-Time mit Konzepten und Technologien der BI niedergeschlagen (Russom et al. 2014; Hackathorn 2004). Eng verknüpft mit der Betrachtung einer Entscheidungsfindung in Echtzeit, wurde eine Informationsbereitstellung zum richtigen Zeitpunkt (Right-Time BI) thematisiert (Davis 2006; White 2004).

Das Ziel, zeitkritische Entscheidungen unter Verwendung von analytischen Informationssystemen zu unterstützen, wurde in Anlehnung an die Begriffe Real-Time BI und Right-Time BI ebenso unter dem Begriff OpBI verfolgt (Russom 2010; Davis et al. 2009; Davis 2007; Eckerson 2007; White 2006; White 2005). Folgende Kernpunkte sind in dieser Diskussion charakteristisch für eine OpBI-basierte Entscheidungsunterstützung:

- Nutzung von Analysewerkzeugen und Methoden der BI im Kontext von operativen Geschäftsprozessen,
- Verkürzung von Latenzzeiten im Entscheidungsprozess,

- Aufbau eines geschlossenen Kreislaufs hinsichtlich Datensammlung und -analyse sowie der Entscheidungsfindung und
- Erweiterung der Nutzergruppe der BI um Endanwender und Entscheidungsträger des operativen Managements.

Einen Anwendungsbereich der OpBI stellt die Leistungsmessung von Geschäftsprozessen dar (Cunningham 2005). In diesem Zusammenhang schlägt das PPM eine Brücke zum Prozesscontrolling. Dieses Konzept ist nicht auf eine spezifische IT-Unterstützung festgelegt (Blasini 2013), jedoch wird gegenwärtig eine Verknüpfung des Geschäftsprozessmanagements mit analytischen Informationssystemen als vorteilhaft angesehen (Vukšić et al. 2013; Allweyer 2012, S. 393ff; Sesselmann und Schmelzer 2008, S. 348). Derartige Beurteilungen einer prozessualen Leistungsfähigkeit haben gleichermaßen Auswirkungen auf die Gestaltung und die Ausführung von Geschäftsprozessen (Hammer 2015). Dabei stellt eine Integration von strukturellen und ablauforientierten Aspekten eine Herausforderung für ein durchgängiges Geschäftsprozessmanagement dar (Scheer et al. 2005, S. 2). In diesem Spannungsfeld hat die IT-Unterstützung von Geschäftsprozessen neben OpBI wiederum weitere Begrifflichkeiten geprägt.

Im Kontext der Prozessausführung wird eine prozessorientierte BI diskutiert (Bucher et al. 2009). Ausgehend von dieser Betrachtungsweise werden analytische Funktionen in Prozessabläufe eingebettet, um die Erfüllung von Aufgaben im Zuge der Prozessausführung zu unterstützen. Diese Aufgabenunterstützung beeinflusst die Prozessleistung z.B. infolge von effizienteren Abläufen. Prozessorientierte BI richtet sich jedoch nicht wie OpBI an eine Analyse der Prozessleistung und eine nachgelagerte Ableitung von leistungsbezogenen Managementmaßnahmen. Der Betrachtungsfokus der prozessorientierten BI liegt ausschließlich auf der Prozessausführung. (Bucher und Dinter 2008)

Komplementär existieren Ansätze, die eine Nutzung von analytischen Informationssystemen für eine Prozessgestaltung aus strategischer und taktischer Managementperspektive adressieren. Dieses Anliegen im Rahmen der prozessorientierten Entscheidungsunterstützung verfolgt das Konzept der BPI (Linden et al. 2011; Felden et al. 2010). Eine derart auf die Prozessgestaltung fokussierende Auffassung von BPI lässt eine Abgrenzung zur OpBI zu. Dieses Verständnis ist jedoch konträr zum ursprünglichen BPI-Verständnis von Jost und Scheer (2002). Der in seinem Ursprung eine Prozessorientierung von BI-Werkzeugen charakterisierende Begriff wurde unter dem Markennamen Process Intelligence für eine Leistungsanalyse von Geschäftsprozessen aus strategischer, taktischer und operativer Sicht fortgeführt (Blickle et al. 2010; IDS Scheer 2008; Kruppke und Bauer 2005).

Eine begriffliche Unschärfe zwischen BPI und OpBI existiert bereits seit dem ungefähr zeitgleichen Aufkommen der beiden Ausdrücke (Linden et al. 2011) und hat partiell zu einem synonymen Gebrauch geführt (Hall 2004). Im Kontext von

Workflow- oder BPM-Systemen wird BPI zusätzlich als eine Zusammenstellung von IT-Werkzeugen diskutiert, um die Qualität der Prozessausführung aus Sicht der Endanwender zu unterstützen (Grigori et al. 2004; Casati et al. 2002). Die IT-Unterstützung umfasst in diesem Zusammenhang analytische Funktionalitäten für eine Analyse, Vorhersage, Überwachung, Steuerung und Optimierung von Geschäftsprozessen auf Grundlage der in BPM-Systemen erfassten Prozessereignisse (Castellanos et al. 2009).

Die kontroverse Diskussion über BI-orientierte Ansätze zeigt, dass analytische Informationssysteme im Kontext des Geschäftsprozessmanagements aus verschiedenen Perspektiven betrachtet werden. Eine weitere Sichtweise auf die prozessorientierte Entscheidungsfindung ergibt sich aus der Berücksichtigung industriespezifischer Ansätze. Die Vorteilhaftigkeit einer Analyse von Prozessdaten in industriellen Anwendungsbereichen hat sich bereits in der Diskussion von Qualitätsmanagementansätzen im Rahmen der kontinuierlichen Prozessverbesserung abgezeichnet.

Zur Planung und Steuerung von Industrieprozessen existieren gegenwärtig verschiedene Konzepte und Systeme, die analytische IT-Funktionalitäten für eine Entscheidungsunterstützung beinhalten. Manufacturing Execution Systems (MES) unterstützen z. B. die Sammlung, Aufbereitung und Darstellung von Produktionsdaten für eine Koordination von industriellen Prozessabläufen (Thiel et al. 2008). Das Konzept der Advanced Process Control (APC) charakterisiert eine Integration von Prozessdaten im Bereich der Halbleiterindustrie und vereint Funktionalitäten für Ablaufkontrollen, Fehlerklassifikationen oder Effizienzberechnungen. Komponenten der Statistical Process Control (SPC) können die analytischen Fähigkeiten von APC-Lösungen um statistische Methoden und Verfahren erweitern. (Yugma et al. 2015)

Eine Nutzung von produktionsspezifischen Daten zum Zweck der Entscheidungsunterstützung spiegelt sich auch im Konzept der Manufacturing Intelligence (MI) wider (Cooley und Petrusich 2013). Dabei wird eine durchgängige Datenintegration in den Mittelpunkt der Betrachtung gestellt, um Industrieprozesse in Echtzeit zu organisieren. Funktionalitäten der MI umfassen eine Analyse, Modellierung und Simulation von Geschäftsprozessen im Produktionsumfeld sowie eine entsprechende Informationsversorgung von Entscheidungsträgern (Cooley und Petrusich 2013; Zehe et al. 2013; Kuo et al. 2011; Chien et al. 2010). Der Begriff Smart Manufacturing baut auf den IT-spezifischen und analytischen Aspekten der MI auf. Dies führt zu einer Intensivierung des Einsatzes und der Vernetzung von Informationssystemen in der Industrie (Davis et al. 2012). Mit Smart Manufacturing geht eine verstärkte Ausstattung von Produktionsumgebungen mit Sensortechnologien und cyberphysischen Systemen einher. Diese Diskussion zielt auf eine Bereitstellung von IT-Lösungen in der Industrie ab, um übergreifende Prozessverbesserungen und eine durchgängige Entscheidungsunterstützung zu erreichen.

Mit einem noch zukunftsweisenderen Charakter ist im deutschsprachigen Raum Industrie 4.0 als visionäre Lösungsüberschrift für eine technische Integration von cyberphysischen Systemen und eine verstärkte Nutzung von internetbasierten Technologien im Produktionsumfeld in die Diskussion getreten. Industrie 4.0 thematisiert die intelligente Vernetzung von produktionsspezifischen Ressourcen, Systemen und Prozessen. Die Steuerung von Industrieprozessen erfolgt durch cyberphysische Produktionssysteme (CPPS). Diese bestehen aus IT-Komponenten, die eigenständig miteinander kommunizieren können. Existierende Systeme (z. B. Maschinen, Roboter) und Produktionsmittel werden mit Sensoren, Aktoren, Mikrocontrollern und Leistungselektronik ausgerüstet. Im Zuge dieser umfassenden Vernetzung entstehen dezentrale, sich selbst regulierende Steuerungs- und Regelungsprozesse. Kennzeichnend für CPPS sind horizontal und vertikal integrierte Produktionssysteme sowie eine durchgängige IT-Unterstützung über den gesamten Produktlebenszyklus. Die Grundlage für die Vernetzung der CPPS bilden interdisziplinäre Datenmodelle, die den Ist- und den Soll-Zustand eines Industriebetriebs abbilden. Die zugrunde liegende Datenorganisation umfasst eine systemübergreifende Sammlung, Analyse und Bereitstellung entscheidungsrelevanter Informationen. (Kagermann et al. 2013)

2.2 Beitrag der Forschungsarbeit

Der Diskursbereich der Forschungsarbeit steht zu einem komplexen Geflecht aus Systemen und Konzepten in Wechselwirkung. Die vorgestellten Konzepte und Systeme für eine industrieorientierte Entscheidungsunterstützung können unter dem Aspekt der Integration und Analyse von Produktionsdaten mit den Funktionalitäten einer OpBI in Verbindung gebracht werden. Ebenso adressieren Begrifflichkeiten aus dem Bereich der analytischen Informationssysteme OpBI-spezifische Facetten. Abbildung 3 fasst die diskutieren Konzepte der Entscheidungsunterstützung und des Geschäftsprozessmanagements zusammen. Die neben der OpBI aus dem Zusammenwachsen der Themenfelder resultierenden Begriffe sind um den Diskursbereich der Arbeit als in Wechselwirkung stehende Begrifflichkeiten dargestellt.

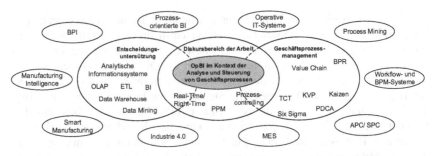

Abbildung 3. Themengebiete im Kontext des Diskursbereichs der Arbeit

Im Diskursbereich der Arbeit wird ein Prozesscontrolling betrachtet, um die Aktivitäten einer unternehmensbezogenen Value Chain kennzahlenbasiert beurteilen zu können. Zu diesem Zweck wird auf Technologien, Konzepte und Werkzeuge der analytischen Informationssysteme zurückgegriffen. Leistungsbezogene Maßnahmen infolge von kennzahlenbasierten Beurteilungen müssen dabei im Sinne des Geschäftsprozessmanagements sowohl für die Gestaltung als auch für die Ausführung von Prozessen ableitbar sein (vgl. z. B. Hammer 2015). Die im Außengürtel von Abbildung 3 dargestellten Ansätze können jedoch die notwendige Integrationsleistung entweder nur teilweise oder lediglich in spezifischen Anwendungsbereichen abdecken. Generalisierbare Erkenntnisse für eine Analyse und Steuerung von Geschäftsprozessen sind auf dieser Basis nur im jeweiligen Betrachtungsfokus zu erreichen. Darüber hinaus sind Smart Manufacturing und Industrie 4.0 Themen mit zukunftsweisendem Charakter.

Aufgrund konzeptioneller Gemeinsamkeiten von Prozesscontrolling, PPM und OpBI wird erwartet, dass in diesem Zusammenhang eine Generalisierung von Erkenntnissen für eine Analyse und Steuerung von Geschäftsprozessen möglich ist. Dies schließt eine zeitkritische Entscheidungsunterstützung für industrielle Produktionsumgebungen und Dienstleistungsbereiche ein, um den Forschungsfokus unabhängig von einem konkreten Anwendungsbereich zu gestalten. Der Beitrag der Forschungsarbeit besteht demzufolge in einer generalisierenden Bewertung von OpBI für eine Analyse und Steuerung von Geschäftsprozessen. Vor diesem Hintergrund thematisiert die Forschungsarbeit zunächst einmal die Betrachtung von Managementaufgaben im operativen, prozessorientierten Entscheidungsumfeld. Dabei wird die Notwendigkeit einer erweiterten Nutzung von analytischen Informationssystemen für Führungsaufgaben im Rahmen von prozessbezogenen Effektivitäts- und Effizienzbetrachtungen zur Diskussion gestellt. Dies umfasst eine Klassifizierung der wissenschaftlichen Literatur hinsichtlich Themen, Trends und Eigenschaften der OpBI. Aufgrund der Vielzahl von Konzepten und Systemen, die zur OpBI in Beziehung stehen, trägt die Forschungsarbeit darauf aufbauend zu einer Begriffsklassifikation der OpBI im Kontext der Analyse und Steuerung von Geschäftsprozessen bei. Im Anschluss daran werden die Gestaltungsbereiche der Wirtschaftsinformatik – Mensch, Aufgabe und IT (vgl. z. B. Felden 2006, S. 5) – hinsichtlich der Diskussion um OpBI präzisiert. Der Beitrag der Forschungsarbeit umfasst zur Charakterisierung dieser IS-spezifischen Elemente eine Exploration der Anwendbarkeit von OpBI im Produktions- und Dienstleistungsumfeld. Schließlich werden Gestaltungsperspektiven für eine IS-spezifische Modellierung und Umsetzung entwickelt, um Geschäftsprozesse mit OpBI im Realweltkontext analysieren und steuern zu können.

Zusammenfassend liefert die Forschungsarbeit einen Beitrag zu den nachfolgenden Gesichtspunkten, um OpBI im Kontext einer geschäftsprozessbezogenen Analyse und Steuerung der wissenschaftlichen Diskussion zugänglich zu machen:

1. Notwendigkeit einer Auseinandersetzung mit OpBI durch Aufzeigen der Entwicklung von BI-Anwendungsfeldern hin zum operativen Fokus,
2. Begriffsklassifikation der OpBI im Kontext der Analyse und Steuerung von Geschäftsprozessen,
3. Untersuchung von fallspezifischen Anwendungsszenarien für OpBI im Kontext der Analyse und Steuerung von Geschäftsprozessen,
4. Erarbeitung von modellierungs- und umsetzungsspezifischen Gestaltungsperspektiven der OpBI im Kontext der Analyse und Steuerung von Geschäftsprozessen.

3 Forschungsrahmen

Der Forschungsrahmen der Arbeit dient der Formalisierung des Erkenntnisweges, um OpBI im Kontext der Analyse und Steuerung von Geschäftsprozessen nach wissenschaftlichen Gesichtspunkten zu untersuchen. Der Entwurf des Forschungsrahmens orientiert sich an Bezugspunkten, die von Becker et al. (2003) vorgeschlagen werden. Die Wahl der Forschungsmethoden resultiert aus einer wissenschaftstheoretischen Positionierung und den aufgestellten Forschungszielen der Arbeit. Die Zielformulierungen und die wissenschaftstheoretischen Grundpositionen weisen dabei eine wechselseitige Abhängigkeit voneinander auf.

Der Zusammenhang zwischen den verschiedenen Gestaltungsbereichen des Forschungsrahmens wird in Abbildung 4 dargestellt. Die einzelnen Bezugspunkte sind Gegenstand der nachfolgenden Betrachtungen. Abschnitt 3.1 stellt die wissenschaftstheoretische Positionierung der Arbeit vor. Daran schließt sich in Abschnitt 3.2 die Positionierung der formulierten Forschungsziele an. Dies umfasst eine Darstellung der Wechselwirkung zwischen den Zielsetzungen der Arbeit und der getroffenen wissenschaftstheoretischen Positionsbestimmung. Unter Berücksichtigung dieses Zusammenwirkens werden in Abschnitt 3.3 die Forschungsmethoden der Arbeit im Gesamtbild vorgestellt.

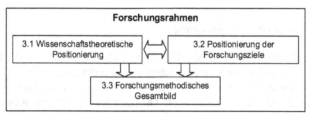

Abbildung 4. Entwurf des Forschungsrahmens in Anlehnung an Becker et al. (2003)

3.1 Wissenschaftstheoretische Positionierung

Die wissenschaftstheoretische Positionierung nimmt zunächst Bezug auf die Leitfragen von Becker et al. (2003). Tabelle 1 beantwortet diese Fragestellungen überblicksartig für die vorliegende Forschungsarbeit. Danach erfolgt eine ausführliche Darstellung hinsichtlich der gewählten ontologischen, epistemologischen und linguistischen Positionen.

Tabelle 1. Wissenschaftstheoretische Positionierung der Arbeit im Überblick

Leitfrage nach Becker et al. (2003)	OpBI im Kontext der Analyse und Steuerung von Geschäftsprozessen
Gibt es eine objektive Welt unabhängig von der Erkenntnis?	Es gibt eine objektive Welt unabhängig von der Erkenntnis.
Wie entstehen Erkenntnisse?	Erkenntnisse entstehen durch Erfahrungen und Verstand.
Auf welchem Weg werden Erkenntnisse erlangt?	Erkenntnisse werden induktiv und deduktiv erlangt.
Wie ist das Verhältnis von Erkenntnis und Gegenstand?	Das Verhältnis von Erkenntnis und Gegenstand ist durch eine stets subjektgebundene Wahrnehmung gekennzeichnet.
Welche Funktion hat Sprache im Rahmen von Denkvorgängen?	Es bleibt offen, ob Sprache das Medium des menschlichen Denkens ist.
Wie erlangen Sprachartefakte Bedeutung?	Die Bedeutung von Sprachartefakten wird durch eine subjektgebundene Wahrnehmung geschaffen.
Ermöglicht Sprache intersubjektive Verständigung?	Sprache unterstützt intersubjektive Verständigung, sofern ein übereinstimmendes Verständnis hinsichtlich der durch Subjekte erlangten Bedeutung von Sprachartefakten vorherrscht.

3.1.1 Ontologische Positionierung

Die ontologische Positionierung der Forschungsarbeit setzt sich mit der Frage auseinander, ob eine objektive Realität unabhängig von der menschlichen Erkenntnis existiert (Becker et al. 2003, S. 8). Diese Auseinandersetzung konzentriert sich allein auf die Existenz einer realen Welt. Die epistemologische Positionierung thematisiert darauf bezugnehmend verschiedene Aspekte hinsichtlich einer Wahrnehmung der Realität durch den Menschen (siehe 3.1.2).

Die Forschungsarbeit untersucht eine IT-basierte Entscheidungsunterstützung zur Analyse und Steuerung von Geschäftsprozessen unter Verwendung von Technologien, Konzepten und Werkzeugen aus dem Bereich der analytischen Informationssysteme. Bezüglich dieses Erkenntnisgegenstands wird von einer real existierenden Welt ausgegangen. Damit nimmt die Arbeit die Position des ontologischen Realismus ein (Becker et al. 2004, S. 4). Ausgehend von der Position des Realismus kann die reale Welt gemäß Popper (1978) in drei Abstraktionsebenen eingeteilt werden, die den Erkenntnis- und Gestaltungsraum der Forschungsarbeit gemeinsam aufspannen:

- Welt 1 ist gekennzeichnet durch physische Objekte, die Naturgesetzen unterliegen und über sensorische Fähigkeiten wahrgenommen werden können. Gegenstände der Welt 1 sind im vorliegenden Forschungskontext z. B. materielle Produkte, Equipment zur Leistungserbringung, technische IT-Komponenten oder instanziierte Modelle. Allgemein sind es alle sensorisch erfassbaren Objekte, die für eine Analyse und Steuerung von Geschäftsprozessen eine Relevanz aufweisen.
- Welt 2 repräsentiert die subjektive Wahrnehmung und das menschliche Bewusstsein. Dies spiegelt im Rahmen der Arbeit die Sicht eines Entscheidungs- und Aufgabenträgers wider, der mithilfe von OpBI-Systemen informationstechnisch unterstützt wird. Hinsichtlich Erkenntnis und Gestaltung derartiger Informationssysteme ist das Bewusstsein eines Forschenden ebenso in Welt 2 angesiedelt.
- Welt 3 stellt Produkte des menschlichen Verstands dar. Dies können Abstraktionen von konkreten Objekten aus Welt 1 sein. In der vorliegenden Forschungsarbeit umfasst Welt 3 beispielsweise Literatur, Ideen, Theorien, IT-Konzepte oder auch Modellierungssprachen. Derartige intellektuelle Artefakte begleiten den Forschungsprozess zum Verständnis und zur Gestaltung von OpBI-Systemen im Anwendungskontext der Analyse und Steuerung von Geschäftsprozessen.

Der Forschungsprozess der Arbeit ist von einer Wechselwirkung dieser drei Welten gekennzeichnet, die gemäß Popper (1978) alle real existieren. Dabei fungiert Welt 2 als Vermittler zwischen Welt 1 und Welt 3. Im Kontext der Forschungsarbeit nimmt die OpBI-getriebene Unterstützung von Aufgaben- und Entscheidungsträgern diese Vermittlerrolle ein. Dadurch wird ein Zusammenhang zwischen allgemeingültigen Technologien, Konzepten und Werkzeugen aus dem Bereich der analytischen Informationssysteme und spezifischen Instanzen einer Analyse und Steuerung von Geschäftsprozessen hergestellt. Der Mensch als zentraler Bestandteil von Informationssystemen ist an allen drei Welten beteiligt.

3.1.2 Epistemologische Positionierung

Die epistemologische Positionsbestimmung zeigt den Ursprung, die Methoden und die Grenzen des Erkenntnisgewinns auf (Becker et al. 2003, S. 6f). Erkenntnisse im Rahmen der Forschungsarbeit entstammen Sinneswahrnehmungen, Erfahrungen und dem menschlichen Verstand. Diese Festlegung der Erkenntnisquellen begründet sich durch den Forschungsgegenstand im Kontext der Wirtschaftsinformatik (Frank 2007, S. 157). Es wird mit OpBI ein betriebliches Informationssystem im Anwendungskontext der Analyse und Steuerung von Geschäftsprozessen untersucht. Um zunächst ein grundlegendes Verständnis für den

Handlungsraum zu erlangen, ist ein Bezug zu unternehmensspezifischen Situationen notwendig. In den Forschungsprozess fließen praxisbezogene Erfahrungen aus Anwendungskontexten gemeinsam mit Beobachtungen von Forschenden ein. Diese Erkenntnisse werden mit apriorischem Wissen reflektiert, um informationstechnologische Gestaltungsparameter zu verstehen, abzuleiten und umzusetzen.

Hinsichtlich des methodologischen Aspekts werden Erkenntnisse induktiv und deduktiv erlangt. Induktion bedient sich Erfahrungen und Beobachtungen, um von Einzelfallbetrachtungen auf die Allgemeinheit zu schließen (Popper 1994, S. 3). Deduktion hingegen leitet primär verstandesgeleitet Einzelaussagen aus allgemeingültigen Sätzen ab (Seifert 1997, S. 45). Eine Grenze des Erkenntnisgewinns liegt im Verhältnis zwischen der Erkenntnis und der objektiv existierenden Welt. In der Arbeit wird der Standpunkt vertreten, dass eine Wahrnehmung der Wirklichkeit nicht ohne subjektive Verzerrungen möglich ist. Damit wird hinsichtlich des Verhältnisses von Erkenntnis und Erkenntnisgegenstand eine konstruktivistische Position eingenommen.

3.1.3 Linguistische Positionierung

Die linguistische Positionierung setzt sich mit der Funktion von Sprache im Rahmen des Forschungsprozesses auseinander (Becker et al. 2003, S. 8). Allgemein betrachtet, wird Sprache als ein System von Zeichen verstanden, die syntaktisch zueinander in Beziehung stehen und eine semantische Bedeutung haben. Hinsichtlich einer pragmatischen Dimension können Zeichen mit Handlungsaufforderungen verbunden sein. (Seiffert 1997, S. 160f)

Im Rahmen der Drei-Welten-Lehre von Popper dient Sprache der Formulierung von subjektiven Wahrnehmungen und menschlichen Gedanken aus Welt 2, um Objekte in Welt 3 zu erschaffen. Damit werden die Objekte der Welt 2 einer kritischen Auseinandersetzung im Sinne einer wissenschaftlichen Diskussion zugänglich gemacht. Popper ordnet Welt 2 Denkprozesse und Welt 3 gedachte Inhalte zu, die sich mithilfe von Sprache persistieren lassen. Zeichenbasiert instanziierte Sprachelemente (z. B. gedruckte Dokumente) sind Objekte der Welt 1. (Popper 1978)

Bereits für von Humboldt (1836) bezweckt Sprache den Ausdruck menschlicher Gedanken. In der Auseinandersetzung von Humboldts hinsichtlich der Funktion von Sprache spiegeln sich ein kognitiver, ein expressiver und ein kommunikativer Aspekt wider (Becker et al. 2003, S. 9). Die kognitive Funktion sieht Sprache als ein Medium der mentalen Tätigkeit. Diese Sichtweise verlangt neben der Existenz von Sprachzentren im menschlichen Gehirn auch Annahmen zu dessen zerebraler Funktionsweise. Derartige Annahmen bleiben im vorliegenden Forschungskontext jedoch unberücksichtigt. Neben dem kognitiven Aspekt kann Sprache expressiv als Ausdrucksmittel für Emotionen, Bewusstseinszustände oder Wahrnehmungen verstanden werden. Der Auffassung von Humboldts folgend, überführt Sprache subjektgebundene Vorstellungen in Objekte. Diese entstandenen Objekte sind dabei wiederum Gegenstand der eigenen oder einer fremden subjektiven Wahrnehmung. Dieser Standpunkt stützt sowohl die Auffassung nach Popper (1978) hinsichtlich der objektiven Existenz von Welt 2 als auch die epistemologische Position einer stets subjektgebundenen Erkenntnis.

Die linguistische Positionierung der Arbeit zur kommunikativen Funktion von Sprache erfordert eine Betrachtung des gegenseitigen Verstehens und der intersubjektiven Verständigung. Die sprachanalytische Grundlage bildet die Logische Propädeutik (Kamlah und Lorenzen 1996). Durch Prädikation werden Gegenstände mit Wörtern einer Sprache bezeichnet. Um die Bezeichnungen zu verstehen, ordnet der Mensch einem Wort eine Bedeutung zu. Die Bedeutungszuweisung ist aufgrund der epistemologischen Position der Arbeit subjektgebunden. Demzufolge kann aus kommunikativer Sicht die reine Existenz von Sprache eine intersubjektive Verständigung nicht ermöglichen (Becker et al. 2003, S. 9). Die wissenschaftliche Prädikation normiert daher Wortbedeutungen durch die explizite Einführung von Prädikatoren. Es entstehen Fachwörter, die als Bestandteil einer Fachsprache zueinander in Beziehung stehen können.

Unter Verwendung von Fachwörtern werden Aussagen unterschiedlicher Komplexität gebildet, die Sachverhalte sprachlich darstellen. Sachverhalte machen als aussagenbasierte Sprachdarstellungen die zwischenmenschliche Verständigung aus. Im Rahmen von Kommunikation erfolgt eine Beurteilung des Wahrheitsgehalts von Aussagen, die einen Sachverhalt bilden. Sachverhalte können jedoch aufgrund ihrer Bindung an Sprache nicht ontologisch festgelegt sein (Seiffert 1996, S. 88). Ein Wahrheitsnachweis von Aussagen ist daher konstruktivistisch an die Erreichung intersubjektiver Übereinstimmungen gebunden (Poser 2001, S. 106). Das Verfahren der interpersonalen Verifizierung (Kamlah und Lorenzen 1996) unterstützt in dieser Hinsicht die Konsensbildung. Die intersubjektive Übereinstimmung hängt dabei von Kriterien und Argumenten ab, die eine sachkundige Sprachgemeinschaft als Wahrheitsnachweis akzeptiert.

Zusammenfassend wird in der Arbeit die kommunikative Position vertreten, dass Sprache die Konsensbildung in einer sachkundigen Gemeinschaft von Kommunikationsteilnehmern unterstützt. Für eine intersubjektive Verständigung müssen Gründe vorliegen, die den Geltungsanspruch von sachverhaltsbezogenen Aussagen rechtfertigen.

3.1.4 Reflektion wissenschaftstheoretischer Ansätze im Rahmen der Positionierung

In der Positionierung der Forschungsarbeit spiegeln sich Elemente des Konstruktivismus und des kritischen Rationalismus wider. Damit folgt die Arbeit zwei wissenschaftstheoretischen Ansätzen, die für die Betriebswirtschaftslehre prägend sind (Kornmeier 2007, S. 38f). Während sich die ontologische Positionierung der

Arbeit an Elementen des kritischen Rationalismus (Popper 1978) ausrichtet, folgt die linguistische Positionierung dem Konstruktivismus (Kamlah und Lorenzen 1996). Die Arbeit ist jedoch nicht dem radikalen Konstruktivismus zuzuordnen, sondern sie zielt vielmehr auf die Konstruktion einer intersubjektiv nachprüfbaren Wissenschaftssprache ab (Schnell et al. 2011).

Sowohl der kritische Rationalismus als auch der Konstruktivismus, in der zuvor erläuterten Form, berücksichtigen Erfahrung und Verstand als Erkenntnisquellen sowie Induktion und Deduktion als Erkenntnismethoden (Kornmeier 2007, S. 38ff). Hinsichtlich der Epistemologie bedeutet dieser Dualismus für die vorliegende Forschungsarbeit, dass Erkenntnisse aus zwei distinkten Perspektiven heraus gewonnen werden. Aus Sicht des Konstruktivismus erfolgt im Sinne der Wirtschaftsinformatik eine zweckmäßige Rekonstruktion von Fachwissen, sodass eine Wissensverarbeitung durch IT-Systeme und eine Wissensnutzung durch den Menschen erreicht werden (Ortner 1999). Es bietet sich jedoch an, die Gültigkeit von Aussagen an der Realität zu überprüfen (Kornmeier 2007, S. 40). Unter dem Blickwinkel des kritischen Rationalismus sind Erkenntnisse im Rahmen der Forschungsarbeit unter dem Aspekt der Falsifizierbarkeit zu gewinnen (Popper 1994, S. 14ff). Demzufolge müssen getroffene Aussagen empirisch überprüft werden können und widerlegbar sein. Es ist dabei zu beachten, dass empirisch bestätigte Erkenntnisse immer nur einen vorläufigen Charakter aufweisen (Kornmeier 2007, S. 41).

3.2 Positionierung der Forschungsziele

Die Forschungsziele der Arbeit thematisieren das Verständnis und die Bereitstellung von Informationssystemen in betrieblichen Anwendungskontexten. In Bezug auf die gestaltungsorientierte Wirtschaftsinformatik (Riege et al. 2009) werden ein Erkenntnisziel und ein Gestaltungsziel unterschieden:

- Das Erkenntnisziel der Arbeit besteht in der Schaffung eines IS-spezifischen Verständnisses von OpBI im Kontext der Analyse und Steuerung von Geschäftsprozessen.
- Das Gestaltungsziel der Arbeit besteht in der Entwicklung IS-spezifischer Gestaltungsperspektiven für OpBI im Kontext der Analyse und Steuerung von Geschäftsprozessen.

Zwischen den Forschungszielen und der wissenschaftstheoretischen Positionierung einer Forschungsarbeit besteht eine gegenseitige Abhängigkeit (Becker et al. 2003, S. 5). Die nachfolgende Tabelle 2 zeigt den Zusammenhang zwischen den gewählten Grundpositionen und den formulierten Forschungszielen auf.

Tabelle 2. Gegenüberstellung der Forschungsziele und der wissenschaftstheoretischen Positionierung

	Erkenntnisziel *Schaffung eines IS-spezifischen Verständnisses von OpBI im Kontext der Analyse und Steuerung von Geschäftsprozessen*	Gestaltungsziel *Entwicklung IS-spezifischer Gestaltungsperspektiven für OpBI im Kontext der Analyse und Steuerung von Geschäftsprozessen*
Ontologie	Interpretation eines Realweltausschnitts	Konstruktion von IT-Artefakten für den Realweltausschnitt
Epistemologie	Analytisches Erkenntnisinteresse	Aktionales Erkenntnisinteresse
Linguistik	Konsensbasierte Kommunikation der zielgeleiteten Ergebnisse	

Aus ontologischer Sicht erfolgt die zielgeleitete Untersuchung in Bezug zu einem Realweltausschnitt, der auf eine Analyse und Steuerung von Geschäftsprozessen fokussiert. Zur Erreichung des Erkenntnisziels ist die Interpretation von Wesensmerkmalen sowie von Ursache-Wirkungsbeziehungen dieses betrieblichen Anwendungskontextes von Bedeutung.

Die erkenntniszielgeleiteten Ergebnisse bilden das Fundament für die Erreichung des Gestaltungsziels. Das aktionale Erkenntnisinteresse setzt sich dabei mit einer Beeinflussung des betrieblichen Anwendungskontextes durch die Schaffung von IS-spezifischen Artefakten auseinander. Die Kommunikation der zielgeleiteten Ergebnisse erfolgt konsensbasiert unter Verwendung von explizit vereinbarten Fachtermini innerhalb der wissenschaftlichen Gemeinschaft. Dies betrifft im Rahmen der vorliegenden Arbeit die deutschsprachige Wirtschaftsinformatik und die internationale Information-Systems-Community. Abbildung 5 fasst die gegenseitige Beeinflussung der Forschungsziele und der wissenschaftstheoretischen Positionen als übergeordnetes Forschungsschema der Arbeit zusammen.

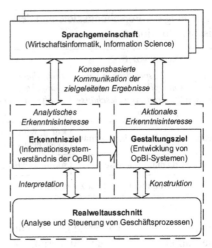

Abbildung 5. Übergeordnetes Forschungsschema der Arbeit

3.3 Forschungsmethodisches Gesamtbild

Die Zielerreichung der Arbeit vollzieht sich unter Verwendung von Methoden der Wirtschaftsinformatik, um OpBI im Rahmen der Analyse und Steuerung von Geschäftsprozessen zu verstehen und zu entwickeln. Tabelle 3 stellt die in der Forschungsarbeit verwendeten Methoden überblicksartig vor. Diese sind zur Verdeutlichung des methodischen Fokus dem Erkenntnisziel oder dem Gestaltungsziel der Arbeit zugeordnet.

Tabelle 3. Forschungsmethoden der Arbeit

	Methode	Beschreibung
Erkenntnisziel	Literatur-Review	Der Literatur-Review untersucht themenspezifische Forschungsbeiträge. Die Inhalte werden beschrieben, zusammengefasst, bewertet, klargestellt und miteinander verknüpft. (Fettke 2006; Cooper 1998)
	Problemzentriertes Interview	Das problemzentrierte Interview ist eine semistrukturierte Expertenbefragung hinsichtlich einer praktischen Problemstellung, die im Vorfeld analysiert wurde (Jaeger und Reinecke 2009).
	Qualitative/ Quantitative Querschnittsanalyse	Diese Methoden umfassen einmalige Erhebungen (z. B. Fragebögen, Interviews, Inhaltsanalysen), die quantitativ oder qualitativ ausgewertet werden (Wilde und Hess 2007).
	Fallstudie	Eine Fallstudie untersucht zeitgemäße und nicht klar abgrenzbare Phänomene in ihrem Realweltkotext (Yin 2009).

	Methode	Beschreibung
Gestaltungsziel	Argumentativ-deduktive Analyse	Die argumentativ-deduktive Analyse adressiert ein logisch-deduktives Schließen im Rahmen eines sprachlich formulierten Theoriemodells (Wilde und Hess 2007).
	Laborexperiment	Das Laborexperiment untersucht Ursache-Wirkungsbeziehungen in kontrollierbaren Umgebungen, um Kausalzusammenhänge aufzuzeigen (Eschweiler et al. 2009).
	Aktionsforschung	Die Aktionsforschung untersucht IS-spezifische Situationen, um praktische Problemlösungen und wissenschaftlichen Erkenntnisgewinn durch die Zusammenarbeit von Forschern und Praktikern zu ermöglichen (Baskerville 1999).
	Prototyping	Das Prototyping umfasst die Entwicklung und Evaluation einer Vorabversion eines Anwendungssystems (Wilde und Hess 2007).

Die Methoden Literatur-Review und Problemzentriertes Interview im Rahmen des Erkenntnisziels lassen sich unter dem Oberbegriff der qualitativen Querschnittsanalyse subsummieren, weil die Auswertungsergebnisse Rückschlüsse auf eine Grundgesamtheit erlauben. Diese Zuordnung ermöglicht die forschungsmethodische Strukturierung der Arbeit unter Verwendung des Methodenprofils von Wilde und Hess (2007). Abbildung 6 stellt dieses Portfolio im Kontext der Arbeit dar.

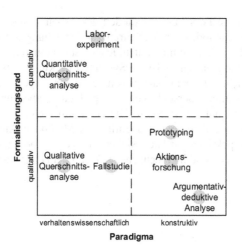

Abbildung 6. Methodenprofil der Arbeit in Anlehnung an Wilde und Hess (2007)

Die Forschungsarbeit bedient sich qualitativer und quantitativer Methoden, um Erkenntnisse unter einem verhaltenswissenschaftlichen und einem konstruktiven

Paradigma zu erzielen. Die in Abbildung 7 dargestellten Methoden sind dabei untereinander kombinierbar. Der Forschungsprozess der Arbeit ist somit von einem Mehrmethodenansatz gekennzeichnet, der nach Nunamaker et al. (1991) in vier forschungsmethodische Schwerpunkte eingeteilt werden kann (siehe Abbildung 7).

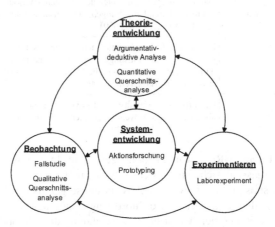

Abbildung 7. Mehrmethodenansatz der Arbeit in Anlehnung an Nunamaker et al. (1990)

Abbildung 7 zeigt die Forschungsmethoden der Arbeit in ihrem Gesamtzusammenhang auf. Die methodischen Verfahren zur Erreichung des Erkenntnis- und Gestaltungsziels der Arbeit kommen nicht losgelöst voneinander zum Einsatz. Der Kern des Mehrmethodenansatzes ist die Systementwicklung in Bezug auf das Gestaltungsziel der Arbeit. Dabei ist der aktionale Erkenntnisgewinn im Rahmen der Schaffung von Gestaltungsperspektiven für OpBI zur Analyse und Steuerung von Geschäftsprozessen qualitativer Natur. Die erkenntniszielgeleitete Untersuchung basiert hingegen auf qualitativen und quantitativen Methoden. Ausgehend von drei verschiedenen Perspektiven wird abgesichert, dass die Informationssystemgestaltung auf Grundlage von und in Wechselwirkung zu dem erreichten Erkenntnisziel steht.

4 Gang der Arbeit

Der Gang der Arbeit richtet sich nach dem übergeordneten Forschungsschema (siehe Abbildung 5, S. 42) und dokumentiert die Forschungsergebnisse der Arbeit. Die analytischen und aktionalen Erkenntnisse wurden in 16 Forschungsbeiträgen einer wissenschaftlichen Diskussion zugänglich gemacht. Für eine umfassende Auseinandersetzung mit den Forschungsergebnissen sind die Beiträge in den Verlauf des vorliegenden Kapitels eingebettet. Dabei werden zunächst die Kernpunkte der Untersuchungen kurz dargestellt und thematisch in einen Gesamtzusammenhang eingeordnet. Die Kurzdarstellungen haben einen zusammenfassenden Charakter und dienen der Überleitung zwischen den einzelnen Forschungsbeiträgen.

Abbildung 8 stellt den Gang der Arbeit schematisch als Architektur eines Hauses dar. Das Fundament bildet eine Themenbegründung. Diese wird unter Verweis auf Beitrag 1 in Abschnitt 4.1 dargestellt. Danach erfolgt eine begriffliche Einordnung der OpBI bezugnehmend auf die Beiträge 2 bis 4. Diese Begriffsklassifikation wird im Kontext von geschäftsprozessorientierten und industriegetriebenen Gesichtspunkten in Abschnitt 4.2 vorgenommen. Hinsichtlich der Allegorie des Hauses kann diese zweiteilige Betrachtung als Säulen aufgefasst werden.

Auf diesen Säulen setzt ein weiterer Baustein auf, der die Anwendbarkeit der OpBI im Kontext der Analyse und Steuerung von Geschäftsprozessen charakterisiert. Abschnitt 4.3 beschreibt zunächst modellierungsspezifische Voraussetzungen unter Verwendung von Beitrag 5 und Beitrag 6. Danach wird anhand der Beiträge 7 bis 12 auf Anwendungen im Produktionsumfeld eingegangen. Abschließend geht Abschnitt 4.3 bezugnehmend zu Beitrag 13 auf OpBI im Dienstleistungsumfeld ein. Die Anwendungsgebiete stehen trotz der unterschiedlichen Anzahl zugrunde liegender Beiträge gleichberechtigt nebeneinander. Abschnitt 4.3 bildet den Abschluss des analytischen Teils im Gang der Arbeit, der auf die Erreichung des Erkenntnisziels gerichtet ist.

Das Dach der Forschungsarbeit bilden Gestaltungsperspektiven der OpBI. Die Ergebnisse des Abschnitts 4.4 zielen auf das aktionale Erkenntnisinteresse der Arbeit ab. Dies umfasst zunächst in Bezug auf Beitrag 14 und Beitrag 15 modellierungsorientierte Gestaltungsparameter. Abschließend werden die Ergebnisse von Beitrag 16 hinsichtlich einer prototypischen Umsetzung eines OpBI-Systems in der Umformtechnik mithilfe von CASE-basierten Werkzeugen vorgestellt.

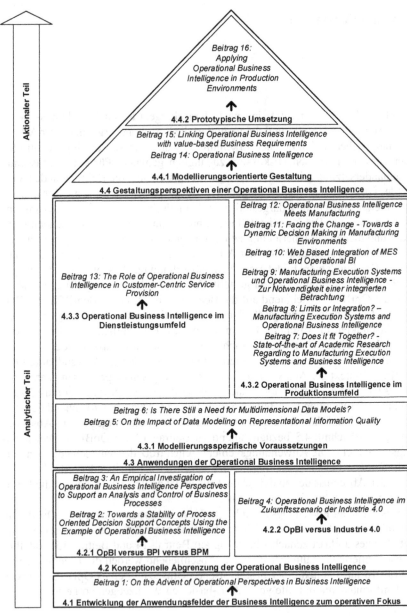

Abbildung 8. Gang der Arbeit

4.1 Entwicklung der Anwendungsfelder der Business Intelligence zum operativen Fokus im Zeitverlauf

Die Anwendungsfelder der Business Intelligence (BI) sind im Zeitverlauf zunehmend operativer geworden. Beitrag 1 stellt diesen Entwicklungsverlauf dar und bildet den thematischen Einstieg in den Gang dieser Arbeit.

4.1.1 Kurzdarstellung Beitrag 1

Als Ausgangspunkt der Betrachtung wird der BI-Begriff eingeführt. Aufgrund der Schwierigkeit eine einheitlich akzeptierte Definition der BI ausfindig zu machen, baut Beitrag 1 auf einem weiten BI-Verständnis auf. Demnach zielt BI zunächst einmal unabhängig von einem spezifischen Aufgabengebiet auf eine datenorientierte Entscheidungsunterstützung ab. Daraus resultiert eine Nutzbarkeit von BI auf allen Managementebenen eines Unternehmens, die in der Literatur üblicherweise in strategisch und operativ unterteilt werden. Diese Unterteilung bringt jedoch die Notwendigkeit mit sich, aufgabenspezifische Informationsanforderungen zu beachten. In diesem Zusammenhang variiert der Fokus einer Entscheidungsunterstützung im Rahmen der BI-Nutzung in Abhängigkeit vom Aufgabenspektrum der jeweiligen Managementebene. Daher analysiert Beitrag 1 die Charakteristika der BI hinsichtlich ihrer Bedeutung für strategische und operative Informationsanforderungen.

Die Ergebnisse von Beitrag 1 basieren auf einem Literatur-Review, der 1057 auswertbare Forschungsarbeiten für eine weiterführende Literaturanalyse identifiziert. Die Aufsätze sind manuell durch eine zweiköpfige Forschergruppe einem strategischen oder einem operativen Fokus zugeordnet worden. In diesen Kategorien erfolgen in Beitrag 1 eine branchenbezogene und eine funktionale Klassifikation. Im Rahmen der Trendbetrachtung stellt sich heraus, dass die Anzahl der operativ klassifizierten Literaturbeiträge mit zunehmender Jahreszahl ansteigt. Ebenso liegt hinsichtlich der zu unterstützenden Aufgabengebiete innerhalb eines Unternehmens (z. B. Logistik oder Marketing) im Zeitverlauf eine Tendenz von BI-spezifischen Themen hin zum operativen Fokus vor. Nach der Trendbetrachtung erfolgt eine inhaltliche Analyse der untersuchten wissenschaftlichen Fachliteratur. Es wird auf Verfahren des Text Mining zurückgegriffen, um automatisiert die Abstracts der Forschungsarbeiten einzelwort- und wortgruppenspezifisch zu analysieren. Die Einzelwortanalyse zeigt auf, dass sowohl strategisch als auch operativ klassifizierte Literaturbeiträge auf gleichen Fachtermini basieren. Jedoch liegt innerhalb dieser Kategorien eine unterschiedliche Häufigkeit der Begriffe vor, sodass der Betrachtungsfokus unterschiedlich ausgeprägt ist.

Aus der sich anschließenden Wortgruppenanalyse resultiert eine Gegenüberstellung von BI-spezifischen Themen mit strategischem und operativem Fokus. Die Auswertung der wissenschaftlichen Publikationen auf Basis des Text Mining zeigt, dass in der Literatur dem Inhalt nach verschiedene BI-spezifische Themen mit strategischen und operativen Managementaufgaben verbunden werden. Im strategischen Kontext sind fachliche Ansätze für eine Definition, Überprüfung und Weiterentwicklung von Unternehmenszielen Gegenstand der Diskussion. Im Gegensatz dazu sind BI-spezifische Themen aus operativer Sicht technologisch ausgerichtet. Beitrag 1 sieht daher einen weiteren Handlungsbedarf zur Klärung, wie BI aus Sicht des operativen Managements eine Entscheidungsunterstützung aufgabenorientiert unterstützen kann.

4.1.2 Beitrag 1: On the Advent of Operational Perspectives in Business Intelligence[1]

Introduction

BI experiences an increasing importance in academia and practice by its expansion on functionalities, available data sets, and its usage on all organizational layers [6]. This provides decision making capabilities to compete in dynamic and uncertain business environments [40]. A decision maker's focus depends thereby on his/her managerial tasks [20]. Different managerial tasks require a different BI support [30, 35]. A systematic reference in this field of discourse leads to benefits for decision makers' understanding to gain a helpful BI capability and a task-oriented application. An identification of trends is also of scientific interest as it allows an overview about potential research topics. The paper's goal is therefore to analyze BI in terms of different management tasks. This paper provides a literature overview of similarities and differences, and development trends.

The characteristics of BI are discussed according to the information needs of decision makers [31, 35]. Currently, there is a discussion of strategic and operational BI capabilities [7, 43]. Especially investigations on operational BI refer exclusively to practical contributions. Scientific publications use without exceptions white papers or research reports of associations of practitioners regarding BI (e.g. [9, 11, 41]) to motivate the research. Methods of reviewing literature to detect knowledge gaps in favor of subsequent research actions [39] are not considered in papers on operational BI. Motivations need an observation of BI from a scientific point of view to achieve a comprehensive basis. But, a classification based on strategic and operational management activities does not occur in the literature, yet. Therefore, the paper contributes to the discussion of BI and information demand-oriented decision making. It provides a literature classification of topics, trends, relationships, and characteristics of strategic and operational BI. It also delivers a

---

1 Hänel, T.: On the Advent of Operational Perspectives in Business Intelligence. In Mayer, J.H.; Quick, R. (Hrsg.): Business Intelligence for New-Generation Managers – Current Avenues of Development, Springer, 2015.

structure of relevant findings to avoid duplication efforts in context of subsequent research activities.

Section 2 discusses BI in context of strategic and operational decisions. This includes an analysis of existing reviews of BI to demonstrate the need for further investigations. The paper uses a phase-oriented approach for a profound literature analysis. Section 3 complements these phases to achieve a resilient classification of BI publications. Section 4 interprets the classification results. A conclusion summarizes the paper and gives further research perspectives.

The understanding of BI in context of data and their managerial usage level

Starting in 1958, BI was introduced to support a decision making in organizations. Luhn discussed a general need of understanding managerial situations to achieve goal-oriented actions [26]. Since this appearance of BI it is challenging to find even today a unique and accepted definition of BI so that for example Hugh Watson pursues a broad definition of BI [36]:

> Business intelligence (BI) is a broad category of applications, technologies, and processes for gathering, storing, accessing, and analyzing data to help business users make better decisions.

This definition focuses on aspects of loading data into a data warehouse and retrieving data out of a data warehouse for decision making [38]. Such a broad classification is also evident in the literature reviews (cf. Table 1).

Table 1. Literature reviews of BI

Source	Summary
[34]	BI gathers, stores, and analyzes data to produce information and knowledge for purposive decisions. Associated technologies are data warehousing, OLAP, knowledge management systems and decision support systems.
[21]	BI can be classified into five distinct categories: artificial intelligence, usage to achieve financial benefits, improvement of overall decision making, BI project management issues and application strategies for BI tools and technologies.
[6]	BI considers structured, unstructured, as well as mobile and sensor based content. The applications are manifold including e-commerce and market intelligence, e-government and politics 2.0, science and technology, smart health and wellbeing, security and public safety. Emerging research is suggested for big data analytics, text analytics, web analytics, network analytics, and mobile analytics.

However, even broad BI perspectives ignore a discussion that a BI support depends on the information needs of business users according to their certain management task [31, 35]. There is a differentiation of strategic and operational BI capabilities [7]. The intersection of BI and strategic decisions deals with organizational performance issues and market orientation to gain competitive advantages or to consolidate a market position [43]. An application of BI techniques within processes is subject of operational BI capabilities [27]. They pursue timely and fast reactions or forecasts to current business situations [43]. Both BI capabilities lead to business value, i.e. a competitive advantage in favor of strategic goals based on internal process improvements in an operational context [33, 51]. Strategic BI capabilities have to be understood as prerequisite for operational BI capabilities [27]. Gorry and Morton [12] provide a detailed classification on the information requirements of strategic and operational management tasks (cf. Table 2).

Table 2. Information requirements according to [12]

	Operational	Strategic
Source	internal	external
Scope	defined, narrow	wide
Level of aggregation	detailed	aggregate
Time horizon	historical	future
Currency	current	old
Required accuracy	high	low
Frequency of use	frequent	infrequent

Strategic information encompasses a wide content and timeline scope and stems rather from external sources. They are usually available on an aggregated level. The demand of strategic information is sporadic and future-oriented. Operational information use is frequent requiring high accuracy and currency on a detailed level of aggregation. Their focus is on reaction of occurrences in a defined scope using primarily internal sources [12].

Hayen [15] for example investigates 48 case study publications of BI applications in context of operational and strategic management levels. The analysis applies the information requirements according to Gorry and Morton [12] (cf. Table 3).

Table 3. Adapted information requirements of BI [15]

	Operational	Strategic
Scope	defined, narrow	wide
Level of aggregation	detailed	aggregate
Required accuracy	high	low
Frequency of use	frequent	infrequent
Range of user	wide	narrow
Operational efficiency	high	low
Duration of use	long	short
Rapid development need	low	high

The applied framework emphasizes on scope, level of aggregation, and frequency of use. Characteristics concerning the range of users, operational efficiency, the duration of use, and the need for rapid developments are added. Hayen's findings do not provide insights about development trends of strategic or operational BI. There is also no assignment of business applications to these categories. Furthermore, a rigorous literature review method is missing so that the case selection is hardly comprehensible.

The discussion demonstrates that the literature is insufficient to apply a conjoint review of BI applications in a strategic or operational context. Considering the circumstances that strategic and operational BI capabilities create business value [33], an analysis is needed to describe fields of BI applications and their characteristics. This is beneficial to consolidate the scientific knowledge regarding meaning and trends of BI in the area of strategic or operational decisions.

Method

The method follows a common phase-oriented approach [9]. A literature search considers the scientific databases of Business Source Complete (BSC), IEEE Xplore, AIS electronic Library (AISeL), ACM Digital Library, Emerald and Science Direct (SD). The search term is "Business Intelligence". Its appearance is limited to abstract, title, or keywords. The date of publication is not later than March 31, 2013. The search leads to an initial data set of 1,322 publications.

A group of two researchers evaluated all papers against the demonstrated understanding of BI. Papers using BI just as an abstract label for business knowledge and know how were excluded. The researchers classified the papers using the Hayen's information requirements and situational characteristics [15]. The evaluation reveals 1,057 publications classified in strategic and operational BI. The first category is also used for papers understanding BI as a holistic concept for an interrelated management of strategic and operational management levels. Each paper was also assigned to an industry and a functional application.

Results

The results encompass 537 papers on strategic BI and 520 papers on operational BI. Figure 1 illustrates the chronology of both categories.

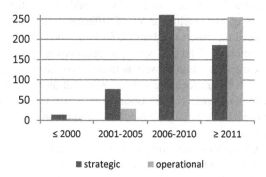

Figure 1. Chronology of investigated papers

The results are described and analyzed in context of industries and functional application areas. This chapter presents subsequently a text mining analysis based on the programming language R [44]. This approach pursues an evaluation of the classification's quality and resilience, and allows a content interpretation. However, the results are not a random sample of practical BI implementations. They reflect the relation of strategic and operational management to BI from a scientific point of view.

Analysis by application areas

The classification's industry profile consists of ten specific groups and one overarching group (cf. Fig. 2).

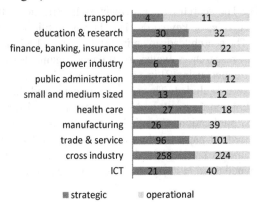

Figure 2. Industries profile of investigated papers

A majority of papers on strategic and operational BI is cross-industry with an ascending trend to strategic considerations. We could not identify any industry within these papers or they include a lot of different industries. The papers on operational BI exceed the papers on strategic BI by 1.5 percent in context of trade and service. The relation of BI and strategic decisions is more pronounced in health care, public administration as well as finance, banking, and insurance. The papers on operational BI are focusing to a larger extent on manufacturing, utility companies, education and research, transport as well as information and communications technology (ICT). Small and medium sized companies are likewise addressed in the papers.

Figure 3 shows industry trends comparing two publication's time periods. The two-section scale is chosen for reasons of readability. The year 2009 serves as split criterion, because there is the most balanced number of the publications. The ratio of papers on operational BI is increased for all industry groups. The focus has changed in seven of eleven groups.

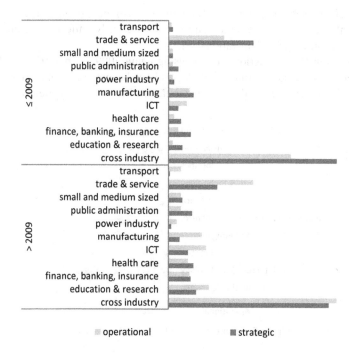

Figure 3. Industry trend of investigated papers

Next to the industry groups, we defined a functional category for each paper (cf. Fig. 4).

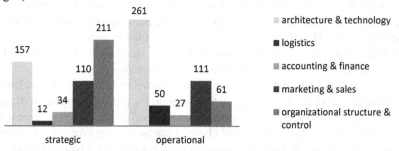

Figure 4. Functional profile of investigated papers

Architecture and technology aspects characterize investigations on operational BI, while activities of organizational structure and control dominate the papers on strategic BI. The papers on operational BI emphasize also more on logistics. Marketing and sales as well as accounting and finance are fairly uniform distributed to the papers on strategic and operational BI.

Figure 5 illustrates functional trends using again 2009 as split criterion for a two-section time scale. All functional classes have become more operational and the focus of marketing and sales changed in favor of an operational decision background.

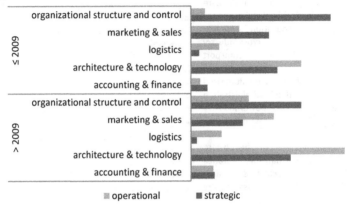

Figure 5. Functional trend of investigated papers

Analysis by text mining

We retrieved the data separately und built two different collections of the papers' abstracts on strategic and operational BI. Every corpus uses the corresponding paper abstracts as vector source. A following text transformation converts the retrieved text elements to lower cases and removed punctuations, numbers, URLs, and stop words. The stop words include a common list of general English terms and an additional list of ca. 200 words considering usual verbs and nouns of abstract writing. A stemming finished the data preprocessing.

Afterwards, we calculated the term frequencies for each data set. Word clouds illustrate the importance of the top 50 terms within the papers' abstracts on strategic and operational BI. The terms *data, business, intelligence,* and *system* are discarded for reasons of readability and clarity, because these are the most frequent words in the papers' abstracts on strategic and operational BI. Figure 6 illustrates the word clouds for papers on strategic BI. The terms *strategic, management, knowledge, competitive, planning, information,* and *decision* have a significant higher percentage in the papers on strategic BI. The most frequent strategic terms are *information, management,* and *decision.* They are interpretable as key elements stretching the relation of BI and strategic decisions. The terms *customer, marketing,* or *competitive* indicate a market orientation.

Figure 6. Word cloud on strategic BI

A wide and comprehensive scope is also evident for organizational concerns. There are aspects such as *maturity, learning, development,* or predictive representing a long-term and future-oriented emphasis. The adjectives *financial* and *economic* allow value and asset interpretations. An aggregated level of information is supported by high percentages of *planning, management,* and *knowledge.* In contrast to the papers on strategic BI, the key issues shift to *process, technology,* and *information* in the papers on operational BI (cf. Fig. 7).

Figure 7. Word cloud on operational BI

The papers on operational BI are notable distinct by *web, queries, process, real-time, traditional, optimization,* and *operational.* The relation of BI and operational decisions is strikingly characterized by the term *process*. It becomes apparent that processes define the source of information and narrow the scope of BI capabilities and operating activities. The importance of *tasks* and *execution* supports this pattern of argument. Thereby, *industrial*, *social* or *risk* indicate trends towards applications in an operational context. The association to technology aspects is strengthened due to operational ratios *web*, *queries*, *algorithm*, *platform*, *network*, and *internet*. The importance of *real-time* shows the demand for current and frequent information. A special distinguishing mark provides a consideration of effectiveness (accuracy and correctness of decisions) and efficiency (decision making cost). The percentage of *effective* is similar for both decision categories with a slight upward trend for the strategic perspective. The terms *efficiency* and *cost* have a higher importance in the operational context. Supporting arguments are time-related, because the time frame of decision making is more limited for operational decisions than in a strategic context. A decision's accuracy (*effective*) is necessary despite the short term background. This circumstance supports in combination with indices of an increasing complexity the higher ratios of analysis terms (*analytics*, *evaluation*, or *OLAP*) for the papers on operational BI.

The discussion demonstrates that the relation of BI and strategic or operational decisions is characterized by the meaning of common terms and not by different term. Papers on strategic and operational BI have next to *data*, *business*, *intelligence* and *system* 39 terms in common. This demonstrates an equal BI understanding for strategic and operational decision backgrounds. Table 4 illustrates this phenomenon by a common terms arrangement according to the definition of Hugh Watson [36] (cf. Sect. 2).

Table 4. Common terms of investigated papers

Part of the BI definition	Common words
BI is a broad category applications, technologies, and processes for gathering, storing, accessing, and analyzing data…	analytics, algorithm, architecture, concept, data, framework, implementation, integration, internet, mining, network, OLAP, platform, queries, report, software, system, technology, tools, warehousing, web
…to help business users make better decisions.	business, complex, customer, decision, development, effective, efficiency, evaluation, information, intelligence, knowledge, management, marketing, measurement, operational, performance, process, product, relationship, service, strategic, support

Discussion of topics on strategic and operational BI

After the single-word analysis has shown content-related characteristics of the papers on strategic and operational BI, we subsequently analyze word groups to discuss topics on strategic and operational BI. Therefore, we modified the text mining transformation by building n-grams with a maximum of four terms. All n-grams with an occurrence greater or equal to ten were scanned for BI topics.

The most frequent word groups of the papers' abstracts on strategic and operational BI are *business intelligence, decision making, data mining,* and *data warehouse.* Such general BI terms are discarded, because the discussion focuses on representative topics.

Topics on strategic BI

The topics on strategic BI address different areas of organizational management and control. Figure 8 illustrates the determined strategic topics.

Strategic decision and *strategic management* [19] consider a management level perspective. *Information management* [21] references to executive functions of topics on strategic BI. There is also a relation to knowledge aspects like *knowledge management* [18] and *knowledge discovery* [2] as well as the use of knowledge to predict future trends or patterns (*predictive analytics* [14]).

The importance of competitiveness and information about actual market trends becomes apparent by *competitive intelligence* or *competitive advantage* [45]. *Business analytics* or *business models* [6] indicate the relevance of business information and analyses. The design and development of organizational aspects according to strategic considerations is pursued by *corporate performance management* [4] or *maturity models* [24].

Figure 8. Topics on strategic BI

The topics on strategic BI encompass concepts to coordinate internal applications (*enterprise resource* planning, *enterprise system*) [46] and the interaction to customers (*customer relationship management, customer data*) [22]. Technical concerns seem to be quality-oriented (*data quality* [42], *information quality* [32]) and secondary in the strategic context.

Topics on operational BI

In contrast to strategic BI, the topics on operational BI focus on technological and application driven aspects (cf. Fig. 9). The study objects of operational BI are *business processes* and *business operations*. These objects are investigated by two perspectives. *Operational business intelligence* [16] represents a BI view of analyzing data and information for decision purposes. *Business process management* [29] defines, implements, monitors, and optimizes business processes and operations. Hence, the combined consideration of BI and operational decisions leads to a merging of originally separated topics - business process management and business intelligence. The existence of *process mining* [1] supports this argumentation.

There are operational topics indicating a relevance of flexibility aspects. This concerns the capability of organizational change due to new market conditions (*organizational agility*) [7] and an architectural flexibility of software systems (*service-oriented architecture*) [28].

Operational applications are characterized by *social media* [10], *sentiment analysis* [13], *risk management* [25], *shop floor* [17] and *situation awareness* [5]. Social media and sentiment analysis address the customer interaction, risk management, and shop floor organizational activities. Situation awareness focuses on the business user.

Figure 9. Topics on operational BI

58

From a data-oriented perspective, there is a relevance of *data management* [47] in operational context associated to *heterogeneous data sources, unstructured data* or *real time data*. The short-term time aspects are also expressed by *real time business intelligence* [37]. The topics of *big data* [6], *cloud computing* [3], *query processing,* and *workload management* [23] indicate a growing amount and complexity of data in an operational BI context.

Conclusion

Strategic and operational management tasks are characterized by different BI topics. The BI support of strategic decisions is associated with managerial concepts regarding corporate governance and information management. From a decision maker's perspective, topics on strategic BI address the definition and adjustment of an organization's objectives. There are approaches to govern the goal accomplishment and to enhance the organizational capabilities in context of strategic management tasks.

Operational BI is not in such a mature state of the art. The topics suggest rather domains of activities than they specify certain tasks of operational management to ensure a proper task execution or to employ tools or resources adequately. It remains unclear, whether and how operational BI provides a task-oriented decision support effectively and efficiently. There is a coexistence of decision making, technology issues, process management, and domain specificity in an operational management context. This forces decision makers to consider manifold perspectives and to examine also e.g. business process-oriented experiences and knowledge. Given a high level of detail and differentiation of operational activities, the corresponding decision making exhibits a high complexity. Faced by the circumstances that BI publications investigate increasingly operational management activities, the research focus has to shift its attention on providing assistance to encounter that complexity and to jointly investigate different perspectives of operational decision making.

The motivation of contributions to operational BI is not only practice-oriented, but also of scientific interest. Decision makers are addressed by a systematic reference of BI topics according to information needs and managerial tasks. The findings are relevant for scientists to guide future research activities. This paper introduces therefore a literature classification to discuss the status quo and development trends of BI towards an operational decision making. It is evident that there is a need for research in this context. Avenues of future BI research are the development and enhancement of organizational analysis and control concepts to support operational tasks. Common use cases concern core processes of manufacturing or service provision, support processes as well as project management activities. Further research on operational BI has to consider specific scenarios from a practical and generalizability from a scientific point of view.

References

1. van der Aalst W (2011) Using Process Mining to Bridge the Gap between BI and BPM. Computer 44(11): 77–80
2. Aggarwal N, Kumar A, Khatter H et al (2012) Analysis the effect of data mining techniques on database. Advances Eng Softw 47(1): 164–169
3. Baars H, Kemper H-G (2011) Ubiquitous Computing – an Application Domain for Business Intelligence in the Cloud? In: AMCIS 2011 Proceedings, Detroit MI, 4–8 August 2011
4. Brynjolfsson E, Hitt L, Kim HH (2011) Strength in Numbers: How does data-driven decision-making affect firm performance? In: ICIS 2011 Proceedings, Shanghai, 4–7 December 2011
5. Castellanos M, Gupta C, Wang S et al (2012) A platform for situational awareness in operational BI. Decis Support Syst 52(4): 869–883
6. Chen H, Chiang RHL, Storey VC (2012) Business Intelligence and Analytics: From Big Data to Big Impact. MISQ 36(4): 1165–1188
7. Chen X, Siau K (2012) Effect of Business Intelligence and IT Infrastructure Flexibility on Organizational Agility. In: ICIS 2012 Proceedings, Orlando FL, 16–19 December 2012
8. Cooper HM (1998) Synthesizing Research: A Guide for Literature Reviews. Sage, Thousand Oaks CA
9. Davis JR, Imhoff C, White C. (2009) Operational Business Intelligence: The State of the Art. Beye NETWORK Research, Boulder CO
10. Dinter B, Lorenz A (2012) Social Business Intelligence: a Literature Review and Research Agenda. In: ICIS 2012 Proceedings, Orlando FL, 16–19 December 2012
11. Eckerson WW (2007) Best Practices in Operational BI: Converging Analytical and Operational Processes. TDWI Best Practices Report, Renton WA
12. Gorry GA, Scott-Morton MS (1971) A framework for management information systems. Sloan Manag Rev 13(1): 55–72
13. Goul M, Marjanovic O, Baxley S et al (2012) Managing the Enterprise Business Intelligence App Store: Sentiment Analysis Supported Requirements Engineering. In: 45th Hawaii International Conference on System Sciences, Maui HI, 4–7 January 2012
14. Hair JF Jr (2007) Knowledge creation in marketing: the role of predictive analytics. Eur Bus Rev 19(4): 303–315
15. Hayen RL (2008) Direction in Business Intelligence: An Analysis of Applications. In: AMCIS 2008 Proceedings, Toronto, 14–17 August 2008
16. Hänel T, Felden C (2012) Towards a Stability of Process Oriented Decision Support Concepts Using the Example of Operational Business Intelligence. Paper presented at the Pre-ICIS BI Congress 3: Driving Innovation through Big Data Analytics, Orlando FL, 16–19 December 2012
17. Hänel T, Felden C (2011) Limits or Integration? – Manufacturing Execution Systems and Operational Business Intelligence. In: AMCIS 2011 Proceedings, Detroit MI, 4–8 August 2011
18. Hertlein M, Smolnik S, Von Kortzfleisch HFO (2011) Towards a Framework for Measuring Knowledge Management Service Productivity. In: ICIS 2011 Proceedings, Shanghai, 4–7 December 2011
19. Isaev D (2010) Information support of corporate governance and strategic management using analytical software. IEEE International Conference on Intelligent Computing and Intelligent Systems 3: 44–48. doi: 10.1109/ICICISYS.2010.5658550
20. Isik O, Jones MC, Sidorova A (2011) Business intelligence (BI) success and the role of BI capabilities. Intell Syst Account Financ Manag 18(4): 161–176
21. Jourdan Z, Rainer RK, Marshall TE (2008) Business Intelligence: An Analysis of the Literature. Inf Syst Manag 25: 121–131

22. Saldanha T, Krishnan M (2011) BI and CRM for Customer Involvement in Product and Service Development. In: ICIS 2011 Proceedings, Shanghai, 4–7 December 2011
23. Krompass S, Kuno H, Dayal U et al (2007) Dynamic workload management for very large data warehouses: juggling feathers and bowling balls. In: Proceedings of the 33rd international conference on Very large data bases, Vienna, 23–28 September 2007
24. Lahrmann G, Marx F, Winter R et al (2011) Business Intelligence Maturity: Development and Evaluation of a Theoretical Model. In: 44th Hawaii International Conference on System Sciences, Kauai HI, 4–7 January 2011
25. Lee G, Kulkarni U (2011) Business Intelligence in Corporate Risk Management. In: AMCIS 2011 Proceedings, Detroit MI, 4–8 August 2011
26. Luhn HP (1958) A Business Intelligence System. IBM J Res Dev 2(4): 314–319
27. Maghrabi RO, Oakley RL, Tambusamy R et al (2011) The Role of Business Intelligence (BI) in Service Innovation: An Ambidexterity Perspective. In: AMCIS 2011 Proceedings, Detroit MI, 4–8 August 2011
28. Mahmoud T, Marx Gómez J, Rezgui A et al (2012) Enhanced BI Systems with On-Demand Data Based on Semantic-Enabled Enterprise SOA. In: ECIS 2012 Proceedings, Barcelona, 10–13 June 2012
29. Marjanovic O (2010) The Importance of Process Thinking in Business Intelligence. Int J Bus Intelligence Res 1(4): 29–46
30. Matei G (2010) A collaborative approach of business intelligence systems. J Appl Collab Syst 2(2): 91–101
31. Mintzberg H (1973) The Nature of Managerial Work. Harper & Row, New York
32. Mueller RM, Coppoolse D (2013) Using Incentive Systems to Increase Information Quality in Business Intelligence: A Quasi-Experiment in the Financial Services Industry. In: 46th Hawaii International Conference on System Sciences, Maui HI, 7–10 January 2013
33. Seddon PB, Constantinidis D, Dod H (2012) How does business analytics contribute to business value? ICIS 2012 Proceedings, Orlando FL, 16–19 December 2012
34. Shollo A, Kautz K (2010) Towards an Understanding of Business Intelligence. In: ACIS 2010 Proceedings, Gardens Point QLD, 1–3 December 2010
35. Simon HA (1960) The new science of management decision. Harper and Row, New York
36. Watson HJ (2009) Tutorial Business Intelligence – Past, Present, and Future. Commun Assoc Inf Syst 25(39): 487–510
37. Watson HJ, Wixom BH, Hoffer J (2006) Real-time Business Intelligence: Best Practices at Continental Airlines. Inf Syst Manag 23(1): 7–18
38. Watson HJ, Wixom BH (2007) The current state of business intelligence. Computer 40 (9): 96–99
39. Webster J, Watson RT (2002) Analyzing the Past to Prepare for the Future: Writing a literature review. MISQ 26(2): xiii–xxiii
40. Wixom BH, Watson HJ (2010) The BI-Based Organization. Int J Bus Intelligence Res 1(1): 13–28
41. White C. (2006) The Next Generation of Business Intelligence: Operational BI. BI Research, Ashland OR
42. Yeoh W, Wang T-W, Verbitskiy Y (2012) Describing Data Quality Problem through a Metadata Framework. In: AMCIS 2012 Proceedings, Seattle, 9–11 August 2012
43. Yogev N, Fink L, Even A (2012) How Business Intelligence Creates Value. In: ECIS 2012 Proceedings, Barcelona, 10–13 June 2012
44. Zhao Y (2012) R and Data Mining: Examples and Case Studies. Elsevier, Amsterdam
45. Zhiqiang Z, Fader P, Padmanabhan B (2012) From Business Intelligence to Competitive Intelligence: Inferring Competitive Measures Using Augmented Site-Centric Data. Inf Syst Res 23(3): 698–720
46. Zhou L (2012) Research on the Integration Application of Business Intelligence and ERP. In: International Conference on Management of e-Commerce and e-Government, Beijing, 20–21 October 2012
47. Zoder S (2011) Analytical Master Data Management 2.0. In: AMCIS 2011 Proceedings, Detroit MI, 4–8 August 2011

4.2 Konzeptionelle Abgrenzung einer Operational Business Intelligence

Beitrag 1 hat die Notwendigkeit einer Auseinandersetzung mit BI zur Unterstützung operativer Managementaufgaben hergeleitet. Im weiteren Forschungsverlauf wird eine Begriffsklassifikation von IT-Konzepten erarbeitet, die eine operative Entscheidungsunterstützung adressieren. Bezugnehmend auf die Ergebnisse von Beitrag 1 ist eine Verschmelzung von BI und BPM zu beobachten. Aufgrund der thematischen Ausrichtung der Forschungsarbeit erfolgt eine Auseinandersetzung mit diesem Verschmelzungsbereich im Hinblick auf eine Analyse und Steuerung von Geschäftsprozessen. Daraus resultieren ein grundsätzliches Verständnis der Begrifflichkeit OpBI sowie eine Abgrenzung gegenüber den Termini BPI und BPM. Darüber hinaus erfolgt eine Differenzierung der OpBI von industriegetriebenen Ansätzen, die entscheidungsunterstützende Funktionaltäten thematisieren.

4.2.1 Operational Business Intelligence versus Business Process Intelligence versus Business Process Management

Die begriffliche Abgrenzung der OpBI zur BPI und zum BPM wird in Beitrag 2 und in Beitrag 3 vorgenommen. Dies erfolgt in Bezug auf den in Beitrag 1 identifizierten Handlungsbedarf zur Klärung einer aufgabenorientierten Entscheidungsunterstützung für ein operatives Management von Geschäftsprozessen.

4.2.1.1 Kurzdarstellung Beitrag 2

Beitrag 2 nimmt als Research in Progress eine qualitative Begriffsklassifikation durch die Methode des problemzentrierten Interviews vor. Die fachliche Annäherung an den Begriff OpBI erfolgt im Kontext der idealtypischen Unternehmenspyramide und der Geschäftsprozessorientierung. Zusätzlich werden funktionale Gesichtspunkte berücksichtigt, die aus verschiedenen Schlagwörtern des Themenbereichs der analytischen Informationssysteme resultieren. Diese Vorüberlegungen zeigen, dass ein einheitliches Begriffsverständnis von OpBI aufgrund einer Menge unterschiedlicher Interpretationsmöglichkeiten nicht gegeben ist. Beitrag 2 untersucht daher Gemeinsamkeiten und Unterschiede in der Wahrnehmung von OpBI.

Den Erkenntnissen von Beitrag 2 liegen 14 Expertengespräche zugrunde. In diesen Befragungen werden Schwerpunkte, Treiber, Potentiale und Herausforderungen für eine Implementierung diskutiert, die sich aus dem Zusammenwachsen von BI und operativen Managementaufgaben ableiten lassen. Das Ergebnis der Expertenbefragung bildet ein aus der Praxis gewonnener Begriffskonsens. OpBI ist dieser Konsolidierung zufolge ein Integrationskonzept für Daten, die in die Geschäftsprozesse einfließen oder während ihrer Ausführung entstehen. Es werden Analysefähigkeiten für Entscheidungsträger zur Verfügung gestellt, um eine Steuerung der unternehmerischen Wertschöpfung zu gewährleisten. Dies erfolgt zu

Gunsten einer kontinuierlichen Verbesserung von Gestaltung und Ausführung der Geschäftsprozesse. Es entsteht ein geschlossener Regelkreis, der den Entscheidungsträgern zeitgenaue Beziehungen zwischen der erreichten Prozessleistung und dem erforderlichen Status der Zielerreichung herstellt.

Die Treiber einer OpBI werden in der Erweiterung klassischer BI-Systeme gesehen, um die Leistungsfähigkeit von Geschäftsprozessen zu verbessern. Beitrag 2 identifiziert kundenspezifische Vertriebsprozesse und Produktionsumgebungen als potentielle Anwendungsfelder. Die Herausforderungen für eine Implementierung der OpBI stellen Wirtschaftlichkeitsbetrachtungen, Datenqualitätsprobleme und verteilte Informationsstrukturen dar. Beitrag 2 sieht abschließend einen weiteren Forschungsbedarf in der Festigung der qualitativ erlangten Erkenntnisse.

4.2.1.2 Beitrag 2: Towards a Stability of Process-Oriented Decision Support Concepts Using the Example of Operational Business Intelligence[2]

Introduction

Operational Business Intelligence (OpBI) is understood as decision support system to gain business process improvements by analyzing daily updated data [26]. That kind of analyzes are particularly relevant in case of a high complexity and diversity of finished products. OpBI supports activities like keeping track of different outputs at real-time, checking the completion, the reached utilization, process bottlenecks, and of course process' performance and its quality indicators. However, there is not much experience about obstacles or benefits of OpBI adoptions in organizations [21]. Practical studies ascertain growing interests of corresponding solutions and demonstrate current and planned investments [22], but there is no project's comparability, yet, because a variety of approaches are subsumed under OpBI and used in those projects [8, 33]. The missing common understanding about bundled OpBI decision support concepts constrains the conceptual foundation and enhancements in favor of a long-term availability and diffusion in organizations. Therefore, the paper's goal is to identify and discuss characteristics influencing the robustness and stability of OpBI as an example of concepts for a process-oriented decision support.

Business Intelligence (BI) is established to integrate and analyze organizational data [32, 36]. The growing maturity of BI within organizations as well as functional enriched BI tools increase the interest in a conceptual development of existing solutions [10]. The discussion about OpBI [35] is pointing out the usage of BI to support operational business processes [1]. OpBI coincides with concepts of Process Performance Management [17, 31] and Business Process Management

---

2 Hänel, T.; Felden, C.: Towards a Stability of Process-Oriented Decision Support Concepts Using the Example of Operational Business Intelligence. In: Procedings of Pre-ICIS BI Congress 3: Driving Innovation through Big Data Analytics, Orlando, Dezember 2012.

(BPM) [7, 29]. But, literature based classifications of OpBI argue rather from an individual perspectives of the adjacent concepts, as they make a meaningful presentation of key messages and benefits for a transparent management of business processes [21]. A heterogeneous representation of OpBI becomes evident by a variety of common, partly marketing driven terms differing in content significantly [8, 33]. The term and its potential to manage business processes remain unclear, which can be understood as an obstacle for the concept's adoption. OpBI seems to become an umbrella for buzzwords disappearing as part of the ephemeral nature of fashion waves. Such an ambiguity limits the willingness of organizations to implement decision support concepts like OpBI. This inhibits the extension of BI to an analysis and control of value adding processes. Therefore, the paper contributes a morphological box to the discussion about the robustness and stability of OpBI in context of a process-oriented decision support. The box methodizes main characteristics of OpBI by referencing on the experiences of preselected experts. The research results meet the need for transparent control mechanisms and opportunities for cross-functional analyses within organizations.

Chapter 2 presents reasons for difficulties to determine a precise definition of OpBI based on the existing literature. Expert interviews are used to discuss the result, because the missing consensus seems to be a main obstacle for bringing such a concept comparably into practice. Chapter 3 explains the structure of the underlying method to meet resilient quality criteria. Chapter 4 presents the results of its application. Finally, the paper is summarized to give conclusions and further research perspectives.

Dimensions of OpBI

OpBI is discussed as a convergence of BI functionalities, operational management tasks, and business process orientation [37]. Three dimensions are classified in the following. They are summarized to propositions in order to set up an initial point for expert interviews.

Hierarchy based dimension of OpBI

Strategic and tactical BI and OpBI are usually differentiated by the organizational hierarchy levels where they are used [8]. But, they are still using same concept shapes, because the techniques used for analysis and reporting remain unchanged. Compared to strategic and tactical BI, the conceptual design of OpBI is contrary discussed in the existing literature. A varying understanding is already recognized for common and therefore in organizations available BI approaches [16]. This issue exacerbates also an unambiguous classification of OpBI.

Strategic BI analyzes long term business goals in time frames from months up to years. Tactical BI focuses on business domains in order to achieve strategic goals. Analysts and business managers decide with data aged between days up to months or years. Strategic and tactical BI refers to historical data based on a user's information demand. [6] Applications supporting strategic and tactical decisions are regarded as classical [1] or traditional BI [37]. OpBI is able to amplify the traditional approaches in order to improve organizational processes in a fast and flexible manner [5]. Conceptual differences of OpBI are characterized by the following aspects:

1. The decision making focus is a single business process. Traditional BI techniques are integrated to facilitate a closed loop environment. Data are collected from operational and external systems, analyzed and combined with appropriate information. The insights get incorporated back within the business process. [6]
2. The pace of decision making has to meet the business process requirements [6]. The spread between the event occurrence and the subsequent decision execution is called action time. A decision's business value depends on three kinds of delay. Data latency characterizes the time for data collection and storage. Insights to control the business process are produced during the analysis latency. The time to finally derive an appropriate action is called decision latency. [19]
3. The initiators of the decision making are lots of different users like internal staff, customers, suppliers or external institutions [6]. The access can be extended to the business processes skirting human interaction by automated control mechanisms [8].
4. The frequency of the decision making is high. This implies that the collective impact of decisions supported by OpBI is equal to strategic significance. [8]

The difference of traditional in organizations available BI approaches and OpBI is concluded differently. Fundamental differences are referred to a huge amount of short dated decisions to be provided for lots of heterogeneous users [1, 8]. This leads to the following proposition:

> P1: OpBI is an independent concept from traditional, available BI approaches.

In contrary to the aforementioned perception, an evolutionary aspect is discussed [37]. This leads to the point that the expansion of mature BI techniques within the scope of business processes is picked out as central issue [6]. This derives the following proposition:

> P2: OpBI represents an advancement of mature BI techniques.

Process-oriented dimension of OpBI

Organizations are able to apply BI in context of BPM [18]. The first phase of BPM deals with the identification, design, and modeling of value creating business processes [4]. Analytical activities are supportable by Business Process Intelligence

(BPI) in order to provide information for tactical and strategic management [11]. Considering a synonymous usage of BPI and OpBI [20], the following proposition is derived from the discussion about BPI:

P3: OpBI focuses on process design/ redesign.

The execution of designed processes transforms input variables to specified output quantities [27]. Analysis capabilities can support this transformation [2]. An embedding of analytical information for a decision support within process execution is called Process centric BI [3]. An equal understanding of OpBI and embedded BI is evident in the existing literature [34] so that a further proposition is built from the process-oriented classification:

P4: OpBI provides analytical information during process execution.

OpBI aims for an integration of analytics and operational processes, too [8]. Information of process states is provided in contrast to a process centric BI [12]. OpBI is understandable as an interface between process design and execution. It offers benefits to control and analyze the process execution. The insights of OpBI are also input for a BPI's tactical or strategic decision making [11]. A consideration of these aspects allows a third proposition of the process-oriented classification:

P5: OpBI supports control activities during process execution.

Functional dimension of OpBI

In a practical perception OpBI functionalities are described by different related terms (cf. Table 1). They are identified by conducted surveys in fields of BI and Data Warehousing [8, 33]. Table 1 shows concepts emphasizing different decision support aspects of operational business process management. There is evidence that OpBI is misunderstood as buzzword and umbrella term for already existing approaches, which is summarized by the following propositions:

P6: OpBI is a buzzword for existing operational analysis functions and disappears as a decision support concept.

P7: There are existing analytical functions allowing a comprehensive management of operational business processes.

The benefits of OpBI are determined just as cross-functional application [8]. Thereby, the organizations focus on sales and finance departments, yet, so that the application intensity is unequally distributed over the functional areas. OpBI seems to be very popular in organizational customer interfaces. The development and growing potential of OpBI in currently not intensely pronounced areas in a cross-industry context is not obvious. This is especially related to production and manufacturing environments. The following propositions serve as a basis for a further investigation of these aspects:

P8: OpBI has current and prospective application domains.

P9: OpBI has a cross-industrial potential to support the operational decision making.

Table 1. Related terms for OpBI functionalities

Related term	Description
Operational reporting (OR)	OR provides detailed information about transactions of daily business processes supporting short term and immediate decisions [23].
Operational Data Warehousing (ODW)	ODW enhances data models and interfaces of data warehouse architectures to facilitate interoperability to operational systems [33].
Operational Data Store (ODS)	The ODS manages the tradeoff between performance and flexibility by an integration of operational applications with a data warehouse [24].
Real time, Right time BI	In context of real time the latencies are reduced on minimum level, while right time requires process specific time value dependencies. [19]
Business critical analytics (BCA)	BCA looks for patterns and relationships in previously collected and processed data. It predicts trends for business critical processes. [9]
Business Activity Monitoring (BAM)	BAM deals with a surveillance of performance indicators and considers multiple information sources to facilitate effective business processes [28].
Active Data Warehousing (ADW)	ADW is popularized by Teradata focusing the interaction of an ODS and a data warehouse to reduce latencies and redundancy [25].

Research model

The paper uses qualitative research [38], because none of the OpBI dimensions provide a certain imagination about the underlying concept. The conceptual design of OpBI depends on an individual understanding, yet. This bias leads to the inadequateness of a quantitative investigation, because the results will not be comparable to each other, if e.g. one perspective leads to different conceptual designs or different understandings. As a method of qualitative research, interviews provide the opportunity to collect expert opinions [13]. In this context, biases have to be accounted and acknowledged [30]. The known circumstances facilitate a collection of diversified opinions regarding OpBI. Thus, the creation of a conceptual consensus is possible taking into account the different understandings.

Expert interviews are divided into phases. They address the problem and eligible experts as well as a guideline based interview conducting and evaluation. Actions to improve the quality accompany the interview research phases permanently. [14] In the present investigation, 14 experts from Switzerland, Germany, and the Netherlands were selected. The used selection criterion was everyone's familiarity with BI, process-oriented decision support, or operational management. The one hour telephone interviews were conducted in September and October 2011. An interview guideline served as impulse for comprehensive remarks of the experts regarding their individual perception of OpBI. All interviews were recorded and transcribed. Afterwards, the participants checked the written conversation records for correctness. An interpretation group of three persons read all transcriptions. The interpreters investigated independent to each other similarities and differences within and across the interviews. They determined generalized statements to derive a consolidation of the qualitative OpBI characteristics. The course of interpretation made apparent that the amount of selected experts is adequate, because no unknown aspects were identified after about 80 percent of the interpreted interviews. There exists no reason that a bigger amount of participants would change this result. The derived generalizations were discussed in regular workshops to gain gradually quality improvements. Figure 1 summarizes the research process.

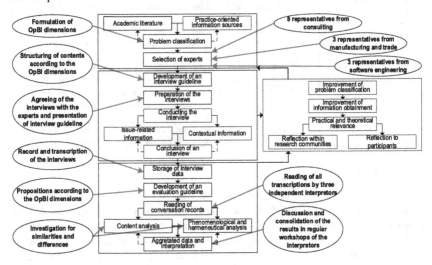

Figure 1. Research model according to [15]

Findings

The interview analysis determines the meaning of OpBI by identifying four classes: key aspects, drivers, potentials and application fields, as well as implementation challenges. Each class is discussed in detail. Finally, the results are systematized using a morphological box and referred to the dimensions of OpBI.

Key aspects of OpBI

The first class describes central factors of OpBI. They could be identified across all interviews. OpBI deals with the integration of process data on instance level to determine primarily non-financial key figures in regular report cycles during process execution. A control effect to core processes of an organization is pursued, while the time reference of underlying decisions is short-dated. Based on the key aspects, the interpretation focuses on the differentiation between OpBI and traditional BI. The majority of the interviews (11) does not support drawing of a clear border. The main argument is that the same functions regarding preparation and analysis of data have to be considered. The adjective *operational* does not require the replacement of existing systems, but merely the usage of BI in context of day to day value creation with higher data granularity and shorter decision times.

Drivers of OpBI

The second class of analysis results describes motivations for an organization to implement OpBI from the expert's point of view. The interpretation discovers that non-technical considerations take precedence (cf. Table 2). They focus on an expansion of existing BI solutions and thereby on an improvement of process performance. The number in brackets characterizes the assignable expert opinions. A complement to these drives is technical maturity of the system environment. The drivers support the assertion that OpBI represents an advancement of traditional BI.

Table 2. Non-technical drivers of OpBI

Enhancement of existing BI solutions	Improvement of process performance
Comprehensive operational process analyses (14)	Realizing cost saving potentials by constant performance level (14)
Fast provision of current information (14)	Adaptiveness to changing basic conditions (12)
Higher transparency requirements (12)	Meeting of increasing demands of process and product quality (11)
Broader range of heterogeneous users (11)	
Clarification of BI potentials to overcome reservations regarding adoptions (9)	Increasing of outcome and output rates (10)
Support of core business processes (7)	Acceleration of production and process cycles (10)
Tapping the higher integration potentials through cross-linked structures and analyzes(6)	Flexible process control (7)
Handling of increasing data volumes (5)	New insights regarding interdependencies between process structures and performance (5)

Potentials and application fields for OpBI

The third class deals with potentials and application fields of OpBI. A growing interest is seen in customer relationship management or marketing. The interpretation could identify certain examples with respect to an analysis of customer intentions, when the success of current offers is monitored and adjusted according to the impact on a target group's behavior.

The perception of the participants regarding the use of OpBI in manufacturing is further analyzed to complement the discussion. All interviews demonstrate a huge OpBI potential for the industrial sector, which is not tapped, yet. The answers refer often to a processing of production data using dashboards. This allows a monitoring and reporting of process performance in terms of operational control.

Manufacturers are able to identify quality variations, weaknesses or machine failures. Such information support time savings or an acceleration of production cycles. Particularly industries with assembly lines, like automotive or packaging industry are seen as appropriate areas. The following statement of one expert sums up the underlying trend of the interviews regarding this aspect:

> *You are interested for use cases, where short dated decisions have to be frequently made?*
> *So, you are automatically in production environments and manufacturing.*

To assess the significance of potentials and application fields, it is necessary to clarify whether the experts grasp OpBI as a buzzword. There is no consensus regarding this aspect. Two experts account OpBI as an umbrella term for already existing concepts of operational process control. In contrast, other participants did not see the term as fashion or were not able to make a specification regarding this aspect. The majority (9) is positioned between the extremes. They mentioned that OpBI is marketing driven, but it pushes new application fields for traditional BI.

Implementation challenges of OpBI

The fourth class of analysis results addresses three key challenges for implementation of OpBI. The interpretation reveals that the determination of cost and benefit in context of OpBI is associated with difficulties. While expenses can be determined by use cases, the assessment of subsequent cost and risks is associated with uncertainties. A benefit analysis is fuzzy, too. Quantitative calculations are frequently backed by qualitative arguments like the obtainment of new data. A couple of participants mentioned that profitability goals often fall short. Economic considerations are eclipsed due to a missing critical analysis.

The further challenge identified across all interviews refers to the assurance of data quality. Poorly met user expectations are a main concern of the experts, because a lack of data quality leads to a great loss of confidence. The huge amount of data and the short-dated decision background of OpBI intensify this issue. Further relevant is transparency of data quality. Maintenance of data is expensive especially in operational context so that 100 percent data quality seems to be not required.

The third challenge refers to fragmented informal networks. In some cases, up to 15 independent decision support applications could be identified. The interpretation discovered different reasons. Departments evaluate data e.g. according to the changing needs. Long wait on required reports reinforce the desire for own solutions. There are also cases, in which transparency is not intentional, because knowledge is seen as part of the raison d'être. Regarding OpBI, the participants identified a clear opposite to fragmented networks, because the business process steps are cross-functional involved in the decision making.

Systematization of interview results

A morphological box [38] presents the main characteristics of OpBI identified within the interview interpretations and arranges them according to the analysis results. The systematization indicates which propositions of the OpBI dimensions are confirmed. They appear bold in Figure 2.

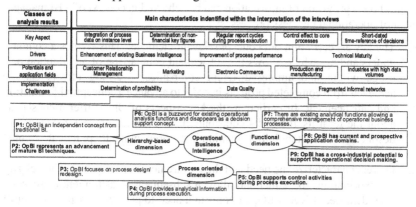

Figure 2. Morphological box of Operational Business Intelligence

The key aspects are mainly supporting P5, thus OpBI supports control activities during process execution. Therewith, the purpose of OpBI in context of process orientation is clarified. This allows a differentiation from the concepts of BPI and embedded BI. OpBI provides analytical capabilities in order to control the organizational value creation in favor of a continuous improvement of process design and execution. Thereby, it is a conductor between the analytical intention and the actual occurrence of a process, while a closed looped system within a process-oriented organization is facilitated. OpBI meets this transmitter role, because a timely adequate relation between the process performance as well as the status of target achievement is made and communicated to the corresponding audience.

The drivers and implementation challenges support P2 declaring that OpBI represents an advancement of mature BI techniques. By supporting decision making, OpBI cannot be seen as a new concept in the sense of breaking away from traditional methods. Moreover, it embodies the trend towards cross-linked operational and analytical systems, so that organizations are able to react fast and flexible on changing conditions in their business environment. The potentials and application fields support the propositions of P8 and P9. There are promising application fields in a cross-industrial context. The highest potential could be identified in the area of manufacturing, where OpBI is currently less pronounced.

Conclusion

The paper presents a morphological box to bring main characteristics into the discussion about the stability and robustness of OpBI. This is a novel arrangement and visualization of the concept characteristics based on experiences of independent experts. The morphological box clarifies the meaning of OpBI and demonstrates how a provision of information can be achieved in context of a BI management of operational business processes:

1. The key aspects point out concept relevant elements. This creates a common understanding, which allows the subsequent comparison of an adoption or a usage within and among different companies. Learning effects can be achieved from completed projects in order to advance a conceptual foundation and enhancement. In particular, the key aspects of OpBI offer a consensus about the term itself and its contribution for business process management despite an inconsistent initial situation in the predominantly practical-oriented literature.
2. Drivers characterize the need and the requirements of a concept. They clarify the expectations to be met and allow a subsequent measurement of success. The identified drivers of OpBI confirm a need to provide transparent control mechanisms for certain processes and within a coherent process management. Current and planned investments are justified from a practical point of view.
3. The potentials and application fields suggest a concept's adaptability and versatility. Especially in production and manufacturing, OpBI has a marginal state, yet, although, it represents a promising application background. An intensive involvement of BI capabilities is required to strengthen this perception. This implies advancements of a future BI usage to analyze and control business processes.
4. The implementation challenges allow conclusions with regard to effort and obstacles of a concept's adoption. Organizations are able to consider already existing experience or external knowledge. The identified implementation challenges in context of OpBI demonstrate the advantage of being able to consider already existing experiences and knowledge of BI.

The paper clarifies the meaning of OpBI to avoid an ambiguity, which can be understood as an implementation obstacle for organizations. The conceptual consensus supports the movement of OpBI into practice. Since BI is established and well known, there is the possibility, now, to apply the mature techniques in context of the daily business' analysis and control. This is especially advantageous faced by the threat to lose the track within the value creation due to high complexity and versatility. The novelty brought by a consensus regarding the meaning of OpBI is the possibility to benchmark existing and planned adoptions. This is especially interesting for organizations relying on learning effects, because their environment is highly competitive or necessary resources are not available to pioneer decision support concepts. The conceptual consensus builds up an initial point for further research actions and to differentiate and classify OpBI to related terms. However, care must be taken in consequence of the inevitable bias due to the qualitative research method. 14 interviews might not represent the mainstream in context of an external validity. But faced by the inconsistency within predominantly practical-oriented literature, the expert interviews provide a suitable approach to reach actually a conceptual consensus. This is also illustrated by the degree of agreement between the interviews.

This paper demonstrates application fields in customer relationship management, marketing, electronic commerce, production and manufacturing, as well as in industries with high data volumes. These potentials should be analyzed in practice to develop future research. Since design and execution of business processes depends on individual characteristics, the implementation of OpBI solutions has to be aligned accordingly. Organizations are able to assign deviations from process targets to causative process steps in order to initiate appropriate corrective actions. There is also the possibility to look for patterns within operational data or to generate decision proposals in situations of repeated or similar occurrence of underlying business events. OpBI supports the decision making as a service provider for data integration and analysis to meet specialist control and analysis requirements against this background. Case specific applications allow a consideration of already existing IT systems in addition in context of further investigations in order to achieve knowledge about certain implementations in organizations. Such references develop the concept's sustainability especially in application fields, in which a lot of benefits are identifiable, e.g. in manufacturing and production environments.

References

1. Blasum, R. 2006. "Operational BI," at: http://www.businesscode.de/cms/uploads/media/ BCD_Operational_BI_01.pdf, last accessed on 2012-09-14.
2. Bucher, T., and Dinter, B. 2008 "Process orientation of information logistics - an empirical analysis to assess benefits, design factors, and realization approaches," in *Proceedings of the 41th Hawaii International Conference on System Sciences*, R. Sprague (ed.), Los Alamitos: IEEE Computer Society.
3. Bucher, T., Gericke, A., and Sigg, S. 2009. "Process-centric business intelligence," *Business Process Management Journal* (15:3), pp. 408-429.
4. Bucher, T., and Winter, R. 2006. "Classification of Business Process Management Approaches - An Exploratory Analysis," *BIT - Banking and Information Technology* (3:7), pp. 9-20.
5. Cunningham, D. 2005. "Aligning Business Intelligence with Business Processes," *What Works - TDWI* (20:1), pp. 50-51.
6. Davis, J., Imhoff, C., and White, C. 2009. *Operational Business Intelligence: The State of the Art*, Boulder CO: Beye NETWORK Research.
7. Dayal, U., Wilkinson, K., Simitsis, A., and Castellanos, M. 2009. "Business Processes Meet Operational Business Intelligence," *IEEE Data Engineering Bulletin* (32:3), pp. 35-41.
8. Eckerson, W. W. 2007. Best Practices in Operational BI: Converging Analytical and Operational Processes, Renton: TDWI Best Practices Report.

9. Eckerson, W. W. 2007a. Predictive Analytics: Extending the Value of Your Data Warehousing Investment, Renton: TDWI Best Practices Report.
10. Evelson, B. 2011. *Trends 2011 And Beyond: Business Intelligence*, Cambridge: Forrester Research.
11. Felden, C., Chamoni, P., and Linden, M. 2010. "From Process Execution towards a Business Process Intelligence," in *Business Information Systems 13th International Conference*, W. Abramowicz and R. Tolksdorf (eds.), Germany, Berlin, pp. 195-206.
12. Ferguson, M. 2008. "Getting Started With Operational BI," at: http://www.beyenetwork.be/print/8399, last accessed on 2012-09-14.
13. Flick, U. 2004. A Companion to Qualitative Research, London: SAGE.
14. Flick, U. 2009. *An Introduction to Qualitative Research*, 4th edition, London: SAGE.
15. Jaeger, U., and Reinecke, S. 2009. "Das Expertengespräch als zentrale Form einer qualitativen Befragung," in Baumgarth, C., Eisend, M., and Evanschitzky, H. (eds): Empirische Mastertechniken der Marketing- und Managementforschung, Wiesbaden: Gabler, pp. 29-76.
16. Gibson, M., Arnott, D. and Carlsson, S. (2004). Evaluating the Intangible Benefits of Business Intelligence: Review & Research Agenda. In Proceeding of the Decision Support in an Uncertain and Complex World: The IFIP TC8/WG8.3 International Conference, Prato, Italy, 295-305.
17. Golfarelli, M., Rizzi, S., and Cella, I. 2004. "Beyond data warehousing: what's next in business intelligence?," in *Proceedings of 7th ACM international workshop on Data warehousing and OLAP*, New York, pp. 1-6.
18. Grigori, D., Casati, F., Castellanos, M., Dayal, U., Sayal, M., and Shan, M.-C. 2004. "Business Process Intelligence," *Computers in Industry* (53:1), pp. 321-343.
19. Hackathorn, R. 2004. "The BI Watch: Real-Time to Real-Value," *DM Review* (14:1), pp.1-4.
20. Hall, C. 2004. "Business Process Intelligence," *Business Process Trends* (2:6), pp. 1-11.
21. Hänel, T., and Felden, C. 2011. "Limits or Integration? - Manufacturing Execution Systems and Operational Business Intelligence," *in Amercias Conference on Informations Systems (AMCIS)*, Detroit, paper 104.
22. Hatch, D. 2009. *Operational Business Intelligence*, Boston, MA: Aberdeen Group.
23. Inmon, W. H. 2000. "Operational and Informational Reporting," at: http://www.information-management.com/ issues/20000701/2349-1.html, last accessed on 2012-09-14.
24. Inmon, W. H. 2005. *Building the Data Warehouse*, Indianapolis: Wiley.
25. Imhoff, C. Active Data Warehousing: The Ultimate Fulfillment of the Operational Data Store, Boulder, CO: Intelligent Solutions, Inc.
26. Imhoff, C., and White, C. 2012. *Operational Analytics Balancing Business Benefits and Technology Costs*, TDWI Checklist Report, Renton: TDWI Research.
27. EN ISO 9000 2005. *Quality management systems: Fundamentals and vocabulary*, Brussels: European Committee for Standardization.
28. McCoy, D., Schulte, R., Buytendijk, F., Rayner, N., Tiedrich, A, 2001. "Business Activity Monitoring: The Promise and Reality," at: http://www.marcusball.com/marcusball/work/TechReference/ Business%20Activity%20Monitoring%20The%20Promise%20and%20Reality.htm, last accessed on 2012-09-14.
29. Marjanovic, O. 2007. "The Next Stage of Operational Business Intelligence: Creating New Challenges for Business Process Management," in *Proceedings of the 40th Annual Hawaii International Conference on System Sciences, IEEE Computer Society*, Washington DC, pp. 215-224.
30. Mehra, B. 2002. "Bias in qualitative research: Voices from an online classroom," *The Qualitative Report (7:1)*, at: http://www.nova.edu/ssss/QR/QR7-1/mehra.html, last accessed on 2012-09-14.
31. Melchert, F., Winter, R., and Klesse, M. 2004. „Aligning Process Automation and Business Intelligence to Support Corporate Performance Management", in *Proceedings of the Tenth Americas Conference on Information Systems,* New York, paper 507.
32. Moss, L. T., and Atre, S. 2003. Business Intelligence Roadmap: The Complete Project Lifecycle for Decision-Support Applications, Boston: Addison Wesley.
33. Russom, P. 2010. Operational Data Warehousing: The Integration of Operational Applications and Data Warehouses, Renton: TDWI Best Practices Report.
34. Sacu, C., and Spruit, M. 2008. "BIDM: The Business Intelligence Development Model," in *Proceedings 12th International Conference on Enterprise Information Systems (ICEIS)*, Portugal, Funchal, pp. 288-293.

35. Ventana Research 2011. *Operational Business Intelligence Benchmark*, San Ramon, CA: Ventana Research.
36. Watson, H. J., and Wixom, B. H. 2007. "The Current State of Business Intelligence", *Computer* (40:9), pp. 96-99.
37. White, C. 2006. The Next Generation of Business Intelligence: Operational BI, Ashland, OR: BI Research.
38. Yin, R. 2009. *Case Study Research Design and Methods*, 4th edition, London: SAGE.
39. Zwicky, F. 1969. Discovery, Invention, Research - Through the Morphological Approach, Toronto: The Macmillan Company.

4.2.1.3 Kurzdarstellung Beitrag 3

Beitrag 3 erweitert das qualitative Begriffsverständnis von OpBI im Rahmen einer theoriegeleiteten Untersuchung. Die in Beitrag 2 explorierten Integrationsaspekte werden einer argumentativ-deduktiven Analyse unterzogen. Diese Methode dient in diesem Zusammenhang der Beschreibung von Determinanten einer integrierten Informationsverarbeitung für OpBI, um die Analyse und Steuerung von Geschäftsprozessen aus technologischer und betriebswirtschaftlicher Sicht zu charakterisieren. Dazu entwickelt Beitrag 3 einen theoretischen Rahmen bestehend aus vier Theorien (Dynamic Capabilities, Organizational Information Processing, Process Virtualization und Work System Lifecycle).

Das Theoriemodell wird anhand einer Stichprobe von 109 prozessorientierten Unternehmen aus dem Produktions- und Dienstleistungssektor empirisch getestet. Die Ergebnisse einer Strukturgleichungsmodellierung bestätigen eine Abhängigkeit der OpBI-spezifischen Integrationsaspekte von externen und internen Unternehmensfaktoren, die eine Analyse und Steuerung von Geschäftsprozessen beeinflussen. Ein volatiles Marktumfeld erhöht die Relevanz von OpBI ebenso wie eine komplexe Gestaltung von Produkten oder Dienstleistungen. Aus IT-technischer Sicht sind vernetzte Systeme erforderlich, die durch entsprechende Kommunikationskanäle einen vertikalen und horizontalen Informationsfluss im Unternehmen gewährleisten müssen. Beitrag 3 kennzeichnet OpBI als Integrationsansatz für Daten, Prozesse und Methoden im Rahmen der Informationsverarbeitung. Als weiterer Forschungsbedarf werden eine Übertragung der theoretischen Erkenntnisse auf praktische Anwendungsfälle und eine kritische Überprüfung der Integrationsaspekte vor diesem Hintergrund identifiziert.

4.2.1.4 Beitrag 3: An Empirical Investigation of Operational Business Intelligence Perspectives to Support an Analysis and Control of Business Processes[3]

Introduction

The analysis and control of business processes is determining the competitiveness of organizations. This facilitates a consideration of and a reaction to changing influencing factors on the organizational business processes. Approaches to integrate IS and, due to this, a technical and a business perspective are seen as beneficial to analyze and control business processes [1]. OpBI is a recent example for an IS-driven integration as it concerns a decision making to improve business processes by analyzing daily updated data [2]. Thereby, a reinforced IS integration of business process information leads to a higher efficiency in terms of business process improvement [1], [3]. It is already stated that the efficiency of IS concepts is conditional and depends on strategic considerations in line with surrounding market conditions [4]. The explanation of influencing factors on IS-driven integration gains insights to justify a choice or a rejection of a concept like OpBI based on a particular organizational strategy. This demands the need to examine and discuss different perspectives on an IS-driven integration of technical and business aspects to analyze and control business processes. This paper's goal is therefore to explain the integration requirements of OpBI for an analysis and control of business processes.

The literature about OpBI encompasses predominantly case studies [5]–[11] and occasional theoretical considerations [7], [12]. However, the literature neither discusses nor clarifies OpBI for the purpose of analyzing and controlling the performance of business processes. This makes it rather impossible to gain general knowledge out of research findings of previous OpBI applications. However, such a discussion is important to validate benefits or obstacles of IS integration aspects for OpBI. The validation of such aspects is interesting to build in particular strategies for business process improvements. We address this research gap by introducing a theoretical model to examine the dependent variable of IS integration for OpBI to be able to analyze and control business processes. We contribute to research with an empirical investigation of 109 process-oriented organizations. This provides a theoretical fundament for the field of operational decision making by a novel combination of dynamic capabilities, organizational information processing, process virtualization, and work system theory. This basis can be used to study the analysis and control of business processes by OpBI in general and to distinguish OpBI from other process-oriented decision support concepts, like business process intelligence [13].

---

3 Hänel, T.; Felden, C.: An Empirical Investigation of Operational Business Intelligence Perspectives to Support an Analysis and Control of Business Processes. In: 48th Annual Hawaii International Conference on System Sciences, Kauai, Januar 2015.

The paper discusses at first the need of IS integration for OpBI to analyze and control business processes. Then, we present a research model to explain this phenomenon by the use of stated theories. Next, the paper describes the results of a cross-sectional survey including a partial least squares (PLS) analysis of the research model. The findings are discussed and summarized in the concluding sections.

Status quo

The context of our study addresses three research areas (cf. Figure 1). These areas cause a following discussion and a choice of findings from previous studies. An integration of IS to combine technical and business perspectives in organizations as well as a business process coordination and improvement was mainly discussed in the 1990s. A consideration of OpBI requires a new investigation.

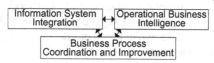

Figure 1. Research areas

The need of IS integration for OpBI to analyze and control business processes

The coordination and improvement of business processes mentioned in Figure 1 has a reference to the value chain discussion [14]. A value chain is understood as an interrelated system of different core and supporting activities [15]. The management of business process information and operational performance is a beneficial strategy to organize the activities of the value chain efficiently [14]. This can be guided by steps to analyze and control process information [16]. The relevance of such a closed loop of analysis and control manifests itself in methods to improve business processes like six sigma [17]. A critical success factor for such a process improvement is an effective use of information technology (IT) [16]. Already [15] discussed that value activities always have an information processing component. This role of IT is still emphasized in recent concepts like e³-value [18]. The efficiency of IT to manage business processes gains thereby evident benefits from a comprehensive IS integration [3]. Consequently, methods for process improvements require an integrative IT-based approach for a closed loop analysis and control of business processes [14].

OpBI is related to the coordination and improvement of business processes (cf. Figure 1). The reason for this relation is the concern of OpBI to analyze the efficiency of daily business processes and to take control actions of process improvement. OpBI integrates analytical information and business processes through an application of common BI functionalities. [2] The inherent IS integration of these BI functionalities [19] is used for an analysis and control of business processes.

These integration efforts are beneficial on an operational level in order to improve business processes [20].

Related studies

A structured literature review reveals that the mentioned integration capability of OpBI is often investigated by case studies. There are cases in manufacturing [5], [10] and in service provision [6], [11]. From another point of view, the success of process improvements depends on a systemic and holistic understanding of organizations. Such systematizations are achievable with theories [21]. However, theoretical investigations regarding OpBI are rare. Previous studies do not intend to explain determinants of IS integration for OpBI to analyze and control business processes. The framework of [7] discusses a theoretical integration of BI and business process management (BPM) to support knowledge-intensive processes. This framework has been used for empirical case studies in service organizations [8], [9]. Another study of [12] considers strategic and operational BI capabilities combined in a theoretical model to explain an incremental BI-driven service innovation and its performance impacts.

Related topics to OpBI are business process intelligence (BPI) [22] and process-centric BI (PCBI) [23]. PCBI concerns a process execution and considers analytical information in order to support the fulfillment of process-related tasks. The study of [23] clearly distinguishes PCBI from using BI to analyze and control business processes. BPI supports strategic and tactical management decisions about a process design or redesign [22]. According to [22] the use of BPI can be investigated by multiple theories. The proposed approach is however not verified. Moreover, the verification approach refers to a mix of empirical and qualitative research actions. The findings of [22] are therefore not easily transferable in the hitherto discussed OpBI context.

Research model and hypotheses

We propose a multi-perspective consideration to explain OpBI in terms of analyzing and controlling business processes. This is reasonable due to the suitability of multiple theoretical frameworks to explain complex relationships [24]. Such a complexity is evident for relationships between IS integration and management control [25], which is in particular the field of an OpBI's decision making. An inherent complexity is also regarded with BPM [26], which is addressed by OpBI [9].

Preliminary considerations

We are going to combine four theories to explain an IS integration in context of OpBI, i.e. dynamic capabilities, organizational information processing, process virtualization, and work system theory. These theories seem to be vaguely related at a first glance. However, the relation can be drawn due to the organizational application context of OpBI. Object of OpBI's interest is the performance of business processes. Performance indicators are measured by analytical models and systems. The analysis results are input for operational decisions to configure actions for a coordination and improvement of business processes.

Hence, OpBI addresses the change of organizational processes, which is a core issue of dynamic capabilities [27]. OpBI provides analytical capabilities to process and communicate information about processes. These are key issues of organizational information processing, which argues that certain organizational design strategies can improve company performance [28]. The analysis and control of business processes with OpBI is an IT-driven approach to collect, transform and communicate information. Such IT capabilities are understood as a main driver and enabler for process virtualization [29]. Thus, a business process needs to be at least partially amenable to virtualization so that a concept like OpBI is generally able to achieve a support in this context. Due to the mentioned information processing capabilities, OpBI can be understood as an IT-reliant work system [30]. Therefore, the dynamic view of how a work system evolves over time is transferrable to OpBI.

The following specifies the preliminary considerations for each theory and derives hypotheses on this basis. This serves as a foundation to confirm or falsify the presented arguments.

OpBI and dynamic capabilities

The theory of dynamic capabilities argues that the achievement of competitive advantages does not depend solely on valuable and rare resources. The resource-based view is extended by a consideration of changing environments. Dynamic capabilities concern the management of competencies in order to buffer change effects on the resources of an organization. Such capabilities require management skills and knowledge to enable the coordination of organizational activities and the usage of firm-specific assets. Dynamic capabilities are referred to organizational routines such as quality assurance or system integration. [27]

Research studies discuss dynamic capabilities within the concurrence of IT capabilities, business process orientation and organizational performance [31], [32]. For example, [32] clarifies the link between operational and dynamic capabilities by examining the impact of organizational knowledge on operational capabilities. The characteristics of dynamic capabilities are attributable to IS, if they influence the development, integration and release of an organization's key resources [33]. As an analysis and control of business processes impacts such key resources [17], dynamic capabilities affect the OpBI's IS integration efforts. Therefore, we examine this relationship by the following hypothesis:

> H1: Dynamic capabilities are positively associated with IS integration for OpBI to control and analyze business processes.

OpBI and organizational information processing theory

The organizational information processing theory discusses aspects of organizations' design to ensure effective and efficient operations. The theory assumes that an increased uncertainty of task execution is associated with an increased amount of information to be processed during a task-oriented decision making. In order to handle such uncertainties, organizations can reduce the need for information processing or they can increase the information processing capacity. [28]

From the beginning of the discussion about BI, the ability of information processing is inherent for BI systems [34]. Information processing networks provide decision making individuals with information to deal with decision situations [35]. The analysis and control of business processes is an example for the decision making needs to be fulfilled by BI capabilities. BI facilitates information processing capacities, but this requires a high quality communication of the corresponding system components [36]. Information processing capacities and needs are thereby discussed in context of BI success [37]. An enhancement of information processing capabilities and a reduction of information processing needs become evident in this discussion. Thus, we hypothesize the following relationships between the OpBI's IS integration and the design strategies of organizational information processing theory:

> H2a: "Information processing needs" is negatively associated with IS integration for OpBI to control and analyze business processes.

> H2b: "Information processing capacities" is positively associated with IS integration for OpBI to control and analyze business processes.

OpBI and process virtualization theory

Process virtualization theory argues that physical interaction between people and objects of business processes are replaced through virtual means. The transition from physical to virtual is regarded as process virtualization. However, not every business process is equally suited for a virtual process environment. The theory proposes main constructs of process virtualization. These are requirements with a counteractive impact on process virtualization, so that a high requirement specification leads to a low possibility of process virtualization. This effect of the main constructs is influenced by moderating constructs of process virtualization. These moderators refer to IT characteristics, which positively affect the relation between the main constructs and the process virtualization. [29]

Process virtualization theory is discussed by application scenarios in electronic commerce [38] or in the public sector [39]. However, there is evidence for an explanation potential of business process analysis and control. [13] discuss aspects of virtualization in BPM systems and BI to enable a management of processes by analysis, prediction, monitoring, control, and optimization. The creation of a virtual value chain allows a consideration of efficiency and effectiveness indicators for physical operations, but this is associated with information integration over the whole value chain [40]. According to this, virtualization entails integration efforts and is relevant for an analysis and control of business processes by OpBI. These efforts are likely to increase in context of diminishing possibilities for process virtualization. Therefore, we hypothesize in context of process virtualization and IS integration for OpBI

> H3a: Process virtualization requirements are positively associated with IS integration for OpBI to control and analyze business processes.

> H3b: The process virtualization moderators counteract the effect of process virtualization requirements on IS integration for OpBI to control and analyze business processes.

OpBI and work system theory

A work system consists of participants (human, machines), information, technology, and business processes, in order to perform work. The aim of this system is the provision of products and services for internal or external customers. Value chains and information systems are considered as special forms of work systems. The existence of a work system is time-dependent. A work system life cycle allows a dynamic view on changes of work systems over time. This model is iterative and considers planned and unplanned changes. The initial point for change decisions is the operation and maintenance of work systems. This phase includes the monitoring of work system performance, the identification and correction of flaws as well as improvement activities. [30]

The analysis and design of work systems requires the awareness of methods for process and data analysis to monitor and improve operational business processes [41]. Decision making capabilities, like the analysis and control of business processes by OpBI, need to be incorporated into organizational work systems in order to implicate certain benefits [42]. Hence, changes on work systems are likely to affect corresponding decision making infrastructures. These are the characteristics of IS integration for OpBI in context of the analysis and control of business processes. Thus, we hypothesize:

> H4: Work system change is positively associated with IS integration for OpBI to control and analyze business processes.

Figure 2 joins the used theories and shows the research model considering the developed hypotheses and their effect on IS integration for OpBI to analyze and control business processes.

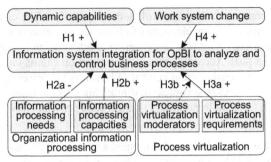

Figure 2. Research model

Research Method

We conducted an empirical study to test our hypotheses. A survey for process-oriented companies was set up to explore the requirements for an analysis and control of business processes. The preparation of the survey instrument referred to literature about the stated theories as well as to empirical studies about BI, BPM and performance management. The initial version of the survey has been pretested by academics and practitioners with expertise in BI and BPM. Based on the answers of 65 respondents, we were able to redefine the survey instrument. Redundancies were condensed and incomprehensibilities were rephrased. We could also improve the survey structure and format-specific issues.

Data collection

Data were collected online in the second half of 2013. A survey invitation was emailed to more than 600 companies out of different industries. Contacts were identified by browsing panels and discussion groups regarding BI and BPM in databases of economic development councils, trade directories and social networks like LinkedIn or Facebook.

256 participants joined the survey and we received 109 completed surveys, which is a completion rate of 42.48%. Table 1 summarizes the general facts of the respondents and illustrates an industry classification.

Table 1. General statistics

Range of Services		Position	
Service companies 48%		Staff 43%	
Manufacturing companies 30%		Executive staff 27%	
Both 22%		CEO 30%	
Industry			
Machine engineering 17%			
IT / Telecommunication 15%			
Automotive engineering 15%			
Manufacturing 13%			
Service provider 13%			
Pharma / Chemical / Biotech 7%			
Electronics 6%			
Financial services 6%			
Other 8%			

("Other" includes several industries, each represented by less than 2% of respondents.)

Operationalization of constructs

The survey combines reflective and formative constructs. The constructs were operationalized by items based on literature about underpinning theories and IS integration. The survey instrument encompasses 24 items. The measurement of the items refers to a six-point Likert scale ranging from (1) strongly agree to (6) strongly disagree [43]. In the following, we discuss the development of the items.

IS integration for OpBI to analyze and control business processes

This construct encompasses five reflective items. The data integration, functional unit integration, and process integration are used to capture areas of IS integration [1], [3], [44]. Furthermore, the direction of information flows is considered by a horizontal and a vertical information structure of firms in order to coordinate operational decisions [45], [46].

Dynamic capabilities

Dynamic capabilities are reflected by three items, which consider the integration, building, and reconfiguration of internal and external competencies. Integration addresses the coordination of specific organizational routines and emphasizes on external factors characterized by strategic alliances, networks or technology collaborations. Learning means a combination of individual and organizational skills to generate knowledge to advance organizational routines and to allow an interorganizational learning. A reconfiguration and transformation of organizational assets is associated with a surveillance of markets and technologies as well as an adoption of best practice. [27]

Process virtualization requirements

The process virtualization requirements are measured reflectively by sensory, relationship, synchronism as well as identification and control requirements. Sensory requirements depend on the need to taste, see, hear, smell, or touch objects or participants during a process including the overall sensation felt in engagement of processes. Relationship requirements illustrate the need for social or professional interaction of process participants. Synchronism refers to delays between process activities. A need for minimal delays leads to high synchronism requirements. Identification and control requirements consider the ability to identify process participants and to control their behavior. [29]

Process virtualization moderators

The measures of process virtualization moderators refer to IT characteristics of representation, reach and monitoring capability. Representation refers to relevant information about characteristics of processes and about interactions between process participants and objects. Reach facilitates a participation in processes independent of time and space. Monitoring capabilities allow authentication of process participants and tracing of process activities. [29]

Information processing needs

Information processing needs is a formative construct. Slack resources encompass the increase of financial budgets and the consideration of buffers for completion times or inventories. The creation of self-contained tasks changes business units to output-based entities with its own authority structure and decentralized information systems. [28]

Information processing capacities

"Information processing capacities" is a reflective construct. Vertical information systems provide capabilities for situational planning based on current requirements and frequent decision making. Lateral relations concern an establishment of communication channels to align the decision making level to information requirements of managerial tasks. [28]

Work system change

Work system change is a formative construct. The work system lifecycle model forces decisions about the existence and enhancement of a work system during operation. This can be a redesign according to a standardized procedure, a continuous improvement or a termination, if the work system and its components do not lead to valuable benefits anymore. [30]

Data analysis

We use Partial Least Squares (PLS) to test our research model. This structural modeling approach is adequate for small sample sizes and it allows a consideration of formative constructs [47]. The model evaluation is done with the SmartPLS software package including a PLS algorithm as well as methods for bootstrapping and blindfolding [48].

The evaluation of measurements follows the rules of thumb and remarks to PLS according to Hair et al. [49]. Therefore, we determined the internal consistency reliability (ICR), indicator loadings, the average variance extracted (AVE) and the discriminant validity for the reflective measures (cf. Table 2).

Table 2. Evaluation of reflective measures

	DC	ISI	IPC	PVR
AVE	0.54	0.57	0.70	0.52
ICR	0.78	0.87	0.82	0.75
CROSS LOADINGS				
Integration	**0.722**	0.316	0.213	0.278
Building	**0.685**	0.320	0.190	0.362
Reconfiguration	**0.793**	0.310	0.194	0.176
Data integration	0.280	**0.763**	0.300	0.489
Function integration	0.384	**0.815**	0.407	0.495
Process integration	0.378	**0.782**	0.421	0.398
Horizontal integration	0.237	**0.776**	0.410	0.423
Vertical integration	0.337	**0.622**	0.373	0.391
Lateral relations	0.207	0.515	**0.921**	0.372
Vertical IS	0.276	0.300	**0.745**	0.316
Sensors	0.163	0.316	0.284	**0.694**
Synchronization	0.379	0.583	0.348	**0.885**
Identification & control	0.202	0.274	0.249	**0.532**
CORRELATION MATRIX				
DC	-			
ISI	0.431	-		
IPC	0.272	0.509	-	
PVR	0.372	0.585	0.410	-

Table 3 summarizes the evaluation of the reflective measures, which comply to the PLS conditions. The ICR values are higher than 0.7 and the AVE of each construct is higher than 0.5. The requirements for discriminant validity are also fulfilled. The highest squared correlation with any other latent construct (0.342) is less than the calculated AVE of the constructs, and the indicator loadings are higher than their cross loadings. The indicator loadings should be higher than 0.7, which is achieved for 9 indicators. We could also consider loadings above 0.5, because the ICR values exceed the suggested threshold values [49].

The evaluation of formative measures includes an examination of the indicator weights. We used the method of bootstrapping with 5000 samples to assess the significance of the indicators. The critical t-value was 1.65 to achieve a significance level of 10 percent. We calculated the variance inflation factor (VIF), which has to be less than 5 for each indicator to avoid multi-collinearity. Table 3 indicates that these conditions are met for our formative constructs.

Table 3. Evaluation of the formative measures

	Item	Weight	t-value	VIF
WSC	Termination	0.413	1.871*	1.20
	Continuous improvement	0.475	1.889*	1.25
	Redesign	0.499	2.118**	1.05
IPN	Slack resources	0.925	4.059***	1.04
	Self-contained tasks	-0.641	2.076**	1.04
	*p < 0.1; **p < 0.05; ***p < 0.01			

The evaluation criteria for the research model are the R^2 value, the Q^2 value and the significance of our path coefficients. Figure 3 illustrates the results of the model evaluation.

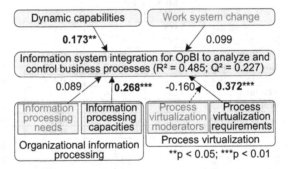

Figure 3: Model results

Our R^2 value indicates that the model explains 49 percent of the dependent construct variance. This leads to a reasonable certainty, because R^2 values of 0.67, 0.33, and 0.19 can be considered as substantial, moderate, and weak [48]. The Q^2 value is larger than zero. This indicates the predictive relevance of the exogenous constructs on information systems integration for OpBI to analyze and control business processes. The effect of dynamic capabilities is positive on a significance level of five percent. This supports H1. The path for reduction of information processing needs is insignificant and indicates a marginal effect on the information systems integration for OpBI. This confutes H2a, while H2b is supported. The structural model shows a positive effect for the information processing capacities, which is significant at a level of one percent. The process virtualization requirements contribute strongest to information systems integration, supporting H3a. This factor has a path coefficient of 0.372 on a one-percent significance level. The hypothesis on work system change is also not supported. The effect is weak with a value of 0.99, and the path coefficient with a t-value of 1.466 only achieves a significance level of less than 20 percent.

In order to test hypothesis H3b, we used the parametric approach for multi-group analysis [50]. We calculated the mean of the process virtualization moderators and used the median of these values (2.33) to split the original data in two groups. Response sets with a mean below 2.33 were grouped with high pronounced moderators and data sets with a mean above 2.33 with low pronounced moderators. Response sets with a mean of 2.33 were equally distributed to both groups. A bootstrapping method was applied to each of the new data sets. Table 4 summarizes the results of the multi-group analysis.

Table 4: Multi-group analysis results

High pronounced moderators (49 samples)			
	Path coefficient	Std. Error	t-value
PVR > ISI	0.278	0.137	2.025**
Low pronounced moderators (60 samples)			
	Path coefficient	Std. Error	t-value
PVR > ISI	0.438	0.123	3.562***
			**p < 0.05; ***p < 0.01

The difference of path coefficients is 0.16. High pronounced moderators seem to reduce the effect on process virtualization requirements. However, the moderating effect is not significant. We calculated a t-value [50] of 0.88, which is far away from the critical t-value of 1.65. For this reason, we cannot support the hypothesis H3b with regard to the moderating effect in context of process virtualization.

Discussion and implications

This study explains the IS integration for OpBI in order to analyze and control business processes. We applied a research model that considers the four theories of dynamic capabilities, organizational information processing, process virtualization, and work systems to examine different perspectives on business process coordination and improvement. We found out that the analysis and control of business processes is influenced by dynamic capabilities, information processing capacities and process virtualization requirements. Aspects of information processing needs, process virtualization moderators and work system change are secondary in this context. The following presents the key observations regarding a business process analysis and control.

Implications from dynamic capabilities

Dynamic capabilities have a significant relationship with IS integration. This result shows that changing environment conditions are associated with integration efforts in order to analyze and control business processes. The need to react fast and flexible on changes to achieve competitive advantages requires a comprehensive view on the organizational value chain. The high load on the reconfiguration item emphasizes this aspect also during the model evaluation. Hence, flexibility and readiness for changes do not act as opponent to the integration of data, functions and processes along the value chain and among the value activities. The impact of a dynamic management of internal and external competencies in process-oriented organizations depends on the possibility to identify leverage points for changes and to bring them into action. This justifies and confirms the relevance of an analysis and control of business processes by OpBI.

Implications from organizational information processing

The concepts of information processing needs and information processing capacity have a different relationship to business process analysis and control. The concept of information processing needs does not seem to be a suitable perspective to explain the IS integration for OpBI to analyze and control business processes. A reason can be seen in inconsistencies of the construct weights. Both are significant, but their relative importance has different signs. According [28], both indicators should have a positive importance for information processing needs. This is only evident for the aspects of slack resources. Organizations seem to consider buffers for completion times or budgets in their processes. However, the creation of self-contained tasks plays only a tangential role and is not estimated as a beneficial design strategy. Likely, the building of output-based business units can be difficult, because changes of service or product portfolio would constantly restructure these autonomous units.

Information processing capacity is significantly related to the analysis and control of business processes and associated integration efforts. An improved utilization of organizational communication channels is positively associated to IS integration and advances therewith an analysis and control of business processes. Such capabilities refer to IT for a connection of transactional and decision-oriented systems. Additionally, information processing capacity focuses on organizational aspects to enable a comprehensive information flow between decision makers. The effect in the structural model indicates that these capacities are relevant and beneficial for an analysis and control of business processes.

Implications from process virtualization

In context of business analysis and control, IS integration highly depends on characteristics of a process-oriented organization. This confirms the significant effect of process virtualization requirements. Synchronism has the highest importance in the structural model followed by sensory requirements. Hence, analysis and control of business processes depends on a high degree on characteristics of products or services and the need to schedule process activities with minimal delays. The importance of identification and control requirements is not as highly pronounced in the structural model. These requirements are likely to be more homogeneous for business processes and seem to depend not to such a high degree on organization specifics as sensory or synchronism requirements. Relationship requirements could not achieve enough importance for consideration in the structural model. Physical interactions between process participants are likely to be unimportant, since IT and communication techniques support the communication within and among organizations.

The process virtualization moderators do not significantly counteract the effect of the synchronism, sensory, and identification and control requirements on IS integration. This observation is surprising, because this is contrary to the origin of process virtualization theory [29]. It is questionable if a consideration of a larger sample size can lead to a necessary doubling of the t-value in order to achieve an adequate significance level. Organizations obviously use IT to manage and perform their processes. Therefore, possibilities to gain benefits from the IT's representation, reach, or monitoring capability are available. The distinct missing significance indicates that the impact of IT on business process analysis and control depends on the design and use in specific cases rather than on a simple availability.

Implications from work systems

Work system change is not significantly related to IS integration for OpBI to analyze and control business processes. This finding can be reasoned by case specifics of organizational work systems. However, the weights of the construct items are above 0.4 and positive. This indicates that the decision alternatives to change and advance work systems have an importance for process-oriented organizations. Therefore, a larger sample size or a concentration on certain industries could be an opportunity to further investigate this relationship of work system change on business process analysis and control.

Conclusions

The practical effect of an analysis and control of business processes by IS-driven integration approaches such as OpBI depends on factors, which characterize the insider's and outsider's view on organizations. A positioning in changing market environments increases the relevance of operational decision making concepts like OpBI. The same effect comes along with strategic considerations to create complex services or products in highly interconnected process organizations. An analysis and control of business processes benefits from capabilities ensuring a convenient information flow through adequate communication channels.

The multi-theoretical framework and its empirical validation allow general implications among which conditions OpBI is able to support an analysis and control of business processes. This enhances case-specific applications of OpBI. The paper proposes a unique consideration of four theories to explain the role of IS integration in a context of business process coordination and improvement. This provides interesting theoretical findings to examine the interactions of business processes, IT-driven decision making and organizational performance. These insights are also worthwhile to evaluate the adequacy of OpBI in a practical context. However, the validation of the research model indicates insignificances for the perspectives of work system change, information processing needs and IT characteristics moderating the influence of process virtualization requirements. Especially in context of work system change, a larger sample size can face this limitation. Furthermore, the choice of a multi-theory approach limits the opportunity for a highly detailed operationalization, which overwhelms survey respondents and reduces the probability of a high number of completed response sets. However, common quality criteria for structural PLS models are met in our research study so that the resilience of the results is confirmed.

Further research activities should investigate the single influence of the presented theory perspectives on OpBI with detailed measurement instruments. This will extend the theoretical knowledge about OpBI to analyze and control business processes. Furthermore, studies which confute the practical effect of an analysis and control of business processes by IS-driven integration approaches are of interest. Such knowledge beyond decision-making benefits enables a more particular discussion of conditions and obstacles of concepts like OpBI for a coordination and improvement of business processes.

References

1. N. Berente et al., "Information flows and business process integration," *Bus. Process Manage. J.*, vol. 15, no. 1, pp. 119-141, 2009.
2. J. Davis et al., *Operational Business Intelligence: The State of the Art*. Boulder, CO: Beye NETWORK Research, 2009.
3. G.D. Bhatt, "An empirical examination of the effects of information systems integration on business process improvement," *Int. J. Operat. Prod. Manage.*, vol. 20, no. 11, pp. 1331-1359, 2000.
4. N.G. Carr, "IT Doesn't Matter," *Harvard Bus. Review*, vol. 81, no. 5, pp. 41-49, May 2003.
5. T. Hänel and C. Felden, "Operational Business Intelligence Meets Manufacturing," *Proc. 19th Amer. Conf. Inform. Syst.*, Chicago, IL, 2013.
6. T. Hänel, and C. Felden, "The role of Operational Business Intelligence in customer-centric service provision," *Proc. 20th Amer. Conf. Inform. Syst.*, Savannah, GA, 2014.
7. O. Marjanovic, "The Next Stage of Operational Business Intelligence: Creating New Challenges for Business Process Management," *Proc. 40th Annu. Hawaii Int. Conf. Syst. Sci.*, Washington DC: IEEE Computer Society, 2007.
8. O. Marjanovic, "Looking Beyond Technology: A Framework for Business Intelligence and Business Process Management Integration," *Proc. 22nd Bled eConference*, Bled, SI, 2009.
9. O. Marjanovic, "Business Value Creation through Business Processes Management and Operational Business Intelligence Integration," *Proc. 43rd Hawaii Int. Conf. Syst. Sci.*, Honolulu, HI, 2010.

10. M. Koch et al., "Manufacturing Execution Systems and Business Intelligence for Production Environments," *Proc. 16th Amer. Conf. Inform. Syst.*, Lima, PE, 2010.

11. E.S. Kyper et al., "Operational Business Intelligence: Applying Decision Trees to Call Centers," *Proc. 15th Amer. Conf. Inform. Syst.*, San Francisco, CA, 2009.

12. R.O. Maghrabi et al., "The Role of Business Intelligence (BI) in Service Innovation: An Ambidexterity Perspective," *Proc. 17th Amer. Conf. Inform. Syst.*, Detroit, MI, 2011.

13. D. Grigori et al., "Business Process Intelligence," *Comput. Ind.*, vol. 53, no. 1, pp. 321-343, Apr. 2004.

14. P. Harmon, *Business Process Change: A Business Process Management Guide for Managers and Process Professionals.* 3rd ed., Boston: Morgan Kaufmann, 2014.

15. M. Porter and V.E. Millar, "How information gives you competitive advantage," *Harvard Bus. Rev.*, vol. 63, no. 4, pp. 149-160, Jul.-Aug. 1985.

16. S.M. Siha, and G.H. Saad, "Business process improvement: empirical assessment and extensions," *Bus. Process Manage. J.*, vol. 14, no. 6, pp. 778-802, 2008.

17. Y.H. Kwak and F.T. Anbari, "Benefits, obstacles, and future of six sigma approach," *Technovation*, vol. 26, pp. 708-715, 2006.

18. J. Gordijn and J.M. Akkermans, "Value-based requirements engineering: exploring innovative e-commerce ideas," *Requirements Eng.*, vol. 8, no. 2, pp 114-134, May 2003.

19. S.T. March and A.R. Hevner, "Integrated decision support systems: A data warehousing perspective," *Decis. Sup. Syst.*, vol. 43, no. 1, pp. 1031-1043, 2007.

20. H. Barkiand and A. Pinsonneault, "A model of organizational integration, implementation effort, and performance," *Org. Sci.*, vol. 16, no. 2, pp. 165-179,Mar.-Apr. 2005.

21. D. Näslund, "Lean, six sigma and lean sigma: fads or real process improvement methods?," *Bus. Process Manage. J.*, vol. 14, no. 3, pp. 269-287, 2008.

22. C. Felden et al., "From Process Execution towards a Business Process Intelligence," *Proc. 13th Int. Conf. Bus. Inform. Syst.*, W. Abramowicz and R. Tolksdorf, Eds., Berlin: Springer, 2010, pp. 195-206.

23. T. Bucher et al., "Process-centric business intelligence," *Bus. Process Manage. J.*, vol. 15, no. 3, pp. 408-429, 2009.

24. R.E. Hoskisson et al., "Theory and research in strategic management: Swings of a pendulum," *J. Manage.*, vol. 25, no. 3, pp. 417-456, Jun. 1999.

25. C.S. Chapman and L.A. Kihn, "Information system integration, enabling control and performance," *Acc. Org. Soc.*, vol. 34, no. 1, pp. 151-169, 2009.

26. P. Trkman, "The Critical Success Factors of Business Process Management," *Int. J. Inform. Manage.*, vol. 30, no. 2, pp. 125-134, 2010.

27. D.J. Teece et al., "Dynamic capabilities and strategic management," *Strat. Manage. J.*, vol. 18, no. 7, pp. 509-533, Mar. 1997.

28. J.R. Galbraith, "Organization design: An information processing view," *Interfaces*, vol. 4, no. 3, pp. 28-36, May 1974.

29. E.M. Overby, "Process Virtualization Theory and the Impact of Information Technology," *Org. Sci.*, vol. 19, no. 2, pp. 277-291, Mar.-Apr. 2008.

30. S. Alter, "The Work System Method for Understanding Information Systems and Information System Research," *Commun. Assoc. Inform. Syst.*, vol. 9, pp. 90-104, Sep. 2002.

31. G. Kim et al., "IT Capabilities, Process-Oriented Dynamic Capabilities, and Firm Financial Performance," *J. Assoc. Inform. Syst.*, vol. 12, no. 7, pp. 487-517, Jul. 2011.

32. G. Cepeda and D. Vera, "Dynamic capabilities and operational capabilities: A knowledge management perspective," *J. Bus. Research*, vol. 60, no. 1, pp. 426-437, Jan. 2007.

33. M. Wade and J. Hulland, "The Resource-Based View and Information Systems Research: Review, Extension, and Suggestions for Future Research," *MIS Quart.*, vol. 28, no. 1, pp. 107-142, Mar. 2004.

34. H. Luhn, "A Business Intelligence System," *IBM J. Research Develop.*, vol. 2, no. 4, pp. 314-319, Oct. 1958.

35. O. Isik et al., "Business intelligence (BI) success and the role of BI capabilities", *Intell. Syst. Acc. Fin. Manage.*, vol. 18, no. 4, pp. 161-176, Oct.-Dec. 2011.

36. R.R. Nelson et al., "Antecedents of Information and System Quality: An Empirical Examination Within the Context of Data Warehousing," *J. Manage. Inform. Syst.*, vol. 21, no. 4, pp. 203-239, Spring 2005.
37. K. McCormack and P. Trkman, "Business Analytics and Information Processing Needs - A Case Study," *Proc. 20th Europ. Conf. Inform. Syst.*, Barcelona, ES, 2012.
38. E.M. Overby and B. Konsynski. (2008). *Process Virtualization: A Theme and Theory for the Information Systems Discipline* [online]. Available: http://dx.doi.org/ 10.2139/ssrn.1138045, last accessed 2014-06-15.
39. M. Barth and D. Veit, "Which Processes Do Users Not Want Online? Extending Process Virtualization Theory," *Proc. 32nd Int. Conf. Inform. Syst.*, Shanghai, CN, 2011, pp. 1-21.
40. J.F. Rayport and J.J. Sviokla, "Exploiting the virtual value chain," *Harvard Bus. Rev.*, vol. 73, no. 6, pp. 75-85, Nov.-Dec. 1995.
41. S. Alter and G.J. Browne, "A Broad View of Systems Analysis and Design: Implications for Research," *Commun. Assoc. Inform. Syst.*, vol. 15, pp. 981-999, Dec. 2005.
42. S. Alter, "A work system view of DSS in its fourth decade," *Decis. Sup. Syst.*, vol. 38, no. 3, pp. 319–327, Dec. 2004.
43. R. Chomeya, "Quality of Psychology Test Between Likert Scale 5 and 6 Points," *J. Social Sci.*, vol. 6, no. 3, pp. 399-403, 2010.
44. D.L. Goodhue et al., "The Impact of Data Integration on the Costs and Benefits of Information Systems," *MIS Quart.*, vol. 16, no. 3, pp. 293-311, Sep. 1992.
45. W. Hasselbring, "Information System Integration," *Commun. ACM*, vol. 43, no. 6, pp. 33-38, June 2000.
46. B. Wanglerand and S. Paheerathan, "Horizontal and Vertical Integration of Organizational IT Systems," in *Information systems engineering: state of the art and research themes*, S. Brinkkemper et al., Eds., London: Springer, 2000, pp. 79-90.
47. W.W. Chin, "The partial least squares approach for structural equation modeling," in *Modern methods for business research*, G.A. Maracoulides, Ed., Mahwah: Lawrence Erlbaum, 1998, pp. 295-336.
48. C.M. Ringle et al. (2005). *SmartPLS* [online]. Available: http://www.smartpls.de, last accessed 2014-06-15.
49. J.F. Hair et al., "PLS-SEM: Indeed a silver bullet," *J. Marketing Theory Practice*, vol. 19, no. 2, pp. 139-152, Nov. 2011.
50. M. Sarstedt et al., "Multigroup Analysis in Partial Least Squares (PLS) Path Modeling: Alternative Methods and Empirical Results," in *Measurement and Research Methods in International Marketing*, vol. 22, *Advances in International Marketing*, M. Sarstedt et al., Eds., Emerald Group Publishing Limited, pp. 195-218, 2011.

4.2.2   Operational Business Intelligence versus Industrie 4.0

Die Aspekte einer OpBI-getriebenen Entscheidungsunterstützung werden auch von industriegetriebenen Ansätzen diskutiert. Die Treiber dieser Diskussion sind z. B. dynamische Wettbewerbsbedingungen oder eine steigende Komplexität von Produkten und Prozessen. Für eine Beherrschung derartiger Herausforderungen wird im deutschsprachigen Raum der Begriff der Industrie 4.0 diskutiert. Diese Lösungsüberschrift thematisiert ein Zusammenwachsen von zeitgemäßen IT-Technologien mit industriellen Prozessen. Industrie 4.0 steht dabei allgemein für eine revolutionäre Veränderung der Produktion, die durch eine technische Integration von cyberphysischen Systemen mit Technologien des Internets der Dinge und Dienste erreicht werden soll.

4.2.2.1 Kurzdarstellung Beitrag 4

Die Nutzung und Integration von IT-Systemen, die von Industrie 4.0 adressiert werden, sind im Produktionskontext von einer dauerhaften Entwicklung gekennzeichnet. Beitrag 4 stellt die verschiedenen Phasen und Konzepte einer IT-Nutzung in der Produktion bis hin zur Industrie 4.0 dar und ordnet OpBI in diesen Entwicklungsverlauf ein. Damit wird das Potential von Produktionsumgebungen als Anwendungsgebiet von OpBI (siehe Beitrag 2) bekräftigt. Des Weiteren liefert die Diskussion um Industrie 4.0 Anwendungsfälle für eine praxisnahe Untersuchung der Integrationsaspekte, die in Beitrag 3 identifiziert werden konnten. Für die Einordnung der OpBI in das Zukunftsbild der Industrie 4.0 erfolgt in Beitrag 4 eine grundlegende Betrachtung von cyberphysischen Systemen sowie des Internets der Dinge und Dienste. OpBI wird danach unter dem Gesichtspunkt der Datenintegration in die IT-Architektur einer Smart Factory eingeordnet. Eine OpBI-spezifische Plattform veranschaulicht in diesem Zusammenhang die Analyse industrieller Prozesse und eine daran gekoppelte Entscheidungsunterstützung im Zukunftsbild der Industrie 4.0. Die in Beitrag 4 skizzierte Plattform nutzt dabei webserviceorientierte Strukturen, die eine internetbasierte Datenintegration und -kommunikation unterstützen. Die Funktionalitäten von OpBI sind Bestandteil eines vielschichtigen Netzwerks, in dem eine Menge von heterogenen Daten verarbeitet wird. Mensch-Maschine-Schnittstellen präsentieren Entscheidungsträgern die Analyseergebnisse der Datenverarbeitung, die direkt in die cyberphysischen Systeme der Produktionsprozesse einfließen können. Es wird aufgezeigt, dass die konzeptionellen Bestandteile der OpBI auch im Rahmen der Industrie 4.0 zu einer produktionsspezifischen Entscheidungsunterstützung beitragen. Abschließend thematisiert Beitrag 4 die Notwendigkeit der Untersuchung von fallspezifischen Anwendungen als zukünftigem Forschungsbedarf.

4.2.2.2 Beitrag 4: Operational Business Intelligence im Zukunftsszenario der Industrie 4.0[4]

Einleitung

Die Leistungsfähigkeit produzierender Unternehmen hängt von ihrer Wettbewerbsfähigkeit auf zunehmend globalisierten Märkten ab. Aus diesem internationalen Wettbewerbsdruck ergibt sich die Herausforderung, fortwährend innovativ zu sein. Eine Konsequenz daraus sind komplexe Produkte sowie aufwändige Her-

---

4 Hänel, T.; Felden, C.: Operational Business Intelligence im Zukunftsszenario der Industrie 4.0. In: Gluchowski, P.; Chamoni, P. (Hrsg.): Analytische Informationssysteme – Business Intelligence-Technologien und -Anwendungen, 5. Auflage, Springer, 2016.

stell- und Logistikprozesse, die einem stetigen Wandel unterliegen. Diese Dynamik wird im Industriesektor durch eine Variantenvielfalt der angebotenen Produkte verstärkt, um individuellen und differenzierten Kundenbedürfnissen gerecht zu werden. Hinzu kommen volatile Bedarfe und abnehmende Produktlebenszyklen. [7] Als möglicher Lösungsansatz für die skizzierten Herausforderungen wird im deutschsprachigen Raum ein Zukunftsprojekt unter der Überschrift Industrie 4.0 diskutiert. Dieser Ausdruck wird mit einer revolutionären Umgestaltung der industriellen Produktion verbunden. Industrie 4.0 ist aus der Perspektive der Informationstechnik (IT) konzipiert und thematisiert ein Zusammenwachsen von zeitgemäßen IT-Technologien mit industriellen Prozessen. [27] Die Nutzung von informationsverarbeitenden Systemen und deren Integration ist im Produktionskontext von einer dauerhaften Entwicklung gekennzeichnet. Der gegenwärtige Entwicklungsstand schließt Automatisierungssysteme, rechnergestützte Werkzeuge und ganzheitliche Ansätze zur Produktentwicklung sowie operative und dispositive IT-Systeme ein [58]. Darüber hinaus existieren Konzepte für eine IT-Unterstützung produktionsspezifischer Entscheidungen [34]. Auf Grund dynamischer und vernetzter Produktionsstrukturen benötigen auch Entscheidungsträger im Produktionsumfeld IT-Systeme, die eine Bearbeitung komplexer Aufgabenstellungen systematisch mit Informationen anreichern. In diesem Kontext wird neben ingenieurgetriebenen Ansätzen wie Manufacturing Execution Systems (MES) auch Operational Business Intelligence (OpBI) als IT-basiertes Konzept zur Entscheidungsunterstützung in der Produktion diskutiert [18]. OpBI schließt Funktionalitäten für eine Erfassung, Konsolidierung und Auswertung von Produktionsdaten ein, um betriebswirtschaftliche und technische Analysen im Hinblick auf operative oder planerische Entscheidungen zu unterstützen [19]. Ein Zukunftsthema wie Industrie 4.0 impliziert neben veränderten Produktionsabläufen und zeitgemäßen Technologien ebenso eine Neuorganisation oder Weiterentwicklung dieser bestehenden Systementwürfe für eine Entscheidungsunterstützung. Das Ziel des Beitrages ist daher die Untersuchung von möglichen Auswirkungen und Veränderungen hinsichtlich der Relevanz und der informationstechnischen Gestaltung von OpBI-Systemen.

Industrie 4.0 thematisiert die intelligente Vernetzung der an der industriellen Produktion beteiligten Ressourcen, Systeme und Prozesse durch Technologien des Internets [27]. Zur Steuerung komplexer Industrieprozesse werden cyberphysische Produktionssysteme (CPPS) geschaffen, deren Komponenten, Objekte und Geräte eigenständig miteinander kommunizieren können. Bereits vorhandene Produktionssysteme (z. B. Maschinen, Roboter) und Betriebsmittel werden mit Sensoren, Aktoren, Mikrocontrollern und Leistungselektronik ausgestattet, um dezentrale, sich selbst regulierende Steuerungs- und Regelungsprozesse zu ermöglichen. [4] Im Rahmen des Zukunftsthemas Industrie 4.0 sind damit Auswirkungen auf die Gestaltung und das Management von Information- und Datenflüssen in den

Produktionsunternehmen zu erwarten. Kennzeichnend für die zu schaffenden CPPS-Lösungen sind horizontal und vertikal integrierte Produktionssysteme sowie durchgängige Technologiekonzepte über den gesamten Lebenszyklus der entstehenden Produkte. Die Grundlage für eine Planung, Simulation, Beschreibung und Bewertung anwenderspezifischer CPPS-Lösungen bilden interdisziplinäre Datenmodelle, die sowohl den Ist- als auch den Soll-Zustand eines Produktionsunternehmens darstellen. Die entsprechende Datenorganisation umfasst Methoden, um entscheidungsrelevante Informationen systemübergreifend zu sammeln, zu analysieren und Entscheidern bereitzustellen. [8] Diese Herangehensweise ist durch eine Überlappung mit dem OpBI-Konzept gekennzeichnet. OpBI unterstützt zunächst einmal, unabhängig von einem bestimmten Anwendungsgebiet, die Abwicklung von täglichen Geschäftsprozessen infolge einer direkten und zeitnahen Verbindung dispositiver und operativer IT-Systeme. [15] Eine derartige Systemintegration unterstützt im Kontext einer hierarchischen Gliederung von Produktionssystemen die Verarbeitung, Verwaltung und den Austausch komplexer Informationen in der Produktions- und Prozessleitebene [32]. Infolge der dezentralen und eigenständigen Organisation von CPPS werden diese Ebenen für eine informationstechnische Strukturierung und damit die aktuelle Einordnung von OpBI infrage gestellt [45]. Der Beitrag nimmt eine zukünftige Positionsbestimmung von OpBI in der IT-Systemlandschaft der Industrie 4.0 vor. Er trägt der sachgebietsübergreifenden Diskussion um intelligent vernetzte Produktionsstrukturen auf Basis von internetbasierten Technologien aus der Perspektive einer operativen Entscheidungsunterstützung bei.

Im Verlauf des Beitrags wird in Kapitel 2 die Entwicklung der IT-Landschaft im Produktionsumfeld vorgestellt. Weiterführend erfolgt die Darstellung des Status Quo von OpBI für eine produktionsspezifische Entscheidungsunterstützung. Kapitel 3 geht auf die technologischen Grundlagen und das Zukunftsbild der Industrie 4.0 ein. OpBI wird in dieses futuristische Szenario eingeordnet. Kapitel 4 fasst den Beitrag zusammen und liefert einen Ausblick.

Entwicklung der IT in der Produktion bis zur Industrie 4.0

In der Industrie kommen verschiedenartige IT-Systeme zum Einsatz, die typische Funktionen der Produktion und der Produktentwicklung ausführen, aufzeichnen, modellieren oder beeinflussen. Diese IT-Systeme haben im Zeitverlauf verschiedene Begriffe und Ansätze begleitet, die in einer groben zeitlichen Einordnung in der nachfolgenden Abbildung dargestellt sind. Der Zweck dieser Darstellung ist die überblicksartige Vorstellung der IT-Unterstützung in der Produktion im Vorfeld der Diskussion um Industrie 4.0 (vgl. [9, 25, 58]). Es werden keine ineinander greifenden zeitlichen Entwicklungsstufen veranschaulicht. Für die nachfolgende

Erläuterung sind die IT-Systeme und konzeptionellen Ansätze vier Phasen zugeordnet.

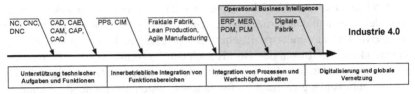

Abbildung 1. IT-Unterstützung in der Produktion im Zeitverlauf

Unterstützung technischer Aufgaben und Funktionen

Die computerbasierte Maschinensteuerung kennzeichnet frühe Ansätze zur Nutzung von IT für die industrielle Fertigung. Sie hat ihren Ursprung in den 1950er
Jahren. Die maschinelle Bearbeitung von Werkstücken ist eine charakterisierende
Aufgabe in der Fertigung. Eine Maschine benötigt Schalt- und Weginformationen,
um mithilfe von geometrischen und technologischen Funktionen ein Werkstück
zu bearbeiten. In diesem Zusammenhang steht NC für Numerical Control und ist
eine Methode zur automatischen Maschinensteuerung auf Basis numerischer Daten (Buchstaben, Ziffern, Sonderzeichen). Diese Daten spiegeln Anweisungen zur
Fertigung eines Werkstückes wider und ergeben entsprechend der Bearbeitungs-
reihenfolge ein NC-Programm. [28] Derartige Steuerungen lassen sich in drei Kategorien einteilen [57]:

- Konventionelle numerische Steuerung (NC),
- Computerisierte numerische Steuerung (CNC) und
- Verteilte numerische Steuerung (DNC).

Konventionelle NC-Steuerungen sind verbindungsprogrammiert und bestehen aus
elektronischen oder elektromechanischen Bauteilen (z. B. Relais oder kontaktlose
Schaltungen), die fest miteinander verdrahtet sind. Die Anpassungsfähigkeit dieser Steuerungen ist eingeschränkt, weil neue Schaltungen und damit verbunden
Änderungen an den festen Verbindungen erforderlich werden. [26] CNC-
Steuerungen weisen eine höhere Flexibilität als konventionelle NC-Steuerungen
auf. Zur Ausübung der Steuerungsfunktion verwenden CNC einen lokalen Rechner, der die numerischen Daten abspeichert. Im Zuge von modifizierten Aufgabenstellungen müssen nur die Speicherinhalte geändert werden. Die Anforderungen der jeweiligen Steuerung werden durch Softwareprogramme gedeckt. Das
Steuerungsprinzip von DNC ist ähnlich. Verteilte numerische Steuerungen nutzen
im Unterschied zu CNC einen gemeinsamen Rechner für eine Vielzahl an nume-
risch gesteuerten Maschinen. [24]

NC, CNC und DNC haben sich als Automatisierungstechniken zur Maschinensteuerung bewährt und werden unter dem Begriff des Computer Aided Manufacturing (CAM) zusammengefasst. Vorgelagert zur Fertigung sind Aufgaben der Konstruktion und Arbeitsplanung von Bedeutung, die sich ebenfalls durch Rechentechnik unterstützen lassen. CAD steht in diesem Zusammenhang für Computer Aided Design und unterstützt die Anfertigung von Konstruktionszeichnungen. Ziel ist die Erstellung, Veränderung oder Erweiterung eines Produktmodells. Die rechnergestützte Auslegung von Produkten sowie deren Komponenten während der Entwicklungs- und Konstruktionsphase wird als Computer Aided Engineering (CAE) bezeichnet. In den Bereich CAE fallen auch die Programme der Finite-Elemente Methode (FEM). Dies dient der Berechnung von Strukturparametern (Festigkeit, Stabilität) von geometrischen Körpern. Durch Zerlegung dieser Körper entsteht das Finite-Elemente Modell. CAE hat eine enge Verbindung zu CAD und wird als Ergänzung zu CAD-Systemen verstanden. Computer Aided Planning (CAP) unterstützt die Arbeitsplanerstellung, indem mithilfe von IT die Reihenfolge der Fertigungsschritte für ein Produkt festgelegt wird. CAD, CAP und CAM werden von einer computergestützten Qualitätssicherung permanent begleitet. Dieses präventive Qualitätsmanagement ist Aufgabe der Computer Aided Quality Assurance (CAQ). Diese aufgabenorientierten Komponenten werden unter dem Begriff der CAx-Systeme zusammengefasst. [22]

Integration von Aufgaben und Funktionen

Neben der alleinigen Nutzung zur Ausführung von einzelnen Fertigungsaufgaben wurde IT im Zeitverlauf für eine übergreifende Aufgabenunterstützung relevant. Gemäß der Definition von Gutenberg kombiniert die Produktion die elementaren Faktoren Arbeit, Material und Betriebsmittel im Rahmen von Planungs- oder Organisationsaufgaben, um Waren und Dienstleistungen herzustellen [16]. Zusätzlich zur eigentlichen Leistungserstellung kennzeichnen die Verfügbarkeit und der Verbrauch von Eingangsressourcen sowie der Absatz der Sachgüter und Dienstleistungen Aufgabenbereiche in der Produktion [40]. In diesem Zusammenhang verfolgt die Produktionsplanungs- und Steuerung (PPS) eine Planung, Durchführung, Überwachung und Korrektur des Produktionsablaufs unter Berücksichtigung von betrieblichen Zielen [61].

Die Computerunterstützung im Rahmen von PPS-Systemen für die operative Planung und Steuerung von Produktionsabläufen reicht bis in die 1960er Jahre zurück. Erste Anwendungssysteme dienten der Materialbedarfsplanung (Material Requirements Planning) und wurden als MRP-Systeme bezeichnet. Durch die Erweiterung um Stufen für eine hierarchische Planung von Absatz-, Produktions- und Bestandsmengen entstand das Manufacturing Resource Planning (MRP II). Dies wurde im deutschsprachigen Raum als PPS aufgefasst. [31]

PPS-Systeme setzen auf einer Grunddatenverwaltung von Stücklisten, Arbeitsplänen und Betriebsmitteldaten auf und gehen in der Planung sukzessiv vor. Die Planungsaufgaben werden in verschiedene Ebenen untergliedert und stufenweise durchlaufen. Zunächst ermittelt eine Hauptproduktionsprogrammplanung aus Kundenaufträgen Primärbedarfe. Diese bilden gemeinsam mit Stücklisten die Grundlage für die Mengenplanung von Endprodukten oder Baugruppen. Damit entstehen Losgrößen für die Produktion, die gemeinsam mit den Arbeitsplänen in die Terminplanung einfließen. Nach Abschluss der Planung liegen Produktionsaufträge für eine Produktionssteuerung vor. [49] Der Übergang zwischen Planung und Steuerung ist fließend und kennzeichnet sich durch die Durchsetzung von Planvorgaben. Die Produktionssteuerung veranlasst, überwacht und sichert die Durchführung von Aufgaben in Bezug auf Mengen, Termine, Qualität und Kosten. Korrekte und aktuelle Rückmeldungen können über eine Betriebsdatenerfassung (BDE) erreicht werden. [61]

PPS erfüllen vorrangig betriebswirtschaftliche Aufgaben im Kontext des Computer Integrated Manufacturing (CIM). CIM ist ein Ansatz zur Integration der Informationsverarbeitung im Industriebetrieb und hat seinen Ursprung zu Beginn der 1980er Jahre [25]. Ein konzeptioneller Rahmen ist das Y-Integrationsmodell nach Scheer.

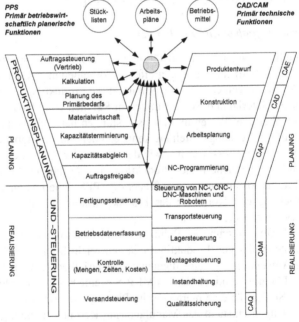

Abbildung 2. Y-Integrationsmodell [44]

CIM sieht vor, während der Planung und der Realisierung von Produktionsaufgaben betriebswirtschaftliche und technische Funktionen (CAx) miteinander zu verknüpfen. Die Verbindung kommt durch gemeinsame Aufgabenobjekte zustande. Die Vorgänge der Produkterstellung durchlaufen verschiedene kaufmännische und ingenieurtechnische Aufgaben, deren Bearbeitungszusammenhänge die Anforderungen an eine Integration der jeweiligen IT-Systeme begründen. Damit ist der Aufbau einer Datenbasis verbunden, die alle Funktionen gemeinsam nutzen können. Durch die Integration der IT-Systeme verfolgt CIM die ganzheitliche Betrachtung von Produktionsprozessen mit dem Ziel sowohl die Kundenorientierung als auch die Reaktionsfähigkeit eines Unternehmens zu verbessern. [44]

Die Integration der Systeme im Rahmen von CIM kann für Unternehmen als anspruchsvoll bezeichnet werden. Eine vollständige Umsetzung von CIM wurde durch technische, organisatorische und wirtschaftliche Gründe beeinträchtigt. Technische Hürden lassen sich auf fehlende leistungsfähige Systeme zur Datensammlung und -übertragung sowie eine unzureichende Standardisierung zurückführen. Organisatorisch verlangt CIM bereichsübergreifende Arbeitsorganisationen und interdisziplinäre Herangehensweisen. Als schädigend wird in diesem Zusammenhang die Vernachlässigung des Faktors Mensch in CIM-Umsetzungen diskutiert. Aus wirtschaftlichen Gesichtspunkten ist die Inflexibilität hochautomatisierter Fertigungsstrecken, wie sie im Rahmen von CIM-Bestrebungen verfolgt wurde, nachteilig. Der Betrieb und die Instandhaltung derartiger Anlagen stellten einen unverhältnismäßigen Aufwand dar, weil Änderungen an Produkten oder Produktionsprozessen mit kostenintensiven Umstellungen verbunden sind. [9, 48]

Integration von Prozessen und Wertschöpfungsketten

Im weiteren Zeitverlauf sind im Anschluss an CIM organisatorische Konzepte sowie die separate Weiterentwicklung der betriebswirtschaftlichen und technischen IT-Systeme in den Mittelpunkt getreten [2]. Durch die Diskussion des Business Reengineering [17] Anfang der 1990er Jahre hat die Prozessorientierung sich sowohl auf die Organisationsstrukturen als auch auf die Gestaltung der IT-Systeme ausgewirkt.

Organisationskonzepte

CIM hat seinen Schwerpunkt auf die Nutzung von Werkzeugen und Methoden der Informationstechnik zur Vernetzung von Funktionsbereichen im Zusammenhang mit der Produktion gelegt. Das Ziel ist die Steigerung der Produktivität und Effizienz von Industriebetrieben. Ein Grund, dass CIM diesem Ziel nur teilweise beitragen konnte, ist die unzureichende Berücksichtigung von personellen und organisatorischen Aspekten.

Die Diskussion um Lean Production (LP) greift diese Gesichtspunkte bezüglich der Arbeitsorganisation Anfang der 1990er Jahre im europäischen Raum auf [30]. LP stellt dabei ein integriertes sozio-technisches System dar. Das wesentliche Ziel ist die Vermeidung von Verschwendungen in der Produktion. Dazu wird die gleichzeitige Reduktion und Minimierung von internen, kundenspezifischen und lieferantenseitigen Schwankungen verfolgt. [47] LP kennzeichnet sich durch ein Prozessdenken über die gesamte Wertschöpfungskette, eine Prozessverantwortung und Kompetenz der Mitarbeiter, einer umfassenden Qualitätssicherung, einer beständigen Orientierung nach Märkten und Kunden, einer Einbindung von Zulieferern sowie einer kontinuierlichen Verbesserung der Produkte und Prozesse [10].

Der Ursprung von LP geht auf das Produktionssystem des japanischen Automobilherstellers Toyota aus den 1950er Jahren zurück. Als US-amerikanische Reaktion ist der Produktionsansatz Agile Manufacturing (AM) entstanden. Während LP operative Methoden für einen optimalen Ressourceneinsatz anbietet, stellt Agilität einen unternehmensweiten strategischen Ansatz dar [41]. Das Ziel ist die möglichst zeitnahe Erfüllung von sich ständig ändernden Kundenbedürfnissen. Die zugrunde liegenden Konzepte des AM sind die Konzentration auf Kernkompetenzen, Anpassungsfähigkeit, wissensbasierte Methoden sowie die unternehmensübergreifende Zusammenarbeit durch eine Virtualisierung von Unternehmensanwendungen [60].

Im europäischen Raum boten LP und AM gleichermaßen eine Orientierung für Produktionsunternehmen. Darauf aufbauend wurde 1991 mit der fraktalen Fabrik ein weiteres Organisationskonzept zur Gestaltung und Steuerung von produzierenden Unternehmen vorgestellt. Fraktale sind selbständige Unternehmenseinheiten, die eindeutige Ziele und Leistungen eigenverantwortlich organisieren und optimieren. Sie agieren im Einklang mit den Zielen des Gesamtunternehmens und sind durch Informationssysteme untereinander vernetzt. Die Organisationsstrukturen der fraktalen Fabrik sind dynamischen Einflussgrößen unterworfen, die wechselseitig ineinander greifen. [55] Eine flächendeckende Durchdringung konnte das Konzept der fraktalen Fabrik allerdings nicht erreichen [25].

IT-Systeme in der Dispositions- und Steuerungshierarchie

Die Funktionalitäten der von CIM ursprünglich adressierten IT-Systeme wurden in neo-logische Systemkonzepte übernommen und weiterentwickelt. Aus den PPS-Systemen sind im Zeitverlauf Enterprise Resource Planning (ERP)-Systeme entstanden. Dies stellt für Industriebetriebe eine integrierte Standardsoftware dar, die modular aufgebaut ist und auch an die Produktion angrenzende Aufgaben unterstützt. Damit ermöglichen ERP-Systeme eine gemeinsame Sicht auf Produktion, Finanz- und Rechnungswesen, Personalwesen sowie Vertrieb und Rechnungswesen. In einem unternehmensweiten Anwendungssystem werden Geschäftsprozesse transaktionsorientiert über eine gemeinsame Datenbank koordiniert und integriert. [31]

ERP-Systeme sind nicht nur auf produktionsspezifische Aufgaben beschränkt. Bei der Einordnung von Leittechnik in die industrielle Fertigung werden ERP-Systeme in die Unternehmensleitebene eingeordnet, weil diese bereichsübergreifend eine mittel- bis langfristige Planung unterstützen. ERP-Systeme haben jedoch keine Steuerungsmechanismen, die eine Rückkopplung zwischen den Planvorgaben und dem tatsächlichen Fertigungsprozess herstellen. Manufacturing Execution Systems (MES) sind aus der Weiterentwicklung elektronischer Leitstände hervorgegangen, um diese Lücke zu schließen. MES werden als Informationssysteme zwischen Unternehmensplanung und der Fertigungsausführung in die Produktionsleitebene eingeordnet. Sie stellen eine Verbindung zwischen den technischen Steuerungssystemen der Fertigung und der betriebswirtschaftlichen Planung her. Die Grobpläne aus den ERP-Systemen werden auf Stunden- bis Minutenebene herunter gebrochen. MES erfassen und bereiten die Ist-Daten der Fertigung auf, um eine fortlaufende Kontrolle und Anpassung der Planungsgrößen zu erreichen. Unterstützt werden Funktionen in den Bereichen der Produktionsausführung, Lagerverwaltung, Instandhaltung und Qualitätsmanagement. [50]

Die Fertigungsausführung wird durch ingenieurtechnische Informationssysteme unterstützt und lässt sich in drei generische Ebenen unterteilen. Die unterste Ebene charakterisiert den realen Herstell- oder Produktionsprozess. Darüber werden Sensoren und Aktoren zur Messung, Überwachung und Einflussnahme auf das Prozessgeschehen eingeordnet. Die oberste Ausführungsebene fasst Instrumente und Rechnereinheiten zur Stabilisierung und Kontrolle der Prozessabläufe zusammen. Die hierarchische Strukturierung findet sich insbesondere bei der Automatisierung komplexer technischer Prozesse wieder. Im MES-Kontext ergibt sich daraus eine Vielzahl heterogener Schnittstellen, die für eine Integration von betriebswirtschaftlicher Planung und technischer Ausführung berücksichtigt werden müssen. [23]

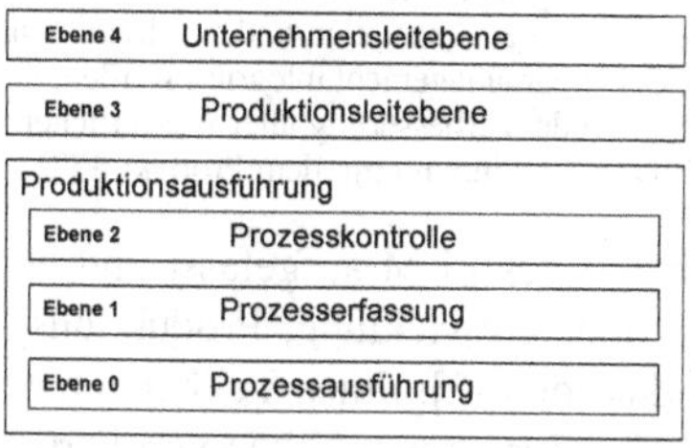

| Ebene 4 | Unternehmensleitebene |
| Ebene 3 | Produktionsleitebene |

Produktionsausführung

Ebene 2	Prozesskontrolle
Ebene 1	Prozesserfassung
Ebene 0	Prozessausführung

Abbildung 3. Funktionale Hierarchie für Aktivitäten in der Produktion entnommen und modifiziert nach: [23]

Produktorientierte IT-Systeme

Ebenso wie die dispositiven Systeme haben sich die rechnergestützten Verfahren im Kontext der Produktentwicklung im Zeitverlauf weiterentwickelt. Dabei wurden die aufgabenorientierten CAx-Systeme durch zentrale IT-Lösungen in ein einheitliches Produktdatenmanagement (PDM) integriert. Gemäß der VDI 2219 steht der Begriff synonym zu Engineering Data Management (EDM). EDM/PDM-Systeme dienen der Speicherung, Verwaltung und Kommunikation von produktdefinierenden Daten (z. B. technische Zeichnungen, digitale Modelle, Textdokumente). Produkte, zugehörige Entstehungsprozesse sowie deren Lebenszyklen werden über ein Produktdatenmodell informationstechnisch abgebildet. Dies verbindet schnittstellenbasiert die notwendigen Anwendungs- und CAx-Systeme zu einem Gesamtsystem für die Produktentwicklung. EDM/PDM-Systeme kommunizieren als Bestandteil der IT-Infrastruktur mit den dispositiven und steuerungstechnischen Systemen. [51]

Product Lifecycle Management (PLM) ist eine Erweiterung der EDM/PDM-Systeme und berücksichtigt sämtliche Informationen aus dem Lebenslauf von Produkten. PLM wird als Sammelbegriff für Management-Ansätze und IT-Systeme im ingenieurtechnischen Bereich verstanden [2]. Es führt die Entwicklungen im Bereich des Produkt- und Prozessdatenmanagements mit den Techniken der Produktmodellierung und Prozessdigitalisierung zusammen. PLM umfasst Methoden, Modelle und IT-Werkzeuge, um Produktinformationen, ingenieurtechnische Prozesse und Anwendungen über alle Phasen des Produktlebenszyklus zu organisieren. Es handelt sich um einen übergreifenden Ansatz für eine interdisziplinäre Zusammenarbeit zwischen Produzenten, Zulieferern, Partnerunternehmen und Kunden. [1]

Digitalisierung und globale Vernetzung

Ende der 1990er Jahre entstand der Begriff der digitalen Fabrik (DF), der gemäß VDI 4499-1 wie folgt definiert ist:

> Die Digitale Fabrik ist der Oberbegriff für ein umfassendes Netzwerk von digitalen Modellen, Methoden und Werkzeugen – u. a. der Simulation und der dreidimensionalen Visualisierung – , die durch ein durchgängiges Datenmanagement integriert werden. Ihr Ziel ist die ganzheitliche Planung, Evaluierung und laufende Verbesserung aller wesentlichen Strukturen, Prozesse und Ressourcen der realen Fabrik in Verbindung mit dem Produkt. [52]

Die DF wird als Bestandteil des PLM aufgefasst und unterstützt die Produktlebenszyklusphasen der Produktentwicklung, Produktionsplanung sowie der Produktherstellung und Produktion [43]. Einen Teilbereich der DF bildet der digitale Fabrikbetrieb, der durch das Zusammenwirken von Fertigungsmanagementsystemen, virtuellen oder realen Anlagensteuerungen sowie virtuellen oder realen Maschinen und Anlagen gekennzeichnet ist. Von der Montage- und Fertigungsprozessplanung bis zur Serienproduktion werden die Phasen eines Produktsystems horizontal über ein durchgängiges Datenmanagement integriert. [53]

Die DF bildet die reale Fabrik mithilfe von rechnergestützten Werkzeugen, Methoden und Technologien digital ab. Das Konzept der Virtuellen Fabrik ermöglicht es, Aussagen über das Verhalten des erzeugten Abbilds auf Grundlage von Simulationen zu generieren. Auf diese Weise können Produktionsabläufe in der tatsächlichen Komplexität für eine Erprobung oder Verbesserung virtuell nachgebildet werden. Die Ergebnisse der Simulation ermöglichen Adaptionen des digitalen Modells sowie eine Umsetzung zukünftiger Produktions- und Fabrikstrukturen. Die Methoden der DF adressieren Aspekte der Modellierung, Simulation, Optimierung, Visualisierung, Dokumentation und Kommunikation, um organisatorische, technische sowie betriebswirtschaftliche Zielstellungen zu erreichen. In den Werkzeugen der DF finden sich zur Unterstützung dieser Methoden die bis hierher dargestellten rechnerbasierten Ansätze aus dem Produktionsumfeld gemeinsam wieder. [37]

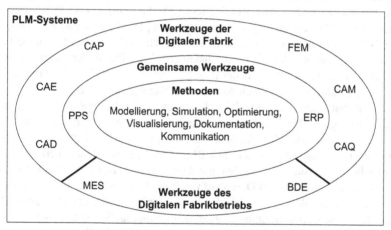

Abbildung 4. Methoden und Werkzeuge der digitalen Fabrik
entnommen und modifiziert nach: [37]

Status Quo der Operational Business Intelligence

Business Intelligence (BI) umfasst Anwendungen, Technologien und Prozesse zum Sammeln, Speichern und Analysieren von Daten, damit Fachanwender bessere Entscheidungen treffen können [56]. Operational BI (OpBI) ist eine begriffliche Erweiterung, die durch folgende Definition präzisiert wird:

Operational BI bezeichnet integrierte geschäftsprozessorientierte Systeme, die mithilfe klassischer Business-Intelligence-Methoden auf der Basis zeitnaher, prozessualer Ablaufdaten und in aller Regel auch historischer, harmonisierter Daten eine Realtime-(Near-Realtime-) Unterstützung für zeitkritische Entscheidungen während des Prozessablaufes bieten. [15]

Produktionsumgebungen eröffnen ein breites Anwendungsfeld für OpBI. Die Zweckmäßigkeit einer derartigen Entscheidungsunterstützung wird durch vergleichbare Funktionen industriegetriebener Ansätze verdeutlicht. So unterstützen MES z. B. die Sammlung, Aufbereitung und Darstellung von Produktionsdaten für eine Koordination der Betriebsabläufe [50]. Die Integration von Prozessdaten ist gleichermaßen charakteristisch für Advanced Process Control (APC) im Bereich der Halbleiterindustrie. APC-Lösungen umfassen Module zur Durchführung von Ablaufkontrollen, Fehlerklassifikationen und Effizienzberechnungen im Produktionsumfeld sowie statistische Methoden zur Analyse und Überwachung von technischen Prozessen. [59]

Eine Extraktion von Informationen aus produktionsspezifischen Daten zum Zweck der Entscheidungsunterstützung spiegelt sich auch in der Terminologie einer Manufacturing Intelligence wider. Im Mittelpunkt steht ein durchgängiger Gebrauch von Datenintegrationstechniken zur Analyse, Modellierung und Simulation, um alle im Unternehmen befindlichen Produktionsprozesse in Echtzeit zu organisieren. Die Anwendung von Manufacturing Intelligence und eine entsprechende Informationsversorgung von Entscheidungsträgern werden aktuell im Kontext eines Smart Manufacturing diskutiert. Diese Diskussion zeigt auf, dass die bestehenden IT-Lösungen in der Industrie nur vereinzelte Prozessverbesserungen und eine lückenhafte Entscheidungsunterstützung mit sich bringen. [11]

Die thematisierten Aspekte hinsichtlich einer durchgängigen Nutzung und Strukturierung von Produktionsdaten erlauben jedoch eine OpBI-getriebene Erweiterung der bestehenden Ansätze für eine produktionsspezifische Entscheidungsunterstützung. So können mit OpBI im Produktionsumfeld generierte Daten konsolidiert und visualisiert werden. Ein Anwendungsbeispiel ist die Analyse von Fertigungsaufträgen, um den Durchlauf von Produkten durch die Anlagen und Arbeitsplätze zu charakterisieren. Die Analyseergebnisse lassen sich als Kennzahlen in Produktionscockpits zusammenführen und veranschaulichen. Die im Netzwerk generierten Kennzahlen geben dann z. B. Auskunft über die Durchlaufzeiten von Fertigungsfolgen, Auslastungsgrade, Engpässe, Materialverbrauche oder die Gesamteffizienz. [33]

OpBI ist in der Lage, die Analyse- und Berichtsfunktionen z. B. von MES zu verbessern und die erzeugten Erkenntnisse in eine unternehmensweite Entscheidungsarchitektur einfließen zu lassen [18], [29]. Damit ermöglicht OpBI eine Integration von analysierbaren Daten aus technischen und betriebswirtschaftlichen Zusammenhängen [34]. Dies ist mit einer Verknüpfung von dispositiven und produktorientierten IT-Systemen in industriellen Unternehmen verbunden. OpBI unterstützt dadurch eine multidimensionale Sichtweise auf die Flexibilitätsanforderungen der Produktionsprozesse [20]. Modularisierung und serviceorientierte Architekturen bilden mit Blick auf die zu erreichende Flexibilität den Ausgangspunkt für eine technische Umsetzung von OpBI [21].

Industrie 4.0

Industrie 4.0 umfasst verschiedene Technologien und Konzepte. Das Thema wird als Zukunftsprojekt im deutschsprachigen Raum diskutiert. Der Kerngedanke ist eine Anwendung moderner IT-Techniken in der produzierenden Industrie, um eine intelligent vernetzte Produktion im Kontext einer Smart Factory zu erreichen. [27]

Technologische Grundlagen

Die technologische Basis für Industrie 4.0 bilden Cyber-Physische Systeme (CPS) sowie das Internet der Dinge und Dienste. Diese Begriffe thematisieren die Vernetzung und Synchronisation von Informationen aus physischen und digitalen Umgebungen. Den Ausgangspunkt dieser Technologien bilden eingebettete Systeme, die informationsverarbeitende Einheiten mit physischen Prozessen oder Gegenständen verknüpfen. Die eingebetteten Systeme wurden in einer weiteren Entwicklungsstufe untereinander vernetzt. Der Erweiterungsaspekt von CPS ist die Vernetzung über das Internet. CPS bilden einen Teilbereich des Internets der Dinge und Dienste. In diesem Zusammenhang werden visionäre Konzepte wie z.B. Smart City oder Smart Factory diskutiert. [14]

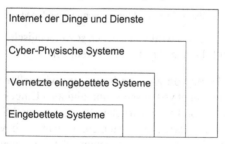

Abbildung 5. Vom eingebetteten System zum Internet der Dinge und Dienste entnommen und modifiziert anch: [14]

Cyber-Physische Systeme

CPS sind in physische Prozesse eingebettete Computer, die über ein Netzwerk miteinander kommunizieren [35]. Dies erlaubt eine regelkreisbasierte Überwachung und Steuerung von realen Prozessen mit digitalen Methoden. Eine acatech Studie aus dem Jahr 2012 präzisiert den Begriff wie folgt:

CPS umfassen eingebettete Systeme, Logistik-, Koordinations- und Managementprozesse sowie Internetdienste, die mittels Sensoren unmittelbar physikalische Daten erfassen und mittels Aktoren auf physikalische Vorgänge einwirken, mittels digitaler Netze untereinander verbunden sind, weltweit verfügbare Daten und Dienste nutzen und über multimodale Mensch-Maschine-Schnittstellen verfügen. [14]

Eine beispielhafte CPS-Struktur ist in der nachfolgenden Abbildung dargestellt. Dabei werden die Kernkomponenten eines CPS deutlich. Dies ist zunächst die physikalische Umgebung, die unabhängig von Computern oder digitalen Netzwerken existiert. Über Schnittstellen wird eine Verbindung zur digitalen Welt hergestellt. Dort finden sich Module mit Rechnereinheiten, Sensoren und Aktoren wieder, die über ein Netzwerk miteinander verbunden sind. [36]

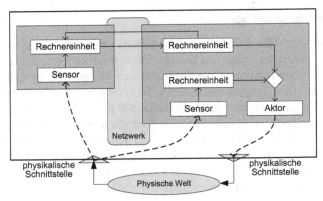

Abbildung 6. Beispielhafte CPS-Struktur [entnommen und modifiziert nach: LeSe11]

Im Zusammenhang mit CPS wird von offenen soziotechnischen Systemen gesprochen, die sich durch folgende Eigenschaften kennzeichnen [14]:

- **Verschmelzung von physikalischer und virtueller Welt:** Die Zusammenführung von physikalischen und digitalen Umgebungen erfordert die Kombination von kontinuierlichen Regelungs- und Steuerungssystemen mit diskreten Informationssystemen. Die mithilfe von Sensoren oder Sensorverbünden erfassten Umgebungsdaten können so parallel verarbeitet und interpretiert sowie anschließend zur Steuerung der physischen Prozesse in Echtzeit benutzt werden.
- *System of Systems* **mit dynamischen Systemgrenzen:** Dieses Merkmal spiegelt wider, dass CPS unterschiedliche Funktionen unterstützen sollen. Dazu entsteht situativ eine temporäre Kommunikation mit zusätzlichen Diensten und CPS-Komponenten.
- **Kontextadaptive und (teil-)autonom handelnde Systeme:** Die Fähigkeit zu kontextadaptivem Handeln erfordert eine umfängliche Kontexter-

fassung, um die gegenwärtige Anwendungssituation umfassend zu modellieren. Das System ist damit autonom in der Lage, sich an wechselnde oder unvorhergesehene Situationen oder Ereignisse anzupassen.

- **Kooperative Systeme mit verteilter und wechselnder Kontrolle:** CPS unterliegen oftmals keiner zentralen Kontrolle. Das Systemverhalten ergibt sich durch die Interaktion und Koordination von softwaregesteuerten Maschinen, Systemen, Diensten, Menschen und sozialen Gruppen. Die Kontrollmechanismen können in Mensch-Maschine-Interaktion, geteilte Kontrolle sowie Kontrolle zwischen verteilten Hardware- und Softwaresystemen eingeteilt werden.

- **Mensch-System-Kooperation:** CPS unterstützen die Interaktion zwischen Mensch und Maschine beispielsweise über multimodale Schnittstellen und können sowohl die Wahrnehmung als auch die Handlungsfähigkeit von einzelnen Personen und Gruppen vergrößern. Eine weitere Fähigkeit stellt die Analyse und Deutung menschlicher Gefühlszustände oder Verhaltensmuster dar. CPS besitzen eine Intelligenz um Entscheidungen oder Handlungen aus der Interaktion von Systemen und Menschen abzuleiten. Dies schließt eine Lernfähigkeit ein.

Internet der Dinge und Dienste

Das Schlagwort Internet der Dinge (Internet of Things) thematisiert seit 1999 die Vernetzung von Gegenständen und Prozessen, die eigenständig interagieren und sich selbst organisieren [5]. Die Erweiterung der Diskussion hinsichtlich Dienste (Services) hat das gemeinsame Begriffsumfeld Internet der Dinge und Dienste geprägt [46]. Dies kennzeichnet im Zusammenhang mit Industrie 4.0 die internetbasierte Vernetzung von CPS mit anderen Computersystemen beliebiger Art. Die Begriffe Internet der Dinge und Internet der Dienste haben jedoch eigenständige Erläuterungen und Basistechnologien, die Gegenstand der nachfolgenden Betrachtung sind.

Das Internet der Dinge bindet eindeutig identifizierbare physikalische Objekte (Dinge) in das Internet oder vergleichbare Netzinfrastrukturen ein [14]. Die ist eng verknüpft mit den Begriffen des Ubiquitous Computing (UC) und des Pervasive Computing (PC). UC thematisiert, dass sich IT und Computersysteme in sämtlichen Bereichen des Alltags wiederfinden, um dort Hintergrundfunktionen auszuüben. PC hat eine vergleichbare Intention wie UC, richtet sich jedoch verstärkt auf die Vernetzung von mobilen oder eingebetteten Computersystemen. Physikalische Objekte werden so in die Lage versetzt, ihre Umgebung wahrzunehmen und miteinander über das Internet zu kommunizieren. Den Übergang zum Internet der

Dinge kennzeichnet ein selbständiger Umgang der Objekte mit den Umgebungs-daten, um eigenständig Aktionen abzuleiten. Diese Fähigkeit wird auch als Ambi-ent Intelligence (Umgebungsintelligenz) bezeichnet. [5]

Die Verwirklichung des Internets der Dinge setzt Technologien [3] voraus, die eine Identifikation, Erfassung und Kommunikation von physikalischen Gegen-ständen unterstützen. RFID (Radio Frequency Identification) ermöglicht in diesem Zusammenhang eine elektronische Objektidentifizierung. Externe Lesegeräte ini-tiieren eine kontaktlose Übertragung von Daten, die auf einem Transponder hin-terlegt sind. Derartige Transponder sind direkt an den Gegenständen angebracht und bestehen aus einem Chip sowie einer Antenne, um mit den externen Lesege-räten kommunizieren zu können. Die Chips enthalten einen elektronischen Pro-duktcode (EPC) zum Zweck der eindeutigen Identifikation und zusätzliche Pro-duktinformationen.

Sensornetzwerke unterstützen die Erfassung von Umgebungsdaten im Kontext des Internets der Dinge. Drahtlose Multihop-Netzwerke verknüpfen eine Vielzahl von Sensorknotenpunkten, deren Messwerte direkt oder über mehrere Knoten-punkte hinweg zu einer oder auch mehreren Basisstationen weitergegeben werden. Derartige Mikrosysteme können über Logik- und Speicherkomponenten verfügen, um Aktoren anzusteuern. Eine Besonderheit stellt die Anwendung von RFID in sensorischen Mikrosystemen dar. Die RFID-Transponder werden mit einer pro-grammierbaren Steuereinheit und einem Sensor ausgestattet. Das Lesegerät fun-giert als Basisstation, die sowohl Sensor- als auch Konfigurationsdaten empfangen kann. Der Transponder arbeitet als passiver Messpunkt, so lange er nur über das Lesegerät mit Energie versorgt wird. Im Falle einer eigenen Energieversorgung, beispielsweise einer Batterie, können die Sensordaten auch im Transponder erfasst werden. [5]

Die Mikrosysteme stellen mit ihren Kommunikationsfähigkeiten verteilte An-wendungssysteme dar, die über eine Middleware vereinheitlicht werden können [38]. Eine Middleware stellt Dienste zur Kommunikation und Integration der An-wendungen bereit, die mithilfe der Infrastruktur des Internets der Dinge entwickelt wurden [3]. Die Eigenschaften und Funktionen der Mikrosysteme werden über Adapter gekapselt, sodass ein zentrales IT-System über bestimmte Schnittstellen auf die Daten der verteilten Anwendungssysteme zugreift, diese zwischen den Systemen austauscht und die Struktur der Daten vereinheitlicht. Middleware-Ar-chitekturen folgen im Zusammenhang mit dem Internet der Dinge dem Prinzip der Serviceorientierten Architektur (SOA). Diese wird als Basiskonzept des Internets der Dienste betrachtet.

Unter dem Internet der Dienste wird ein Teilbereich des Internets verstanden, in dem Dienstleistungen und Funktionalitäten in Form eigenständiger Software-komponenten mit webbasierten Technologien abgebildet werden [14]. In diesem

Zusammenhang wird SOA als zugrunde liegendes Architekturkonzept herangezogen. Es ist ein Ansatz zur Gestaltung und Umsetzung von Unternehmensanwendungen, der eine Vernetzung von lose gekoppelten IT-Services zur Unterstützung von Geschäftsprozessen adressiert. Ein IT-Service unterstützt eine abgrenzbare Funktion oder führt diese aus. Als Konsequenz der losen Kopplung ist es möglich, funktionale Komponenten je nach fachlichem Bedarf unterschiedlich zu kombinieren. Dies wird als Orchestrierung bezeichnet. Die Services sollen in diesem Zusammenhang wiederverwendbar sein und über eine plattformunabhängige Schnittstelle verfügen. [13]

Das Konzept einer SOA ist mithilfe von Web Services umsetzbar. Ein Web Service ist ein Softwaresystem, das eine vollständig kompatible Maschine-zu-Maschine-Interaktion über ein Netzwerk unterstützt. Der Web Service verfügt dazu über eine in maschinenlesbarer Form beschriebene Schnittstelle. Dabei hat sich die Web Service Description Language (WSDL) etabliert. Die WSDL beschreibt die Schnittstelle eines Web Services und definiert seine Funktionalitäten sowie technische Details. Derartige Beschreibungen werden in einem Service Repository hinterlegt. UDDI (Universal Description, Discovery and Integration) stellt in diesem Zusammenhang einen Verzeichnisdienst dar, der die Veröffentlichung von Web Services ermöglicht. Andere Systeme können mit Web Services interagieren. Für die Kommunikation und Interaktion von Web Services ist ein Nachrichtenaustauschformat erforderlich, das eine Suche, Erkennung und Nutzung unterstützt. Dafür kommt mit SOAP (Simple Open Network Protocol) ein Netzwerkprotokoll zum Einsatz, das sich auf XML (Extensible Markup Language) und weitere webbezogene Standards stützt. Der Transport erfolgt durch zugrunde liegende Protokolle wie dem Hypertext Transfer Protocol (HTTP) oder dem File Transfer Protocol (FTP). [39]

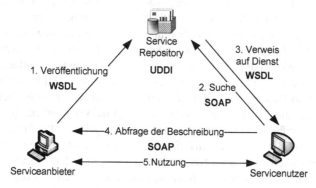

Abbildung 7. Funktionsweise einer SOA entnommen und modifiziert nach: [39]

Ein Web Service eines Anbieters wird durch ein WSDL-Dokument beschrieben und in einem Service Repository (UDDI) veröffentlicht. Ein potentieller Dienstnutzer durchsucht das Service Repository mithilfe von SOAP und findet durch das passende WSDL-Dokument einen Verweis auf den gewünschten Dienst. Damit wird auf Basis der SOAP-Nachricht eine Kommunikation zwischen Dienstnutzer und Dienstanbieter hergestellt. [39]

Cloud Computing ist ein weiterer Ansatz, der zur Umsetzung des Internets der Dienste diskutiert wird [12]. IT-Infrastrukturen, Anwendungen oder Plattformen verteilen sich auf verschiedene Systeme, die der jeweilige Anwender nicht lokal betreibt. Die Nutzung erfolgt über Dienste auf die über das öffentliche Internet (Public Cloud) oder über spezifische Intranets (Private Cloud) zugegriffen wird. Mithilfe von virtuellen Ressourcen sind die Dienste dynamisch skalierbar und abhängig vom Bedarf flexibel einsetzbar. Aus Anwendersicht bleibt der technische Unterbau verborgen, sodass der Zugriff über Schnittstellen oder standardisierte Programme erfolgen muss. Im Zusammenhang des Cloud Computing lassen sich drei generische Ebenen unterscheiden [6]:

- Infrastructure as a Service (IaaS) umfasst bestimmte Dienste, um Kapazitäten für Server, Speicher und Netzwerke sowie Sicherheitsaspekte abzudecken.

- Platform as a Service (PaaS) adressiert die Bereitstellung von Entwicklungs- und Laufzeitumgebungen von webbasierten Anwendungen.

- Software as a Service (SaaS) bezeichnet webbasierte Anwendungen, die als Dienstleistung bezogen werden.

Das Zukunftsszenario „Smart Factory"

Das Ziel von Industrie 4.0 ist die Smart Factory. Die Systeme der Smart Factory sind vertikal mit den betriebswirtschaftlichen Prozessen integriert und verbinden horizontal alle Bereiche der Wertschöpfung in den Unternehmen und entlang der Wertschöpfungskette. Einzelne Unternehmen oder Unternehmensverbünde nutzen IT zur Entwicklung von Produkten, für die Gestaltung von Produktionssystemen, für Logistik- und Produktionsaufgaben sowie zur Interaktion mit ihren Kunden. Die Smart Factory zielt auf die flexible Bearbeitung von individuellen Kundenwünschen, die Beherrschung komplexer Produktionsaufgaben, die Minimierung der Störanfälligkeit und die Effizienzsteigerung in der Produktion ab. Den Schwerpunkt bildet die Kommunikation von Menschen, Maschinen und Ressourcen in einem internetbasierten Netzwerk. Intelligente Produkte (Smart Products) stellen Informationen über ihren Kontext (Identifikation, Ort, Zustand, Historie, alternative Wege zum Zielzustand) selbst zur Verfügung. Die Ressourcen der Smart Factory umfassen Maschinen, Roboter, Förderanlagen, Lagersysteme und

Betriebsmittel einschließlich der angegliederten Planungs- und Steuerungssysteme. In der Smart Factory bilden diese Einheiten ein komplexes miteinander vernetztes System. Eine jeweils inhärente Intelligenz ermöglicht den Ressourcen, sich selbst zu steuern und zu konfigurieren sowie Informationen zu erfassen und diese über räumliche Entfernungen zu kommunizieren. [27]

Technologisch basiert die Netzinfrastruktur der Smart Factory auf dem Internet der Dinge und Dienste. Die Intelligenz der Produktionsressourcen ist eine Folge des Einsatzes von CPS in Produktionssystemen. Aus der Anwendung von CPS in der produzierenden Industrie resultiert der Begriff Cyber-Physisches Produktionssystem (CPPS). Dieser Term beschreibt flexible, adaptive, selbstorganisierende und selbstkonfigurierende Produktionsanlagen. Daten, Dienste und Funktionen werden zu Gunsten einer effizienten Entwicklung und Produktion an einer geeigneten Stelle in der Smart Factory vorgehalten, abgerufen und ausgeführt. Die damit verbundene Vernetzung sowie die ubiquitäre Verfügbarkeit von Daten, Diensten und Funktionen bringen Veränderungen hinsichtlich der Produktionsstrukturen mit sich. Die bestehenden funktionalen Hierarchieebenen in der Produktion brechen auf und werden durch vernetzte, dezentrale Systeme ersetzt [45].

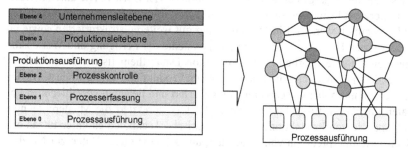

Abbildung 8. Auflösung der hierarchischen Struktur in der Produktion entnommen und modifiziert nach: [54]

Neben den technischen Veränderungen erfolgt im Rahmen der Industrie 4.0 eine intensive Auseinandersetzung mit der Rolle des Menschen in der Smart Factory im Hinblick auf die Steuerung, Regelung und Gestaltung der Produktionsressourcen. Der Mensch berücksichtigt in der Rolle des Entscheiders kontextbezogene Zielvorgaben zur Kontrolle der Produktionsabläufe und für die Qualitätssicherung. [27] In diesem Zusammenhang wird die Relevanz von Wissensmanagement und Wissenstransfer in den Vordergrund gestellt. Die Architektur einer Smart Factory ist modular aufgebaut, um das notwendige Wissen mithilfe von Menschzentrierten IT-Lösungen anwendungsfallspezifisch bereitzustellen. [42]

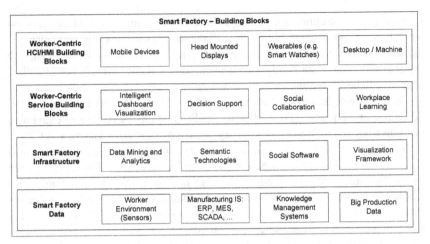

Abbildung 9. Mensch-zentrierte IT-Architekturbausteine einer Smart Factory entnommen und modifiziert nach: [42]

Die schematisch dargestellte Architektur umfasst vier Ebenen. Die unterste Ebene charakterisiert Daten der Smart Factory, die mithilfe von Sensoren im Arbeitsumfeld gesammelt werden. Eine Verknüpfung mit weiteren strukturierten sowie unstrukturierten Daten ist über Informationssysteme der Fertigung und Wissensmanagementsysteme möglich. „Big Production Data" thematisiert, dass durch die steigende Digitalisierung die Datenmenge im Produktionsumfeld wächst. Die Daten werden mit hoher Geschwindigkeit generiert und liegen in verschiedenen Formaten vor. Die Infrastruktur der Smart Factory adressiert die Mustererkennung und Analyse von Produktionsdaten. Semantische Technologien unterstützen eine IT-basierte Interpretation von Bedeutung und Kontext dieser Daten zur Nutzbarmachung von digitalem Wissen. In der Smart Factory kommt Social Software zum Wissensaustauch zwischen den Beschäftigten zum Einsatz. Einen weiteren Aspekt der Infrastruktur bildet die Visualisierung der Produktionsdaten. Die Dienste der Smart Factory sind in die Bereiche Visualisierungsdashboards, Entscheidungsunterstützung, Zusammenarbeit von Beschäftigten sowie das Lernen am Arbeitsplatz eingeteilt. Die oberste Ebene kennzeichnet Schnittstellen und Interaktionsmittel zwischen Mensch und Maschine, z. B. Anzeigen an Geräten, mobile Geräte oder intelligente Endgeräte. [42]

Operational Business Intelligence in der Industrie 4.0

Unter dem Gesichtspunkt der Datenintegration lässt sich OpBI in das Zukunftsbild der Industrie 4.0 einordnen. Im Zusammenhang mit CPS und dem Internet der Dinge richtet sich das Potenzial von OpBI auf die Analyse und Weiterverarbeitung von Sensordaten. Die erzeugten Ergebnisse können dann von Entscheidungsträgern und technischen Aktoren gleichermaßen genutzt werden. Die bereits existierende Diskussion von OpBI im Rahmen von SOA stellt einen Zusammenhang zum Internet der Dienste her. Die Funktionen von OpBI können demzufolge als Dienste im Kontext einer Datensammlung, Datenaufbereitung, Leistungsanalyse und Informationsdarstellung umgesetzt werden. Damit fungiert OpBI als Bestandteil der Kommunikationsinfrastruktur von CPPS in der zukünftigen Smart Factory. Die nachfolgende Abbildung stellt die von OpBI unterstützten Architekturbausteine diesbezüglich dar.

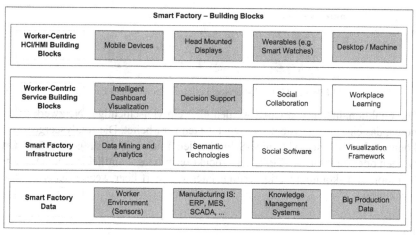

Abbildung 10. OpBI in der IT-Architektur einer Smart Factory

Die Architekturbausteine, die sich mit OpBI unterstützen lassen, sind in der obigen Abbildung durch eine graue Markierung hervorgehoben. Die Datengrundlage bilden Sensordaten aus dem Arbeitsumfeld der Mitarbeiter, aufgabenspezifische IT- und Wissensmanagementsysteme sowie eine Menge an Produktionsdaten. OpBI unterstützt mit Funktionen hinsichtlich Data Mining, Datenanalyse, Visualisierung und Entscheidungsunterstützung eine Mensch-Maschine-Interaktion in der Smart Factory. Die nachfolgende Darstellung ordnet diese Bausteine in eine serviceorientierte Plattform im Hinblick auf das Internet der Dienste ein.

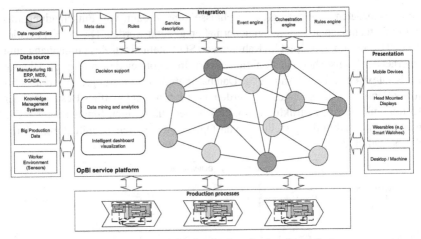

Abbildung 11. OpBI-Serviceplattform in einer Smart Factory

Die Funktionalitäten von OpBI werden über ein vielschichtiges Netzwerk ange-
boten, das eine Menge von heterogenen Daten verarbeitet. Die Analyseergebnisse
können über Mensch-Maschine-Schnittstellen Entscheidungsträgern präsentiert
werden oder direkt in die CPPS der Produktionsprozesse einfließen. Die Datenintegration und -kommunikation erfolgt internetbasiert über webserviceorientierte
Strukturen.

Fazit

Der Beitrag nimmt eine Einordnung und Positionsbestimmung von OpBI im Rahmen des Zukunftsprojekts Industrie 4.0 vor. Diese Diskussion basiert auf der Darstellung des Entwicklungstands von IT-Systemen in Produktionsumgebungen und
der Beschreibung des Status Quo von OpBI für eine produktionsspezifische Entscheidungsunterstützung. Der Beitrag zeigt daraufhin das Zukunftsbild der Industrie 4.0 als komplexes Zusammenspiel von CPPS über das Internet der Dinge und
Dienste auf. In einem derartigen Netzwerk aus intelligenten Ressourcen, Produk-
tionsmaschinen und Entscheidungsträgern besteht die Notwendigkeit für eine Datenverarbeitung und Informationsstrukturierung. OpBI kann vor diesem Hintergrund dienstbasiert eine Mensch-Maschine-Interaktion von Entscheidungsträgern
unterstützen. Dabei wird eine Infrastruktur der Smart Factory zugrunde gelegt, die
aus Mensch-zentrierten IT-Bausteinen besteht.

Industrie 4.0 und die damit verbundene CPPS-Strategie adressiert eine horizontale und vertikale Integration von produktionsbezogenen IT-Systemen sowie ein
durchgängiges Datenmanagement über die Produktlebenszyklen hinweg. Im Ver-

lauf des Beitrages hat sich gezeigt, dass diese Aspekte sich ebenso im OpBI-Konzept widerspiegeln. Die aktuell umfassende Diskussion zur Industrie 4.0 mindert jedoch nicht die Relevanz einer OpBI-getriebenen Entscheidungsunterstützung im Produktionsumfeld. Diese Erkenntnis stützt sich auf die durch den Beitrag initiierte Gegenüberstellung der Technologien einer Industrie 4.0 mit OpBI. Die Betrachtung aus Perspektive der operativen Entscheidungsunterstützung regt eine Neugestaltung von bestehenden Systementwürfen an. Die Berücksichtigung von serviceorientierten Architekturen ist dabei aus Sicht der IT schon länger Gegenstand der Diskussion. Diese wird aber von den sich in der Entwicklung befindlichen CPPS-Lösungen beeinflusst. Industrie 4.0 blickt in dieser Hinsicht ungefähr 10 bis 15 Jahre in die Zukunft [7]. Der bis dahin erreichte Entwicklungsstand wird ein Gestaltungsfaktor für entscheidungsunterstützende Systementwürfe wie OpBI sein. Im weiteren Verlauf der Forschung sollten daher prototypische OpBI-Umsetzungen die Entwicklung der CPPS-Lösungen und damit die Diskussion um Industrie 4.0 begleiten.

Literaturverzeichnis

1. Abramovici, Michael: Future Trends in Product Lifecycle Management (PLM), in: Krause, Frank-Lothar (Hrsg.): The Future of Product Development; Proceedings of the 17th CIRP Design Conference, Heidelberg 2007, S. 665-674.
2. Abramovici, Michael; Schulte, Stefan: PLM - Neue Bezeichnung für alte CIM-Ansätze oder Weiterentwicklung von PDM?, in: Konstruktion - Zeitschrift für Produktentwicklung und Ingenieur-Werkstoffe 1/2, 2005.
3. Atzori, Luigi; Iera, Antonio; Morabito, Giacomo: The Internet of Things: A survey, in: Computer Networks, 54. 2010, S. 2787-2805.
4. Bauernhansel, Thomas: Die Vierte Industrielle Revolution - Der Weg in ein wertschaffendes Produktionsparadigma, in: Bauernhansel, Thomas; ten Hompel, Michael; Vogel-Heuser, Birgit (Hrsg.): Industrie 4.0 in Produktion, Automatisierung und Logistik, Wiesbaden 2014, S. 5-36.
5. Brand, Leif; Hülser, Tim; Grimm, Vera; Zweck, Axel: Internet der Dinge - Perspektiven für die Logistik, Düsseldorf 2009.
6. Baun, Christian; Kunze, Marcel; Nimis, Jens; Tai, Stefan: Cloud Computing - Web-basierte dynamische IT-Services, 2. Aufl., Berlin 2011.
7. Bundesministerium für Bildung und Forschung: Zukunftsbild „Industrie 4.0", abrufbar unter: www.bmbf.de/pubRD/Zukunftsbild_Industrie_40.pdf, (16.03.2015).
8. Bundesministerium für Bildung und Forschung: Richtlinien zur Förderung im Themenfeld Industrie 4.0, abrufbar unter: http://www.bmbf.de/foerderungen/24078.php, (16.03.2015).
9. Bracht, Uwe; Geckler, Dieter; Wenzel, Sigrid: Digitale Fabrik - Methoden und Praxisbeispiele, Heidelberg 2011.
10. Bullinger, Hans-Jörg: Lean Production, in: Mertens, Peter (Hrsg.) Lexikon der Wirtschaftsinformatik, 4. Aufl., Berlin, Heidelberg 2001.
11. Davis, Jim; Edgar, Thomas; Porter, James; Bernaden, John; Sarlie, Michael: Smart manufacturing, manufacturing intelligence and demand-dynamic performance, in: Computers and Chemical Engineering, 47. 2012, S. 145-156.
12. Dufft, Nicole: Das wirtschaftliche Potenzial des Internet der Dienste, Berlecon Research GmbH, Berlin 2010.
13. Erl, Thomas: SOA Entwurfsprinzipien für serviceorientierte Architektur, München 2008.
14. Geisberger, Eva; Broy, Manfred: Integrierte Forschungsagenda Cyber-Physical Systems, München 2012.

15. Gluchowski, Peter; Kemper, Hans-Georg; Seufert, Andreas: Innovative Prozesssteuerung, in BI-Spektrum, 4. 2009, S. 8-12.
16. Gutenberg, Erich: Grundlagen der Betriebswirtschaftslehre, Band 1: Die Produktion, 24. Aufl., Berlin, Heidelberg 1983.
17. Hammer, Michael; Champi, James: Business Reengineering - Die Radikalkur für das Unternehmen, 6. Aufl., Frankfurt am Main, New York 1996.
18. Hänel, Tom; Felden, Carsten: Limits or Integration? Manufacturing Execution Systems and Operational Business Intelligence, in: 17th Amercias Conference on Informations Systems, Detroit 2011.
19. Hänel, Tom; Felden, Carsten: Towards a Stability of Process-Oriented Decision Support Concepts Using the Example of Operational Business Intelligence, in: Pre-ICIS BI Congress 3: Driving Innovation through Big Data Analytics, Orlando 2012.
20. Hänel, Tom; Felden, Carsten: Operational Business Intelligence Meets Manufacturing, in: 19th Americas Conference on Information Systems, Chicago 2013.
21. Hänel, Tom; Pospiech, Marco; Felden, Carsten: Web-based integration of MES and Operational BI, in: 8th International Conference on Web Information Systems and Technologies, Porto 2012.
22. Hehenberger, Peter: Computergestützte Fertigung, Berlin, Heidelberg 2011.
23. ISO 62264-3: Integration von Unternehmens-EDV und Leitsystemen, Teil 3: Aktivitätsmodelle für das operative Produktionsmanagement, Berlin 2008.
24. ISO 2806: Numerische Steuerung von Maschinen, Berlin 1996.
25. [Jacobi, Hans-Friedrich: Computer Integrated Manufacturing (CIM), in: Westkämper, Engelbert; Spath, Dieter; Constantinescu, Carmen; Lentes Joachim (Hrsg.): Digitale Produktion, Berlin, Heidelberg 2013, S. 51-92.
26. Karaali, Cihat: Grundlagen der Steuerungstechnik, 2. Auf., Wiesbaden 2013.
27. Kagermann, Henning; Wahlster, Wolfgang; Helbig, Johannes: Umsetzungsempfehlungen für das Zukunftsprojekt Industrie 4.0, Frankfurt am Main 2013.
28. Kief, Hans B.; Roschiwal, Helmut A.: CNC-Handbuch 2013/2014, München 2013.
29. Koch, Margarete T.; Lasi, Heiner; Baars, Henning; Kemper, Hans-Georg: Manufacturing Execution Systems and Business Intelligence for Production Environments, in: 16th Americas Conference on Information Systems, Lima 2010.
30. Kuhn, Heinrich: Konfigurationsplanung bei Zentrenproduktion, in: Arnold, Dieter; Isermann, Heinz; Kuhn, Axel; Tempelmeier, Horst; Furmans, Kai (Hrsg.): Handbuch Logistik, 3. Aufl., Berlin, Heidelberg 2008, S. 123-136.
31. Kurbel, Karl: Produktionsplanung und -steuerung im Enterprise Resource Planning und Supply Chain Management, 6. Aufl., München 2005.
32. Langmann, Reinhard: Prozesslenkung - Grundlagen zur Automatisierung technischer Prozesse, Wiesbaden 1996.
33. Laqua, Ingo: Der sinnvolle Einsatz von Business Intelligence-Systemen in der Produktion, abrufbar unter: http://www.cim-aachen.de/showpub.php? show=read_zwf1003.html, (16.03.2015).
34. Lasi, Heiner: Industrial intelligence - a BI based approach to enhance manufacturing engineering in industrial companies, in: 8th CIRP conference on intelligent computation in manufacturing engineering, Gulf of Naples 2012.
35. Lee, Edward Ashford: Cyber Physical Systems: Design Challenges, in: 11th IEEE International Symposium on Object Oriented Real-Time Distributed Computing, Orlando 2008.
36. Lee, Edward Ashford; Seshia, Sanjit Arunkumar: Introduction to Embedded Systems - A Cyber-Physical Systems Approach, LeeSeshia.org 2011.
37. Landherr, Martin; Neumann, Michael; Volkmann, Johannes; Constantinescu, Carmen: Digitale Fabrik, in: Westkämper, Engelbert; Spath, Dieter; Constantinescu, Carmen; Lentes Joachim (Hrsg.): Digitale Produktion, Berlin, Heidelberg 2013, S. 107-132.
38. Lucke Dominic: Smart Factory, in: Westkämper, Engelbert; Spath, Dieter; Constantinescu, Carmen; Lentes Joachim (Hrsg.): Digitale Produktion, Berlin, Heidelberg 2013, S. 251-270.
39. Melzer, Ingo: Service-orientierte Architekturen mit Web Services, 4. Aufl., Heidelberg 2010.
40. Plümer, Thomas: Logistik und Produktion, München 2003.
41. Sanchez, Luis M.; Nagi, Rakesh: A review of agile manufacturing systems, in: International Journal of Production Research, 39. 2001, S. 3561-3600.

42. Stocker, Alexander; Brandl, Peter; Michalczuk, Rafael; Rosenberger Manfred: Mensch-zentrierte IKT-Lösungen in einer Smart Factory, in: Elektrotechnik und Informationstechnik, 131. 2014, S. 207-211.
43. Schack, Rainer Jürgen: Methodik zur bewertungsorientierten Skalierung der Digitalen Fabrik, München 2008.
44. Scheer, August-Wilhelm: Computer Integrated Manufacturing, 4. Aufl., Berlin 1990.
45. Schlick, Jochen; Stephan, Peter; Greiner, Thomas: Kontext, Dienste und Cloud Computing - Eigenschaften und Anwendungen Cyber-physischer Systeme, in: atp edition, 55. 2013, S. 32-41.
46. Sendler Ulrich: Industrie 4.0– Beherrschung der industriellen Komplexität mit SysLM (Systems Lifecycle Management), Berlin, Heidelberg 2013.
47. Shah, Rachna; Ward, Peter T.: Defining and Developing measures of lean Production, in: Journal of Operations Management, 25. 2007, S. 785-805.
48. Soder, Johann: Use Case Production: Von CIM über Lean Production zu Industrie 4.0, in: Bauernhansel, Thomas; ten Hompel, Michael; Vogel-Heuser, Birgit (Hrsg.): Industrie 4.0 in Produktion, Automatisierung und Logistik, Wiesbaden 2014, S. 85-102.
49. Stadtler, Hartmut: Hierarchische Systeme der Produktionsplanung und -steuerung, in: Arnold, Dieter; Isermann, Heinz; Kuhn, Axel; Tempelmeier, Horst; Furmans, Kai (Hrsg.): Handbuch Logistik, 3. Aufl., Berlin, Heidelberg 2008, S. 194-214.
50. Thiel, Klaus; Meyer, Heiko; Fuchs, Franz: MES - Grundlage der Produktion von morgen, München 2008.
51. VDI 2219: Informationsverarbeitung in der Produktentwicklung Einführung und Wirtschaftlichkeit von EDM/PDM-Systemen, Düsseldorf 2002.
52. VDI 4499-1: Digitale Fabrik - Grundlagen, Düsseldorf 2008.
53. VDI 4499-2: Digitale Fabrik - Digitaler Fabrikbetrieb, Düsseldorf 2011.
54. VDI/VDE-Gesellschaft Mess- und Automatisierungstechnik (GMA): Cyber-Physical Systems: Chancen und Nutzen aus Sicht der Automation, abrufbar unter: www.vdi.de/uploads/media/Stellungnahme_Cyber-Physical_Systems.pdf, (16.03.2015).
55. Warnecke, Hans-Jürgen: Revolution der Unternehmenskultur - Das Fraktale Unternehmen, 2. Aufl., Berlin, Heidelberg 1993.
56. Watson, Hugh J.: Tutorial Business Intelligence - Past, Present, and Future, in: Communications of the Association for Information Systems, 25. 2009, S. 487-510.
57. Werner, Hartmut: Supply Chain Management - Grundlagen, Strategien, Instrumente und Controlling, 4. Aufl., Wiesbaden 2010.
58. Westkämper, Engelbert: Struktureller Wandel durch Megatrends, in: Westkämper, Engelbert; Spath, Dieter; Constantinescu, Carmen; Lentes Joachim (Hrsg.): Digitale Produktion, Berlin, Heidelberg 2013, S. 7-10.
59. Yugma, Claude; Blue, Jakey; Dauzere-Peres, Stephane; Vialletelle, Philippe: Integration of Scheduling and Advanced Process Control in Semiconductor Manufacturing: Review and Outlook, in: IEEE International Conference on Automation Science and Engineering, Taipei 2014.
60. Yusuf, Yahaya Y.; Sarhadi, Mansoor; Gunasekaran, Angappa: Agile manufacturing: The drivers, concepts and attributes, in: International Journal of Production Economics, 62. 1999, S. 33-43.
61. Zäpfel, Günther: Grundzüge des Produktions- und Logistik-Management, 2. Aufl., München 2001.

4.3 Anwendbarkeit der Operational Business Intelligence

Der bisherige Forschungsverlauf zeigt, dass OpBI neue Anwendungsfelder für den Einsatz von analytischen Informationssystemen im Rahmen einer Analyse und Steuerung von Geschäftsprozessen erschließen kann. Neben diesem erweiterten Aufgabenspektrum von BI-Anwendungen sind ebenso organisatorische und technische Veränderungen hinsichtlich der Integration und der Gestaltung von analytischen Systemen Gegenstand der begrifflichen Diskussion um OpBI. Diese dargestellten Entwicklungen adressieren gleichermaßen die Strukturelemente Mensch, Aufgabe und IT eines Informationssystems. Im weiteren Forschungsverlauf erfolgt eine Untersuchung dieser IS-spezifischen Gestaltungsbereiche hinsichtlich der Anwendbarkeit des OpBI-Konzepts für eine Analyse und Steuerung von Geschäftsprozessen (siehe Abbildung 9). Es werden zunächst Voraussetzungen aus der Perspektive einer endanwenderbezogenen Datenmodellierung betrachtet, um das Zusammenwirken von Mensch und IT in einem Informationssystem zu untersuchen. Die Ergebnisse dieser Untersuchung fließen daraufhin in eine Betrachtung von Anwendungsszenarien der OpBI im Produktions- sowie im Dienstleistungsumfeld ein.

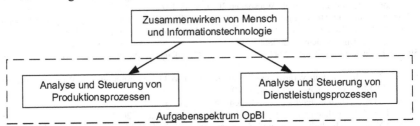

Abbildung 9. Untersuchung der Anwendbarkeit von OpBI als Mensch-Aufgabe-Technik-System

4.3.1 Modellierungsspezifische Voraussetzungen

Beitrag 5 und Beitrag 6 diskutieren modellierungsspezifische Voraussetzungen für eine Anwendbarkeit der OpBI im Rahmen der Analyse und Steuerung von Geschäftsprozessen. Im Mittelpunkt der Untersuchung steht der Einfluss einer formalen Abbildung von Informationsobjekten in IT-gestützten Analysewerkzeugen auf die wahrgenommene und die beobachtete Informationsqualität aus Sicht der Endanwender. Als Darstellungsmöglichkeiten für die zugrunde liegenden Daten werden multidimensionale, transaktionale und flache Datenstrukturen berücksichtigt (siehe Abbildung 10).

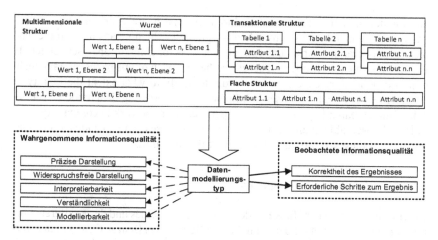

Abbildung 10. Informationsqualität in Abhängigkeit des Datenmodellierungstyps

4.3.1.1 Kurzdarstellung Beitrag 5

Die Untersuchung von Beitrag 5 und Beitrag 6 basiert auf der Methode des Laborexperiments. Beitrag 5 leitet zunächst das zugrunde liegende Forschungsmodell her und erläutert verschiedene Arten der Datenmodellierung im Rahmen der Erstellung von Ad-hoc-Analysen mit BI-Werkzeugen. Das Forschungsmodell berücksichtigt sowohl die vom Benutzer wahrgenommene Informationsqualität eines spezifischen Datenbestands als auch die nachprüfbare Qualität der erstellten Berichte. Hinsichtlich des vermuteten Zusammenhangs zwischen den vorgestellten Datenmodellierungstypen und den diskutierten Qualitätsaspekten werden Hypothesen formuliert. Mit dem Ziel einer Qualitätsverbesserung wurde die Experimentkonzeption vorläufig als Research in Progress zur Diskussion gestellt. Für eine Weiterverwendung der inhaltlichen Bestandteile erfolgte nur die Publikation des Abstracts von Beitrag 5.

4.3.1.2 Beitrag 5: On The Impacts of Data Modeling on Representational Information Quality (Abstract Only)[5]

Organizational and technical changes challenge standards of data warehouse design and initiate a redesign of contemporary Business Intelligence and Analytics

---

5 Schulz, M.; Hänel, T.: On The Impacts of Data Modeling on Representational Information Quality. In: Multikonferenz Wirtschaftsinformatik, Paderborn, Februar 2014.

environments. Hence, the use of multidimensional models for performance-oriented reasons is not necessarily taken for granted, which means that simple data models or operational structures emerge as a basis for complex analyses especially in context of ad hoc reporting. Therefore, the approach of this paper refers to techniques of laboratory experiments in order to verify to what extent the quality of analysis of a non-technical user is influenced by alternating data models. The result of this research in progress is an experimental framework to compare perceptible and observable quality aspects of ad hoc analyses. This includes a formulation of hypotheses to provide a basis for further research.

4.3.1.3 Kurzdarstellung Beitrag 6

Unter Zuhilfenahme der Hinweise des Gutachtenprozesses und des Konferenzvortrags konnten weiterführend die Inhalte von Beitrag 5 in Beitrag 6 eingebettet werden. Dieser beschreibt neben den Vorarbeiten auch die Ergebnisse der Experimentdurchführung. Es stellt sich heraus, dass Endanwender unter Verwendung einer multidimensionalen Datenstruktur qualitativ hochwertigere Ergebnisse mit weniger Aufwand erzielen als mithilfe von transaktionalen oder flachen Datenstrukturen. Die wahrgenommene Informationsqualität hinsichtlich der im BI-Werkzeug dargestellten Daten weist im Gegensatz zu den nachprüfbaren Qualitätsgrößen keine Unterschiede auf. Beitrag 6 schließt daher auf die Vorteilhaftigkeit von multidimensionalen Datenstrukturen in operativen Entscheidungsumgebungen. Die Teilnehmer des Laborexperiments sind jedoch im Umgang mit BI-Werkzeugen nicht vertraut gewesen. Unerfahrene Anwender können demzufolge die Wirkung eines zugrunde liegenden Datenmodells auf die Qualitätsgüte der zu erreichenden Analyseergebnisse nicht einschätzen. Im Hinblick auf die Erkenntnisse der Beiträge 2 bis 4 ist an dieser Stelle festzuhalten, dass OpBI die Nutzergruppe um Entscheider und Anwender erweitert, deren Aufgaben bisher noch nicht von BI-spezifischen Analysewerkzeugen unterstützt wurden. Daher wird die Modellierung von multidimensionalen Datenstrukturen als charakterisierende Voraussetzung für eine Anwendbarkeit der OpBI in Produktionsumgebungen und im Dienstleistungsumfeld angesehen.

4.3.1.4 Beitrag 6: Is there still a need for multidimensional data models?[6]

Introduction

Business Intelligence (BI) systems process data they receive by an integration of various data sources to provide business insights for decision making [20]. An

---

6 Hänel, T.; Schulz, M.: Is There Still a Need for Multidimensional Data Models. In: 22nd European Conference on Information Systems, Tel Aviv, Juni 2014.

important aspect of data integration is data modeling, which eventually affects the analysis opportunities for end users [3]. Data models need to illustrate business domains according to user requirements in order to make accurate decisions [30]. Multidimensional models have thereby gained acceptance in BI contexts [8]. The data therefore have to be prepared and they are typically stored in an integrated data store, namely the data warehouse [38]. The modeling and transformation of data in data warehouse contexts is costly, so that alternatives are under discussion due to current technical and organizational changes of BI environments. Such changes result in an extension of analytical functions and user groups. Business users recently are able to access manifold information sources and analytical options [28]. This leads to a discussion about changes on architectures of analytic tools and questions distinct data modeling types. For instance, a replacement of multidimensional models by simpler data structures seems to be a beneficial strategy to avoid additional efforts, especially to establish and maintain data transformation processes. Therefore, this paper's goal is to investigate whether the quality of an analysis will suffer from changing the underlying data model. Thereby, this research examines the extent to which a data modeling type influences the representation of information perceived by an end user performing analysis tasks as well as the actual impact observed by impartial measures. The research question is whether multidimensional data models are still needed and beneficial for a decision making in context of ad hoc analysis.

The discussion about representational information quality on decision tasks was mainly completed twenty years ago, but the consideration of differences in data modeling requires an investigation from a new perspective. We consider multidimensional models, transactional models and flat file models, which are commonly used data modeling types in context of BI and Analytics [10, 38]. Previous studies investigate multidimensional and transactional models with a dominant focus on the database design perspective [12, 15, 36, 37]. Existing usability studies are rather technical driven than application-oriented [42] so that they are less conclusive to estimate the impact of a certain data model on the decision quality of end users from a non-technical perspective. However, especially an end user needs to understand new approaches in order to assess a potential usefulness of advanced analytic forms. This is in particular necessary to substantiate subsequent implementations. The paper contributes therefore to a discussion about data models and new analytical trends. This discussion will gain insights regarding understandability and expressiveness of certain data models in an ad hoc analysis context. The paper's arguments address practitioners and researchers from a database design and focus on the non-technical perspective of end users.

Section 2 discusses technological and organizational reasons for analytical advances of BI to show the current relevance of the topic. In the following, we point out the relevance for analysis of the considered data models. The paper refers to laboratory experimentation, because this approach allows quality evaluations by independent participants [30]. The research model is presented in Section 3. This includes a formulation of hypotheses in terms of an observed and a perceived representational information quality. Section 4 introduces the participants and the data collection procedure of the experiment. We describe the software environment and the constraints that guided our experimental design. In Section 5, the collected data are analyzed so that the explanatory power of the research model can be evaluated. The paper concludes with a discussion of the results and an outlook on further research activities.

Status Quo

Problem refinement

Since the last decade, the term BI is under scrutiny and the term Business Analytics is becoming more important. Statistical analysis is emphasized more in Business Analytics than in BI, but a separate consideration of the terms is not beneficial [14]. Therefore, we follow the arguments of [9] to use BI and Analytics (BI&A) as a unified term.

The debate on a common term indicates a continuous change of business analysis over time as well as a progressive emergence of new requirements. An increasing amount of data generated by a large number of different data sources is available to organizations intending to use the data to learn more about their business [28] and to create competitive advantages. The focus of analysis has shifted partially from a support of strategic and tactical decisions to operational issues [6]. This requires detailed and recent information and leads also to new user groups with different demands and not only to traditional users of BI&A tools. If standard reports do not cover such information requirements, users are recently able to create their own analysis. Related trends like self-service BI are driven by an accelerating change of market demands for data analysis and provisioning [17]. Technical restrictions diminish due to advances in hardware, like large main memory, parallelized hardware platforms, solid state disks [40] and faster networks. New software architectures are discussed for analysis environments, in particular in-memory databases [32] and cloud computing [2].

As a consequence of the arguments mentioned above the research problem is that organizational and technical changes challenge existing standards of data warehouse design and initiate a redesign of existing BI&A environments. [40] for example, proposes a data virtualization to unify current data from various sources. [32] and [26] discuss a possible combination of transactional and analytical databases in that context. Considering further big data analytics, organizations have to deal with data that is in general not structured according to traditional data models. Faced by such proceedings, performance-oriented reasons based on software and hardware issues for a special data modeling of analytical environments [11] seem to be insufficient. In line with this, research findings point out that technical considerations of BI&A software are rather secondary from an end user's perspective.

The intention to use an analytical system depends to a higher degree on the suitability of information to fulfill existing information requirements [33]. Especially representational information quality is recognized as one of the most important factors to create a source for BI&A [31].

The goal of our research activities is therefore to examine how different data models affect the representational information quality in analytical tools from the non-technical viewpoint of end users. This non-technical perspective assumes that users do not necessarily need experiences with data modeling. They access data structures via a user interface to answer questions based on the information presented. In particular, we want to investigate a perceived representational information quality in relation to an observed representational information quality. The perceived quality is a subjective assessment of an end user about the information presented. The observed quality concerns impartial measurable indicators of an analysis result. This distinction allows us to examine whether the actual unbiased quality of the analysis corresponds to the evaluation of the participants or if there is a discrepancy. The outcome of this investigation renders assistance to justify the creation of special data models for analytical activities.

Data models and their relevance for analysis

We focus on the creation of ad hoc reports in order to examine the refined problem by an experiment so that we are able to obtain reliable results with a reasonable anticipated number of participants. Multidimensional models are popular to support the analysis of managerial issues. Therefore, Online Analytical Processing (OLAP) provides operations in order to filter, aggregate, pivot, rollup, or drill-down [8]. The concept was introduced by [11] and originates from the inadequateness of Online Transaction Processing (OLTP) systems to represent decision relevant information according to the analysis needs of business users. The reason is that OLTP systems are intended to support operational applications commonly conceptualized by normalized transactional models [13]. However, advances in technology like in-memory [32] and the increasing discussion of big data analytics [34] have shifted the analysis focus beyond the OLAP concept. Arguments considering advantages in processing time do not have much relevance anymore. Direct access to transactional databases supersedes a need for transformation processes and a redundant storage in OLAP and OLTP systems [32]. Benefits of such a strategy are lower cost for data processing through the omission of data cleansing and structuring, which leads to time savings and a more up to date decision making.

Multidimensional and transactional models are common design techniques in data analysis contexts [38]. However, the creation of such a structure can be very complex and changes of displayed information are time consuming. This justifies the question whether a comparable representational information quality can be achieved by using simpler structures like flat files ignoring structured relationships of data [10]. In context of big data, software vendors (e.g. [35]) already offer similar products without fixed table structures. Flat file models can be created easily, even if the data is stored in different sources.

Transactional and flat file models represent solely metadata so that actual data values are only visible in corresponding reports. A multidimensional model allows for a representation of data and metadata on the model level. This structure assumes a hierarchical data organization so that measures can be summarized at all hierarchy levels by different rules [5]. A hierarchy value is an attribute or a combination of various attributes, e.g. first name and surname. Such information items are usually not combined in transactional models and flat file models. The multidimensional model provides the highest degree of structuring from the perspective of an end user. Transactional models are also very structured, but usually from a more technical point of view. The structure of a flat file model can only be derived at the level of a single record. Figure 1 shows a simple example to visualize the different modeling approaches from an end user perspective.

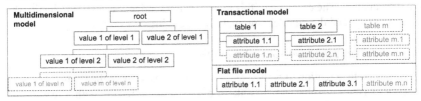

Figure 1. Examples of data model representation

Related studies

The majority of the previous studies focus on design issues of transactional and multidimensional models. Flat file models are not considered by any previous study. There are experiments dealing with a content reproduction depending on a data modeling type [12, 15]. The findings confirm beneficial effects of multidimensional structures for a data model comprehension. [22] explore positive impacts on modeling time and correctness by dint of dimensional design patterns. Further studies compare the understandability of transactional and multidimensional models in context of content identification and modification [36, 37]. A preliminary study reveals that inexperienced users understand multidimensional models easier, while the results did not achieve significance [37]. However, an additional experiment neglects a better user understanding in context of multidimensional models [36]. The findings suggest the consideration of technical aspects for choosing either multidimensional or transactional models.

The most recent study investigates the usability of multidimensional and transactional models in an analysis-oriented context [42]. The focus shifts to the use of data models to facilitate decision support in a business context. The study reveals higher accuracy values, faster completion times, as well as a better holistic view and subjective perception in favor of the usability of multidimensionally modeled data. However, the underlying software prototype reflects rather a technical perspective and provides no analysis interface for an end user.

Technical limitations have left no room to investigate the impact of a specific prepared data structure on aspects of information representation. This constrained studies about representations of an underlying problem. Overall, we reviewed about 100 articles on the representational information quality in decision making situations. More than 80 percent were published in the 1980s and 1990s. Previous experiments focused on a comparison of tabular and graphical views (e.g. [1, 18, 41]), a differentiation of graphical representations (e.g. [16, 21, 39]) or an analysis of advanced forms of presentation (e.g. [4, 7]).

All these studies mentioned above address an end user perspective, which means that their research design can guide our research intention, too. Five of the selected experimental studies are limited to observed values [1, 16, 18, 21, 39], while two contributions took an end user perception into account [4, 7]. Next to various observed values, an accuracy measure was always considered. Four experiments recorded the time for problem solving [7, 18, 21, 39].

Research Design

The independent construct of our research model is the data modeling type (DMT) that influences the quality of an ad hoc analysis. We differentiate between a perceived representational information quality of an end user and an observed representational information quality (cf. Figure 2).

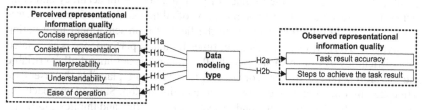

Figure 2. Research model

The perceived representational information quality considers to what extent a DMT leads to information according to end user needs. The information quality a system produces is distinguishable into intrinsic, contextual, representational and accessibility-related information quality [25]. In order to achieve comparable results, different DMTs have to consider a consistent business context, content and accessibility for any end user. Therefore, the representational information quality is suitable for an investigation of the perceived analysis quality influenced by a given DMT. This means in particular how a data structure provides information to the end users.

[25] distinguish representational information quality into concise and consistent representation, interpretability, understandability as well as ease of operation. Concise representation concerns how compact the information is provided. A representation should encapsulate the main aspects precisely to the point in order to avoid overwhelming and unnecessary information. A further quality attribute is consistent representation. Information should be presented in a coherent and invariant format. Appropriate units, definitions or labels have to characterize information in terms of interpretability. Another representational information quality aspect is understandability. This considers unambiguousness and comprehensibility of information. Finally, ease of operation means that information needs to be managed and manipulated easily. We formulate the following hypotheses in context of the perceived analysis quality by the end users:

- H1a: The DMT affects the concise representation of information perceived by an end user.
- H1b: The DMT affects the consistent representation of information perceived by an end user.
- H1c: The DMT affects the interpretability of information perceived by an end user.
- H1d: The DMT affects the understandability of information perceived by an end user.
- H1e: The DMT affects the ease of operation of information perceived by an end user.

Apart from the perceived quality, we need to introduce measures for an observed quality, too. According to the findings of [42], the task result accuracy and completion time are suitable measures in context of ad hoc analyses. These measures were also used in other experiments in the field of representational information quality. However, the documentation of times for a task performance is associated with difficulties. A time measurement by the end user is not impartially verifiable and therefore a potential source of error. It is furthermore plausible that users are influenced by time tracking, e.g. by pressure or distraction. Such an approach excludes as well the possibility to conduct experiments online and implies additional efforts. A system side time recording neglects breaks of users and interruptions during task performance. Hence, we use the steps an end user needs to achieve the task result. This measure is expressed by the number of task related clicks, which are logged during the task performance. Consequently, we formulate two hypotheses for the observed analysis quality:

- H2a: The DMT affects the observed task result accuracy of an ad hoc analysis.
- H2b: The DMT affects the observed steps of an end user to achieve the task result of an ad hoc analysis.

A support of the hypotheses indicates differences of the observed and perceived representational information quality for different DMTs. We expect an increasing

126

representational information quality with an increasing degree of structuring. This would be in line with existing studies of [33] or [42]. A missing support suggests that different DMTs do not influence an end user in any way. This would advance the findings of [36] from the data base design to an end user perspective.

Experimental Design

We decided to use an experimental design of independent measures [29], in which each design option needs a separate group of participants. Three groups are required in our study, since we intend to compare transactional, multidimensional and flat file structures. 20 participants are considered as a minimum number for each group [19]. The experiment was conducted online from June until July 2013. We asked 600 undergraduate students of business administration from Germany to participate. Experts are familiar with multidimensional structures, because this has evolved into a de facto standard for analysis [8]. Thus they may be affected by previous experiences. [18] demonstrate a decision makers' preference for an initially used representation of information, so that efforts are required to learn new representation patterns or to adapt heuristics. Therefore, we performed the experiment among students without prior knowledge in the use of BI&A systems to achieve homogeneous results from unbiased participants.

The students were requested via e-mail to participate voluntarily in the experiment. One reminder was sent after 14 days to those who did not respond to the first e-mail. The participation allowed the students to take part at a raffle of vouchers. The students were informed that the experiment intends to study the representational information quality of certain data structures and not to evaluate personnel skills in dealing with software. All results were saved anonymously. The survey was accessed by 197 persons. 93 students participated, which is a response rate of 15.5 percent. Nine participants stopped processing before enough information for evaluation was collected. Incomplete responses were eliminated. Response sets with an unusual short processing time and apparent fill out patterns are also not considered for evaluation. The resulting data set includes 78 records, in equal parts male and female participants. The average age is 24.

Each participant was confronted with a software user interface that was specifically programmed for this experiment. It includes a toolbar as well as a data source and a working area (cf. Figure 3). No vendor-specific characteristics were displayed so that the participants could understand the system quickly. The software served needs to understand efforts and usability aspects in data modeling. Therefore, technical considerations played only a minor role in the choice of the data model. The software modeled a reporting tool of a sales scenario. The working area allowed a creation of reports in a simple grid form. The participants needed to click on attributes or hierarchy elements in the data source. The working area displayed grouped attributes and aggregated measures. A selection of particular expressions within the working area set a report filter. The filter expression appeared in the toolbar. The toolbar had two buttons to clear the working area and to insert/delete a total column sum. Any column could be sorted in ascending or descending order by clicking on the column name.

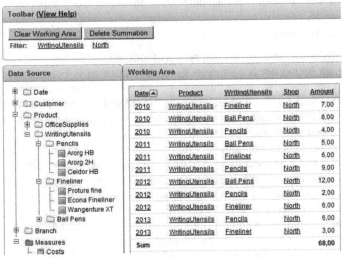

Figure 3. User interface for the multidimensional structure

The specific characteristics of the DMT options were represented by the data source, which was the only difference of the three user interfaces. The left hand side of figure 3 is thereby an example for the structure of the multidimensional model. Figure 4 illustrates and compares additionally the structures of the three different DMTs.

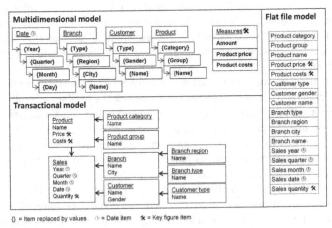

Figure 4. Data structures used in the experiment

All DMT options used the same sample data set and data granularity. We chose a sales scenario because this is a typical data warehouse issue (see, for example [23]). The number of attributes, metrics, and data sets were chosen so that they could be understood by the participants in a reasonable time. In the multidimensional case, the data source included hierarchies for time, customers, products, geography and a folder for measures. The transactional data source consisted of several folders with attributes of entities and relationship tables, while the flat file structure only listed attributes and metrics. We made simplifying modeling decisions to measure only the differences in the handling of the data structures. We chose field names that identify the contents clearly and did not use calculated measures. The date field was divided into year, quarter, month and day. The fields were thematically grouped and no technical keys were displayed. If appropriate, individual attributes were combined into values.

A participant was randomly assigned to a DMT option. Using a specific DMT, the participants had to solve ten tasks in the course of the experiment. The tasks could be solved clearly and represented typical questions to a BI&A system in the context of a sales scenario. One task asked for example: *How many franchise stores are in Hamburg?* Another task was formulated as: *Which female customers of customer type B bought pencils on 2012-01-23?* These examples show that the tasks have differed in their complexity. A higher complexity was created by longer and nested tasks, by more attributes and metrics that had to be used to solve the task and by the need to use filters and summations. The tasks were equivalent for each DMT. The result for each task had to be written in a text box in the task area. Tasks could be left out. After answering all tasks the participants were asked to assess the information content of the data structure (not of the reports).

Findings

In line with our research question and the singularity that the multidimensional model has a wide awareness, we compare this data modeling type to the flat file model and to the transactional model. The results support H2b and partly H2a. The observed quality measures behave in favor of the multidimensional model. The hypothesis H1b remains unsupported. H1a, H1c, H1d and H1e are supported only partly, so that an influence of the differing DMTs on the perceived representational information quality cannot be certainly confirmed from a statistical point of view. The detailed results are described and analyzed in the following.

Impacts on observed representational information quality

The participants had to solve ten tasks that can be divided into four result groups. We measured observed quality of each task by a system side record of steps needed by a user to achieve the result and a comparison against the correct result. A correct result is marked with one point, while zero points is the rating for incorrect, incomplete or non-existent results.

We calculated the means of observed quality measures for each task across the users (cf. Table 1). The users of the multidimensional model achieved the best results on average viewing all tasks. The accuracy is however only statistically significant in comparison to the flat file model. In contrast, the single tasks lead to a differentiated consideration.

Task 1 and 10 asked for a specific list of attributes (customers, products). Thereby, the number of steps to achieve the result is significantly less for the multidimensional model in comparison to other models. Users needed on average half as many steps in both tasks and achieved a clearly higher accuracy in task 1. The transactional model lead to the most correct answers in task 10, but the difference is not statistically significant in comparison with the multidimensional model.

Task 2 and 3 required the counting of stores in a city and the number of a group of customers. Users of the multidimensional model needed again the fewest steps to achieve their results. The participants using this model had also the most correct results. However, this mean is not significant in task 3.

The volume of sold products was the subject of three tasks (no. 4, 5 and 7). Only in 2 tasks, a significant result could be achieved for the number of steps. The participants using the flat file model needed the fewest number in task 4 compared to the other data modeling types. The user of the multidimensional model achieved the result faster in task 7.

In three tasks (no. 6, 8 and 9), participants had to determine customers, sales regions and stores for a maximum or a minimum value of sold products. Statistically significant differences between the models were found in task 8 and 9 by comparing the multidimensional and the transactional model. Thereby, users of the transactional model achieved more correct result in task 8 and a worse accuracy in task 9. The flat file model allowed the fewest steps for users to the result also in task 9.

Table 1. List of tasks and mean comparison for the observed quality measures. The best result for each row is shown in **bold**, non-significant values are shown grayed.

Task	Result group	Observed measure	Multidim. model	Comparison to flat file model		Comparison to transactional model	
			Mean	Mean	Sig. (2-tailed)	Mean	Sig. (2-tailed)
1	Attribute listing	Steps	**5.00**	10.58	0.000	11.35	0.001
		Accuracy	**0.96**	0.73	0.021	0.77	0.043
2	Attribute counting	Steps	**2.65**	8.88	0.000	9.88	0.000
		Accuracy	**0.92**	0.69	0.035	0.46	0.000
3	Attribute counting	Steps	**3.42**	7.96	0.000	9.00	0.000
		Accuracy	0.88	0.85	0.692	0.73	0.166
4	Quantitative value selection	Steps	5.69	**3.15**	0.093	3.88	0.223
		Accuracy	0.96	1.00	0.327	0.96	1.000
5	Quantitative value selection	Steps	9.04	**8.08**	0.518	8.46	0.694
		Accuracy	0.73	0.62	0.385	**0.81**	0.520

Task	Result group	Observed measure	Multidim. model	Comparison to flat file model		Comparison to transactional model	
			Mean	Mean	Sig. (2-tailed)	Mean	Sig. (2-tailed)
6	Attribute selection according to a quantitative value	Steps	10.58	11.15	0.828	11.65	0.678
		Accuracy	0.62	0.62	1.000	0.77	0.238
7	Quantitative value selection	Steps	5.23	8.73	0.000	9.42	0.000
		Accuracy	0.92	0.81	0.231	0.85	0.395
8	Attribute selection according to a quantitative value	Steps	9.08	9.65	0.733	10.73	0.313
		Accuracy	0.81	0.88	0.452	1.00	0.022
9	Attribute selection according to a quantitative value	Steps	8.88	6.00	0.020	6.50	0.045
		Accuracy	1.00	0.92	0.155	0.88	0.077
10	Attribute listing	Steps	6.00	13.38	0.000	11.54	0.000
		Accuracy	0.92	0.85	0.395	0.96	0.561
	Average of all tasks	Steps	6.56	8.76	0.001	9.24	0.000
		Accuracy	0.87	0.80	0.027	0.82	0.145

Table 2 summarizes the properties of the final reports, i.e. the representations which were displayed before the participant entered the results of the ten tasks. The users of the multidimensional model required fewer columns and fewer filters on average in comparison to the other two models. A summation was most frequently used in the multidimensional model. Between the flat file model and the transactional model, only small differences were measured.

Table 2. Properties of the final reports

	Multidimensional Model	Flat file model	Transactional model
Columns used on average	1,98	3,08	3,11
Reports in which one or more filters were used	8,08%	77,69%	78,46%
Reports in which one or more summations were used	14,61%	6,54%	7,69%

Impacts on perceived representational information quality

We used items according to [25] to compare the perceived representational information quality of the data models. Thereby, we have not considered such items which were determined in [25] by reverse coding techniques. A seven-point Likert scale was used to rate each item statement including response options from 'strongly disagree' (1) to 'strongly agree' (7). The Likert scale design is chosen based on measurement instruments of information quality [25] and conceptual models [27]. Table 3 shows the mean comparison of the rated item statements and the statistical significance. Thereby significant results arise only for less than half of the used items. The differences of the means are smaller than in case of the observed quality measures. The perceived representational information quality of the users tends always to an over-average or high degree for each data modeling type. The lowest mean is 4.8 and the highest averages 6.3.

Table 3. List of items and mean comparison for the perceived quality measures. The best result for each row is shown in **bold**, non-significant values are shown grayed.

	Item	Multidim. model Mean	Comparison to flat file model		Comparison to transactional model	
			Mean	Sig. (2-tailed)	Mean	Sig. (2-tailed)
Concise representation	This information is formatted compactly in the database.	5.8	5.5	0.284	**6.1**	0.202
	This information is presented concisely in the database.	5.7	5.8	0.911	**6.0**	0.263
	This information is presented in a compact form in the database.	**6.1**	5.5	0.068	5.7	0.115
	The representation of this information is compact and concise in the database.	**5.9**	5.3	0.068	6.0	0.786
	Average of concise representation	5.9	5.5	0.133	6.0	0.682
Consistent representation	This information is consistently presented in the same format in the database.	5.9	5.7	0.655	6.0	0.745
	This information is presented consistently in the database.	5.9	5.6	0.472	6.3	0.241
	This information is represented in a consistent format in the database.	5.5	5.9	0.326	6.0	0.161
	Average of consistent representation	5.8	5.7	0.931	6.1	0.199
Understandability	This information of the database is easy to understand.	5.4	5.7	0.519	**6.1**	0.046
	This information of the database is easy to comprehend.	5.2	5.3	0.866	5.7	0.183
	The meaning of this information is easy to understand.	5.6	5.9	0.228	5.9	0.268
	Average of understandability	5.4	5.6	0.507	**5.9**	0.092
Interpretability	It is easy to interpret what this information means.	5.2	**5.8**	0.061	5.7	0.133
	This information is easily interpretable.	5.4	**6.1**	0.053	5.9	0.175
	The measurement units for this information are clear.	4.9	**5.1**	0.618	5.1	0.691
	Average of interpretability	5.2	**5.7**	0.053	5.6	0.206
Ease of operation	This information is easy to manipulate to meet the user's needs.	5.0	5.3	0.447	**5.8**	0.034
	This information is easy to aggregate.	4.8	5.2	0.467	**5.7**	0.014
	This information is easy to combine with other information.	5.5	6.0	0.355	6.1	0.152
	Average of ease of operation	5.1	5.5	0.351	**5.9**	0.023

Concise and consistent representation is perceived at the highest average for the transactional model, while the averages are not statistically significant. The single means range from 5.7 to 6.1 in context of concise representation. However, only two items are statistically significant. The compact form and representation of information is thereby perceived more concisely by users of the multidimensional model than by users of the flat file model.

In terms of consistent representation, the user perception ranges from 5.5 to 6.3. The means of all items are highest for the transactional model, but none of the values has statistical significance. The values of the multidimensional model are in between those of the flat file and the transactional model in context that information is presented in same format and consistently. In terms of representation in a consistent format, the multidimensional model has the lowest mean compared to the other models.

The transactional model is perceived as most understandable and thereby the average and the single mean for ease of understanding are significant in comparison to the multidimensional model. The interpretability is perceived significantly higher by users of the flat file model in comparison to the multidimensional model. Only clearness of the measurement units achieves no statistical significance. The transactional model is perceived as easiest to operate. The values are significant excluding the aspect information combination.

The values range from 5.2 to 6.1 in context of understandability, from 4.9 to 6.1 in terms of interpretability and from 4.8 to 6.1 regarding the ease of operation. Thereby, the multidimensional model is perceived as least understandable, interpretable and easy to operate compared to the other models. However, statistical significance is achieved only by comparing the multidimensional model to either the flat file or the transactional model. A statistically significant comparison of the perceived representational quality regarding the transactional and the flat file model is not possible.

Discussion

The goal of the experiment is to find out whether different data models affect the analysis quality of end users. The need of classical multidimensional models is questioned. Thereby, the experiment investigates if models that can be made more readily available provide comparable or better insights into data with same or a better level of intuitiveness. We consider common data modeling types by a comparison of a multidimensional model with a flat file model and a transactional model. The focus is on representational information quality. The experiment addresses effectiveness and quality in processing tasks and the perceived assessment of participants.

The experiment was conducted among students who do not have experience in data analysis. With this group of participants, it was possible to carry out the quality independent of existing experiences. For a long-term orientation of the BI&A strategy, this is more important than the short-term advantage of models that are known by the use in the past. In recent years, new user groups are able to use

BI&A systems to solve complex problems. This leads to new data requirements, so that data structures need to be extended in favor of user-friendly and analysis-oriented data structures. However, models with less structure are increasingly used for the analysis, yet.

Data modelers cannot directly influence the subsequent usage of data models by a non-technical end user, but an incorrect and inconsistent sharing of data has to be avoided. Decision makers should be able to use a representation of data without adaptations to specific needs [24]. The hierarchies in a multidimensional model represent the logical data structure. This helps to identify relevant information quickly. In transactional models, the relationships are defined, but they are not represented in a form that is understandable to a non-technical end user. In flat file models, the relationships are only available at the level of a single record. This increases the risk that relevant information is not considered and analysis options are not recognized [12]. Therefore, less structured data sources from the perspective of an end user require a high level of domain knowledge.

Multidimensional models usually entail cost for data processing. There is a potential to save cost of data transformation for analysis purposes in case of flat file models and transactional models. However, the experiment indicates a higher reporting complexity and higher probability to make wrong decisions in case of using these models (H2a, H2b). This is associated with a danger to eat up the potential savings of data processing or even to incur losses.

In contrast to previous studies, our approach is responsive to end users, who actually perform ad hoc analyses with a certain user interface. Although we consider another perspective, the results confirm that the multidimensional model is more appropriate for analysis purposes than the transactional model. This is in line with four previous studies [12, 15, 22, 42]. Flat file models also have weaknesses compared to the multidimensional model.

[41] argue that the problem representation has to be suitable for a task to be fulfilled. This does not seem to apply to the representation of the data source: In our experiment, the different numbers of steps to get a result and the task accuracy cannot be attributed to a task type or the complexity of a task. However, the observable quality measures indicate advantages of the multidimensional model considering all tasks together. The results regarding the properties of the final reports show that the reports that have been built using the multidimensional model contain overall fewer elements and have a lower complexity. This is one reason why fewer mistakes are made using the multidimensional model.

We have not expected that only a few differences are perceived by the participants of the experiment (H1a – H1e). [4] also find out that a change in the representation does not result in a change of end user satisfaction. A possible explanation is that the participants are not experienced to judge whether an achieved result is correct or not.

Limitations and future research

One experiment can hardly consider all aspects, which can be usefully tested in context of representational information quality of different data models. This experiment discusses a problem area that can be investigated by further studies. Therefore, we have conducted a small-scaled experiment to provide a basis for a meaningful interpretation. The participants were not overwhelmed by a large information source and they were able to perform the tasks in a timely manner. Further investigations can enhance our experimental design to examine the effects of different information loads in conjunction with various data structures.

We chose a simple model to assign the results clearly to their source. Participants of the experiment are students, who are in the same phase of their studies. This is an attempt to keep individual differences as small as possible. [18] have considered this issue in more detail by typology of personality of participants. In future studies, such aspects should be considered.

A laboratory experiment has limitations to prove a general practicality. Therefore, we cannot bring forward the argument that decision makers benefit more from the use of multidimensional models in comparison to flat files or transactional models. However, our results point out that the model used for data analysis is important for quality of a derived decision. Thereby, the laboratory experiment leads us to the opportunity to control the confounding variable of unequally distributed experiences of end users.

In general, students are not familiar with the preparation of business reports. Therefore, we chose tasks so that a substantial understanding is very simple and cognitive differences do not have any relevance. The focus is on preparation of reports. However, the inexperience of the participants is not negligible. Further research activities should examine how the results will change when experienced users are asked. This includes situations, in which problem domains are already known beforehand or decision tasks are used that require not only simple extractions of information but decisions under uncertainty.

Conclusion

Companies have more data available than ever before [28]. However, this is only an advantage for analysis activities if the data is presented in a structure so that correct information can be drawn easily. The paper's contribution takes the usefulness of data structures and the viewpoint of end users of a BI&A system into account in order to enhance a discussion about organizational and technical aspects in context of integrating new analytical systems. We have conducted an experiment that compares the representational information quality of multidimensional models, transactional models, and flat file models.

The observed representational information quality was measured by task result accuracy and steps to achieve task results. Although newer data models have relevance for specific issues (e.g. analyzing data without internal structure), we have shown that the omission of technical restrictions does not mean that a particular analysis-oriented data preparation and a dimensionally oriented representation is no longer necessary. The less structured data are made available, the more possibilities exist for the users to prepare reports and to gain analysis results. This increases the complexity of report preparation and hence the search for information. Companies must decide whether to tolerate higher costs during processing of data or in course of data preparation for analysis purposes.

An important finding of the experiment is that end users are commonly not able to assess the representational information quality of a data source. This shows that end users of BI&A systems cannot make a decision for the appropriateness of the underlying data model. An end user's perception seems to be not suitable to select a certain analysis system. The results of a laboratory experiment cannot be readily transferred to practice and the findings cannot be generalized without limitations. However, there is evidence that the experiment provides useful implications and that multidimensional data models are still needed. We have formed a basis, which includes further research aspects.

References

1. Anderson, J. C. and Mueller, J. M. (2011). The Effects of Experience and Data Presentation Format on an Auditing Judgment. Journal of Applied Business Research, 21, 53-63.
2. Baars, H. and Kemper, H.G. (2010). Business Intelligence in the Cloud? In Proceedings of the Pacific Asia Conference on Information Systems, Paper 145, Taiwan, Taipeh.
3. Ballard, C., Farrell, D. M., Gupta, A., Mazuela, C. and Vohnik, S. (2006). Dimensional Modeling: In a Business Intelligence Environment. International Business Machines Corporation. http://www.redbooks.ibm.com/redbooks/pdfs/sg247138.pdf, Accessed 12/03/2014.
4. Bharati, P. and Chaudhury, A. (2004). An Empirical Investigation of Decision-Making Satisfaction in Web-based Decision Support Systems. Decision Support Systems, 37, 187-197.
5. Boehnlein, M. and Ulbrich vom Ende, A. (1999). Deriving Initial Data Warehouse Structures from the Conceptual Data Models of the Underlying Operational Information Systems. In Proceedings of the 2nd ACM International Workshop on Data Warehousing and OLAP, 15-21.
6. Böhringer, M., Gluchowski, P., Kurze, C. and Schieder, C. (2010). A Business Intelligence Perspective on the Future Internet. In Proceedings of the Americas Conference on Information Systems, Paper 267, Peru, Lima.
7. Cao, Y., Theune, M. and Nijholt, A. (2009). Decision Making with a Time Limit: The Effects of Presentation Modality and Structure. In European Conference on Cognitive Ergonomics: Designing beyond the Product - Understanding Activity and User Experience in Ubiquitous Environments (p. 8). VTT Technical Research Centre of Finland.
8. Chaudhuri, S., Dayal, U. and Narasayya, V. (2011). An Overview of Business Intelligence Technology. Communications of the ACM, 54, 88-98.
9. Chen, H., Chiang, R.H. and Storey, V.C. (2012). Business Intelligence and Analytics: From Big Data to Big Impact. MIS Quarterly, 36, 1165-1188.
10. Cios, K.J., Pedrycz, W., Swiniarski, R.W. and Kurgan, L.A. (2007). Data Mining: A Knowledge Discovery Approach. Springer, New York.
11. Codd, E.F., Codd, S.B. and Salley, C.T. (1993). Providing OLAP to User-Analysts: An IT Mandate. Codd & Associates, Ann Arbor.
12. Corral, K., Schuff, D. and St. Louis, R.D. (2006). The Impact of Alternative Diagrams on the Accuracy of Recall: A Comparison of Star-Schema Diagrams and Entity-Relationship Diagrams. Decision Support Systems, 42, 450-468.

13. Datta, A. and Thomas, H. (1999). The Cube Data Model: A Conceptual Model and Algebra for On-Line Analytical Processing in Data Warehouses. Decision Support Systems, 27, 289-301.
14. Davenport, T.H. (2012). Enterprise Analytics: Optimize Performance, Process, and Decisions Through Big Data. FT Press, Upper Saddle River.
15. Dowling, K., Schuff, D. and St. Louis, R.D. (2001). Dimensional Data Models versus Entity Relationship Models: Does it Make a Difference to End-Users? In Proceedings of the Americas Conference on Information Systems, Paper 80, USA, Boston.
16. Dull, R. B. and Tegarden, D. P. (1999). A Comparison of Three Visual Representations of Complex Multidimensional Accounting Information. Journal of Information Systems, 13, 117-131.
17. Evelson, B. (2012). The Forrester Wave™: Self-Service Business Intelligence Platforms. http://www.forrester.com/The+Forrester+Wave+SelfService+Business+Intelligence+Platforms+Q2+2012/fulltext/-/E-RES71902?objectid=RES71902, Accessed 12/03/2014.
18. Ghani, J. and Lusk, E. J. (1982). The Impact of a Change in Information Representation and a Change in the Amount of Information on Decision Performance. Human Systems Management, 3, 270-278.
19. Hair, J.F., Black, W.C., Babin, B.J., Anderson, R.E. and Tatham, R.L. (2006). Multivariate Data Analysis. 6th edition. Prentice Hall, Upper Saddle River.
20. Hamilton, J. (2009). A Customer Centric Approach to Front-End-Business Intelligence Deployment. E-Business Review, 9, 58-68.
21. Jarvenpaa, S. L. (1989). The Effect of Task Demands and Graphical Format on Information Processing Strategies. Management Science, 35, 285-303.
22. Jones, M.E. and Song, I.Y. (2005). Dimensional Modeling: Identifying, Classifying & Applying Patterns. In Proceedings of the 8th ACM International Workshop on Data Warehousing and OLAP, Germany, Bremen.
23. Kimball, R., Reeves, L., Ross, M. and Thornthwaite, W. (1998). The Data Warehouse Lifecycle Toolkit: Expert Methods for Designing, Developing, and Deploying Data Warehouses, John Wiley & Sons, New York.
24. Larcker, D. F. and Lessig, V. P. (1980). Perceived Usefulness of Information: A Psychometric Examination. Decision Sciences, 11, 121-134.
25. Lee, Y.W., Strong, D.M., Kahn, B.K. and Wang, R.Y. (2002). AIMQ: A Methodology for Information Quality Assessment. Information and Management, 40, 133-146.
26. Loos, P., Lechtenbörger, J., Vossen, G., Zeier, A., Krüger, J., Müller, J., Lehner, W., Kossmann, D., Fabian, B., Günther, O. and Winter, R. (2011). In-memory Databases in Business Information Systems. Business & Information Systems Engineering, 3, 389-395.
27. Maes A. and Poels, G. (2007). Evaluating quality of conceptual modelling scripts based on user perceptions. Data & Knowledge Engineering, 63, 701-724.
28. McAfee, A. and Brynjolfsson, E. (2012). Big Data: The Management Revolution. Harvard Business Review, 90, 60-66.
29. McLeod, S.A. (2007). Experimental Design - Simply Psychology. http://www.simplypsychology.org/experimental-designs.html. Accessed 12/03/2014.
30. Moody, D.L. (2005). Theoretical and Practical Issues in Evaluating the Quality of Conceptual Models: Current State and Future Directions. Data & Knowledge Engineering, 55, 243–276.
31. Nelson, R.R., Todd, P.A. and Wixom, B.H. (2005). Antecedents of Information and System Quality: An Empirical Examination within the Context of Data Warehousing. Journal of Management Information Systems, 21, 199-235.
32. Plattner, H. (2009). A Common Database Approach for OLTP and OLAP Using an In-Memory Column Database. In Proceedings of the 2009 ACM SIGMOD International Conference on Management of data, USA, Providence.
33. Popovic, A. and Jaklic, J. (2010). Benefits of Business Intelligence System Implementation: An Empirical Analysis of the Impact of Business Intelligence System Maturity on Information Quality. In Proceedings of the European, Mediterranean & Middle Eastern Conference on Information Systems (EMCIS), Late Breaking Papers, Abu Dhabi.
34. Russom, P. (2011). Big Data Analytics. TDWI Research, Renton.

35. SAS (2013). Visual Analytics: Visually Explore Your Data for Better, Faster Insights, Create Reports and Share Results to the Web and Mobile Devices. http://www.sas.com/resources/factsheet/sas-visual-analytics-factsheet.pdf. Accessed 12/03/2014.
36. Schuff, D., Corral, K. and Turetken, O. (2011). Comparing the Understandability of Alternative Data Warehouse Schemas: An Empirical Study. Decision Support Systems, 52, 9-20.
37. Schuff, D., Turetken, O. and Corral, K. (2005). Comparing the Effect of Alternative Data Warehouse Schemas on End User Comprehension Level. In International Conference on Information Systems: Third Annual Pre-ICIS SIGDSS Workshop on Decision Support Systems, USA, Las Vegas.
38. Sen, A. and Sinha, A.P. (2005). A Comparison of Data Warehousing Methodologies. Communications of the ACM, 48, 79-84.
39. Tan, J. K. and Benbasat, I. (1993). The Effectiveness of Graphical Presentation for Information Extraction: A Cumulative Experimental Approach. Decision Sciences, 24, 167-191.
40. van der Lans, R. (2012). Data Virtualization for Business Intelligence Systems: Revolutionizing Data Integration for Data Warehouses. Morgan Kaufmann, Waltham.
41. Vessey, I. (1991). Cognitive Fit: A Theory-Based Analysis of the Graphs Versus Tables Literature. Decision Sciences, 22, 219-240.
42. Vujošević, D., Kovačević, I., Suknović, M. and Lalić, N. (2012). A Comparison of the Usability of Performing Ad hoc Querying on Dimensionally Modeled Data Versus Operationally Modeled Data. Decision Support Systems, 54, 185–197.

4.3.2 Operational Business Intelligence im Produktionsumfeld

Die Notwendigkeit einer Entscheidungsunterstützung im Produktionsumfeld, die bereits in Beitrag 4 identifiziert wurde, motiviert eine weiterführende Betrachtung der OpBI in diesem Kontext. Die Beiträge 7 bis 12 setzen sich daher mit den Möglichkeiten einer Anwendung der OpBI zu Gunsten einer Analyse und Steuerung von Produktionsprozessen auseinander. Dabei besteht die Herausforderung, dass neben OpBI ebenso industriegetriebene IT-Konzepte entscheidungsunterstützende Funktionalitäten adressieren (siehe Beitrag 4). Als beispielhafte Vertreter für derartige Konzepte aus dem Produktionsumfeld werden MES zum Einstieg in die Anwendbarkeitsuntersuchung herangezogen.

4.3.2.1 Kurzdarstellung Beitrag 7

MES unterstützen eine Analyse von Produktionsdaten, um operative Steuerungsmaßnahmen ausführen können. Aufgrund dieser Ähnlichkeit zur OpBI diskutieren Beitrag 7 und Beitrag 8 Unterschiede und Gemeinsamkeiten zwischen beiden Systementwürfen. Beitrag 7 charakterisiert zunächst als vierseitiger Kurzbeitrag die Funktionalitäten und die Anwendungssystemarchitektur von MES. Diese Systeme ermöglichen eine vertikale Integration von ERP-Systemen und industriespezifischen Automatisierungssystemen. Beitrag 7 bestimmt einführend einen State-of-the-Art hinsichtlich MES in der wissenschaftlichen Literatur und stellt die Grenzen von MES im Kontext einer unternehmensweiten Entscheidungsunterstützung dar. Darauf aufbauend wird eine Eingrenzung der Literaturbeiträge über MES hinsichtlich BI-spezifischer Themen (siehe Beitrag 1) vorgenommen. Es stellt sich heraus, dass eine gemeinsame Betrachtung von BI und MES Vorteile für eine Integration und eine Analyse von Produktionsdaten mit sich bringt. Beitrag 7 sieht in dieser Hinsicht weiteren Forschungsbedarf aufgrund der geringen Anzahl wissenschaftlicher Untersuchungen, die dieses Verbesserungspotential adressieren.

4.3.2.2   Beitrag 7: Does it fit Together? – State-of-the-art of Academic Research Regarding Manufacturing Execution Systems and Business Intelligence[7]

Introduction

Manufacturing Execution Systems (MES) close the gap between an Enterprise Resource Planning (ERP) layer and an automation layer [1]. This is relevant for organizations of manufacturing and process technology forced to restructure their production due to increased competitive pressure. Reasons are networking, dynamic sampling and an ongoing product individualization, which requires permanent adaption capabilities in production, information management, and process control [2]. A challenge is the integration of MES within the overall organizational decision making [3], because the data of the shop floor level are needed for decisions in all enterprise levels, for instance to operate plants and machines, to control quality, for accounting or to appraise new technologies. Business Intelligence (BI) describes concepts to support management decisions by usage of a data warehouse and online analytical processing (OLAP). A data warehouse is a persistent database decoupled from operational systems to support reporting and analysis activities within the whole organization [4]. The integration of BI and MES led to the generation of performance indices for production influencing operational, middle management and strategic decisions [5]. Motivated by the introduced issue, the paper intends to give a state-of-the-art of MES and BI in academic literature, which is defined as an overview about scientific questions and stimulates further research [6]. This provides a basis to investigate the role of BI in context of MES and production environments. This is useful for collaboration of organizational entities between different enterprise levels, which is especially relevant for organizations realizing value creation in production.

As depicted in Fig. 1 the amount of published research in field of MES has been increased over the last period of 18 years. This includes several articles giving an overview about scientific issues and expediting further research [3], [7], [8]. None of these publications, which are comparable to the definition of state-of-the-art, consider the term or concepts of BI. Furthermore they are not reviewing the

---

7 Hänel, T., Felden, C.: Does it fit together? - State-of-the-art of Academic Research regarding Manufacturing Execution Systems and Business Intelligence. In: International Conference on Mechanical, Industrial, and Manufacturing Engineering, Melbourne, Januar 2011.

underlying literature according to a dedicated method. Therefore, this paper contributes a state-of-the-art by analyzing the literature in field of MES under consideration of BI using an appropriate approach [6], [9], [10]. This is important for researchers and practitioners, so that duplication can be avoided and relevant findings can be considered.

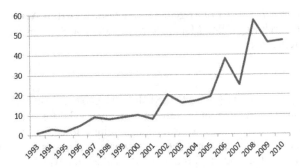

Figure 1. Publications in field of MES from 1993-2010

The paper is organized as follows: Section II defines the term of MES as concept between ERP layer and automation layer and as submodule of BI. Furthermore, the functions and architecture of MES are described. The method of literature review is explicated in Section III by presenting a staged process. Section IV highlights results of the literature review with an evaluation and an analysis of located publications in context of MES and BI. Finally, the paper is summarized in Section V giving conclusions and further research perspectives.

Background

This section defines the term MES. After the definition, basic functions of MES are described. Finally, this section points out architecture requirements of MES.

Definition of MES

The MES is placed between the layer of ERP and automation as shown in Fig. 2. It realizes a vertical integration by enabling task-oriented compaction, communication and access to data [2]. The ERP system is responsible for order and resource planning. It communicates desired quantities to the MES, which reports the results back to the ERP. Therefore, the MES has to execute target-performance comparisons permanently. This is to be done over the full production cycle by using real-time data. Operational performance shall be improved by reporting of crucial information regarding the production process. MES deliver decision relevant information on shop floor level. Therefore, MES can be considered as a submodule of BI, which provides decision relevant information to the whole organization [11].

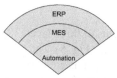

Figure 2. MES as concept between ERP and automation layer

Functions of MES

Manufacturing environments are manifold depending on complexity of products and underlying production processes. To meet different production conditions, a MES has to cover eleven functions (see Fig. 3) [12].

Dispatching production units reacts on occurrences of the ongoing production. Orders and work plans are changed and adjusted if necessary. Data collection gathers and monitors all relevant data regarding materials, operators, machines and processes. Quality management analyzes measured data to avoid non-conformity. Maintenance management ensures functionality of machines and plants by recording consumption of resources and hours of operation. Performance analysis compares achieved efficiency of the production environment with desired quantities of the business or ERP level. Scheduling means a planning of sequences of process steps under consideration of available resources and capacities. Document control manages that all relevant information regarding products, processes and design are accessible to employees. Labor management records and organizes working time. Process management monitors the production process and provides information to operators about production activities. Product tracking and genealogy creates a product history for the progress of production units. Resource allocation manages and monitors production relevant resources.

Data collection, quality management, performance analysis, document control, process management as well as product tracking and genealogy coincide with BI, because these functions of MES allegorize data aggregation and analysis to support the collection and distribution of decision relevant information. This is equal to the intention of BI [12]. Considering the aforementioned aspects there are intersections between both concepts, but the MES concept is more versatile than BI, because of its focus on the shop floor level.

Figure 3. Functions of MES

Architecture of MES

The architecture of MES consists of three layers [8]: application layer, functional layer, and data interface layer (see Fig. 5). The data interface layer enables access to one or more databases, where persistent data are stored. The heart of a MES is the functional layer. It implements the aforementioned eleven functions of the MES especially scheduling or document control. This layer consists of single functional components and can be extended according to production requirements. The application layer presents the MES functions on several clients. Users are able to interact with the system by sending requests and getting desired results. In addition to the described layers the architecture of MES has to consider interfaces to ERP and control systems.

BI is based on the extraction, loading and transformation of data from several operational databases as for instance ERP, supply chain management, customer relationship management and other external data sources within a data warehouse [13]. Since the architecture of MES proposes a data interface layer, an interface to the data warehouse and therewith integration within BI can be achieved.

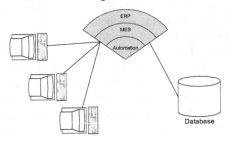

Figure 4. Architecture of MES

Method of Literature Review

A review is defined by the following characteristics: Based on primary investigations to one or more similar research questions, the review intents to describe, summarize, evaluate or integrate findings of previous research [6]. From this it follows that a review identifies gaps within a research topic and raises new issues in a scientific field [9]. The review follows a process consisting of five stages as depicted in Fig. 5 [6]. During the stage of problem formulation, the question that has to be answered by the review gets formulated, delimited and further specified. The next stage of literature search makes suitable literature for the given problem available. The third stage evaluates located literature. The focus is to examine identified literature concerning its relevancy. Subsequently, literature has to be processed and proper systemized. After this, analysis and interpretation of literature take place. Within this stage, the findings of literature evaluation will be explored and rated. This has to be done against the formulated problem. Finally, the research results are to be edited and presented to general public.

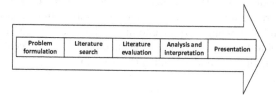

Figure 5. Review process according to Ref. [6]

Results

Since the problem formulation is been explicated in the introduction, this section presents the results of further steps regarding the review process of literature.

Literature search

The scientific databases of IEEE Xplore, ACM Digital Library, Science Direct, EBSCOHOST, Emerald and AIS electronic Library (AISeL) are the basis of literature search. This has been done, because the databases are covering a wide range of scientific publications. The search considered double-blind reviewed articles of the databases and references of them focusing on MES. The search terms were *Manufacturing Execution System, MES* or *Manufacturing Execution System MES*. Fig. 6 shows the result of literature search. Altogether 340 articles are found, where the most (183) are listed in the IEEE Xplore database.

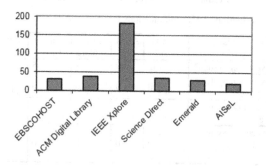

Figure 6. Matches in selected databases

Literature evaluation

All of the 340 articles are evaluated for their relevance in context of BI. Therefore, the articles were searched in for the keywords of *Business Intelligence, BI, Data*

Warehouse and *Operational Business Intelligence*. After this limitation the selected articles have been compared to the narrow understanding of BI, which equalizes the term with data warehousing and OLAP [11]. This has been done, because in broader sense, BI considers applications used for direct and indirect decision support including evaluation and presentation functionality as well as data storage and processing [13]. Due to this understanding, a MES itself is a BI application. Table 1 shows the results of evaluation. Only 2 percent of the articles consider BI in the narrow understanding (see Fig. 7).

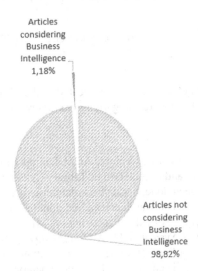

Figure 7. Articles considering MES and BI

Table1. Evaluation of MES publications for their relevance in context of BI

Database / Keywords	EBSCO-HOST	ACM DL	IEEE Xplore	Science Direct	Em-erald	AI-SeL	TOTAL
"Manufacturing Execution System"	32	39	183	35	30	21	340
"Manufacturing Execution System" + "Business Intelligence"	0	0	0	0	0	2	2
"Manufacturing Execution System" + "Data Warehouse"	1	0	2	0	0	0	3
"Manufacturing Execution System" + "Operational Business Intelligence"	0	0	0	0	0	1	1

Analysis and interpretation

The number of publications regarding MES is increasing. This indicates the relevance of MES for practitioners and researchers. Considering the integration of

MES within BI, the relationship between the concepts is hardly investigated, because the percentage of publications has a marginal value of 1.8 percent. Table II summarizes content and findings of articles considering BI. Implementation and integration aspects are addressed. The term BI is only used in the last three articles. Previous articles consider data warehousing and OLAP, which is consistent to a narrow understanding of BI [11].

Table 2. Summary of the articles considering BI

Ref.	Year	Summary
[14]	2005	The article presents a multi-dimensional data model and snowflake schema for MES data warehouse. Furthermore OLAP cubes are designed for an implementation case to analyze production indices.
[15]	2006	The article discusses an enterprise yield management (EYM) system, which loads data from MES and from ERP into a centralized data warehouse to identify problem areas in production.
[16]	2006	The article discusses an integration of MES, data warehouse, OLAP and data mining.
[17]	2010	The article investigates the relationship between operational BI and MES and proposes an integration framework.
[18]	2010	The article presents an architecture to integrate MES data in a BI tool of an ERP system. The investigation is based on a case study, in which a prototype is modelled for extraction of MES data in real-time.
[5]	2010	The article presents a concept for operational management to organize the production process according to restrictions of original equipment manufacturers. Integration of BI and MES is part of the research framework and base for operational decision support.

Conclusion

The role of BI to integrate MES in the overall decision making of organizations is hardly investigated, although it is advantageous for the following reasons:

- consideration of production performance indices within all organizational levels,
- real-time analysis in the shop floor to improve operational performance and
- integration of isolated applications to ensure a comprehensive operational decision making.

To close the identified gap, scientific approaches for an integration of BI and MES have to be investigated and validated. This is needed to confirm the conclusions of this paper and to get further insights to the presented topic.

References

1. ISA ANSI/ISA-95.00.01-2000, "Enterprise Control System Integration, Part 1: Models and Terminology," 2000.
2. J. Kletti, *Manufacturing Execution System – MES*, Berlin: Springer, 2007.
3. B. Saenz de Ugarte, A. Artiba, and R. Pellerin, "Manufacturing execution system – a literature review," *Production Planning and Control*, vol. 20, no. 6, pp. 525-539, September 2009.

4. P. Gluchowski, "Data Warehouse," in Enzyklopädie der Wirtschaftsinformatik – Online-Lexikon, 4th ed., K. Kurbel, J. Becker, N. Gronau, E. Sinz, and L. Suhl, Eds. Munich: Oldenbourg, 2010, http://www.enzyklopaedie-der-wirtschaftsinformatik.de, last access: 2010-12-28.
5. P. Louis and S. Olbrich, "Architecture for analyzing manufacturing execution data – using Business Intelligence logic," *Proceedings of the Sixteenth Americas Conference on Information Systems,* Lima, Peru, August 12-15, 2010.
6. P. Fettke, „State-of-the-Art des State-of-the-art – Eine Untersuchung der Forschungsmethode 'Review' innerhalb der Wirtschafts-informatik," *Wirtschaftsinformatik,* No.4, 2006, pp. 257-266.
7. M. Younus, C. Peiyong, L. Hu, and F. Yuqing, "MES Development and Significant Applications in Manufacturing – A Review," *2nd International Conference on Education Technology and Computer (ICETC),* 2010.
8. L. Fei, "Manufacturing Execution System Design and Implementation," *2nd International Conference on Education Technology and Computer (ICETC),* 2010.
9. J. Webster and R. Watson, "Analyzing the past to prepare for the future: Writing a literature review," *MIS Quarterly,* vol. 26, no. 2, pp. 13-23, 2002.
10. J. vom Brocke, et al. "Reconstructing the Giant: on the importance of rigour in documenting the literature search process," in S. Newell, E. Whitley, N. Pouloudi, J. Wareham, and L. Mathiassen, Eds. *17th European Conference on Information Systems,* Verona, 2009.
11. C. Felden and G. Chamoni, "Project Blueprints as Basis for Business Intelligence Projects – Towards an Applicable Business Intelligence Maturity Model," unpublished.
12. MESA, "MES Functionalities and MRP to MES Data Flow Possibilities," *MESA International – White Paper Number 2,* Pittsburgh, 1997.
13. H.-G. Kemper, W. Mehanna, and C. Unger, *Business Intelligence Grundlagen und praktische Anwendungen,* 2nd ed., Wiesbaden: Vieweg, 2006.
14. K.-Y. Chen and T.-C. Wu, "Data warehouse design for manufacturing execution systems," *Proceedings of the 2005 IEEE international Conference on Mechatronics,* Taipei, Taiwan, July 10-12, 2005.
15. S. Griffith, "It takes an enterprise to manage yield," *Electronic Engineering Times,* May 2006.
16. R.-S. Chen, Y.-S. Tsai and C.-C. Chang, "Design and Implementation of an Intelligent Manufacturing Execution System for Semiconductor Manufacturing Industry," *IEEE International Symposium on Industrial Electronics,* 2006.
17. M. Koch, H. Baars, H. Lasi, and H.-G. Kemper, "Manufacturing Execution Systems and Business Intelligence for Production Environments," *Proceedings of the Sixteenth Americas Conference on Information Systems,* Lima, Peru, August 12-15, 2010.
18. P. Hollstein and H. Lasi, "A CHANGEBILITY APPROACH FOR PROCESS MANAGEMENT AND DECISION SUPPORT ON THE SHOP FLOOR," *Mediterranean Conference on Information Systems (MCIS),* Paper 41, 2010

4.3.2.3   Kurzdarstellung Beitrag 8

Beitrag 8 baut auf den Erkenntnissen von Beitrag 7 auf und stellt das Management von Geschäftsprozessen in den Vordergrund der weiteren Betrachtung. Gegenstand der Diskussion ist die Untersuchung inwieweit MES aus industriegetriebener und OpBI aus managementorientierter Perspektive einander ähneln oder ergänzen. Dazu werden die Funktionen von MES und OpBI zueinander in Beziehung gesetzt. Diese Klassifikation zeigt die Vorteilhaftigkeit einer gemeinsamen Betrachtung auf. Der in Beitrag 7 begonnene State-of-the-Art wird weiterentwickelt, um den Forschungsstand zur Assoziation von MES und OpBI darzustellen. Die untersuchten Literaturbeiträge zeigen Aspekte der Vorteilhaftigkeit einer gemeinsamen Betrachtung von OpBI und MES auf. Hinsichtlich einer datenorientierten Entscheidungsunterstützung im Produktionsumfeld können jedoch nur einzelne Facetten dargestellt werden. Die analysierten Literaturbeiträge liefern aufgrund ihrer geringen Anzahl nur marginale Erkenntnisse hinsichtlich der gemeinsamen Betrachtung von OpBI und MES im Kontext einer Analyse und Steuerung von Geschäftsprozessen. Daher sieht Beitrag 8 weiteren Forschungsbedarf, um neue Erkenntnisse für eine Analyse und Steuerung von Geschäftsprozessen im Produktionsumfeld zu erlangen.

4.3.2.4 Beitrag 8: Limits or Integration? – Manufacturing Execution Systems[8]

Introduction

The design of business processes is a determining competitive factor. Increased informal networks not only influence processes within an organization, but changes also relationships to customers and suppliers. Therefore, companies have to keep their business processes flexible, which requires a consistently optimization. The range of conformable concepts allowing efficient support is large and manifold. But recently, MES and OpBI came into discussion since they are a promising support of process flexibility. However, such aforementioned concepts come from different perspective – the engineering and the decision support point of view. This raises a discussion whether the concepts are equal or have at least such similarities so that a combined approach seems to be more promising. Therefore, the paper's goal is to analyze the concepts of MES and OpBI to show overlapping or differences as basis for a conjoint process-oriented and flexible decision support oriented infrastructure.

Decision making in real-time has provoked business-oriented concepts like OpBI [9]. OpBI is an integrative approach for information delivery using traditional BI-techniques like e.g. Data Warehousing or Online Analytical Processing (OLAP) to organize and improve business processes [6, 7, 25]. Popular application fields are sales and marketing [7]. An engineering driven concept is used for IT-support of control and analysis activities especially in production environments. MES coordinate operational activities across the whole production lifecycle to enhance the performance and quality of plants or processes based on generated information for real-time decisions [27]. Both, OpBI and MES are integrative approaches to facilitate operational control and analysis of processes in real-time, but they are used in different organizational fields. The investigation of reasons for boundary of the concepts on domain-specific conditions gives implications

---

8 Hänel, T.; Felden, C.: Limits or Integration? - Manufacturing Execution Systems and Operational Business Intelligence. In: 17th Amercias Conference on Informations Systems, Detroit, August 2011.

how far company-wide process control is supportable by OpBI and MES. Therefore, the paper contributes a state-of-the-art giving a literature based classification of OpBI and MES, which is important in academic research to avoid duplication and to consider relevant findings.

Section 2 sheds light on reasons for the domain-specific application of MES and OpBI. Hence, academic literature is analyzed regarding the interrelation of the concepts. While MES is defined by several associations as MESA or ISA [18, 27], the perception of OpBI is fuzzy due to related terms like e.g. Real-time BI or Active Data Warehousing [7]. Therefore, the literature review is not fixed on OpBI. General BI-related terms are also considered to ensure profundity. The underlying method to build this state-of-the-art is explained in Section 3 and the results of its application are presented in Section 4. Finally, the paper is summarized to give conclusions and further research perspectives.

Status Quo of Operational Business Intelligence and Manufacturing Execution Systems

The scope of OpBI and MES is the analysis of processes to recognize weak points, malfunctions or business interruptions. Organizations are able to improve their management of business processes continuously and to generate interdisciplinary process information. The section shows an extension of traditional BI to OpBI and explains thereafter the concept of MES. Finally, analysis of the concepts results in a classification within the organizational structure of an enterprise.

Traditional BI-systems are focusing on management decisions [33]. The support reaches from operational planning level up to top management, nowadays. It is a bottom-up approach in the organization. Relevant data are collected from external sources or from internal operational systems [11]. From these sources, data are extracted, loaded and transformed (ETL-process) into a data warehouse [2]. This is a persistent database decoupled from operational systems to support reporting and analysis activities within the whole organization [21]. The systematically gathered data are used so that management is able to make suitable decisions. Techniques like OLAP or data mining characterize the analysis of the data [12, 15]. The following table comprises functions of BI:

Table 1. Functions of BI [34]

Function	Description
Business-relevant information	BI concentrates on business-relevant information. This is a balancing act, because it is complex to find a compromise between incomplete information and unnecessary memory usage.
Data collection	Operational data are collected from external and internal sources. This leads to the task of connecting data sources with a centralized data store. Access rights and security aspects need to be considered.
Data preparation	Data preparation generates usable information from raw data. To accomplish this, data have to be interrelated, expertise has to be implemented and mathematical procedures have to be applied.

Function	Description
Decision support	BI is designed to improve decision fundamentals by providing adequate information. It is important to focus on information certainly influencing a decision in order to avoid unnecessary expenses.
Information representation	Information is to be presented, so that users are able to manage their organizational tasks. Therefore, it is essential to understand the user's business model for offering adequate information.

Corporate Performance Management (CPM) enhances the concept of BI considering the organization as closed-loop system, in which strategic, tactical, and operational management is interrelated [13, 26]. This implicates the trend to Real-time Analytics next to Business Process Automation and Process Performance Management [26]. In context of real-time, the spread between occurrence of an event and execution of the subsequent decision is important. The so called action time involves three kinds of delay: data latency, analysis latency, and decision latency [14]. Latency and real-time characterizes OpBI [35]. This development of BI has the same functions as traditional systems, but its focus is on analysis and control of business processes [6]. Data consolidation can be realized by the Operational Data Store (ODS) [35]. The ODS has to manage the trade-off between performance and flexibility by an integration of operational applications with a data warehouse [17]. The knowledge of operational process execution is linked to the management supporting BI-system. In result, OpBI is advantageous in process analysis in real-time by dint of mature techniques of traditional BI-systems and integration of operational key figures in tactical or strategic decision making for instance in context of process design [9]. Examples of application represent an analysis of customer behavior to avoid migration or a fraud detection. This suggests the business context of OpBI. While sale, finance, marketing, or service is mainly supported, the concept is moderately driven within the field of manufacturing [7]. A related term to OpBI and ODS is Operational Data Warehousing (ODW) intending to enhance data models and interfaces of prevalent data warehouse architectures to facilitate interoperability to operational systems (Russom, 2010). The application fields are similar to them of OpBI. ODW is often used in financial application or Customer Relationship Management (CRM) and seldom applied in field of manufacturing [31].

A common approach to support the decision making on the shop floor is the MES [36], which is placed between the layer of Enterprise Resource Planning (ERP) and the layer of process, controls and automation [18]. It realizes vertical integration by enabling task-oriented compaction, communication and access to data [22]. Between these layers, a bi-directional data stream is preceded. The ERP-system responsible for order and resource planning communicates desired quantities to the MES, which has to execute permanent target-performance comparisons and must report the results back to ERP. The target-performance comparison is to be done over the full production cycle using real-time data [27]. So, operational performance is enhanced by reporting crucial information regarding the production process. The MES architecture consists of application layer, functional layer, and data interface layer [8]. The data interface layer enables access of MES database on machines and plants to gather relevant data. The application layer presents information generated out of a MES database on several clients. Users are able to send requests and to get desired results. Therefore, MES functions have to be implemented considering that manufacturing environments are manifold depending on the complexity of products and the underlying production process. To meet different production conditions, MES are covering eleven functions [28]:

Table 2. Functions of MES according to MESA

Function	Description
Data collection	All relevant data regarding materials, operators, machines and processes of a company are gathered and organized in real-time. The data are used to figure out possible improvements.
Dispatching production units	Production units are managed with work orders and instructions assigned to dedicated parts of the shop floor. To react on occurrences of the ongoing production, adjustments have to be taken.
Document control	All relevant information regarding products, processes and design have to be accessible to employees. Also certification statements regarding work and other conditions are gathered.
Labor management	Labor management ensures that every shift is properly recorded and organized. This is done under consideration of employees' qualifications, structure of the work and current business needs.
Maintenance management	Machines, plants and other operational assets have to be kept in state of functionality. Failures and malfunctions must be repaired by documenting of problems and corrective actions.
Performance analysis	Performance analysis compares achieved efficiency of the production environment with desired quantities of business coming from ERP level. Process and quality parameters are provided.
Process management	The monitoring of process activities provides information to operators about production activities. The goal is to optimize planning and provide a real-time control for actual production.
Product tracking and genealogy	A full product history for progressing production units is to be created for single units, lots or batches. Process transparency over the whole product lifecycle can be achieved.
Quality management	Products and processes of manufacturing value creation are analyzed to avoid non-conformities. Abnormalities are identified and corrected. Information of laboratory studies is also incorporated.
Resource allocation	The state of production-relevant resources is managed and monitored in real-time. Detailed history information of the resources is provided, too, in order to realize that a plant is properly equipped.
Scheduling	Planning of operational sequences in production proceeds under consideration of available resources and capacities. Overlapping operations are managed to minimize setup time.

MES and OpBI have comparable functions regarding data management and analysis, while MES have a broader range of tasks. Figure 1 summarizes the present analysis in context of organizational structure of an enterprise:

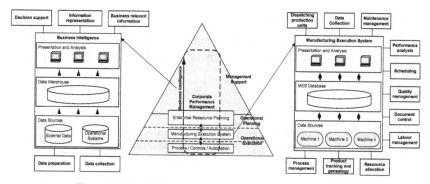

Figure 1. Classification of MES and BI within the organization

The functions of BI/OpBI and MES consider an integrated provision of data as well as purposive reporting and analysis. While a traditional BI-system delivers decision relevant information on management support level, the MES has a comparable intention in operational execution. If the MES gets more complex by including a high number of operational processes, the similarity to OpBI will grow. This is associated with a performance lost and limitation of decision making in real-time, because an increasing complexity requires a higher degree on interfaces [32]. Furthermore, the limited analysis capabilities of MES [1] question the benefits of such a strategy. OpBI also forces the decision making in real-time, has comprehensive analysis capabilities and facilitates company-wide process control. But as already mentioned in this section the concept is seldom applied in manufacturing. A possible reason is that the MES covers more functions than operational BI, because it is especially designed for production environments [29]. Hence, OpBI cannot compensate a MES and vice versa. From this it follows that the concepts are insulated applications, if they are not integrated.

The classification of the concepts shows, that there is a need for combined consideration. Thereby, the integration of OpBI and MES notably supports business process management in a whole organization, because implementation of performance indicators is enriched with information from process analysis. This leads to improvements of business processes itself and allows an interdisciplinary synchronization. In addition to the benefits for process-oriented decision support in organizations, new market potential for IT vendors of BI and MES solutions is generated. Research is needed to base the achievement of these benefits on comprehensive investigations. Therefore, information is necessary how far the topic has been discussed in academics to date. The next section presents a literature research to give an overview about published studies in these fields.

Method of Literature Review

The literature review intents to describe, summarize, evaluate or integrate findings of previous research based on primary investigations and can follow a process consisting of five phases [10]:

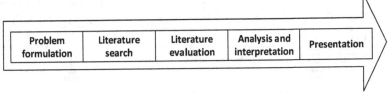

Figure 2. Phase-oriented process to realize a literature review

During problem formulation, the question that has to be answered by the review gets formulated, delimited and further specified. The next phase of literature search makes suitable contributions to a given problem available. A pool of literature sources is defined, in which contributions are extracted. The third phase evaluates located literature to examine the relevancy of identified literature. Subsequently, the literature has to be processed and proper systemized. Analysis and interpretation of the literature take place thereafter. Within this phase, the findings of literature evaluation will be explored and rated. This has to be done against the formulated problem. Finally, the research results have to be presented.

Results

There are significant results from the various phases of the review process. Since the problem is explained in the introduction and refined in Section 2, the subsequent description focuses on a presentation of search, evaluation as well as analysis and interpretation of literature considering integration aspects of MES and BI.

Literature search

The scientific databases of Business Source Complete (BSC), IEEE Xplore, AIS electronic Library (AISeL), ACM Digital Library, Emerald and Science Direct (SD) are the basis of literature search, because they cover a wide range on scientific publications. To ensure comparability, there are some restrictions:

- Terms are entered full and in quotation marks.
- The appearance of the terms is limited to abstract, title or keywords of the article.
- The date of publication is not later than December 31, 2010.

Initially, the search is split in two categories: MES and BI-related terms. The first category includes only the term *Manufacturing Execution System* to distinguish it from previous concepts as e.g. *Computer Integrated Manufacturing (CIM)* or adjacent areas as *Manufacturing Resource Planning (MRP)*. This procedure ensures that extracted contributions consider MES according to the definition in section two. To get a representative number of articles for the BI-related category, the following terms have been chosen: *Business Intelligence (BI), Data Warehouse (DW), Online Analytical Processing (OLAP), Operational Business Intelligence (OpBI), Operational Data Store (ODS)* and *Operational Data Warehouse (ODW)*. The search leads to a total number of articles as depicted on the following chart:

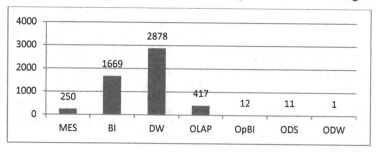

Figure 3. Total Number of Articles in all Databases

250 articles deal with MES. Substantial results are also reached for *BI, DW* and *OLAP*. Based on this intermediate result of literature search, the BI-related terms are combined with *MES*, while at least one has to be included in abstract, title or keyword of a particular article. The final result represents the following table, which includes duplicates. The highest compliance could be found upon the combination of the search items *MES* and *DW*. The search result reflects almost no relation in context of research activities regarding MES and OpBI. Since it is questionable whether an intensification of searching changes this fact significantly, the review process continues by analyzing all of the extracted articles.

Table 3. Evaluation of MES publications for their relevance in context of BI

Database / Search Term	BSC	IEEE	AISeL	ACM	Emerald	SD	Total
MES + BI	0	0	4	0	0	1	5
MES + DW	0	3	4	0	0	0	7
MES + OLAP	0	2	2	0	0	0	4
MES + OpBI	0	0	1	0	0	0	1
MES + ODS	0	0	1	0	0	0	1
MES + ODW	0	0	0	0	0	0	0

Literature evaluation

The literature evaluation eliminates duplicates within the search results. After elimination, seven articles remained. These were exactly the articles that could be found when searching MES in combination with DW. The following table shows the remaining articles and describes their key aspects. The remaining articles are examined whether the core of their attention is integration of BI and MES after elimination of duplicates. This examination reveals that the articles Nr. 1, Nr. 5 and Nr. 7 are not longer relevant.

Table 4. Remaining articles after elimination of duplicates

Nr.	Author, Year: Title	Key Aspects
1	Cheng and Lin, 2004: A Holonic Information Exchange System for e-Manufacturing	A proposal for information exchange between operational systems with different formats is presented. The role of so called holons (association of software agent and physical device) is investigated regarding MES, ERP and Data Warehouse to facilitate the information exchange.
2	Chen and Wu, 2005: Data Warehouse Design for Manufacturing Execution Systems	A multi-dimensional data model and snowflake schema for a MES-related data warehouse is developed. Based on this OLAP-cubes are used to analyze production indices.
3	Chen et al., 2006: Design and Implementation of an Intelligent Manufacturing Execution System for Semiconductor Manufacturing Industry	The article discusses integration of MES, data warehouse, OLAP and data mining to build up an intelligent MES.
4	Koch et al., 2010: Manufacturing Execution Systems and Business Intelligence for Production Environments	The focus is on investigation of the relationship between ODS and MES. Based on qualitative and quantitative exploration an integration framework is derived.
5	Hollstein and Lasi, 2010: A Changeability Approach for Process Management and Decision Support on the Shop Floor	A concept for operational management to organize the production process according to restrictions of original equipment manufacturers is presented.
6	Louis and Olbrich, 2010: Architecture for analyzing manufacturing execution data - using Business Intelligence logic	Architecture to integrate MES data into the BI-Tool of an ERP system is described. The investigation is based on a case study, where a prototype is modelled for extraction of MES data in real-time.
7	Olbrich, 2010: Warehousing and Analyzing Streaming Data Quality Information	Problems of data quality influencing the decision support in case of distributed applications are investigated.

Analysis and interpretation

The amount of published research in field of MES has been increased over the last period of 18 years (see Figure 4). Referring to BI, the huge amount of scientific publications is emphasized, too (e.g. [20]).

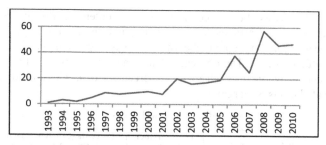

Figure 4. Publications in field of MES

Four of the evaluated articles address integration aspects of MES and BI. The term BI is used in two publications (Nr. 4 and Nr. 6 of table 4). [23] explore how the concepts of BI and MES are integrated in a practical context. Therefore, they present two case studies, in which the connection of MES, ERP and BI is investigated in automotive and chemical industries. In addition, a survey is conducted to identify benefits of MES for organizational-wide reporting with BI. An integration framework is derived based on the case study and survey results, in which the ODS is the interface between operational systems and a BI solution. This framework considers a lot of operational systems, which ensures organizational-wide integration. Certain information regarding technical implementation are missing. Louis and [30] focus on architecture requirements to separate the MES analysis function from operational execution level. Therefore, they carry out a case study to implement a prototype, in which the shop floor data are integrated into an ERP-related BI system. For implementation technical configuration aspects for data extraction is given. Unfortunately, the prototype requires the availability of a BI-supported ERP system. Other operational systems are not explicated. Worthy of criticism is also the decoupling of the analysis function from MES, because this limits the versatility of concept and standardization efforts.

The other two contributions consider data warehousing and OLAP (Nr. 2 and Nr. 3 of table 4). This is consistent to a narrow understanding of BI, because these are central components for an integrated management and a preparation of data. [3] propose a multidimensional database for MES. They define categories for further queries and design snowflake schemas for these categories. An implementation environment is proposed and query pages are presented for the so called *MES-Data Warehouse*. [4] aim to design, implement and operate an intelligent MES. This includes frameworks and procedures to integrate MES, data warehouse, decision making, analysis and data mining. Both contributions (Nr. 2 and Nr. 3 of table 4) neglect the organizational-wide context, because they do not consider other operational systems for e.g. ERP, supply chain or customer relations. The focus is on multidimensional analysis of MES data, which supports decision making on shop floor level, but not for the whole organization. Nevertheless, these findings show that there is a basis for an integration of BI and MES.

For statistical analysis, the four contributions, the content has just lit, are referred to the total number of articles for the single search terms of *MES, BI, DW* and *OLAP*. Due to the insufficient number of matches for *OpBI, ODS* and *ODW*, these terms are not considered. Table 5 demonstrates the state of investigation regarding the single and the whole research area. The percentage of articles considering MES and BI-related terms is marginal.

Table 5. Statistical analysis

Single term	Total number of articles	Percentage of articles considering MES and BI-related terms
Manufacturing Execution System	250	1,60
Data Warehouse	2878	0,14
Business Intelligence	1669	0,24
Online Analytical Processing	417	0,96
Total	5214	
	mean	0,31
	std. dev.	0,71

Conclusion

MES and OpBI are not equal. They deliver information regarding process analysis in different application fields. The integration of MES and OpBI to realize a process-oriented decision support in real-time is hardly investigated. The literature review covering a representative but not all-embracing pool of publications has made four articles available. The contributions consider multi-dimensional analysis of shop floor data and the role of MES for company-wide decision making. These are single aspects of integration, while the benefits of interrelations between OpBI and MES are only strived in one publication. This fact can be caused by the different roots of the concepts. OpBI is economic-driven. The MES comes from an engineering perspective and the awareness level only recently increases in business. This explains different application fields of the concepts. In academics, OpBI seem to be a novel topic, because of the manageable amount of matches in literature review. A reason is that the term is non-exhaustive defined, which is confirmed through availability of related terms e.g. Real-time BI or Active Data Warehousing.

The marginal state of research requires further investigation to provide new insights regarding the analysis and control of business processes. The integration of OpBI and MES enables an enhanced process management, in which processes are comprehensively coordinated and optimized. So, organizations are able to react fast and flexible on business occurrences increasing their competitiveness.

References

1. Alpar, P. and Louis, J.P. (2007) Eine empirische Untersuchung der Softwareunterstützung bei der Fertigung und Qualitätssteuerung - Implikationen für Manufacturing Execution Systeme, Philipps-Universität Marburg, Marburg.

2. Berson, A., Smith, S. and Thearling, K. (2002), Building Data Mining Applications for CRM, Tata McGraw-Hill, Delhi.
3. Chen, K.-Y. and Wu, T.-C. (2005) Data warehouse design for manufacturing execution systems, *Proceedings of the 2005 IEEE international Conference on Mechatronics*, Taipei, Taiwan, July 10-12.
4. Chen, R.-S. Tsai, Y.-S. and Chang, C.-C. (2006) Design and Implementation of an Intelligent Manufacturing Execution System for Semiconductor Manufacturing Industry, *IEEE International Symposium on Industrial Electronics*.
5. Cheng, F.-T. and Lin C.-T. (2004) A Holonic Information Exchange System for e-Manufacturing, *The 30h Annual Conference of the IEEE Industrial Electronics Society*, November 2 -6, 2004, Busan, Kora.
6. Cunningham, D. (2005) Aligning Business Intelligence with Business Processes, *What Works (TDWI)*, 20, 50-51.
7. Eckerson, W.W. (2007) Best Practices in Operational BI: Converging Analytical and Operational Processes, TDWI Best Practices Report, Renton (WA).
8. Fei, L. (2010) Manufacturing Execution System Design and Implementation, *2nd International Conference on Education Technology and Computer (ICETC)*.
9. Felden, C., Chamoni P. and Linden M. (2010) From Process Execution towards a Business Process Intelligence, in Abramowicz, W. and Tolksdorf, R. (Eds.) *Business Information Systems 13th International Conference*, May 3-5, Berlin, Germany, 195-206.
10. Fettke, P. (2006) State-of-the-Art des State-of-the-Art – Eine Untersuchung der Forschungsmethode 'Review' innerhalb der Wirtschaftsinformatik, *Wirtschaftsinformatik*, 4, 257-266.
11. Gangadharan, G. R. and Swamy, N. S. (2004) Business intelligence systems: design and implementation strategies, *Proceedings of 26th International Conference on Information Technology Interfaces*, Cavtat, Croatia.
12. Gluchowski, P., Gabriel, R. and Dittmar, C. (2008) Management Support Systeme und Business Intelligence: Computergestützte Informationssysteme für Führungskräfte und Entscheidungsträger, Springer, Heidelberg.
13. Golfarelli, M., Rizzi, S. and Cella, I. (2004) Beyond data warehousing: what's next in business intelligence? *Proceedings of 7th ACM international workshop on Data warehousing and OLAP*, ACM Press, New York, 1-6.
14. Hackathorn, R. (2004), The BI Watch: Real-Time to Real-Value (Whitepaper), URL: http://www.information-management.com/issues/20040101/7913-1.html, published January 2004, last accessed on 2011-02-28.
15. Han, J. and Kamber, M. (2001) Data Mining: Concepts and Techniques, Academic Press, San Diego.
16. Hollstein, P. and Lasi, H. (2010) A Changeability Approach for Process Management and Decision Support on the Shop Floor, *Mediterranean Conference on Information Systems (MCIS)*, Paper 41.
17. Inmon, W. H. (2005) Building the Data Warehouse, Wiley, Indianapolis.
18. ISA ANSI/ISA-95.00.01-2000 (2000) Enterprise Control System Integration, Part 1: Models and Terminology, ISA technical paper.
19. ISO 9000 (2005) Quality management systems: Fundamentals and vocabulary, European Committee for Standardization, Brussels.
20. Jourdan, Z., Rainer, R. K. and Marshall, T. E. (2008) Business Intelligence: An Analysis of the Literature, *Information Systems Management*, 25, 121-131.
21. Kimball, R. and Ross, M. (2002) The Data Warehouse Toolkit: The Complete Guide to Dimensional Modeling, Wiley, New York.
22. Kletti, J. (2007) Manufacturing Execution System – MES, Springer, Berlin.
23. Koch, M. et al. (2010) Manufacturing Execution Systems and Business Intelligence for Production Environments, *Proceedings of the Sixteenth Americas Conference on Information Systems*, Lima, Peru, August 12-15, 2010.
24. Louis, P. and Olbrich, S. (2010) Architecture for analyzing manufacturing execution data - using Business Intelligence logic, *Proceedings of the Sixteenth Americas Conference on Information Systems*, Lima, Peru, August 12-15.

25. Marjanovic, O. (2007) The Next Stage of Operational Business Intelligence: Creating New Challenges for Business Process Management, *Proceedings of the 40th Annual Hawaii International Conference on System Sciences*, IEEE Computer Society, Washington DC.
26. Melchert, F., Winter, R. and Klesse, M. (2004) Aligning Process Automation and Business Intelligence to Support Corporate Performance Management, *Proceedings of the Tenth Americas Conference on Information Systems*, New York, New York, August 2004.
27. MESA (1997a) MES Explained: A High Level Vision for Executives, MESA International – White Paper Number 6, Pittsburgh.
28. MESA (1997b) MES Functionalities and MRP to MES Data Flow Possibilities, MESA International – White Paper Number 2, Pittsburgh.
29. Meyer, H., Fuchs, F. and Thiel K. (2009) Manufacturing Execution Systems (MES): Optimal Design, Planning, and Deployment, McGraw Hill, Columbus (OH).
30. Olbrich, S. (2010) Warehousing and Analyzing Streaming Data Quality Information, *Proceedings of the Sixteenth Americas Conference on Information Systems*, Lima, Peru, August 12-15.
31. Russom, P. (2010) Operational Data Warehousing: The Integration of Operational Applications and Data Warehouses, TDWI Best Practices Report, Renton (WA).
32. Saenz de Ugarte, B., Artiba, A., and Pellerin, R. (2009) Manufacturing execution system – a literature review," *Production Planning and Control*, 20, 6, 525-539.
33. Sahay, B.S. and Ranjan, J. (2008) Real time business intelligence in supply chain analytics, Information Management & Computer Security, 16, 1, 28-48.
34. Schrödl, H. (2006) Business Intelligence, Hanser, München, Wien.
35. White, C. (2006) The Next Generation of Business Intelligence: Operational BI, BI Research, Sybase White Paper, URL: http://certification.sybase.com/content/1041416/Sybase_OperationalBI_WP-071906.pdf, last accessed on 2011-02-28.
36. Younus, M., Peiyong, C., Hu, L. and Yuqing, F. (2010) MES Development and Significant Applications in Manufacturing – A Review, *2nd International Conference on Education Technology and Computer (ICETC)*.

4.3.2.5   Kurzdarstellung Beitrag 9

Beitrag 9 baut auf der in Beitrag 7 identifizierten und in Beitrag 8 gefestigten Forschungslücke auf. Es wird die Zusammenführung von MES und OpBI in einer operativen Informationsplattform skizziert und ein Vorgehen zur Entwicklung einer Infrastruktur für eine produktionsspezifische Entscheidungsunterstützung vorgestellt. Die angestrebte Integration der Konzepte adressiert Fähigkeiten, um schnell und flexibel auf Geschäftsereignisse zu reagieren und damit die Wettbewerbsfähigkeit eines Industrieunternehmens zu steigern. Die Integrationsaspekte infolge der gemeinsamen Betrachtung von OpBI und MES stehen in Zusammenhang mit den Erkenntnissen von Beitrag 3.

4.3.2.6   Beitrag 9: Manufacturing Execution Systems und Operational
Business Intelligence – Zur Notwendigkeit einer integrierten
Betrachtung[9]

Einleitung

Die Gestaltung von Geschäftsprozessen ist ein entscheidender Wettbewerbsfaktor.
Dabei werden nicht nur die Prozesse innerhalb eines Unternehmens durch die zu-
nehmende Vernetzung beeinflusst. Es ändern sich ebenfalls die Beziehungen zu
Lieferanten und Kunden. Dies zwingt Unternehmen dazu, Geschäftsprozesse flexibel zu halten und immer wieder anzupassen. Konzepte, die wirksame Unterstützung anbieten, sind vorhanden (z. B. SOA/service-oriented Business Intelligence
[6], Real-Time Analytics [16], Active Data Warehousing [13]). In den vergange-
nen zehn Jahren sind dazu ergänzend Manufacturing Execution Systems (MES)
und Operational Business Intelligence (OpBI) parallel aus unterschiedlichen
Blickrichtungen in die Diskussion getreten. Beide Ansätze versprechen Unterstützung in der Prozessflexibilität, argumentieren jedoch aus ihrer jeweiligen Perspektive heraus – der ingenieurwissenschaftlichen und der entscheidungsunterstüt-
zungsorientierten Sichtweise. Im Unklaren verbleibt, inwiefern OpBI und MES
überlappend sind oder zumindest solche Ähnlichkeiten aufweisen, als dass eine
kombinierte Betrachtung einen höheren Beitrag für die Flexibilität von Geschäftsprozessen und der Unterstützung unternehmerischer Tätigkeiten leistet. Ein Bedarf an entsprechenden Lösungen ist erkennbar, weil z. B. gemäß einer Studie der
Aberdeen Group 85 Prozent der befragten Unternehmen mit ihren Anwendungen
keine adäquate Flexibilität erreichen können [20]. Ein Ziel des Dissertationsprojektes ist eine Zusammenführung von MES und OpBI unter Berücksichtigung der
Gemeinsamkeiten aber auch der Unterschiede, um zu einer interdisziplinären, prozessorientierten und flexiblen Entscheidungsunterstützung beizutragen.

OpBI stellt mithilfe von BI-Techniken, wie Data Warehousing oder OLAP,
Echtzeitinformationen zur Verfügung, um Geschäftsprozesse zu koordinieren [3,
15]. Hauptanwendungsgebiete sind Vertrieb und Marketing [5]. Innerhalb von
Produktionsumgebungen erfolgt die IT-Unterstützung der Prozesse vorrangig
durch ingenieurwissenschaftlich-orientierte Konzepte, insbesondere dem MES,
welche die Abläufe von Produktionsanlagen in Echtzeit organisieren [18]. OpBI
und MES sind integrative Ansätze, die eine flexible Echtzeitsteuerung von Geschäftsprozessen fördern. Sie kommen jedoch in verschiedenen Segmenten der
Wertschöpfungskette zum Einsatz. In diesem Kontext leistet die Forschung durch
die Zusammenführung von MES und OpBI in eine operative Integrationsplattform

---

9 Hänel, T., Felden C.: Manufacturing Execution Systems und Operational Business Intelligence -
Zur Notwendigkeit einer integrierten Betrachtung. In: 3. Workshop "Business Intelligence" der GI-
Fachgruppe Business Intelligence, Stuttgart, Oktober 2011.

einen Beitrag hinsichtlich der unternehmensweiten Steuerung und Analyse von Geschäftsprozessen.

Kapitel 2 stellt MES und OpBI vor, ordnet die Konzepte in die Organisationsstruktur eines Unternehmens ein und diskutiert Folgen einer gemeinsamen Betrachtung für die Integration der Informationsverarbeitung. Ein methodisches Raster wird in Kapitel 3 beschrieben. Kapitel 4 präsentiert erste Arbeitsergebnisse. Abschließend erfolgen eine Zusammenfassung und ein Ausblick.

Status Quo

Operational Business Intelligence und Manufacturing Execution Systems

OpBI und MES analysieren Geschäftsprozesse, um Schwachstellen, Fehlfunktionen oder Störfälle zu erkennen. Unternehmen können ihre Abläufe kontinuierlich steuern, überwachen und verbessern. In die Struktur eines Unternehmens lassen sich die vorgestellten Konzepte wie folgt einordnen:

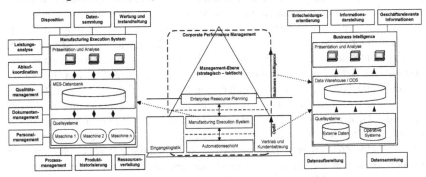

Abbildung 1. Organisationsstrukturelle Einordnung der Konzepte

BI und OpBI bedienen sich Funktionen, die auf Aspekte der Datensammlung, Datenaufbereitung sowie der Informationsdarstellung hinsichtlich Entscheidungsorientierung und geschäftlicher Relevanz fokussieren [22]. Daten werden aus operativen Quellsystemen in ein zentrales Data Warehouse übertragen [8] und z. B. mit OLAP oder Data Mining analysiert [9]. Die Ergebnisse fließen im Weiteren in die dispositive Entscheidungsunterstützung des strategischen und taktischen Managements ein. Konzepte wie Corporate Performance Management betrachten die dispositive und operative Ebene im Zusammenspiel [10]. Neben der integrierten Sammlung und Auswertung von operativen Daten im dispositiven Bereich ist ein Steuerungseffekt der operativen Prozesse in zumindest teilautomatisierter Form verbunden. In diesem Kontext findet sich das Konzept der OpBI wieder, welches vorrangig auf die Steuerung von Prozessabläufen auf Basis von Prozesskennziffern abzielt. Dies bringt neben Automation und Leistungsmessung von Geschäftsprozessen auch Trends zur Echtzeitanalyse mit sich [16]. Hinsichtlich des Anwendungskontextes weißt OpBI einen betriebswirtschaftlichen Fokus auf und findet wenig Beachtung im Fertigungsbereich [5].

MES übernehmen die Prozesssteuerung und damit auch Funktionen für eine Entscheidungsunterstützung im Fertigungsbereich [24]. Diese Systeme agieren zwischen unternehmensweiten ERP-Systemen sowie der fertigungsspezifischen Automatisierungsebene [14] und stellen den Soll-Vorgaben der ERP-Systeme permanent die Ist-Werte der Produktion gegenüber. Funktional müssen MES abhängig von der Komplexität des Produktionsprozesses vielseitig ausgelegt sein. Die MESA [18] schlägt dafür elf Kernfunktionen vor (siehe linker Teil der Abbildung 1).

OpBI und MES ermöglichen beide eine integrierte Bereitstellung von Daten sowie deren zielgerichtetes Berichten und Auswerten in unterschiedlichen Unternehmensbereichen. Ein MES könnte zusätzlich die Aufgaben von OpBI ausführen. Dazu müsste eine höhere Schnittstellenanzahl berücksichtigt werden. Derartige Komplexitätssteigerungen können die Systemleistungsfähigkeit einschränken [21]. Zusätzlich stellen die begrenzten Analysefähigkeiten eines MES [1] den Nutzen einer solchen Strategie infrage. OpBI dagegen fehlt es an der funktionalen Vielfältigkeit von MES, die speziell auf Produktionsumgebungen ausgerichtet sind [19].

Im Kontext ihrer Anwendungsspezifik können sich OpBI und MES nicht gegenseitig ersetzen, aber im Hinblick auf eine unternehmensweite Entscheidungsunterstützung nutzenbringend ergänzen. Dazu sind die Konzepte gemeinsam zu betrachten, da sonst Insellösungen das Resultat sind. Eine Integrationsplattform zur Kombination von Informationen aus Lieferkette, Produktion und Kundenbetreuung stellt eine Zusammenführung dieser Verinselungen dar, wobei die spezifischen Funktionalitäten innerhalb der Anwendungsgebiete erhalten bleiben. Prozessleistungskennziffern erfahren eine Anreicherung mit Informationen aus der gesamten Wertschöpfungskette. Dies ermöglicht eine übergreifende Synchronisation der Geschäftsprozesse mit flexibilitätssteigernder Wirkung. Durch die Erhöhung der Transparenz in den operativen Prozessen sind Verbesserungen im Bereich der Leistungsfähigkeit der Prozesse und im Kontext der Prozessgestaltung denkbar.

Folgen für die Integration der Informationsverarbeitung

In diesem Abschnitt werden die Folgen für die Ausprägungen der Integrierten Informationsverarbeitung (vgl. [17]) auf Grund einer gemeinsamen Betrachtung von MES und OpBI diskutiert. Die betroffenen Ausprägungen sind grau hinterlegt. Die Kennzeichnung resultiert aus der Zielstellung des Dissertationsprojektes, zu einer interdisziplinären, prozessorientierten und flexiblen Entscheidungsunterstützung beizutragen.

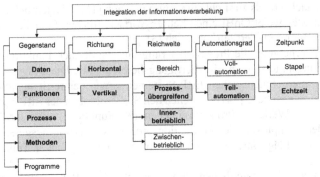

Abbildung 2: Ausprägungen der Integrierten Informationsverarbeitung entnommen und modifiziert nach [17]

Gegenstand der Integration sind Daten, Funktionen, und Methoden, um der Forderung nach einer flexiblen Entscheidungsunterstützung nachzukommen. Ein Entscheidungsunterstützungssystem verlangt das Vorhandensein einer Daten-, Methoden- und Modellbank. Der Begriff der Flexibilität erfordert die Anpassungsfähigkeit hinsichtlich sich ändernder Funktions- und Leistungsanforderungen [12]. Der interdisziplinäre Charakter kennzeichnet sich durch horizontale und vertikale Integrationsrichtung sowie durch die prozessübergreifende und innerbetriebliche Integrationsreichweite. Prozessorientierung bedeutet die Ausrichtung des Unternehmens an Geschäftsprozesse [12] mit dem Ziel, deren Leistungsfähigkeit und die Flexibilität zu Gunsten einer transparenten Prozessbeherrschung zu steigern [4]. Daher sind auch Prozesse Gegenstand der Integration. Um die Flexibilität auch im Hinblick auf eine erhöhte Anpassungsgeschwindigkeit zu verbessern, erscheint eine teilautomatisierte Integration in Echtzeit sinnhaft.

Methodik

Das methodische Raster lässt sich in drei Bereiche differenzieren. Im ersten Bereich wird der Stand der Forschung ermittelt. Dazu erarbeitet ein State-of-the-Art (siehe dazu grundlegend [7]) eine literaturbasierte Klassifikation der Begriffe MES und OpBI, um existierende Forschungsergebnisse hinsichtlich einer gemeinsamen Betrachtung der Konzepte zu ermitteln. Im zweiten Bereich erfolgt mithilfe von Fallstudien (siehe dazu grundlegend [23]) eine Anforderungsbestimmung für eine operative Integrationsplattform von OpBI und MES zu Gunsten einer Steuerung und Analyse von operativen Geschäftsprozessen. Dabei werden zu berücksichtigenden Prozesse abstrakt definiert sowie erforderliche Datenobjekte und Informationsflüsse analysiert. Auf Basis der Anforderungen erfolgt eine Ableitung von Hypothesen bezüglich eines Modells zur theoretischen Fundierung der Integrationsplattform, die auch einem Hypothesentest zuzuführen sind. Im dritten Bereich wird auf Basis der qualitativen Erkenntnisse eine Implementierung und Validierung der konzipierten Integrationsplattform angestrebt.

Erste Ergebnisse

Zum gegenwärtigen Zeitpunkt ist die Literaturrecherche abgeschlossen und publiziert [11]. Für den zweiten Schritt ist zur Planung der Fallstudien mit der Erarbeitung eines Forschungsprotokolls begonnen worden. Dieses geht auf Problemstellung und Zielsetzung, Definition und Auswahl der Fälle, die anzuwendenden Datenerhebungsmethoden sowie auf die Durchführung einer exemplarischen Studie ein [2].

Die Literaturrecherche konnte vier Publikationen identifizieren, die eine gemeinsame Betrachtung von BI und MES thematisieren. Die Beiträge berücksichtigen die multidimensionale Analyse von Produktionsdaten und die Rolle des MES im Rahmen der unternehmensweiten Entscheidungsfindung. Dies sind jedoch nur einzelne Facetten der Integration. Der Zusammenhang zwischen MES und OpBI wird lediglich in einer Publikation gestreift. Die unterschiedlichen Wurzeln der Konzepte bieten hierfür ein Erklärungspotenzial. Die Wahrnehmung von MES ist im entscheidungsorientierten Umfeld erst in letzter Zeit stärker ausgeprägt. Andererseits zeigt OpBI eine geringe Menge an Suchergebnissen, was auf eine Neuartigkeit des Begriffs schließen lässt. Eine weiterführende Auseinandersetzung mit dem Thema bietet die Möglichkeit, zur Schärfung des Begriffsverständnisses beizutragen.

Fazit und Ausblick

MES und OpBI sind nicht identisch - sie liefern aber beide Informationen im Zuge der Prozessanalyse in unterschiedlichen Arbeitsgebieten. Die Konzepte lassen eine gemeinsame Betrachtung für eine flexible operative Entscheidungsunterstützung zu, wobei der Integrationsaspekt bisher kaum wissenschaftlich betrachtet ist.

Die Ergebnisse der Literaturrecherche motivieren eine weitere Betrachtung des Themas entsprechend der vorgeschlagenen Methodik. Dabei besteht die Möglichkeit, neue Erkenntnisse bezüglich der Analyse und Steuerung von Geschäftsprozessen im Kontext des aktuellen Tagesgeschehens zu sammeln. Die Integration von OpBI und MES zu einer operativen Informationsplattform unterstützt die Fähigkeit, schnell und flexibel auf Geschäftsereignisse zu reagieren und die unternehmensindividuelle Wettbewerbsfähigkeit zu steigern.

Literaturverzeichnis

1. Alpar, P. und Louis, J.P. (2007). Eine empirische Untersuchung der Softwareunterstützung bei der Fertigung und Qualitätssteuerung - Implikationen für Manufacturing Execution Systeme. *Philipps-Universität Marburg*. Marburg.

2. Borchardt, A. und Göthlich, S. (2009). Erkenntnisgewinn durch Fallstudien. In Albers, S. et al. (Hrsg.), Methodik der empirischen Forschung(S. 33 – 48). Wiesbaden: Gabler.
3. Cunningham, D. (2005). Aligning Business Intelligence with Business Processes. *What Works (TDWI)*. 20, S. 50-51.
4. Derszteler, G. (2000). Prozeßmanagement auf Basis von Workflow-Systemen: Ein integrierter Ansatz zur Modellierung, Steuerung und Überwachung von Geschäftsprozessen. Lohmar: EUL.
5. Eckerson, W.W. (2007). Best Practices in Operational BI: Converging Analytical and Operational Processes. *TDWI Best Practices Report*. Renton: WA.
6. Erl, T. (2005). Service-Oriented Architecture: Concepts, Technology, and Design. Upper Saddle River: Prentice Hall.
7. Fettke, P. (2006). State-of-the-Art des State-of-the-Art – Eine Untersuchung der Forschungsmethode 'Review' innerhalb der Wirtschaftsinformatik. *Wirtschaftsinformatik*. 4, S. 257-266.
8. Gangadharan, G. R. und Swamy, N. S. (2004). Business intelligence systems: design and implementation strategies. *Proceedings of 26th International Conference on Information Technology Interfaces*. Cavtat. Croatia.
9. Gluchowski, P., Gabriel, R. und Dittmar, C. (2008). Management Support Systeme und Business Intelligence: Computergestützte Informationssysteme für Führungskräfte und Entscheidungsträger. Heidelberg: Springer.
10. Golfarelli, M., Rizzi, S. und Cella, I. (2004). Beyond data warehousing: what's next in business intelligence? *Proceedings of 7th ACM international workshop on Data warehousing and OLAP*. New York: ACM Press. S. 1-6.
11. Hänel, T. und Felden, C. (2011). Limits or Integration? – Manufacturing Execution Systems and Operational Business Intelligence. *AMCIS 2011 Proceedings*.
12. Heinrich, L.J., Roithmayer, F. und Heinzl, A. (2004). Wirtschaftsinformatik-Lexikon. 7. überarbeitete Auflage. München: Oldenbourg.
13. Imhoff, C. (2001). Active Data Warehousing the Ultimate Fulfillment of the Operational Data Store. *Intelligent Solutions, Inc.* Boulder.
14. ISA ANSI/ISA-95.00.01-2000 (2000). Enterprise Control System Integration, Part 1: Models and Terminology. *ISA technical paper*.
15. Marjanovic, O. (2007). The Next Stage of Operational Business Intelligence: Creating New Challenges for Business Process Management. *Proceedings of the 40th Annual Hawaii International Conference on System Sciences*. Washington DC: IEEE Computer Society.
16. Melchert, F., Winter, R. und Klesse, M. (August 2004). Aligning Process Automation and Business Intelligence to Support Corporate Performance Management. *Proceedings of the Tenth Americas Conference on Information Systems*. New York.
17. Mertens, P. (2009). Integrierte Informationsverarbeitung 1: Operative Systeme in der Industrie.17. überarbeitete Ausgabe. Wiesbaden: Springer.
18. MESA. (1997). MES Functionalities and MRP to MES Data Flow Possibilities. *MESA International – White Paper Number 2*. Pittsburgh.
19. Meyer, H., Fuchs, F. und Thiel K. (2009). Manufacturing Execution Systems (MES): Optimal Design, Planning, and Deployment. Columbus (OH): McGraw Hill.
20. Rodriguez, R. A. (2007). Aligning IT to Business Processes: How BPM is Complementing ERP and Custom Applications. *Aberdeen Group*.
21. Saenz de Ugarte, B., Artiba, A., und Pellerin, R. (2009).Manufacturing execution system – a literature review. *Production Planning and Control*. 20, 6, S. 525-539.
22. Schrödl, H. (2006). Business Intelligence. München, Wien: Hanser.
23. Yin, R. K. (2009). Case Study Research: Design and Methods. Los Angeles: SAGE.
24. Younus, M., Peiyong, C., Hu, L. und Yuqing, F. (2010). MES Development and Significant Applications in Manufacturing – A Review. *2nd International Conference on Education Technology and Computer (ICETC)*.

4.3.2.7 Kurzdarstellung Beitrag 10

Beitrag 10 diskutiert als Positionsbeitrag eine serviceorientierte Architektur zur technischen Bereitstellung von MES- und OpBI-Funktionen. Diese Diskussion spezifiziert die in Beitrag 9 skizzierte Integrationsplattform und greift deren Gestaltung mithilfe von Web Services auf (vgl. Beitrag 4). Das Ergebnis von Beitrag 10 bildet eine Konzeption, die aus fünf Komponenten besteht. Eine Datenquellenkomponente dient als Grundlage für leistungsbezogene Analysen und eine produktionsspezifische Entscheidungsunterstützung. Daneben stellt eine Prozesskomponente einen Bezug zu den Ereignissen der Fertigungsprozesse her, deren Leistung kontinuierlich gemessen wird. Eine Integrationskomponente koordiniert die Web Services und die Ereignisse im Gesamtsystem. Das zentrale Element der Plattform ist die Servicekomponente. Sie fasst alle notwendigen MES- und OpBI-Funktionalitäten zusammen. Darauf aufbauend ermöglicht die Präsentationskomponente eine flexible Darstellung der Analyseergebnisse für Entscheidungsträger.

4.3.2.8 Beitrag 10: Web Based Integration of MES and Operational BI[10]

Introduction

The design and control of business processes based on coherent information is a determining competitive factor. Internet and web-based technologies influence the business processes of an organization as well as its relationships to customers and suppliers. These increasing informal networks accelerate changing basic conditions. Companies are forced to embrace emerging web technologies in order to keep their business processes flexible by corresponding adjustments. However, research indicates that organizations are not able to meet flexibility demands. According to a survey of the Aberdeen Group, 85 percent of companies do not provide an adequate flexibility within their applications [20]. This lack of flexibility implies high cost due to delayed decisions and low productivity associated with negative effects in terms of customer satisfaction and service orientation. With respect to the given issue, the position paper discusses whether a web service (WS) based integration approach is beneficial for a conjoint process-oriented and flexible decision support oriented infrastructure.

The range of conformable concepts allowing efficient support is large and manifold. Recently, MES and OpBI came into the discussion promising both support of process flexibility. These concepts are integrative approaches for operational process control and analysis, but they come from different perspectives – the engineering and the decision support point of view. A combined approach of

---

10 Hänel, T.; Pospiech, M.; Felden, C.: Web Based Integration of MES and Operational BI. In: 8th Web Information Systems and Technologies, Porto, April 2012.

MES and OpBI facilitates overarching analyses to comprehensively coordinate and optimize processes so that organizations are able to react fast and flexible on business occurrences [13]. Considering the state-of-the-art, the integration potential of WS to combine MES and OpBI is not investigated, although especially service-oriented architectures (SOA) are beneficial to support flexibility [9]. Therefore, we contribute to the research of WS and decision support by proposing a discussion about opportunities and potentials of a web-based integration regarding engineering and economic driven systems.

Chapter 2 sheds light on the integration potential of OpBI and MES. Furthermore, the ability of WS and SOA in context of a flexible operational decision making is discussed. Chapter 3 joins the separately considered aspects and presents an architecture scheme for a web based integration of MES and OpBI. Finally, the paper is summarized to give conclusions and further research perspectives.

Status quo

The scope of OpBI and MES is the analysis of processes to recognize weak points, malfunctions or business interruptions in order to improve the management of business processes continuously and to generate overarching process information. This chapter explains the concepts of OpBI and MES as well as its potential of complementation. Thereafter, WS are put in context to the demonstrated decision support to support flexible architecture requirements.

OpBI and MES

OpBI is aiming for an integrated ensemble of analytical activities and operational processes [8]. The main focus is on reducing times to collect, report, and analyze data as well as to take appropriate decisions [27]. Information regarding process states during progress is provided [3]. Due to this reason, OpBI analyzes, controls, and improves organizational core processes in a fast and flexible manner [4]. Thereby, a Corporate Performance Management is facilitated [22] considering the organization as closed-loop system, in which strategic-tactical and operational management is interrelated [11]. Figure 1 comprises the functionality of OpBI.

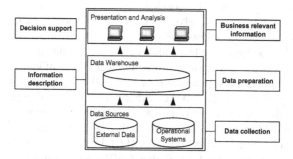

Figure 1. Functions of OpBI.

OpBI provides analytical capabilities in order to control the organizational value creation in favor of a continuous improvement of process design and execution. Thereby, it is a moderator between the analytical intention and the actual occurrence of a process. A timely adequate relation between process performance and states of target achievement get communicated to the corresponding audience.

A comparable approach to support the decision making on the shop floor is the MES [28]. It is placed between the layer of Enterprise Resource Planning (ERP) and the layer of process execution [14]. A vertical integration by enabling task-oriented compaction, communication and access of data is realized [19]. The ERP system responsible for order and resource planning communicates desired quantities to the MES executing a permanently target-performance comparison and a feedback to ERP. This is to be done over the full production cycle using real-time data [17]. The MES-architecture consists of application layer, functional layer, and data interface layer [10]. The data interface layer enables the access of MES database on machines and plants to gather relevant data. The application layer presents the information generated out of a MES database on several clients. Users are able to send requests and to get desired results. Therefore, MES are covering eight functions [23]:

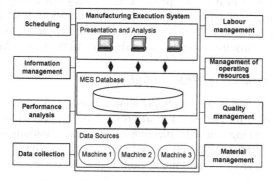

Figure 2. Functions and architecture of MES.

The functions of OpBI and MES consider an integrated provision of data as well as its purposive reporting and analysis. If the MES gets more complex by including a high number of operational processes, the similarity to OpBI will grow. This is associated with a performance lost and limitation of decision making in real-time, because an increasing complexity requires a higher degree of interfaces [21]. Furthermore, the limited analysis capabilities of the MES [2] question the benefits of such a strategy. OpBI forces also the decision making in real-time, has comprehensive analysis capabilities and facilitates company-wide process control. But, this concept is seldom applied in manufacturing [8]. A possible reason is that the MES covers more functions than operational BI, because it is especially designed for production environments [18]. Hence, OpBI cannot compensate a MES and vice versa, but they have beneficial intersections to support an enterprise-wide decision making. Table 1 demonstrates this functional complementation potential.

Table 1. Overlapping and complementation possibilities for MES and OpBI.

OpBI functions / MES functions	Decision Support	Business relevant information	Data preparation	Data collection	Information description
Scheduling	M	M			
Quality management	M	M			
Labour Management	M	M			
Materials management	M	M			
Management of operating resources	M	M			
Data collection				O	
Performance analysis			O		O
Information management			O		O

An integration approach is required to provide a basis for a conjoint process-oriented and flexible decision support oriented infrastructure using MES in combination with OpBI. Therefore, the presented monolithic driven and data warehouse oriented architecture of the concepts are contradictory. Flexibility and reduction of complexity is possible by modularization, which means to structure a system in semi-autonomous and straightforward subsystems [1]. To support such a modular design Section 2.2 discusses WS to gain a flexible information architecture.

Web Services in context of MES and OpBI

The technology of WS is commonly implemented in a SOA, representing the current state-of-the-art for flexible IT structures [9]. A SOA can be understood as „ … a way of designing and implementing enterprise applications that deals with the intercommunication of loosely coupled, coarse grained (business level), reusable artifacts (services). Determining how to invoke these services should be through a platform independent service interface ..." [25]. It is possible to combine (orchestration) the existing components depending on flexibility requirements in consequence of loosely coupled services. Thus, business functionalities are to be abstracted and assembled according to the process logic. This leads to new processes, which can be easily redefined or created. Especially, vendor independent specifications enable a consistent integration of heterogeneous systems and an open communication between various components. A SOA is understood as an abstract concept, supportable by WS [9]. According to the W3C, a WS is defined as follows:

> A Web service is a software system designed to support interoperable machine-to-machine interaction over a network. It has an interface described in a machine-processable format (specifically WSDL). Other systems interact with the WS in a manner prescribed by its description using SOAP messages, typically conveyed using HTTP with an XML serialization in conjunction with other Web-related standards. [26]

Nowadays, SOAP and WS Description Language (WSDL) specifications are state-of-the-art based on Extensible Markup Language (XML) [16]. WSDL describes the WS interface and specifies service functionalities, restrictions and conventions. Furthermore, it refers to an endpoint that corresponds to a software component. Those descriptions can be stored in a Universal, Description, Discovery and Integration (UDDI) repository. The UDDI is based on XML and serves as directory service that is responsible for WS publication and detection. SOAP allows as message exchange format the discovery, searching, finding and usage of WS. Thereby, the transport occurs by an underlying protocol like HTTP or FTP. In this context, a WS gets described by a WSDL document and published in a UDDI. A potential service consumer will search through SOAP in the UDDI and retrieves the matching WSDL. Afterwards, the service consumer will start the communication to the service provider by the SOAP protocol.

The main concept of a SOA is the encapsulation of business functionalities. In this context, OpBI and MES functionalities have to be encapsulated into WS, so that they act either as service user or service provider. Performance analysis services provide analytical business logic and correspond to mature BI techniques [15]. The data collection services provide the required operational, tactical and strategic data. They are divided into data access, transformation and infrastructure services, corresponding mainly to encapsulate extract, transform and load (ETL) functionalities [6]. The data access service includes four basic operations, namely create, read, update and delete. They allow universal access to all connected systems and all systems to request demanded analyses [24]. Source and target exist likewise as service or database e.g. the DWH. If persistently storing is not required, the data get promptly accessed by a service from any operational system on demand and will be used for further analysis [7]. Transformation services represent the encapsulated transformation phase of ETL. Thus, tasks like aggregation, encoding, filtering, conversion, join and mapping have to be fulfilled by services. [5, 15] There are existing cross-cutting tasks in addition to the presented services that are realized through infrastructure services [6] including data security and data protection features as well as aspects of data quality, master data, and meta-data management [12]. Furthermore, the data collection services provide all MES relevant data regarding materials, operators, machines and processes in real-time through specific decision support services. On this basis, the labour management service ensures that every shift is properly organized and recorded. The material management handles the need-driven supply and disposal with material on schedule, as well as the management of work in process. Here, quality information, schedule and material data are considered. In this context, the quality management services sustain the guarantee of product quality and the capability of the process, by quality planning and inspection. The service for management of operating resources provides a demand-actuated availability on schedule and functionality of equipment (machines, operating utilities) in a historical, current and further view. The scheduling service plans operational sequences in manufacturing under consideration of available resources and capacities. [23]

Web based Integration Platform

The platform is divided into five components (cf. Figure 3), which gets successively refined. The data storage component holds data sources and serves as fundament for further analyses. Here, process changes get noticed by the event engine and will be instantly inserted by orchestrated data collection services placing target data into the data source. In addition, performance analysis and decision support services accessing available data through the same services. The enterprise-wide consolidation of information exceeds in most cases IT budget and manageable complexity [16]. Therefore, it appears adversely to follow the traditional BI architecture concept, since a data warehouse (DWH) exists no longer in a monolithic pillar, but rather in an embedded IT infrastructure [15]. Thus, the DWH lose its role as central data storage component [7]. The historical data stored by the DWH are combined and synchronized with real-time information from operational processes. This provides an input flow for decision support and performance analysis services. There is the danger that redundant and distributed storage lead to individual application terminologies ending in inconsistencies and duplication. Due to this reason, a central meta-data repository is required.

The service platform component reflects all encapsulated and presented functionalities of OpBI and MES. In this context, both have to be implemented in a WS-oriented way. Here, OpBI and MES take the role as service provider or service consumer. This integrates analytical functions into processes and operational applications affecting the operational detailed planning. All services are event-driven and transfer real-time data. Thereby, WS are endpoints, which react to or produce new events. [24] In this context, a WS-oriented platform promises the integration of OpBI services into MES processes and systems, avoids redundant implementations, enables an unproblematic integration, improves scalability, and allows an open communication between all components.

The integration component realizes coordination of all services and events in the total system. The service repository (UDDI) manages and publishes all service descriptions, which are presented in form of WSDL. Furthermore, the service repository selects WS in cooperation with the orchestration engine. The selection is based on the service description, which makes the service available for the orchestration engine. The orchestration executes a service sequence that can be embedded in other systems or processes. In addition, the orchestration engine contains mechanisms that allow status management, logging and monitoring of sequences. The orchestration engine is requested by events that are triggered from the event engine. Here, the event engine is based on publish-and-subscribe. It receives and processes events from all components, which are sent to registered users. Furthermore, the event engine holds analytical operations. The analysis is enriched by business process events [24]. Therefore, defined business rules are required, which are provided by the corresponding repository. This prevents a redundant implementation of business rules, increases their reusability and separates process logic from decision logic.

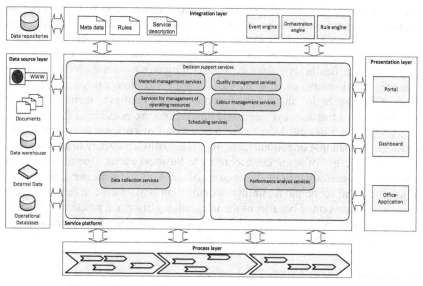

Figure 3. Web-based integration architecture for OpBI and MES

The core of process component is the process itself. Here, the event engine analyzes continuously business process events in real-time. Required process states are received by data collection services and passed through WS for decision support and performance analysis. Hereby, a timely adjustment of the manufacturing process in consequence of unpredictable circumstances can be established. Complex events or causal, temporal or spatial relationships are detected by the event engine and lead to defined reactions in process execution. Thus, decisions can be automated and done in shortest time. Consequently, the approach enables monitoring of critical process key figures in MES or OpBI analyses and hereupon tailored events. A so called closed-loop can be established that provides reduced decision latency.

The top level is represented by a presentation component. This enables a flexible integration of different visualization options. The fundament is performance analysis and decision support services, which allow graphical representations in portals, dashboards, or office applications. [24] The user can be informed about circumstances by events or send its decision directly to the event engine.

Conclusions

The position paper discusses an integration platform to consolidate economic and engineering driven information across the whole value creation. The proposed architecture joins concepts of MES and OpBI, while their domain specific functions are conserved. Thereby, during the paper's discussion, the advantages of WS are evident in favour of a flexible process-oriented decision support. Process performance indices are enriched by information from all segments of value chain as part of technical-economic analyses. This reduces the effort of information gathering and provides the ability for a comprehensive synchronization of business processes with flexibility-enhancing effects. Organizations are able to consider changing requirements of customers and suppliers contemporary to adjust their production, distribution and purchase processes. This implies an increased process transparency so that improvements and innovations are possible in fields of process and product design. Next to the introduction of completely new products, there are for example opportunities to improve quality characteristics of products or to tailor the use of resources according to business needs. Due to knowledge about process performance in all segments of value creation, the necessity as well as technical and economic feasibility of innovation is assessable in detail. In order to realize the presented benefits of the integration platform, a practical validation of the arguments is required. Thereby, the discussed insights of this position paper serve as guidance and basis for further research.

References

1. Aier, S., Dogan, T., 2005. Indikatoren zur Bewertung der Nachhaltigkeit von Unternehmensarchitekturen. *In Wirtschaftsinformatik 2005*, 607-626.
2. Alpar, P., Louis, J.P., 2007. *Eine empirische Untersuchung der Softwareunterstützung bei der Fertigung und Qualitätssteuerung*. Philipps-Universität Marburg.
3. Bauer, A., Schmid, T., 2009. Was macht Operational BI aus? *BI-Spektrum*, 4 (1), 13-14.
4. Cunningham, D., 2005. Aligning Business Intelligence with Business Processes. *TDWI*, 20, 50-51.

5. Dinter, B., 2008. Einsatzmöglichkeiten serviceorientierter Architekturen in der Informationslogistik. In *Töpfer, J. and Winter, R. (Eds.), Active Enterprise Intelligence, 1st Edition.* Springer, Berlin.
6. Dinter, B., Stroh, F. 2009. Design Factors for Service-oriented Architecture Applied to Analytical Information Systems: an Explorative Analysis. In *Proceedings of the 17th European Conference on Information Systems ECIS, Verona.*
7. Dittmar, C., 2007. Latenzzeiten von Business Intelligence-Systemen. In *Gluchowski, P. et al. (Eds.), Schlaglichter der Wirtschaftsinformatik, 1st Edition. GUC,Chemnitz, 131-142.*
8. Eckerson, W.W., 2007. Best Practices in Operational BI: Converging Analytical and Operational Processes. *TDWI Best Practices Report.* Renton (WA).
9. Erl, T., 2009. *SOA Design Patterns,* 1st Edition, Prentice Hall, Boston.
10. Fei, L., 2010. Manufacturing Execution System Design and Implementation, 2nd *International Conference on Education Technology and Computer (ICETC).*
11. Golfarelli, M., Rizzi, S., Cella, I., 2004. Beyond data warehousing: what's next in business intelligence? In *Proceedings of 7th ACM international workshop on Data warehousing and OLAP, ACM Press, New York.*
12. Gordon, S. et al., (2006). Service-Oriented Business Intelligence. In *The Architecture Journal.* 6,23-32.
13. Hänel, T., Felden, C., 2011. Limits or Integration? - Manufacturing Execution Systems and Operational Business Intelligence. In *Americas Conference on Information Systems AMCIS 2011, Detroit, USA.*
14. ISA ANSI/ISA-95.00.01-2000, 2000. Enterprise Control System Integration, Part 1: Models and Terminology, ISA technical paper.
15. Martin, W., 2011. Performance Management and Analytics – Business Intelligence meets Business Process Management, *Retrieved 2011-11-21, from: http://www.wolfgang-martin-team.net/BI-BPM-SOA.php.*
16. Melzer, I., 2010. *Service-orientierte Architekturen mit Web Services,* 4th Edition, Spektrum Verlag, Heidelberg.
17. MESA, 1997. *MES Explained: A High Level Vision for Executives,* MESA International – White Paper Number 6, Pittsburgh.
18. Meyer, H., Fuchs, F., Thiel K., 2009. *Manufacturing Execution Systems (MES),* McGraw Hill, Colum.
19. Kletti, J., 2007. *Manufacturing Execution System – MES,* Springer, Berlin.
20. Rodriguez, R. A., 2007. *Aligning IT to Business Processes: How BPM is Complementing ERP and Custom Applications.* Aberdeen Group.
21. Saenz de Ugarte, B., Artiba, A., Pellerin, R., 2009. Manufacturing execution system – a literature review. *Production Planning and Control,* 20, 6, 525-539.
22. Schwingel, J. (2010). Strategien für Process Performance Management. *BI-Spektrum* 4 (3), 14-18.
23. VDI 5600, 2007. *Manufacturing Execution Systems,* VDI Verlag, Duesseldorf, Germany.
24. Vogt, T. et al., 2008. Business-Intelligence-Konzept auf Basis einer Event-Driven Service-Oriented Architecture. In *Dinter, B. et al. (Eds.), Synergien durch Integration und Informationslogistik Proceedings DW 2008.*
25. Wilkes, S., Harby, J., 2004. A move to drive industry standardization of SOA. *Retrieved 2012-01-21, from: http://xml.coverpages.org/SOA-BlueprintsConceptsV05.pdf.*
26. W3C (2004), W3C Web Services Glossary. *Retrieved 2012-01-27, from: http://www.w3.org/TR/2004/NOTE-ws-gloss-20040211.*
27. White, C., 2006. The Next Generation of Business Intelligence: Operational BI. (White Paper). *Retrieved 2012-01-21, from: http://certification. sybase.com.*
28. Younus, M. et al., 2010. MES Development and Significant Applications in Manufacturing – A Review, 2nd *International Conference on Education Technology and Computer (ICETC).*

4.3.2.9 Kurzdarstellung Beitrag 11

Die Ergebnisse der Beiträge 7 bis 10 adressieren IT-spezifische Aspekte hinsichtlich der Anwendbarkeit von OpBI im Produktionsumfeld unabhängig von einem bestimmten Anwendungsfall. Um darauf aufbauend fallspezifische Aussagen ableiten zu können, untersuchen Beitrag 11 und Beitrag 12 die Unterstützung von produktionsspezifischen Entscheidungen durch OpBI unter Realweltbedingungen.

Beitrag 11 diskutiert als Research in Progress die Vorteilhaftigkeit eines Zusammenwirkens von MES und OpBI für eine dynamische Entscheidungsunterstützung am Beispiel eines Instandsetzungsunternehmens für IT und Kommunikationsgeräte. Angesichts dynamischer Wettbewerbsbedingungen und sich ständig ändernder Kundenanforderungen zeichnet sich die Notwendigkeit von umfassenden Analysefunktionen für eine flexible Steuerung von Prozessabläufen im Produktionsumfeld ab. MES und OpBI können in diesem Zusammenhang als integrierter Ansatz die Erreichung von Flexibilitätsanforderungen unterstützen, um die Leistungsfähigkeit von Produktionsprozessen aufrecht zu erhalten. Es zeigt sich, dass Flexibilität im Produktionsumfeld ein mehrdimensionales Phänomen darstellt. Hinsichtlich der Betrachtung einer Fertigungsflexibilität aus verschiedenen Perspektiven kann OpBI dabei eine Unterstützungsleistung erbringen, deren Untersuchung im Ausblick von Beitrag 11 als zukünftiger Forschungsbedarf identifiziert wird.

4.3.2.10 Beitrag 11: Facing the Change – Towards a Dynamic Decision Making in Manufacturing Environments[11]

Introduction

Manufacturing is essential for value creation especially in industrial organizations. Globalization and increased informal networks have created highly dynamic competitive environments in this area. As a consequence, organizations focus on customer orientation forcing them to align and adjust their product and process design accordingly. Hence, a manufacturing has to consider varying demands, which are consistently changing. In order to address such uncertainties, dynamic planning and decision making processes are essential for a successful organizational existence [19]. However, an adequate manufacturing flexibility is not achieved [18], while the management of such volatilities challenges growth and sustainability of organizations [16]. Therefore, the paper investigates the phenomenon of manufacturing flexibility in changing competitive environments aiming to detect a strategy for a conjoint process-oriented and dynamic decision support.

---

11 Hänel, T.; Felden, C.: Facing the Change - Towards a Dynamic Decision Making in Manufacturing Environments. In: 4th Conference on Knowledge Management and Information Sharing, Barcelona, Oktober 2012.

The range of conformable concepts allowing a dynamic decision support is manifold. Currently, MES and OpBI are discussed, because they promise improvements of process flexibility. Both are integration approaches dealing with analysis and control of operations, but they address either an engineering or a decision-oriented point of view. A combined consideration of MES and OpBI is advantageous, because cross-linked analyses are possible to coordinate and improve business processes [15]. Organizations are able to recognize weaknesses, failures, and business interruptions in order to respond in a flexible manner. However, a literature review reveals that a dynamic decision making capability of the concepts named above is limited, yet. Especially the complementary integration potential of MES and OpBI is not tapped to support the flexibility demands of industrial organizations [9]. The refinement of complementarities and its affirmation in an organizational context give implications how far a combined consideration of MES and OpBI is necessary and beneficial for an industrial organization to compete in challenging environments. Therefore, the paper contributes to an initial discussion in providing empirical insights on reasons and support strategies for a dynamic decision making based on a comprehensive process analysis in favour of manufacturing flexibility.

Section 2 discusses beneficial effects of MES and OpBI for a dynamic decision making to achieve a comprehensive manufacturing flexibility. A methodological structure to affirm the illustrated support potential is explained in Section 3 and results of its application are presented in Section 4. Finally, the paper is summarized giving conclusions and further research perspectives.

Status quo

Manufacturing flexibility has been intensively discussed in the 1980s and 1990s [3]. Incorporating a strong influence on organizational competiveness [10], it deals with uncertainties in multiple dimensions [4] and refers to the ability of change without lost in performance, time, cost, or effort [23]. Manufacturing flexibility improves firm performance in dynamic markets depending on strategy, environmental factors, organizational attributes, and existing technology [24].

Despite of numerous findings, a renewed discussion is identifiable. According to Aberdeen Group in 2007, 85 percent of surveyed companies do not provide an adequate flexibility and especially manufacturing applications are not designed to handle rapid business changes [19]. The lack of flexibility implies high cost due to delayed decisions and low productivity associated with negative effects in terms of customer satisfaction and service orientation. Recent surveys confirm this relevance of aligning flexibility to manufacturing operations to face steady changing customer demands [2]. The ability of managing volatilities is discussed to grow and sustain in dynamic market environments [16]. Manufacturers are faced by an increased complexity, so that they need innovation capabilities to achieve a constant manufacturing performance [17]. Therefore, flexible planning and decision processes are essential to assure existence of an organization in competitive environments. This is challenged by the multi-dimensional character of manufacturing flexibility [19].

MES contribute to success of manufacturing flexibility [20] improving a decision making based on measurement of production key figures [27]. Placed between the layer of Enterprise Resource Planning (ERP) and process execution, a vertical integration of shop floor information is realized [14]. The MES allows a decision making by detailed scheduling, dispatching, resource management, definition management, execution management, tracking, data collection, and analysis in the subareas of production, quality, maintenance as well as inventory operations management [11]. However, current MES solutions are limited in offering an integrated production support covering all of these subareas. Manufacturing gets more complex due to an increased customer orientation triggering a multiplication of product characteristics [19]. The existing informal networks in manufacturing environments consider a heterogeneous software application landscape. This forces MES to process and analyze a higher amount of information. [21] The limited analysis capabilities of MES are challenging in this context [1].

OpBI provides those analytical capabilities to control organizational value creation in favour of a continuous improvement of process design and execution [6]. The focus is on reducing times to collect, report, and analyze data as well as to take appropriate decisions [25]. OpBI is understandable as an integrated business process-oriented system approach, supporting time critical decisions during process execution based on process-related and historical data using mature traditional BI functions [8]. These functions are classifiable to decision support, business-relevant information, information description, data preparation and data collection [22]. OpBI and MES have beneficial intersections supporting dynamic decisions in manufacturing (cf. Table 1).

Table 1. Complementation of MES and OpBI.

MES functions/ OpBI functions	Decision support	Business-relevant information	Information description	Data preparation	Data collection
Detailed scheduling	MES	MES			
Dispatching	MES	MES			
Resource management	MES	MES			
Definition management	MES	MES			
Execution management	MES	MES			
Tracking			OpBI		
Analysis				OpBI	
Data collection					OpBI

The MES provides the background for decision support and business-relevant information, while OpBI is able to fulfil tracking, analysis, and data collection. During a process, input is transformed to specified output according to quality and quantity measures [12]. This transformation is influenced by uncertainties due to changing basic conditions e.g. demand volatilities or varying customer and supplier relationships. To cope with these indeterminations a closed loop approach is able adjust targets of a corresponding value creation (cf. Figure 1). The following hypotheses summarize the interrelation of MES and OpBI:

- H1: Organizations have a comprehensive flexibility demand in manufacturing due to consistently changing basic conditions.
- H2: Organizations need comprehensive analysis functions and dynamic decision making capabilities to fulfill the complex manufacturing flexibility requirements.
- H3: MES provide dynamic decision making capabilities to achieve manufacturing flexibility.
- H4: OpBI is able to strengthen a MES in context of comprehensive analysis functions.

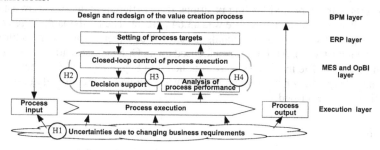

Figure 1. MES and OpBI in context of a process-oriented decision support architecture influenced by uncertainties

Methodology

The methodology follows a phase-oriented approach (cf. Figure 2). The first phase classifies the problem of manufacturing flexibility and the contribution of MES and OpBI. The results are further investigated by a case study [26]. Subsequently, expert interviews [13] enrich the discussion clarifying an OpBI potential in production environments. Actions to improve the quality are facilitated by a critical reflection.

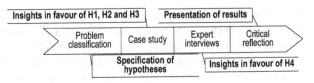

Figure 2. Research phases

Case study design

The case study organization is an IT and communication products distributor. Process-related roles, components and decision relevant information could be acquired in workshops with responsible persons of manufacturing department and supplemented by observations of processes. This leads to a consolidation of information flows illustrating the demand for a manufacturing flexibility. Finally, the benefits of a MES to support a flexible process-oriented decision making were discussed.

Expert interview design

22 experts with IT-related leading positions from different industries were asked for participation. The response rate was 63.64 percent. The participants were consultants (8) and software professionals (3) as well as experts from manufacturing and trade industry (3). All interviews focused on an OpBI classification and application potential. The interviews were conducted in September and October 2011. They lasted typically on hour. Each interview was guided by predefined questions, recorded and transcribed.

Results

The subsequent description focuses on a critical reflection of the case study and the expert interviews.

Exploration of a need for flexibility

The following discusses flexibility requirements at the manufacturing department of the case study organization. The company refines IT and communication products by implementation of software updates, prefabrication of returns and packaging of finished goods. Suppliers are manufacturers and service provider, while a subsidiary performs maintenance and repair of returns. The products are predominantly distributed to specialized trade, wholesale and online retailers. The structure of the value creation is demonstrated in Figure 3.

There are four core processes. The customizing is characterized by assembly and remodelling of mobiles, e.g. a change of keyboards, covers or software updates. The new configuration depends on customer requirements differing in individual orders. A refreshing pursues quality assured maintenance and repair of products. Devices are sent by customers and refreshed for the purpose of resale. This includes a completeness check of receipts and if necessary an ordering of missing devices. Thereafter, a reset to factory settings, a functional check and a corrective maintenance of defect devices by the subsidiary is executed.

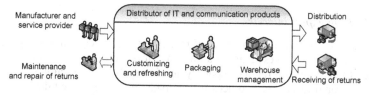

Figure 3: Value creation structure of the case study

Multiple key accounts are served, while the process scope differs. There are customers passing through the whole process, while others just order reset and test activities. After conditioning, products are finished for shipping. A blistering and a foliation of item boxes are executed for different product sizes. Blisters allow the buyer to see the items consisting usually of a device and its accessories. They are packaged in boxes getting foiled and stacked on pallets. The packaging has to consider multiple peculiarities. Order specific barcode labels and security chips are generated for the items and pallets. Campaign stickers and additional information have to be attached. Intermittent, product bundles must be equipped with extra packaging bands. A warehouse management system is responsible for material storage, shipment and assumption of returns.

The processes are characterized by complex requirements regarding planning, coordination and analysis. This is reinforced by the current order situation. On average, 20,000 products are processed during a week. However, there are enormous seasonal fluctuations. In boom phases like Christmas trade, weekly quantities are reduplicated. The throughput is marginal in silly seasons. It is important to adjust the staff according to the order situation. Due to a perennial growing of quantities within boom phases, readiness of delivery has to be increased next to a reduction of throughput time. This is associated with dynamic routing and resource utilization by maintaining a consistent quality. An intensive tracking of process states and demand situations is necessary to achieve time and cost efficiency. Given to dynamic market environment and complex process parameters of organizational value creation, a comprehensive need for manufacturing flexibility is evident, especially in terms of output volumes and highly customized products. The case study participants affirmed a need for dynamic decision making in the final consultation. They mentioned that IT systems should consider order fluctuations especially by a flexible staff planning. Provided that a consistently quality level has to be met, the suitability of a MES was analyzed to support flexibility demands. The analysis reveals a MES's ability to beneficially complement the existing IT systems in terms of scheduling and dispatching. Furthermore, overarching analysis and reporting capabilities were notably emphasized. The discussion casted doubts, that a MES is able to forecast customer behaviour or to predict current market developments. These are popular application fields of OpBI [5]. Hence, the next section investigates its potential to support the MES analysis capabilities.

Results from expert interviews

The analysis of interview transcriptions reveals main characteristics of OpBI. The concept integrates process data on an instance level to determine primarily non-financial key figures in regular report cycles during process execution. A control effect of organizational core processes is pursued by a short-dated time reference of decisions. This is similar to the MES definition and focuses on an event-oriented analysis. The identified drivers for OpBI support this aspect (cf. Table 2).

Table 2. Drivers of OpBI

Enhancement of process analysis solutions	Improvement of process performance
• Comprehensive process analyses • High transparency requirements • Support of core processes • Broader range of users • Handling of increasing data volumes • Fast provision of current information • Tapping the integration potential through cross-linked structures	• Flexible process control • Adaptiveness to changing basic conditions • Achieving higher process and product quality • Acceleration of production times and process cycles • Increasing of output rates • Realizing cost savings • Obtaining of new insights regarding interrelations between process structures and performance

Current application fields named by the participants are customer relations or marketing. Certain examples with respect to the analysis of customer behaviour were provided. Offers can be displayed and adjusted according their impact on customer behaviour to manage marketing campaigns. A further example is a flexible staffing in case of new product placing. Often, there is a high usage of customer services, and in terms of capacity overload, staff can be expanded.

Furthermore, the participants were asked for use of OpBI in manufacturing. The quintessence across the interviews is that the short-dated time reference of decision making in context of OpBI leads to a big potential. Examples are the processing of production data using dashboards. This allows a monitoring and reporting of process performance in terms of operational control. Manufacturers are able to identify quality deviations, weaknesses or machine failures to facilitate time savings and to accelerate production. Particularly industries with manufacturing bands, such as automotive or packaging industry were called as appropriate areas. Further applications like staffs work time logging, maintenance and surveillance of production equipment, inventory management for raw materials and supplies, or product lifecycle management came in mind of the interview participants. The potential to use gathered information for improvement of logistics processes was also mentioned, e.g. timing of loading cycles to reach optimal transport capacity utilization.

Discussion of results

The case study reveals that customer-oriented value creation leads to planning and decision making uncertainties in manufacturing. Flexibility is required to react accordingly, while the management of tremendously changing order quantities is important. However, it has to be noted that the focus on respective flexibility depends on the specific value creation. This differs according to specialist fields of industrial organizations.

Nevertheless, a universal valid need for comprehensive analysis functions and dynamic decision making capabilities in manufacturing is evident. Since flexibility is defined as ability to change by a constant performance level [23], counteracting adjustments necessitate an awareness of current situations to execute adequate control mechanisms. The case study confirms that actuating interventions are supportable by a MES to support a dynamic decision making. The functional design will vary depending on requirements of the respective value creation. Such an asking for a case dependent alignment is also true for analysis capabilities, which are required for a closed-loop process control. Therefore, the expert interviews affirm a support potential of OpBI enabling comprehensive descriptions of information, data preparation and collection in manufacturing.

Summing up, MES and OpBI are jointly able to support a manufacturing flexibility. However, they have to be aligned to value creation in order to achieve a closed-loop control approach. Considering that a lack and an excessive flexibility are discussed as reducing effect of process performance [7], a case specific awareness of flexibility becomes beneficial for dynamic decision making and the IT support in manufacturing.

Conclusion

The paper investigates the demand of manufacturing flexibility in competitive environments and explores benefits of a closed loop approach using MES and OpBI in a conjoint manner. This facilitates a dynamic decision making to face steady changing customer requirements. These are uncertainties for manufacturing, while their successful handling cast a positive light on growth and sustainability especially in industrial organizations. A closed-loop approach of MES and OpBI is able to achieve these benefits, because decision making is directly attached on execution of the value creation process. The MES provides control mechanisms for production, quality, maintenance and inventory operations management, while OpBI complements with capabilities for a customer-oriented analysis of process performance.

Lessons learned from the paper reflect complex and multidimensional characteristics of manufacturing flexibility. Its achievement challenges especially industrial organizations to establish a dynamic decision making based on comprehensive performance analyses. The issue is supportable by MES and OpBI, but there is no unisonous and abstract procedure universally valid across all manufacturing industries. This sheds an ambiguous light on flexibility, because of its presence regarding manufacturing itself as well as underlying decision support.

Considering subsequent research actions, the paper gives an impulse for case specific implementations and for benchmarking studies of all-embracing industries. Thereby, the initial discussion gets enriched by further insights including comprehensive statistical evaluations with respect to a particular and a global view on manufacturing flexibility in context of a dynamic decision making.

References

1. Alpar, P., Louis, J.P., 2007. *Eine empirische Untersuchung der Softwareunterstützung bei der Fertigung und Qualitätssteuerung.* Philipps-Universität Marburg.
2. Barret, J., Barger, R., 2010. *Supply Chain Strategy for Industrial Manufacturers: The Handbook for Becoming Demand Driven.* Retrieved April 16, 2012, from www.gartner.com/id=1430728.
3. Beach, R., Muhlemann, A.P., Price, D.H.R., Paterson, A., Sharp, J.A., 2000. A review of manufacturing flexibility. *European Journal of Operational Research,* 122, 41-57.
4. Browne, J., Dubois, D., Rathmill, K., Sethi, S.P., Stecke, E., 1984. Classification of flexible manufacturing systems. *The FMS Magazine,* 22, 114–117.
5. Eckerson, W.W., 2007. *Best Practices in Operational BI: Converging Analytical and Operational Processes.* TDWI Best Practices Report, Renton.
6. Felden, C., Chamoni P., Linden M., 2010. From Process Execution towards a Business Process Intelligence. In Abramowicz, W. and Tolksdorf, R. (Eds.) *Business Information Systems 13th International Conference,* May 3-5, Berlin, Germany, 195-206.
7. Gebauer, J., Lee, F., 2005. Towards an "Optimal" Level of Information Systems Flexibility: A Conceptual Model. *In Proceedings of the 13th European Conference on Information Systems,* May 26-28, Regensburg.
8. Gluchowski, P., Kemper, H., Seufert, A., 2009. Innovative Prozess-Steuerung. *BI-Spektrum,* 4, 1, 8-12.
9. Hänel, T., Felden, C., 2011. Limits or Integration? Manufacturing Execution Systems and Operational Business Intelligence. *In Amercias Conference on Informations Systems,* August 05-07, Detroit, USA.
10. Hayes, R.H., Wheelwright, S.C., 1984. *Restoring our Competitive Edge: Competing Through Manufacturing.* Wiley, New York.
11. ISA ANSI/ISA-95.00.01-2000, 2000. *Enterprise Control System Integration, Part 1: Models and Terminology.* ISA technical paper.
12. ISO 9000, 2005. *Quality management systems: Fundamentals and vocabulary.* European Committee for Standardization, Brussels.
13. Flick, U., (2006). *An introduction to qualitative research.* SAGE Publications, London.
14. Kletti, J., 2007. *Manufacturing Execution Systems.* Springer, Berlin.
15. Koch, M., Lasi, H., Baars, H., Kemper, H.G., 2010. Manufacturing Execution Systems and Business Intelligence for Production Environments. *In Proceedings of the Sixteenth Americas Conference on Information Systems,* August 12-15, Lima, Peru.
16. KPMG, 2011. *Global Manufacturing Outlook: Growth while Managing Volatility.* Retrieved April 16, 2012, from www.kpmg.com/global/en/issuesandinsights/ articlespublications/global-manufacturing-outlook/ pages/growth-while-managing-volatility.aspx.
17. Patel, P.C., Terjesen, S., Li, D., 2012. Enhancing effects of manufacturing flexibility through operational absorptive capacity and operational ambidexterity, *Journal of Operations Management,* 30, 201–220.
18. Rodriguez, R.A., 2007. *Aligning IT to Business Processes.* Retrieved April 16, 2012, from www.appian.com/bpm-resources/papers_reports/report_aberdeen1.pdf.
19. Rogalski, S., 2011. *Flexibility Measurement in Production Systems,* Springer, Berlin.

20. Rolón, M., Martínez, E., 2012. Agent-based modeling and simulation of an autonomic manufacturing execution system. *Computers in Industry*, 63, 53-78.
21. Saenz de Ugarte, B., Artiba, A., Pellerin, R., 2009. Manufacturing execution system: a literature review. *Production Planning and Control*, 20(6), 525-539.
22. Schrödl, H., 2006. *Business Intelligence*. Hanser, München, Wien.
23. Upton, D., 1994. The management of manufacturing flexibility. *California Management Review*, 36, 72-89.
24. Vokurka, R.J., O'Leary-Kelly S.W., 2000. A review of empirical research on manufacturing flexibility. *Journal of Operations Management*, 18, 485-501.
25. White, C., 2006. *The Next Generation of Business Intelligence: Operational BI*. Retrieved April 16, 2012, from certification.sybase.com/content/ 1041416/Sybase_OperationalBI_WP-071906.pdf.
26. Yin, R.K., 2009. *Case Study Research: Design and Methods*. SAGE, Los Angeles.
27. Younus, M., Peiyong, C., Hu, L., Yuqing, F., 2010. MES Development and Significant Applications in Manufacturing - A Review. *In 2nd International Conference on Education Technology and Computer*, June 22-24, Shanghai, China.

4.3.2.11   Kurzdarstellung Beitrag 12

Beitrag 12 setzt sich weiterführend zu den Erkenntnissen von Beitrag 11 mit der Mehrdimensionalität von Flexibilität im Produktionsumfeld auseinander. Es wird deutlich, dass neben logistisch geprägten Informationssystemen, wie z. B. MES oder ERP, ebenso konstruktionsorientierte Systeme für ein Produktdatenmanagement (PDM) im Rahmen einer produktionsspezifischen Entscheidungsunterstützung zu berücksichtigen sind. Beitrag 12 stellt einen Bezug zwischen den verschiedenen Flexibilitätsdimensionen und der IT-Unterstützung durch industriespezifische Informationssysteme her. Es stellt sich heraus, dass bestehende IT-Systeme im Produktionsumfeld (MES, ERP und PDM) die Perspektiven einer Fertigungsflexibilität immer nur teilweise unterstützen können. Die Ursache dafür ist ein unterschiedlicher Systemfokus. MES und ERP unterstützen die stückbasierte Betrachtung von Produkten. Im Gegensatz dazu sehen PDM-Systeme Produkte als ein Bündel von Produkteigenschaften (Features) an. Sämtliche Features eines Produkts werden im Vorfeld der Herstellungsprozesse im Rahmen des PDM definiert. Danach erfolgt eine produktbezogene Wertschöpfung durch das Hinzufügen oder das Ändern der Produkteigenschaften. Die damit verbundenen Aktivitäten werden durch ERP und MES unterstützt, sodass die Leistungserbringung für ein Produkt stückbasiert abgerechnet wird. Infolge der fehlenden Verknüpfung von konstruktiven und logistischen IT-Systemen, lassen sich im Fertigungsprozess erzeugte oder veränderte Produkteigenschaften betriebswirtschaftlich nicht detailgetreu nachvollziehen. Ebenso wenig können ökonomische Betrachtungsparameter im Rahmen der Produktgestaltung berücksichtigt werden.

Motiviert von dieser Problemstellung untersucht Beitrag 12 die Möglichkeiten einer OpBI-basierten Integration der vorgestellten IT-Systeme im Produktionsumfeld. Die in Beitrag 11 gewonnenen Erkenntnisse hinsichtlich der Instandsetzung von IT- und Kommunikationsgeräten werden mit fallspezifischen Untersuchungen aus der Metallverarbeitung und dem Werkzeugmaschinenbau erweitert. Im Rahmen einer vergleichenden Fallstudie zeigt sich, dass OpBI eine multidimensionale Betrachtung der Fertigungsflexibilität umfassend unterstützt und eine Analyse von Fertigungsprozessen auf Basis von spezifischen Produkteigenschaften ermöglicht. Die Erkenntnisse von Beitrag 12 bekräftigen die Vorteilhaftigkeit von multidimensionalen Datenstrukturen (Beitrag 5 und Beitrag 6) im Hinblick auf die Anwendbarkeit von OpBI im Produktionsumfeld. OpBI ist in der Lage, sowohl logistische als auch konstruktive Aspekte in die Entscheidungsfindung einfließen zu lassen. Der Wert eines bestimmten Produkts kann anhand seiner zugrunde liegenden Eigenschaften bemessen werden. Durch den Einsatz von OpBI besteht die Möglichkeit, Produkte derart zu entwerfen und herzustellen, sodass sie einen maximal möglichen Mehrwert für die Kunden aufweisen. Es sind Kosten bestimmbar, die eine bestimmte Produkteigenschaft bei ihrer Herstellung verursacht. Führungskräfte und Prozessmanager können dadurch unnötige Kosten identifizieren und somit den Wertbeitrag von einem expliziten Produktmerkmal bis hin zum endgültigen Produkt kundenspezifisch erhöhen.

Beitrag 12 zeigt mögliche Perspektiven auf, die bei einer multidimensionalen Analyse von Fertigungsprozessen zu berücksichtigen sind. Diese Perspektiven stehen in Wechselwirkung zu verschiedenen Aufgabengebieten, die Gegenstand einer OpBI-getriebenen Entscheidungsunterstützung sind. Diese Entscheidungsfelder können im Rahmen einer multidimensionalen Datenmodellierung als Analysewürfel abgebildet werden. In diese entscheidungsrelevanten Analysen fließen Daten ein, die von logistischen und konstruktionsorientierten IT-Systemen generiert werden. Der Einsatz von OpBI führt demzufolge nicht zu einem Austausch der bestehenden IT-Systeme im Produktionsumfeld. Vielmehr bilden ERP, MES und PDM die Datengrundlage für ein integratives Analysesystem zum Zweck einer Entscheidungsunterstützung.

4.3.2.12   Beitrag 12: Operational Business Intelligence Meets Manufacturing[12]

Introduction

The capability to design and control manufacturing processes is a determining competitive factor of industrial organizations. Dynamic market conditions enforce flexibility and readiness for changes in order to maintain a durable product excellence. [23] A product's value depends on specific product features embodying particular attractiveness for the customer. The design of those features is engineering-driven, but logistical processes accomplish a customer-oriented provision of corresponding products. These two different points of view coincide during a manufacturing process, in which the actual feature creation happens. The manufacturing

---

12 Hänel, T.; Felden, C.: Operational Business Intelligence meets Manufacturing. In: 19th Americas Conference on Information Systems, Chicago, August 2013.

process design has to be aligned and adjusted so that a created product feature merits to customer requirements. However, there is a lack of decision support systems for an appropriate control of manufacturing processes in consideration of engineering design data and logistical key figures, yet [16]. Therefore, the paper's goal is to investigate need and benefits of a dynamic decision support strategy, which allows an analysis of manufacturing processes in its logistical and engineering perspective. This is pursued to control and improve the value contribution of a specific product feature created during a manufacturing process activity.

Separate IT systems differing in their area of responsibility characterize decision support in manufacturing. Product Data Management (PDM) systems manage engineering design features e.g. technical drawings or machine tool specifications throughout the whole product life cycle [18]. Enterprise Resource Planning (ERP) systems support an operational planning in manufacturing and its adjacent management areas. They focus in particular on managerial key figures for a comprehensive market and resource-oriented planning of e.g. sales, production or inventory volumes [20]. This spanning view of ERP systems does not allow control or analysis of manufacturing process activities on execution level. Manufacturing Execution Systems (MES) bridge this gap between planning and execution layer [15]. These systems maintain and improve performance and quality of manufacturing processes using contemporary information [21]. MES support the intersection of PDM and ERP responsibilities, but they show shortcomings for decisions about adaption strategies especially to address a customer's changing value perceptions [24]. An approach to overcome these obstacles in decision making of manufacturing is OpBI [13]. OpBI is defined as provisioning of analytical capabilities to control organizational value creation in favor of continuous improvement of process design and execution [9]. It refers to established BI techniques and builds up a closed loop to analyze contemporary relations between process performance and status of goal achievement [3]. This research contributes to the discussion about dynamic decision making in manufacturing and delivers practical insights regarding motives and benefits of OpBI applications. It demonstrates an OpBI's suitability to jointly analyze logistical and engineering perspectives on a product's feature creation. This enables a value driven control and improvement of manufacturing processes.

The status quo chapter discusses reasons for specificity of currently existing IS in manufacturing. The exposition of certain advantages regarding an OpBI-oriented integration of these systems follows this discussion. The paper adopts a case study approach for profound exploration of reasons and benefits of OpBI in three different industrial organizations. The results chapter presents each case in detail and analyzes replications for an OpBI-oriented decision support in manufacturing. A conclusion summarizes the paper's insights and provides further research directions.

Status Quo

Over last decades, information systems (IS) are discussed to plan and realize manufacturing processes. Computer integrated manufacturing (CIM) introduced an integration of data and processes for economic and technical activities in the 1980's [26]. CIM could not become prevalent e.g. due to insufficient standardization or a marketing driven use [15], but IS still support manufacturing processes. [1] classify electronic data interchange (EDI) to share information with customers or suppliers, operations management systems (OMS) to control and monitor manufacturing processes, and resource planning systems (RPS) for a spanning management of business processes. RPS and OMS support a control and disposition of value-added activities on different organizational hierarchy levels. The nature of decisions differs with respect to time horizon of corresponding levels and integration reach of supporting systems.

The highest level encompasses a medium and long-term enterprise-wide planning [11]. ERP systems allow an integrated view of e.g. procurement, production and sales [10]. The ERP commits certain target figures to MES for contemporary decisions [29]. The MES performs a permanent target-actual comparison in terms of volumes, deadlines and quality and reports achieved results of shop floor back to the ERP [15]. The shortest time horizon has the actual manufacturing process, which transforms inputs into outputs [4]. The output results from consecutive occurrences, in which specific product features are created, added or changed. PDM defines corresponding characteristics and is responsible for product engineering and design data during the whole product lifecycle [22]. This includes technical aspects, digital models of products, or even machine data used for simulation and development purposes [18].

The increasing time horizon redeploys a decision's subject from actual creation of a technical feature, to partial product components and finished products. Value considerations are usually performed in terms of manufactured products or its components, because agreed prices and sum of all costs incurred are taken into account due to ERP integration strategies [17]. The value creation is done in course of adding or modifying a product feature by different methods and tools during manufacturing process. The determination and accounting of achieved values relates to resulting product components using ERP functionalities [19]. However, it is not possible to amount the value contribution of a specific process activity (add on or modification of product features) and to use it for control purposes of a manufacturing process. The existing systems are not able to give any information about the value proposition of a process activity, if a process activity is worthwhile in certain circumstances, how malfunctions, failures or interruptions influence the value proposition of a process activity, or about the impact of design changes to the value proposition of a process activity.

The missing information limits flexibility of industrial organizations, because earning capacities are not certainly estimable for product or process-related changes on execution level. But, flexibility in manufacturing context deals with the ability to handle changes in multiple dimensions [27]. Table 1 summarizes such dimensions for manufacturing processes according to a literature review of [14]. Decision support capabilities are advantageous to avoid negative influences on profitability or fatal performance changes.

Table1. Manufacturing flexibility dimensions

IS	Flexibility dimension	Description
MES	Machine	Machines execute various and heterogeneous operations.
	Labor	Workers execute various and heterogeneous operations.
	Material handling	Various materials are transported along paths between different processing centers.
	Routes	Products can have variable routes, if processing machines are changeable.
	Operations	Operations' sequence can change, if multiple processing plans are possible.
ERP	Expansion	Expansions increase capacities and capabilities of manufacturing processes.
	Volumes	Manufacturing processes are exposed to changes or fluctuations of aggregated output levels.
	Mix	Manufacturing processes create various products categorized to different product groups.
PDM	New products	Innovativeness is characterized by number and variety of new products.
	Modifications	Product modifications represent changes of product design and its features.

All dimensions are relevant to manufacturing flexibility [14], but an IT support refers to different systems. An advantageousness of BI is subject of discussion in order to support conjoint decision making of industrial organizations [9]. BI provides a multidimensional analysis environment using established techniques of data provision, storage, and presentation [25]. External sources or internal operational systems provide relevant data [5]. The ETL process extracts, transforms, and loads these data into the data warehouse (Berson et al., 2002), which is a persistent database decoupled from operational systems to support multidimensional reporting and analyses [12]. Techniques like online analytical processing or data mining can advance a data analysis [7].

A consideration of ERP, MES, and PDM within a BI environment allows an investigation of flexibility-related changes according to technical and economic aspects within different perspectives of manufacturing processes. This provides analysis capabilities in terms of OpBI in order to analyze and control the value contribution of certain process activities, i.e. creation, adding and modification of product features. However, there is not much experience about OpBI's decision support capabilities in industrial organizations, yet [8]. The research objective is therefore to investigate reasons and benefits of an OpBI application in practical context. This leads to the following research questions:

RQ1: Why does an application of OpBI contributes to a decision making in manufacturing processes?

RQ2: How does OpBI analyze the value contribution of process activities for controlling and improvement purposes?

Method

The method is based on case study research and follows a multiple structure with a single unit of analysis [28]. Planning and design activities develop research questions, which are derived in the previous section. The selection of corresponding cases encompasses three industrial organizations. Two organizations have a repeatable manufacturing process design so that benefits of OpBI are expectable due to theoretical considerations. One organization has in contrast a project-oriented structure, in which a comparability of performed projects is not given. These different characteristics are chosen to provide eclectic input for a detailed investigation about an OpBI's contribution for decision making in manufacturing.

The case based method is able to provide tried and tested results in first place. The insights are necessary to evaluate advantageousness of subsequent research actions and to provide guidance for similar cases. [28] emphasizes demand of three or four cases for literal replications. This allows an identification of recurring patterns referring in the present investigation about reasons and benefits of OpBI application in manufacturing. Figure 1 illustrates the research process.

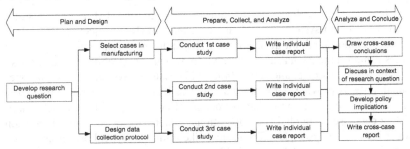

Figure 1. Case study method

Results

The result's chapter presents cases of three industrial organizations, i.e. an IT and communication product manufacturer, a machine tool modernizer and a hydraulics engineering company located in Germany. A discussion of cross-case conclusions follows in order to make a point about the OpBI's contribution for decision making in industrial organizations.

Case one: Manufacturing of IT and communication products

The first organization refines IT and communications products including a customizing and a refurbishment. A packaging of shipping finished products happens in course of blistering and foliation of item boxes. Blisters allow the buyer to see packaged items consisting usually of a device and accessories. The foliation enables affixing of security chips and creation of product bundles.

Customizing refers to assembling and remodelling of mobiles e.g. keyboard changes or software updates. Individual configurations and settings are performed according to specific customer requirements. The refurbishment executes a quality assured maintenance, repair and overhaul of returns. A customer orders the service to resale outdated or defective devices. The process includes completeness checks of incoming devices, resets to factory settings and functional checks. External partners repair defective components as the circumstances require. Figure 2 illustrates the refurbishment process.

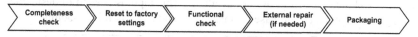

Figure 2. Refurbishment

The monthly throughput is more than 100,000 products of different brands and categories. But, the order situation has seasonal fluctuations. In boom phases like Christmas trade, weekly sales quantities are doubled, while throughput is marginal in silly seasons. This fluctuating situation determines the number of employees so that shop floor staff changes accordingly. It is important to maintain high product quality during boom phases. The processes have to be quick and cost efficient independent who is executing the process. Refurbishment and customizing need access to customer order-specific and product-related data. A joint consideration is advantageous for controlling purposes of processes, because this provides the opportunity to analyse, if the add-on of a specific product feature has improvement potential regarding time, quality, or cost.

OpBI facilitates analyses with respect to changing staff and to heterogeneity of customer-specific product features. Process managers are able to identify, how a specific product feature merits to a customer order, which expenses are associated to creation, and if processes are well executed by employees. Customizing needs those capabilities to shift attention to eminently worthwhile product features of certain customers. The refurbishment process benefits also from an integrated analysis of order and product design data. The first step checks completeness of devices including an ordering of missing parts or accessories. The purchaser reviews current product data needed to update old devices for design or functional changes. Reset and test activities are responsible for early detection of defective devices. A refurbishment board has to decide who is able to repair the respective device, which expenses are associated and if it is worthwhile at all. An analysis of defect causes, order information and product data supports decision making, because this demonstrates the amount of affected devices across all orders in a refurbishment cycle categorized by features to be restored. Production control can decide about scrap or repair. Early sharing of those insights with purchase avoids ordering of redundant materials for final packaging and unnecessary expenses.

Case two: Project-oriented decision support in machine tool manufacturing

The second organization modernizes gear hobbing machines by reviewing machine components and replacing worn parts. This happens in different individual projects with fixed budgets and limited time frames in order to restore desired machine states. Projects passing several phases as illustrated in Figure 3. The employees remove cover panels and disassemble a machine in assemblies and single components. Assemblers list all standard and specific parts. They take pictures of units, if technical drawings are not available. This input is needed to design necessary adjustments, to purchase standard parts and to reassemble machines.

Figure 3. Modernization process of gear hobbing machines

An assessment about assembly states takes place during dismantling. A project board decides about an overhaul sequence of components or whether a new production is required. A responsible board analyzes availability and suitability of in house capabilities and capacities. They have to find out if external organizations offer required services. An overhaul must be cheaper than purchase or new production. The board needs accurate information about expenses to renew or reproduce features of a given component. However, the organization process different kinds of gear hobbing machines including various assemblies and components. Expense considerations on part level are difficult due to this complexity and multiplicity. Actual features which are added or restored have indeed a high comparability, but their expenses depend on several factors influencing feature creation e.g. type of material or processing equipment.

OpBI is able to point out expenses of feature creation from these perspectives to a varying level of detail. This is beneficial to plan and manage different project workflows. The project board can execute comprehensive cost estimations already during stocktaking in course of dismantling. Number and heterogeneity of a gear hobbing machine's features lead to a determination of cost, duration or quality measures, although this machine type must not necessarily be modernized before. Those planning parameters provide also decision support to control occurring activities of feature creation. Employees are able to intervene in the overhaul process at concerning points in case of target/actual deviations. Causes can be related to perspectives of feature creation. This leads to continuous process improvements and adjustments of planning parameters.

Case three: Value adding analyses and quality management in hydraulics engineering

The third organization produces various hydraulics cylinders. An engineering department designs new products and customer specific enhancements. Each product consists of several components to be manufactured internally or externally, and purchased parts. An assembly, a possible coloring and a preparation for shipment conclude the value creation. Order withdrawals, missing materials, troubles of external manufacturers, unavailable labors, machine failures or quality reductions constantly disturb the value creation. Malfunctions of e.g. automatic welders or CNC machining centers delay planning cycles, so that product features cannot be created as scheduled. A continuous planning is associated with large uncertainties and corresponding adjustments imply disproportional expenses. Unfortunately, the process includes many cleaning steps to assure leakproofness of cylinders. This leads often to impossibility of proponing subsequent activities.

A workaround is consideration of monthly value creation targets. Alternative outputs have to compensate adverse circumstances if an order fulfillment is impossible. This necessitates a measurement of added values in order to use variations for control purposes. An analysis based on finished products is not favorable, because created values are only measureable during assembly shortly before delivery. The value contribution of actual component's manufacturing remains unclear, although it is useable for controlling the process and its influencing perspectives. Figure 4 illustrates incremental feature creation and value adding for a cylinder head.

Figure 4. Cylinder head manufacturing

OpBI supports measurement of incremental accretion within a component's manufacturing process. Production manager enrich their decisions by consideration of expenses and benefits regarding a specific feature creation. This allows an improved allocation of e.g. resources, materials, and available technologies to create a product feature, because inhouse production of the product's components has to be cheaper than external procurement. The engineering department gets also information about expenses of specific feature creation e.g. to punch a hole in a certain material. This allows determination of cost and prices for new products or product enhancements in advance during design phase based on needed features.

A quality assurance board investigates issues according to cost-by-cause principles using different process perspectives. OpBI records quality-related complaints in each process step and calculates expenses for rework, sorting or scrap. A cost comparison to monthly revenues supports decisions for quality assurance measures, e.g. changing of feature design, processing equipment or materials supplier, and a mix of it.

Cross-case conclusions

This section analyzes the presented cases in order to identify replications for an OpBI-oriented decision support in manufacturing processes. The business scope of the investigated industrial organizations is indeed different, but explored analysis requirements are quite similar. All cases benefit from an integrated view on logistical and engineering information in order control organizational value creation.

RQ 1 conclusions – Reasons for an OpBI application to contribute a decision making in manufacturing processes

A product's value refers not only to the difference between cost and selling price, but rather depends on underlying product features. This provides the opportunity to design and manufacture products, so that they incorporate a maximum value for the customer. An appropriate control of value creation needs to know expenses that a specific feature causes during its production. OpBI represents various perspectives of a product creation. Executives and process managers are able to consider technical and economic information on different detail levels. This supports decisions looking for causes of unnecessary cost in order to increase the value contribution from an explicit product feature up to final products and product groups. Figure 5 illustrates several perspectives of a manufacturing process concerning and joining different decision support areas addressed by OpBI.

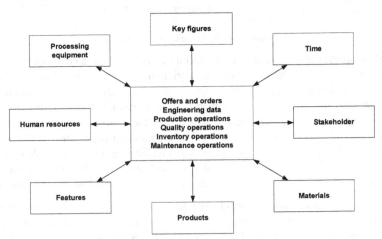

Figure 5. Perspectives and decision support areas

The middle square of Figure 5 represents decision support areas, which are representable by fact tables or analysis cubes in a multidimensional data model. They include situational transaction data originating from IT systems of supply chain, product engineering and certain operations of manufacturing control.

RQ 2 conclusions – OpBI benefits to analyze value contribution of process activities

An OpBI solution is able to analyze information jointly within various perspectives surrounding the decision support areas in Figure 5. The characteristics of these perspectives to control organizational value creation of manufacturing processes result from similarities of the presented case studies.

Table 2. Characteristics of manufacturing process perspectives

Perspective	Characteristics explored due to replications of the case studies
Stakeholder	Customer, supplier, and external manufacturers
Materials	Raw materials and supplies, purchased parts, and external manufactured features or components
Products	Sales items produced categorized to product groups
Feature	Geometric and qualitative properties of products added in the course of a manufacturing process
Human resources	Executives, responsible persons, operators distinguishable into departments
Processing equipment	Machines, tools, plants, or IT systems applied during a manufacturing process
Key figures	Metrics and calculation rules determining the value contribution of manufacturing process activities
Time	Calendar hierarchy to track chronology of manufacturing process activities

The basic objects of analysis are features that are created for a specific product using materials and appropriate processing equipment. The chronology of corresponding occurrences describes a manufacturing process in its actual behavior. Responsible boards controlling process behavior are able to consider expenses of a specific feature, most efficient manufacturing alternatives situationally, and the value a feature merits to the customer. These capabilities of OpBI complement existing decision support concepts in manufacturing beneficially. Table 3 compares effects of OpBI to ERP, MES and PDM systems with respect to value contribution assessment of manufacturing process activities.

Table 3. Comparison of OpBI and existing IS for decision support in manufacturing

		Supporting IS			
		OpBI	**ERP**	**MES**	**PDM**
Assessment of value contribution	**Flexibility dimension**	Expansion, volume, mix, machine, labor, material handling, routes, operations, new products, modifications	Expansion, volume, mix	Machine, labor, material handling, routes, operations	New products, modifications
	Activity perspective	Logistics and engineering	Logistics	Logistics	Engineering
	Activity scope	Planning, monitoring and controlling, improvement	Planning	Monitoring and controlling	Definition and improvement
	Activity focus	Process- and product-oriented	Process-oriented	Process-oriented	Product-oriented
	Product characterization	Components and features	Components	Components	Features
	Reach of decisions	Domain-specific and enterprise-wide	Enterprise-wide	Domain-specific	Domain-specific

OpBI is not a new software application or system approach, which replaces existing systems for decision making in manufacturing. To a greater degree, OpBI facilitates an integration effect regarding flexibility dimensions, product characterization, reach of decisions as well as perspective, scope and focus of manufacturing process activities. This integration effect is demonstrated by certain examples of industrial organizations confirming theoretical considerations of OpBI. This is especially expectable for case one and three due to an underlying standardized and repeatable manufacturing processes. However, case two reveals this integration effect also for a project-oriented context. OpBI processes according to that corresponding information allowing a comparability of tasks and activities, in which standardization and repeatability is not given at a first glance. This novel capability is particularly advantageous for industrial organizations, because existing systems have not been able to respond dynamically to uncertainties during performance execution.

Conclusions

OpBI is able to provide beneficial decision support capabilities in industrial organizations. An application contributes to a decision making in manufacturing, because OpBI enables a conjoint analysis of concerned process perspectives in context of managerial, engineering and manufacturing operation information. A product value is described, measured, and managed according to conspicuous features from a customer's point of view. OpBI investigates expenses for each feature creation within manufacturing process perspectives. Executives and responsible persons get decision support capabilities to justify corresponding efforts. Industrial organizations are able to face dynamic market conditions by adaptations of their product design and manufacturing, so that a customer perceives durable excellent products.

The raison d'être of OpBI for a decision support in manufacturing results from insufficiency of existing IT systems to combine logistical and engineering information of a product's feature creation. OpBI debuts a multidimensional understanding about value relations between corresponding manufacturing process activities and influencing factors. Features and activities that do not contribute to creation of a customer value can be redesigned or modified. Necessary interaction of product engineering design, manufacturing operations and logistics gets transparent. This is particularly interesting for managers deciding about changes or redesigns in manufacturing as OpBI provides input for profitability analyses of new and existing products. However, care must be taken in consequence to the number of case studies restricted only to industrial organizations. Three cases represent not a large share of industrial organizations, but they are sufficient for literal replications. Despite an indeed different scope of concerned organizations, the case studies provide resilient congruencies to explore advantageousness of OpBI for decision support in manufacturing.

There are opportunities for further research based on these qualitative insights about OpBI's decision support in manufacturing. Further qualitative or quantitative analyzes are able to achieve a broader level of knowledge in favor of a result's generalizability. A value orientation is also discussed in context of service provision and e-Business activities (Gordijn, 2004) next to creation of physical products. Achieved insights of this paper provide therefore also starting points for further research within the scope of services.

References

1. Banker, R., Bardhan, I., Chang, H. and Lin, S. (2006) Plant Information Systems, Manufacturing Capabilities, and plant performance, *MIS Quarterly*, 30, 2, 315-337.
2. Berson, A., Smith, S. and Thearling, K. (2002) Building Data Mining Applications for CRM, McGraw-Hill, New York.
3. Davis, J., Imhoff, C. and White, C. (2009) Operational Business Intelligence: The State of the Art, Beye NETWORK Research, Boulder CO.
4. EN ISO 9000 (2005) Quality management systems: Fundamentals and vocabulary, European Committee for Standardization, Brussels.
5. Gangadharan, G. R. and Swamy, N. S. (2004) Business intelligence systems: design and implementation strategies, in Proceedings of 26th International Conference on Information Technology Interfaces, Croatia, Cavtat.
6. Gordijn, J. (2004) e-Business value modelling using the e³value ontology, Value Creation from e-business models (Currie, W.). Elsevier, Osford, 98-127.
7. Han, J. and Kamber, M. (2001) Data Mining: Concepts and Techniques, Third edition, Academic Press, San Diego.
8. Hänel, T. and Felden, C. (2011) Limits or Integration? Manufacturing Execution Systems and Operational Business Intelligence, in Amercias Conference on Informations Systems, August 05-07, USA, Detroit.

9. Hänel, T. and Felden, C. (2012) Towards a Stability of Process-Oriented Decision Support Concepts Using the Example of Operational Business Intelligence, in Pre-ICIS BI Congress 3: Driving Innovation through Big Data Analytics, USA, Orlando.

10. Hossain, L., Patrick, J. D. and Rashid, M. A. (2002) Enterprise Resource Planning: Global Opportunities & Challenges, IGP, London.

11. ISA ANSI/ISA-95.00.01-2000 (2000) Enterprise Control System Integration, Part 1: Models and Terminology, ISA technical paper, Research Triangle Park.

12. Kimball, R. and Ross, M. (2002) The Data Warehouse Toolkit: The Complete Guide to Dimensional Modeling, 2nd edition, Wiley, New York.

13. Koch, M., Lasi, H., Baars, H. and Kemper, H.G. (2010) Manufacturing Execution Systems and Business Intelligence for Production Environments, in Proceedings of the Sixteenth Americas Conference on Information Systems, Peru, Lima.

14. Koste L.L. and Malhotra M.K. (1999) A theoretical framework for analyzing the dimensions of manufacturing flexibility, *Journal of Operations Management* 18, 75–93.

15. Kletti, J. (2007) Manufacturing Execution System: MES, Springer, Berlin and Heidelberg.

16. Lasi, H. (2012) Decision Support within Knowledge-Based Engineering – A Business Intelligence-Based Concept,0 in Proceedings of the Eighteenth Americas Conference on Information Systems, Paper 12, USA, Seattle.

17. Lea, B.-R. (2007) Management accounting in ERP integrated MRP and TOC environments, *Industrial Management & Data Systems*, 107, 8, 1188-1211.

18. Liu, D.T. and Xu X.W. (2001) A review of web-based product data management systems, *Computers in Industry*, 44, 251-262.

19. Markus M.L., Tanis C. and van Fenema, P.C. (2000) Multisite ERP Implementation, *Communications of the ACM*, 43, 4, 42-46.

20. Monk, F. E. and Wagner B. J. (2007) Concepts in Enterprise Resource Planning, Third Edition, Course Technology Cenage Learning, Boston (MA).

21. MESA (1997) MES Explained: A High Level Vision for Executives, MESA International White Paper Number 6, Pittsburgh.

22. Peltonen H., Pitkänen, O. and Sulonen R. (1996) Process-based view on product data management, *Computers in Industry*, 31, 195-203.

23. Rogalski, S. (2011) Flexibility Measurement in Production Systems, Springer, Berlin.

24. Saenz de Ugarte, B., Artiba, A. and Pellerin, R. (2009) Manufacturing execution system: a literature review, *Production Planning and Control*, 20, 6, 525-539.

25. Sahay, B.S. and Ranjan, J. (2008) Real time business intelligence in supply chain analytics, *Information Management & Computer Security*, 16, 1, 28-48.

26. Scheer, A.W. (1988) CIM: Computer integrated manufacturing: computer steered industry, Springer New York, Berlin and Heidelberg.

27. Upton, D. (1994) The management of manufacturing flexibility, *California Management Review*, 36, 2, 72-89.

28. Yin, R.K. (2009) Case Study Research: Design and Methods, 4th edition, SAGE, Los Angeles.

29. Younus, M., Peiyong, C., Hu, L. and Yuqing, F. (2010) MES Development and Significant Applications in Manufacturing – A Review, in 2nd International Conference on Education Technology and Computer (ICETC), China, Shanghai.

4.3.3 Operational Business Intelligence im Dienstleistungsumfeld

Eine Anwendbarkeitsuntersuchung von OpBI im Dienstleistungsumfeld ist in Beitrag 13 erfolgt, um Erkenntnisse hinsichtlich einer Analyse und Steuerung von Dienstleistungsprozessen zu gewinnen.

4.3.3.1 Kurzdarstellung Beitrag 13

Beitrag 13 diskutiert die Herausforderung einer Integration von heterogenen Informationen aus Kunden- und Dienstleistersicht während der Erbringung von Dienstleistungen. Diese Integrationsproblematik konnte bereits in Beitrag 2 als potentielles Anwendungsgebiet der OpBI identifiziert werden. Beitrag 13 macht deutlich, dass verschiedenartige Zielstellungen aus Perspektive eines Kunden und eines Dienstleisters in Einklang zu bringen sind. Dabei werden die Aspekte hinsichtlich des Austauschs von Informationen sowie der Interaktion von Kunden und Dienstleistern weiterführend am Fallbeispiel einer Versicherungsagentur betrachtet. Die Untersuchung konzentriert sich auf die Tätigkeitsbereiche Neukundenakquise, Kundenbetreuung und Schadenregulierung. In einer Konzeptionsphase erfolgen die Beschreibung der Dienstleistungsprozesse, die Strukturierung der Informationen aus Kundensicht und der Perspektive der Versicherungsagentur sowie die Definition von Steuerungsparametern. Im Ergebnis der Konzeption liegt ein multidimensionales Datenmodell vor, das die Analyse und Steuerung der Prozesse in der Versicherungsagentur fachlich strukturiert. Das Modell nutzt die Notation von ADAPT (Application Design for Analytical Processing Technologies), um die fachlichen Analyseaspekte der Versicherungsagentur in den Vordergrund zu stellen. Im Rahmen der Modellierung werden fallspezifische Beschreibungsperspektiven mit operativen Steuerungsgrößen in Zusammenhang gebracht. Durch die Nutzung von Hierarchien lassen sich Informationen auf verschiedenen Verdichtungsstufen darstellen. Im weiteren Verlauf von Beitrag 13 werden zwei Anwendungsszenarien beschrieben, die die Datensammlung und die Datenanalyse sowie die Ableitung und die Bewertung von geeigneten Managementmaßnahmen auf Grundlage des fachlichen Datenmodells kennzeichnen. In der Quintessenz zeigt die Fallstudie auf, dass OpBI die Analyse und Steuerung von Dienstleistungsprozessen wie folgt unterstützen kann:

- Strukturierung einer Menge von heterogenen Kundeninformationen,
- eindeutige Zuordnung der Kundeninformationen zu den Tätigkeitsbereichen der Dienstleistungserbringung,
- Bestimmung von Parametern zur Bewertung der Prozessabläufe,
- Herunterbrechen von komplexen Sachverhalten auf unkomplizierte Managementmaßnahmen und
- eine kritische Bewertung der Prozessanalysen auf Grundlage von gesammelten Erfahrungen und Fachwissen.

4.3.3.2 Beitrag 13: The Role of Operational Business Intelligence in Customer Centric Service Provision[13]

Introduction

The interaction of customers and service industry's companies characterizes the provision of services. Differing and regularly changing customer requirements lead to a complexity so that service providers need to continuously adapt design and control of their services. Thereby, integration and consideration of customer information for service decisions is challenging. Customers expect a high service quality, while service provision has to be beneficial in terms of economical key figures from service provider perspective. Business processes and operations of service providers are deterministic and repeatable. However, results are different for changing service contexts and customer situations. Important factors are integration and consideration of internal and external information emerging within and flowing into a service provision. This requires a measuring and a structuring of different information perspectives in a service context in order to facilitate a situational configuration of service actions. Therefore, the paper's goal is to discuss need and benefits of a dynamic decision support strategy, which allows an analysis and control of service processes. This is pursued to configure and improve service provision in dependence of differing customer information.

The literature of business intelligence (BI) discusses services rather from a technological perspective. BI capabilities supporting decision making are understood, designed, and provided as services [3]. This is expressed by discussions about cloud computing [11] as well as service-oriented architectures (SOA), or web services [15]. However, decision makers need to analyze business impact of decisions on efficiency of service provision and customer perception. This provides capabilities to make decisions and to take actions in terms of affected customers, service costs, and potential revenues. In context of an organizational performance management, business processes force organizations to make such decisions based on key performance indicators at different management levels [9]. A constitutive element of performance management is thereby the operational level, in which BI information are used to monitor, control and optimize business processes in favor of strategic performance analyzes by the management [19]. [18] take up this combined consideration of BI and business processes and provides theoretical insights, which address the concept of OpBI by coincidence of BI and knowledge intensive business processes. OpBI is able to provide analytical capabilities in order to improve design and execution of such business processes [10]. Established BI techniques are used in a closed loop to analyze process performance and status of goal achievement [4]. However, this potential of OpBI is not

---

13 Hänel, T.; Felden, C.: The Role of Operational Business Intelligence in Customer Centric Service Provision. In: 20th Americas Conference on Information Systems, Savannah, August 2014.

considered in context of service provision, yet, in order to determine customer-tailored service actions. There is a lack of professional discussion about OpBI in order to solve the translucent complexity regarding integration of different customer information. This discussion will gain insights about decision making to break knowledge intensive processes down into manageable facts, which can be handled by straightforward management approaches. This research contributes therefore to a dynamic decision making in field of service provision. It delivers practical insights regarding benefits of an OpBI application to jointly analyze service quality and service efficiency aspects by integration and configuration of service actions according to customer information.

The following chapter discusses interaction of service providers and customers during service provision and points out reasons for a technological focus on services from a BI perspective. The exposition of related studies and certain advantages regarding an application of OpBI in context of service provision completes this discussion. The paper adopts a case study approach for a profound exploration of reasons and benefits of OpBI in a general agency of a large insurance group. The results chapter presents the creation of an operational data model and its application for an OpBI-oriented decision support to manage insurance operations.

The understanding of BI and service provision

Customers and service providers interact and exchange information during process of service provision [7]. For example, there is an exchange of information in banking, in which consultants and clients are in direct contact to customize financial products. From a supplier's perspective customer information has to be considered, so that a customer experiences high service quality [21]. Thereby, the service provider intends to keep down cost and to increase incomes (cf. Figure 1).

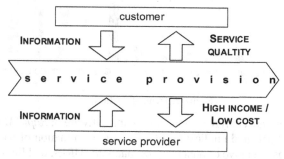

Figure 1. Interaction of customers and service providers

Due to personality and diversity, customer information differ in quantity and quality. This leads to complex and multilayered combinations of customer and supplier information. These combinations are crucial to structure service provision. Perceived service quality of a customer depends thereby on performed service actions. Hence, customer information is important for identification, evaluation, and evolution of actions during the process of service provision.

BI supports a decision making by integration of internal and external information [25]. However, the potential of BI to organize and advance services is not exploited. [24] study a BI support of strategic decisions to analyze business impacts of changes in software engineering. Thereby, they take up also the operational issue that use of BI in service contexts is challenged by an identification of relevant data about service provision and affected customers [24]. In order to pursue this issue we provide in the following results of a literature review regarding BI approaches in service contexts.

Status quo of BI and service in academic literature

We conducted a literature search in academic databases of Business Source Complete, IEEE Xplore, AIS electronic Library, ACM Digital Library, Emerald and Science Direct, since they allow us access to scientific publications of top journals according to MIS journal rankings [1]. Search terms (*business intelligence* and *service*) were entered full and in quotation marks limited to abstract, title, or keywords. This widespread, but not overall search leads to 250 articles published between 1999 and 2014. The number of publications is increasing over time (cf. Figure 2).

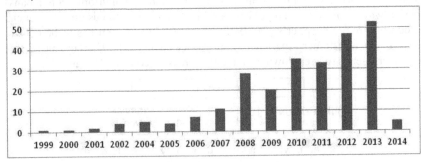

Figure 2. Trend of publications

The publications are analyzed using text mining software of *Rapid Miner*. We preprocessed abstracts and publication titles by a transformation of letters to lower cases as well as a remove of punctuations, numbers, URLs, and English language stop words. Data preprocessing was finished by a stemming and building of n-grams with a maximum length of four characters. The text mining reveals a word list containing 2,177 individual or grouped terms. This word list was scanned for topics regarding BI and service. The corresponding topics were finally categorized in context of application, field of application, technical driven, and functional driven topics (cf. Table 1).

Table 1. Classification of topics

	Topic	total	doc.	Topic	total	doc.	
context of application	cost	46	36	cloud computing	57	34	**technical driven focus**
	business process	44	35	data mining	66	30	
	innovation	30	16	data warehouse	52	28	
	service level	21	15	web service	34	23	
	business performance	17	13	OLAP	34	22	
	strategic decision	12	12	service-oriented architecture	30	19	
	supply chain	13	9	ETL	25	16	
	business models	13	7	algorithm	13	11	
	customer satisfaction	8	5	text analytics	20	11	
	social network	13	5	dashboard	16	10	
	business value	5	4	data mart	17	9	
	performance indicators	5	4	data model	9	8	
	social media	10	4	big data	12	6	
	churn	11	3	software as a service	16	6	
	operational efficiency	4	3	OLTP	7	5	
	service quality	5	3	RFID	11	4	
	value creation	4	3	complex event processing	4	3	
field of application	marketing	33	25	data visualization	3	3	
	commerce	54	23	EAI	3	3	
	telecommunications	32	21	service-oriented BI	6	3	
	transport	20	11	web mining	10	3	
	banking	16	11	workload management	7	3	
	financial services	15	9	knowledge management	22	12	**functional-driven fo-**
	purchase	14	9	CRM	25	11	
	customer service	10	8	performance management	15	9	
	logistics	16	8	operational BI	9	6	
	manufacturing	14	7	supply chain management	6	5	
	insurance	11	6	business process management	6	4	
	healthcare	11	5	change management	3	3	
	education	4	3	predictive analytics	5	3	

Table 1 indicates a technical focus in the discussion about BI and service. This technical discussion includes facets and architecture components of BI. Examples for these architecture components are the ETL process and the data warehouse in context of data delivery as well as OLAP and data mining concerning data analysis tasks. An illustrative example for the application of data analytics is given by [20]. They demonstrate benefits of data mining and BI dashboards to predict and avoid customer churn in business operations. Additionally, BI capabilities are under-stood, designed, and provided as services [3]. This is primarily discussed by cloud computing containing approaches to provide BI infrastructures, platforms, and software components as a service. The high term and document occurrences for service-oriented architectures (SOA) and web services confirm this relevance. Intention is a deployment of SOA in BI systems to address flexibility requirements and architecture innovations [5].

Main fields of application are marketing, commerce, and telecommunications. High value-added services such as financial services, banking or insurance are fewer discussed. Cost and business processes are main topics regarding context of application. However, approaches like performance management, operational BI, or business process management are only marginally discussed in comparison to technical topics. There is obviously a gap of functional approaches to support decision making in mainly discussed application contexts.

Related studies

This section discusses conceptual approaches in favor of integrating customer information to support an efficient service provision. Related studies were identified by scanning publications regarding a functional-driven focus classified in Table 1 and a corresponding backward search based on these publications. They address the functional focus of performance management as well as coincidence of BI and business process management.

Corporate performance management (CPM) is synonymously used for business performance management (BPM) and enterprise performance management [9]. CPM is an extension of BI by a performance measurement based on performance indicators. CPM defines performance targets on the level of strategic management decisions and compares achieved business values to those targets. This comparison is used to evaluate impact of business decisions on a given management strategy. However, this concept does not focus on creation of process-related information in order to derive suitable actions to fulfill and improve an efficient service provision.

[13] provide experiences about process performance management (PPM) in order to analyze structures of business processes for continuous improvement purposes. Analysis of processes happens subsequently to process execution. Emerging deviations are used to define appropriate modifications in process execution. The use of BI in context of PPM was originally not designated, but PPM can be understood as a convergence of business process modeling and BI, since performance indicators are used to improve business processes [19]. PPM assumes thereby comparison of *to-be* business process models to *as-is* processes. However, this definition of *to-be* models constrains a flexible and customer individual provision of services.

The debate about PPM indicates potentials of a conceptual merge of BI and business process management. There are further process-oriented BI approaches capturing this issue. Thereby, business process intelligence (BPI) concerns a support of process design and redesign activities for strategic and tactical management

decisions [6]. BPI guides rather design strategies for a service provision than identification of operational actions. [2] discuss a process-centric business intelligence
(PCBI). PCBI focuses on process execution and integrates BI applications within
this. Thereby, analytical information is provided in order to support fulfillment of
process-related tasks. However, this analytical information stem not necessarily
from the concerned process. The analysis results are not used to identify actions
for process improvement or to evaluate the impact of derived actions from a business efficiency perspective.

Interaction of business processes and analytical information is also a concern
of OpBI. OpBI analyzes efficiency of process activities and involves influencing
perspectives into consideration [10]. This determines the (in)efficiency of actions
and opportunities to improve these actions. Existing studies of OpBI consider services from a technological and an organizational point of view. There are two contributions on achievement of service level agreements by providing cloud-based
solutions [22, 23]. [14] study usability of OpBI for an incremental service innovation from organization's perspective, i.e. use of BI to develop and provide new
services. In context of resource allocation, [12] provide a decision tree application
to support call center operations. This examines the need of OpBI for measurement
and controlling of indicators influencing service levels. However, these findings
cannot be used to estimate the role of OpBI for configuration or evaluation of
actions in service provision.

Especially contributions of Marjanovic emphasize an integration potential of
OpBI regarding knowledge intensive processes in service provision [16] and provide an integration framework beyond technological aspects in order to get a holistic view on service decisions [17, 18]. This provides a theoretical basis for interaction of business processes and analytical information about customers. [18]
points out that this basis needs to be enriched by exploring practical-oriented BI
applications in service organizations.

Research method

The paper follows principles of case study research according to [26]. We use
thereby a single case including two embedded units of analysis. The case study
approach is chosen according to *future work suggestions* of [18] in order to explore
experiences about integrating external customer knowledge. We conduct therefore
a representative case study concerning service processes of a general agency of a
large insurance group. Representative status refers to the circumstance that insurance companies typically execute services by a multitude of general agencies performing commonly acquisition of new customers, support of existing customers
and claim settlement. There is a conceptual and an application phase in the method
of this case study (cf. Figure 3).

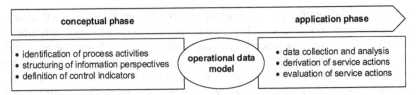

Figure 3. Research method

The conceptual phase contains an identification of business process activities, a structuring of corresponding information perspectives and a definition of control indicators. These research actions were guided by semi-structured expert interviews according to [8]. In two separate 1 to 2 hour interviews with respectively a senior manager, two sales representatives, and one back office employee, we recorded and documented all insurance activities, in which customer information needs to be integrated. After this activity identification, we conducted a second round of interviews, in which we consulted two individual clients and one business client additionally in order to structure different perspectives involved in the business process. The insights of all interviews were consolidated. Together with the senior manager, we defined control indicators in context of service quality and process efficiency. We set up an operational data model including two analysis contexts for service quality actions and actions to sustain or increase business volumes based on the given information. This model was finally discussed and consolidated together with the senior manager and the sales representatives.

During application phase, the operational data model was used to collect and analyze data for different insurance scenarios. The operational data model provided a functional/organizational reference in order to assign and integrate different process perspectives of insurance operations. The actual collection and analysis was realized by existing software and hardware components of the insurance agency. The analysis results of the collected data provided input for derivation of service actions regarding customer liaison and support. Impact and efficiency was evaluated by cost comparisons and personal expertise of the senior manager and the sales representatives.

Results

The case study company is a general agency of a large insurance group. The company is a self-contained sales partner and distributes insurance products on behalf of the insurance group. Strategic goals for exclusive distribution are targeted by the insurance group. These strategic goals concern expansion of profit yielding customer portfolios, optimization of trading results, and establishment of excellent business processes. Activities of the general agency have an operational character to fulfill the strategic goals by efficient service actions. They defined the need to conclude insurance contracts for different product lines with commercial and individual customers. Certain premium targets must be achieved for each product line. A key indicator is the cross-selling ratio, which reflects the ratio of subscribed contracts and supported customers. But additionally, the general agency coordinates and supervises insurance claims of their customers.

Three freelancing sales representatives are organized in the case study company, in which one sales representative is heading the general agency. He employs one back office staff member. The agency supports more than 1,800 customers and achieves a cross-selling ratio of 1.8 contracts per customer. An important management issue is the compensation of expiring insurance contracts. This affects the beginning of payment periods or loss of customers. Therefore, the agency needs to increase the cross-selling rate so that a customer subscribes a couple of long-term insurance contracts. Additionally, sales representatives have to avoid premature dismissals. For that reasons, the general agency needs an IT system for a comprehensive consideration and analysis of their customers. The following sections demonstrate the conceptualization of such an IT system.

Conceptual insights to build an operational data model in an insurance context

The major concern of the general insurance agency is interaction of sales representatives, customers, and back office. Customers interact with sales representatives, back office employees, or call center agents of the insurance group. This requires a coordination and unification of customer information from general agency's perspective. It is important to consider diverse requirements and situational aspects of customers in context of product line specific insurance contracts.

Integrating customer information into service provision will be possible, if the insurance staff comes into contact with their customers. A communication can be initiated from both parties. The insurance agency needs an establishment of contacts and agreement to conversation dates in order to maintain existing contracts or to offer new insurance products. Thereby, integration of customer information guides an initiation and conducting of those sales conversations. Customers contact the insurance agency in case of informal requests, loss occurrences, or claim settlements. Table 2 contains typical concerns from insurance agency and from customer perspective in order to structure different information perspectives and in order to define control indicators.

Table 2. Concerns of insurance agency and their customers

		interaction from	
		insurance agency to customer	**customer to insurance agency**
concerns from the perspective of the	insurance agency	Which customer information (core data, customer history) are already available? How much premium results from a customer? Which customers have not been consulted, yet? Were there any appointments with the customer before? When is the customer on call? Why do customers refuse calls for conversations? What are the appointment costs? What will be the potential income of a sales conversation? What are optimal access paths to new customers? What is the ratio of initiation to answering about an insurance contract?	Which customer is calling and what are the reasons for the call? Have there been similar requests? Has the customer reported on this matter before? What information provides the customer? Can the insurance agency manage the matter for its own or do they need to forward the request to the head quarter of the insurance group? Are there tasks or information, which have to be coordinated in context of the customer request? Does the customer signal problems to pay the insurance premiums? Does the customer want to cancel an insurance contract?
	customer	What is the reason for the call? What are the benefits and the necessary premiums for the new product? How long is the conversation? What information needs to be provided?	What and how much the insurance will pay? How long takes the processing of insurance claims? Are the cases completed in a timely manner? Who is authorized to remedy the damage?

The customer is interested in characteristics of insurance products and the nature of handling claims and requests. It becomes evident during the interviews that these are significant issues related to perceived service quality. In comparison, the insurance agency has complex issues to measure performance of service provision and to clearly assign responsibilities. This requires a comprehensive and consistent consideration of premiums and economically important cost factors. The control levels encompass customers, insurance contracts, time-related scenarios, and sales partners on a varying level of detail. Figure 4 demonstrates relationships to achieve an integrative control in context of insurance agency operations.

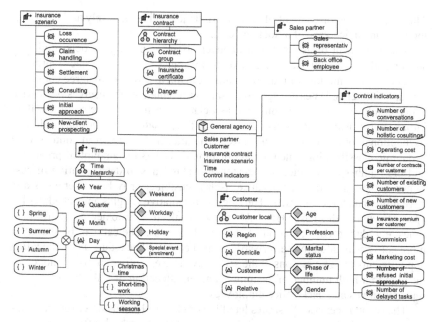

Figure 4. Operational data model for the insurance agency

The operational data model is represented by using ADAPT notation to focus on non-technological aspects of the insurance agency. The model combines four functional dimensions, a time dimension, and one dimension for control indicators. Time periods and special events play an important role within the model to determine reachability aspects of customers. Time-related information need to be considered together with different scopes of customer information. Insurance scenarios consider interaction from insurance agency to customer and vice versa. The dimension sales partner demonstrates contact interfaces of customers to the insurance agency. This illustrates organizational units, which have to integrate and exchange customer information. Thereby, insurance contracts are the relevant sales and maintenance objects. These contracts need to be analyzed on a different level of detail from risk up to contract clusters. Control indicators represent measurement parameters for service quality and efficiency. The following section describes an application of the operational data model in order to configure and evaluate service actions.

Application scenarios of OpBI in insurance agency operations

Two different scenarios of the insurance agency exemplify the application of OpBI. The first scenario concerns planning and scheduling of sales conversations.

The focus is on improvement of service efficiency and respectively an increase of incomes and a decrease of associated cost.

The agreement of as many sales conversations as possible is determining to sustain and increase business success of the insurance agency. The sales representatives need information for reasons of unsuccessful approaches to agree conversation appointments. Dates are agreed by sale representatives themselves or by back office employees. Time, reasons, and associated expenses will be recorded, if an initial approach fails. Reasons can be of different nature, e.g. holidays, illness, occupational, or personal circumstances. The information are set in context to an economic classification. Such a classification considers the amount of premiums and the number of contracts per customers. This leads to determination of customer groups, in which for instance A-class-customers pay high premiums and have more than three contracts. The sales representative weights and schedules his appointments on this basis. He is able to avoid calls to a customer at inconvenient times, e.g. due to consideration of shift work periods. The call can be placed in more convenient situations afterwards. Travel costs will be reduced by scheduling appointments in same regions at the same day. These configurations are not obvious due to a high number of customers and an allocation of tasks between sales representatives and back office employees.

The second scenario illustrates handling of claims. The customer reports damages to central office employees, sales representatives, or back office employees of the insurance agency. The damage gets recorded and indicated for further handling. If the customer calls the central office of the insurance group, damage information will be forwarded to the insurance agency. During damage recording, it has to be clear whether the customer has already reported the damage elsewhere and whether these statements coincide. The back office employee creates a claim file and checks conditions for regulation. Depending on amount of loss or damage, regulation is carried out by the insurance agency or the central office of the insurance group. The agency has to meet deadlines in context of claim file preparation and verification. It is important to identify and record reasons for any delays in order to accelerate handling times. The state of reported claims will be monitored and controlled, if the central office processes the claim settlement. The insurance agency has to broach the subject in case of delay. If a full loss adjustment is not possible (as a result of claim review), the insurance agency will use the economic classification of customers (A-class-customers) for a consideration of goodwill aspects. The configuration of service actions in context of claim settlement differs by type or extent of damage, underlying policy as well as customer information and behavior. The insurance agency processes more than 50 claims per month on average. Thereby, loss or damage occurrences concentrate within different periods of the year (e.g. automobile or personal accidents during winter months). This requires a customer-specific control to achieve a fast and well-founded claim settlement.

Both illustrated application scenarios can be abstracted to a closed loop as it is constituted in Figure 5.

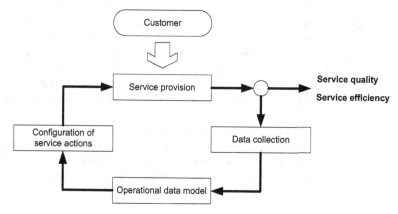

Figure 5. Closed loop to manage insurance agency operations

The controlled system is the service provision in an insurance context, which is influenced by customer information. The control variables are representing service quality to meet customer expectations and service efficiency from insurance agency perspective. During service provision, a collection and integration of customer information happens for different insurance contexts. The control unit is the operational data model. This model allows a combination of customer and agency information in consideration of control indicators. This enables configuration of service actions according to analysis results derived from the operational data model. These service actions have an influence on the service provision and an impact on service quality, and service efficiency aspects, too.

Discussion of the application scenarios

The sales representatives experience a better coordination of dates. This is expressed by a decrease of cost for initial approaches. The agency could achieve savings of cost and time of about approximately 15 percent. An essential point in the opinion of the sales representatives is that they attracted their customers more efficiently than before. The interviewed customers gave also a positive feedback so that claims were handled to their satisfaction and handling times could be accelerated. The senior manager and the sales representatives agreed that the service actions would not be taken without analyzing and processing customer information by the use of the operational data model.

However, the derived service actions differ in their effect. The configuration was not always equally successful. The insurance agency has initially assumed that integration of customer information and especially data collection is the main issue in the application phase. This assumption can be reasoned by the high amount of information, which needs to be recorded by the back office employee or the sales representatives. But, there were less integration points and data collection problems than previously thought. It was surprising that inherently consistent and obviously customer-tailored service actions remained unsuccessful. Sometimes, the sales representatives have consciously decided against a configured service action, because they were able to estimate the customer and his behavior due to their wealth of experience. There are obviously cases, in which a customer behaves different to that what is derived from provided information. This points out that an evaluation of customer information is beneficial next to integration concerns.

The senior manager of the insurance agency expects also an increase of global key indicators like cross selling rate and annual bonus. However, these effects cannot be measured due to the rather short period of application, yet. The insurance agency posits therefore an application period of at least one year to achieve certain effects.

Conclusion

OpBI supports service provision of a general insurance agency in favor of an increased service quality and higher process efficiency. It allows identification of customer-tailored service actions. Due to application of OpBI, the customer is reached more efficient. This increases new business volume by a customer-specific initiation and service scheduling and customer requests are treated faster and more efficient. An interaction between conceptualization and application of OpBI happens. This enables a continuous improvement of process controlling by adaptations of the underlying data model.

The considered customer information (e.g. reasons for conversation dismissals or statements to claims) in the investigated insurance context is thereby not complicated and complex. Complexity arises instead, because information needs to be combined, assigned, and coordinated constantly recurring but in changing circumstances. The benefit from the demonstrated case study is that OpBI provides decision making capabilities in services through

- a structuring and a clear assignment of different information perspectives,

- and a facilitation of straightforward management actions,

- which is guided by a stringent necessity for a critical appraisal of analysis results based on gained experiences.

The case study consolidates and enhances theoretical considerations regarding OpBI and knowledge intensive service processes. This allows a consideration of OpBI beyond a technological point of view. Thereby, an issue is investigated, which was not discussed in the scientific literature, yet. For this reason, this is the first case study allowing a detailed understanding of OpBI's application in service provision. This is relevant for researchers, because it builds up a reference for further applications of OpBI in service industry. Decision makers can learn about opportunities to reduce uncertainties in a customer-focused and also value-oriented service process control. This is thereby only a single case study, which provides adaptable results for insurance industry. Further case studies in different industries are beneficial in order to achieve generalizable results for OpBI in customer-centric service provision. However, the conducted case study represents a typical case in insurance industry with inherent interaction of customers and service providers that characterizes any service provision context. Therefore, especially elements of the conceptual approach have a general relevance in order to explain an application of OpBI in service provision.

Further research activities should investigate more applications of OpBI. Next to further successful applications, cases are of interest, in which application is impossible or inadequate. This will provide knowledge about reasons, preconditions, and basic conditions for a BI-oriented decision making in business processes of service providers.

References

1. AIS 2014. "MIS Journal Rankings," available online: http://aisnet.org/?JournalRankings, last accessed: 2014-04-16.
2. Bucher, T., Gericke, A., and Sigg, S. 2009. "Process-centric business intelligence," *Business Process Management Journal* (15:3), pp. 408-429.
3. Clavier, P. R., Lotriet, H. H., and van Loggerenberg, J. J. 2012. "Business Intelligence Challenges in the Context of Goods- and Service-Dominant Logic," in *Proceedings of the 45th Hawaii International Conference on System Science (HICSS)*, Maui, HI, pp. 4138-4147.
4. Davis, J., Imhoff, C., and White, C. 2009. *Operational Business Intelligence: The State of the Art*, Boulder, CO: Beye NETWORK Research.
5. Dinter, B., and Stroh, F. 2009. "Design factors for service-oriented architecture applied to analytical information systems: An explorative analysis," in *Proceedings of the 16th European Conference on Information Systems*, Galway, Ireland, Paper 27.
6. Felden, C., Chamoni P., and Linden M. 2010. "From Process Execution towards a Business Process Intelligence," in *Proceedings of the 13th International Conference on Business Information Systems*, W. Abramowicz, and R. Tolksdorf (eds.), Berlin, Germany, pp. 195-206.
7. Fitzsimmons, J. A., and Fitzsimmons, M. J. 2001. *Service Management: Operations, Strategy, and Information Technology*, 3rd Edition, New York, NY: McGraw-Hill.
8. Flick, U. 2004. *A Companion to Qualitative Research*, London: SAGE.
9. Golfarelli, M., Rizzi, S., and Cella, I. 2004. "Beyond data warehousing: what's next in business intelligence?," in *Proceedings of 7th ACM international workshop on Data warehousing and OLAP*, New York, NY: ACM Press, pp. 1-6.
10. Hänel, T., and Felden, C. 2012. "Towards a Stability of Process-Oriented Decision Support Concepts Using the Example of Operational Business Intelligence," in *Proceedings of the Pre-ICIS BI Congress 3: Driving Innovation through Big Data Analytics*, Orlando, FL, Paper 118.
11. Juan-Verdejo, A., and Baars, H. 2012. "Decision support for partially moving applications to the cloud: the example of business intelligence," in *Proceedings of the 2013 international workshop on Hot topics in cloud services*, New York, NY, pp. 35-42.
12. Kyper, E. S., Douglas, M. J., and Lievano, R. J. 2009. "Operational Business Intelligence: Applying Decision Trees to Call Centers," in *Proceedings of the Proceedings of the 15th Americas Conference on Information Systems*, San Francisco, CA, Paper 101.

13. Kueng, P., and Krahn, A. 1999. "Building a Process Performance Measurement System: some early experiences," *Journal of Scientific & Industrial Research* (58:3/4), pp. 149-159.
14. Maghrabi, R. O., Oakley, R. L., Thambusamy, R., and Iyer, L. 2011. "The Role of Business Intelligence (BI) in Service Innovation: An Ambidexterity Perspective," in *Proceedings of the 17th Americas Conference on Information Systems*, Detroit, MI, Paper 319.
15. Mahmoud, T., Marx Gómez, J., Rezgui, A., Peters, D., and Solsbach, A. 2012. "Enhanced BI Systems With On-Demand Data Based On Semantic-Enabled Enterprise SOA," in *Proceedings of the 20th European Conference On Information Systems*, Barcelona, Spain, Paper 184.
16. Marjanovic, O. 2007. "The Next Stage of Operational Business Intelligence: Creating New Challenges for Business Process Management," in *Proceedings of the 40th Annual Hawaii International Conference on System Sciences*, Washington DC: IEEE Computer Society, p. 215c.
17. Marjanovic, O. 2009. "Looking Beyond Technology: A Framework for Business Intelligence and Business Process Management Integration," in *Proceedings of the 22nd Bled eConference*, Bled, Slovenia, Paper 18.
18. Marjanovic, O. 2010. "Business Value Creation through Business Processes Management and Operational Business Intelligence Integration," in *Proceedings of the 43rd Hawaii International Conference on System Sciences (HICSS)*, Honolulu, HI, pp. 1-10.
19. Melchert, F., Winter, R., and Klesse, M. 2004. „Aligning Process Automation and Business Intelligence to Support Corporate Performance Management," in *Proceedings of the 10th Americas Conference on Information Systems*, New York, NY, Paper 507.
20. Padmanabhan, B., Hevner A., Cuenco, M., and Shi, C. 2011. "From information to operations: Service quality and customer retention," *ACM Transactions on Management Information Systems (TMIS)* (2:4), pp. 1-21.
21. Parasuraman, A., Zeithaml, V. A., and Berry, L. L. 1985. "A Conceptual Model of Service Quality and Its Implications for Future Research," *Journal of Marketing* (49:4), pp. 41-50.
22. Seibold, M., Kemper, A., and Jacobs, D. 2011. "Strict SLAs for Operational Business Intelligence," in *Proceedings of the IEEE International Conference on Cloud Computing (CLOUD)*, Washington, DC, pp. 25-32.
23. Seibold, M., Jacobs, D., and Kemper, A. 2013. "Operational Business Intelligence: Processing Mixed Workloads," *IT Professional* (15:5), pp. 16-21.
24. Silva, E., Becker, K., Galante, R. 2013. "Supporting Strategic Decision Making on Service Evolution Context Using Business Intelligence," in *Proceedings of the IEEE International Conference on Services Computing (SCC)*, Santa Clara, CA, pp. 240-247.
25. Wixom, B. H., and Watson, H. J. 2010. "The BI-Based Organization," *International Journal of Business Intelligence Research*, (1:1), pp. 13-28.
26. Yin, R. K. 2009. *Case Study Research: Design and Methods*, 4th edition, Los Angeles: SAGE.

4.4 Gestaltungsperspektiven einer Operational Business Intelligence

Die untersuchten Charakteristika der OpBI im Rahmen einer Analyse und Steuerung von Geschäftsprozessen bilden das Fundament für eine gestaltungsorientierte Betrachtung im weiteren Forschungsverlauf. Dabei liegt der Fokus auf der Erarbeitung eines fachlichen Modellierungsansatzes (Beitrag 14 und Beitrag 15) sowie in der prototypischen Umsetzung eines OpBI-Systems (Beitrag 16), um die Leistungsfähigkeit von Geschäftsprozessen zu bestimmen und darauf aufbauend Steuerungsmaßnahmen abzuleiten.

4.4.1 Modellierungsorientierte Gestaltung

Beitrag 14 und Beitrag 15 diskutieren eine fachliche Strukturierung operativer Informationen zur Modellierung von OpBI-Systemen im Kontext von praktischen Anwendungsfällen. Diese Diskussion hinsichtlich modellierungsorientierter Aspekte baut auf den Erkenntnissen der Beiträge 5 bis 13 auf. Im Mittelpunkt der Betrachtung steht eine multidimensionale Aufbereitung von operativen Daten (Beitrag 5 und Beitrag 6), die sowohl im Produktionsumfeld (Beiträge 7 bis 12) als auch im Dienstleistungsbereich (Beitrag 13) Anwendung finden kann.

4.4.1.1 Kurzdarstellung Beitrag 14

Beitrag 14 diskutiert als dreiseitiger Aufsatz für eine Praktikerzeitschrift die Notwendigkeit einer fachlichen Strukturierung von operativen Informationen, um die Leistungsfähigkeit wertschaffender Prozesse zu unterstützen. Dadurch kann ein Unternehmen den Einsatz von OpBI an seinen konkreten betriebswirtschaftlichen Problemstellungen ausrichten. Beitrag 14 beschreibt anhand einer einführenden Fallstudie aus der Metallverarbeitung (vgl. Beitrag 12), wie ein operatives Geschäftsszenario in ein fachliches Datenmodell überführt werden kann. Die Untersuchungsergebnisse implizieren einen weiteren Forschungsbedarf hinsichtlich der Modellierung von OpBI-Systemen, um die Integration analytischer Systeme und operativer Geschäftsszenarien zu verbessern.

4.4.1.2 Beitrag 14: Operational Business Intelligence[14]

Einleitung

Operational Business Intelligence (OpBI) adressiert die Analyse des aktuellen Tagesgeschäfts, um das Leistungspotential wertschaffender Prozesse auszuschöpfen [1]. Derartig umgesetzte Konzepte müssen mit der betriebswirtschaftlichen Motivation eines Unternehmens im Einklang stehen, so dass Entscheider ein System wie OpBI für die Leistungsanalyse der täglichen Aufgabenerfüllung nutzen. Das Ziel des Beitrages ist daher die Überführung von Geschäftsszenarien in ein fachliches Datenmodell im Rahmen einer Anwendung der OpBI.

Der Literatur über OpBI fehlt es gegenwärtig an einer Diskussion von fachlichen Ansätzen, die eine Ableitung von Analysestrukturen aus Geschäftsszenarien adressieren. Diese Diskussion ist wichtig, um den Nutzen oder die Hürden für eine Anwendung der OpBI ausgehend von der betriebswirtschaftlichen Motivation ei-

---

14 Hänel, T.; Felden, C.: Operational Business Intelligence. In: ERP Management 3, 2014.

nes Unternehmens abschätzen zu können. Es bedarf eines fachlichen Bezugs zwischen dem analytischen Modell für eine Datenverarbeitung im Rahmen von OpBI und der Wertschöpfungslogik eines Unternehmens. Zu diesem Zweck tragen wir zu einer Diskussion über die Strukturierung von Geschäftsszenarien zu Gunsten einer Leistungsanalyse von wertschaffenden Prozessen bei.

Kapitel 2 zeigt die Relevanz einer fachlichen Strukturierung in operativen Entscheidungssituationen auf. Anschließend erfolgen die Darstellung einer Fallstudie aus der metallverarbeitenden Industrie und ein Fazit.

Status quo

OpBI integriert und analysiert Daten zur Unterstützung operativer Entscheidungen [1]. Daraus lässt sich schließen, dass das Entscheidungsumfeld durch Anforderungen des operativen Managements bestimmt wird. Die Erfüllung wiederkehrender Aufgaben ist an dieser Stelle charakteristisch. Informationen sind detailliert vorzuhalten und der betreffende Sachverhalt präzise darzustellen. Operative Tätigkeiten beziehen schon aufgrund ihrer Position in der Unternehmenspyramide viele Anwender ein, die häufig Entscheidungen treffen. Ebenfalls charakterisierend ist, dass die Anwendungssysteme über längere Zeiträume genutzt und kontinuierlich angepasst werden.

OpBI-Systeme müssen Informationen aus dem operativen Entscheidungsumfeld derart aufbereiten, als dass ein Entscheidungsträger zeitnah sein Handlungserfordernis erkennen und geeignete Maßnahmen ableiten kann [1]. Mit abnehmender Strukturierung der Informationen besteht die Gefahr, dass fehlerhafte Entscheidungen getroffen werden und der Aufwand der Entscheidungsfindung zunimmt [2]. Diese Gefahr bezieht sich auf Entscheidungen, die aufgrund ihrer Häufigkeit einen signifikanten Einfluss auf ein Unternehmen haben.

OpBI ist hinsichtlich der Aufbereitung entscheidungsrelevanter Informationen mit dem Anspruch einer Reduktion von Latenzzeiten bis hin zu einer Datenverarbeitung in Echtzeit verbunden [1]. Allerdings begegnen IT-Systeme dieser Anforderung aus technischer Sicht schon eine längere Zeit. Seien es ursprünglich Datenbanktrigger und Spiegelungsmechanismen, so sind es heutzutage Frameworks wie Hadoop, die beispielsweise den Zugriff auf große Datenmengen ermöglichen [3]. In-Memory-Datenbanken können transaktionale und analyseorientierte Datenstrukturen gleichermaßen berücksichtigen [4]. Die Integration von Daten lässt sich ebenso durch eine Virtualisierung verbessern [5]. Die technischen Entwicklungen fokussieren aber nur auf die Bereitstellung von Daten und sind anwendungsneutral hinsichtlich der Analyse eines operativen Entscheidungsumfelds. Dieses Umfeld hängt jedoch von der Wertschöpfungslogik eines Unternehmens ab und ist nicht per se für ein technisches System zugänglich. Daher wird im Folgenden anhand einer Fallstudie aufgezeigt, wie ein operatives Geschäftsszenario in ein fachliches Datenmodell überführt und als IT-basiertes Arbeitssystem beschrieben werden kann.

Fallstudie Metallverarbeitung

Das hier betrachtete Unternehmen führt Lohnfertigungsaufträge für den allgemeinen und spezialisierten Maschinenbau aus. Die Untersuchung erfolgt in drei Phasen: (1) Beschreibung des Geschäftsszenarios, (2) Erstellung des fachlichen Datenmodells und (3) Beschreibung des IT-basierten Arbeitssystems.

Beschreibung des Geschäftsszenarios

Die Beschreibung des Geschäftsszenarios wird mit e³value [6] durchgeführt. Es schließt die wertschaffenden Aktivitäten eines Unternehmens sowie extern beteiligte Akteure und Marktteilnehmer ein. Das Geschäftsszenario des metallverarbeitenden Unternehmens ist in Bild 1 dargestellt.

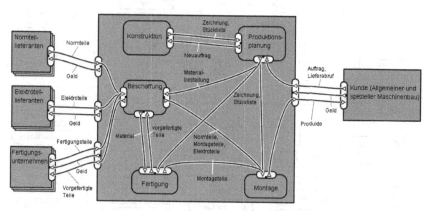

Bild 1. Beschreibung des Geschäftsszenarios

Die Fertigung umfasst typische Aktivitäten der Metallverarbeitung, die in entsprechenden Bearbeitungszentren ausgeführt werden. Die gefertigten Einzelteile werden zu Baugruppen oder Endprodukten montiert. Die Montage schließt eine Farbgebung und Funktionstests ein. Die fortlaufende Qualitätskontrolle ist Aufgabe der ausführenden Mitarbeiter. Ein Qualitätsmanager entscheidet über das Verfahren bei Qualitätsmängeln und nimmt Zwischen- und Endkontrollen vor.

Die Herstellung der Produkte wird von verschiedenen Faktoren beeinträchtigt. Zu nennen sind hier von externer Seite der Widerruf von Kundenaufträgen oder Schwierigkeiten von Lieferanten und externen Fertigungsunternehmen. Intern werden die Vorgänge von Fehlfunktionen oder Ausfällen von Maschinen sowie mitarbeiterbedingt beeinflusst. Bild 1 zeigt die Abhängigkeiten zwischen den Aktivitäten und beteiligten Akteuren. Dies spiegelt den Austausch von Objekten wider, die zur Produktherstellung unerlässlich sind. Die in Bild 1 dargestellten Komponenten der Wertschaffung und deren Abhängigkeiten sind Kernelemente für eine Analyse des Geschäftsszenarios.

Erstellung des fachlichen Datenmodells

Zu Gunsten der Modellerstellung wird auf die ADAPT-Notation [7] zurückgegriffen, welche die Erstellung eines fachlichen Datenmodells zur Strukturierung von Informationen hinsichtlich der wertschaffenden Aktivitäten unterstützt. Bild 2 zeigt das Datenmodell des metallverarbeitenden Unternehmens. Die zugrunde liegende IT-Infrastruktur umfasst ein ERP-System mit einer integrierten Maschinen- und Betriebsdatenerfassung. Jeder Arbeitsplatz erfasst die Ist-Daten der Produktion an einem Terminal.

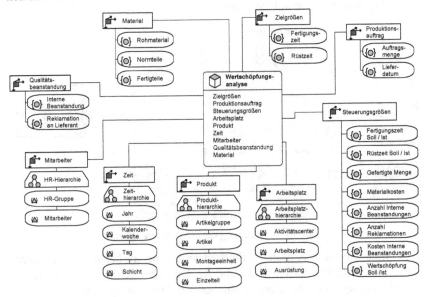

Bild 2. Fachliches Datenmodell

Das Datenmodell ermöglicht die anteilige Verrechnung der erzielten Wertschöpfung eines Zeitraums auf Aktivitäten zur Herstellung eines Produkts. Dies misst den schrittweisen Wertzuwachs bei der Herstellung eines Bauteils und während der Montage des Endprodukts. Die Erfüllung von Wertschöpfungszielen ist über den gesamten Herstellungsprozess nachvollziehbar. Damit können z. B. Gegenmaßnahmen oder Kompensationsleistungen eingeleitet werden, insofern die Zielvorgaben nicht erreichbar sind. Die in Bild 2 gezeigten Dimensionen unterstützen eine Ursachenanalyse auf unterschiedlichen Detaillierungsstufen.

Beschreibung des IT-basierten Arbeitssystems

Die dritte Phase stellt einen Bezug zum Arbeitssystem-Ordnungsrahmen her, der sich für eine Beschreibung von IT-basierten Arbeitssystemen eignet [8]. Die Wertschaffungslogik eines Unternehmens wird als Arbeitssystem verstanden. Die Innensicht bilden Mitarbeiter, die Aktivitäten oder Prozesse unter Verwendung von Technologien und Informationen ausführen. Dies ist vergleichbar mit den wertschaffenden Aktivitäten im Kontext von e³value. Das Ergebnis der Aktivitäten sind Produkte oder Services für den Kunden. Die Innensicht sowie der Wertaustausch werden von den Marktteilnehmern, den Ressourcen der Infrastruktur und den strategischen Zielen beeinflusst. Bild 3 zeigt das Zusammenspiel des Geschäftsszenarios mit dem fachlichen Datenmodell des metallverarbeitenden Unternehmens unter Berücksichtigung des Arbeitssystem-Ordnungsrahmen.

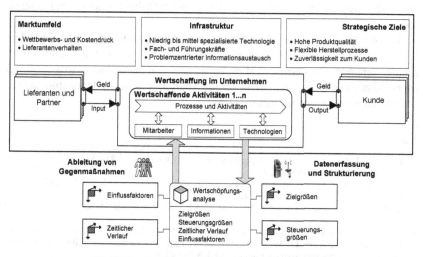

Bild 3. Beschreibung des IT-basierten Arbeitssystems

Das Unternehmen bietet Fertigungsprodukte für Geschäftskunden an. Die untersuchten Prozesse und Aktivitäten sind deterministisch und wiederholbar. Trotzdem ist der Ablauf der durchzuführenden Tätigkeiten variabel und hängt vom Wissen der ausführenden Mitarbeiter ab. Die zur Analyse des Szenarios notwendigen Informationen sind Zielgrößen und Steuerungsparameter sowie betroffene Ressourcen, Produkte oder Akteure. Aus IT-Sicht sind Systeme zur Verwaltung und Erfassung von Produktionsdaten im betrachteten System involviert.

Die Anforderungen des Marktumfeldes wachsen stetig. Damit ist ein erhöhter Wettbewerbs- und Kostendruck verbunden. Eine wesentliche Rolle spielt dabei das Verhalten der Zulieferer und externen Fertigungsunternehmen. Strategische Ziele des Lohnfertigers sind eine hohe Produktqualität, flexible Herstellprozesse und Zuverlässigkeit zum Kunden. Die Infrastruktur des Arbeitssystems umfasst niedrig bis mittel spezialisierte Technologien. Fach- und Führungskräfte tauschen Informationen problemzentriert untereinander aus.

Fazit

Unternehmen können ihre operative Entscheidungsfindung durch analytische Konzepte wie OpBI unterstützen. Allerdings wird dies nur von Vorteil sein, wenn das analytische Modell mit der Wertschöpfungslogik eines Unternehmens übereinstimmt. Der Beitrag nimmt daher eine betriebswirtschaftliche Perspektive ein, um eine fachliche Diskussion zur Integration von Analysesystemen mit operativen Geschäftsszenarien anzuregen. Methodisch wird auf die Modellierung mithilfe von e³value und ADAPT zurückgegriffen. Der Ansatz wurde im Rahmen einer Fallstudie angewendet und mit dem Arbeitssystem-Ordnungsrahmen in Bezug gesetzt.

Es besteht weiterer Forschungsbedarf in der Konsolidierung fachlicher Überlegungen zu Gunsten einer Integration analytischer Systeme und operativer Geschäftsszenarien. Dies ermöglicht es, ausgehend von der betriebswirtschaftlichen Motivation eines Unternehmens, neuartige Analysesysteme zur Unterstützung von operativen Entscheidungen einzusetzen.

Literatur

1. Davis, J., Imhoff, C., White, C.: Operational Business Intelligence: The State of the Art. Beye NETWORK Research, Boulder, 2009
2. Hänel, T., Schulz, M.: Is There Still a Need for Multidimensional Data Models. In: 22nd European Conference on Information Systems, Tel Aviv, 2014
3. McAfee, A., Brynjolfsson, E.: Big Data: The Management Revolution. Harvard Business Review 90, 60–66, 2012
4. Loos, P., Lechtenbörger, J., Vossen, G., Zeier, A., Krüger, J., Müller, J., Lehner, W., Kossmann, D., Fabian, B., Günther, O., Winter, R.: In-memory Databases in Business Information Systems. Business & Information Systems Engineering 3, 389–395, 2011
5. Van der Lans, R.: Data Virtualization for Business Intelligence Systems: Revolutionizing Data Integration for Data Warehouses. Morgan Kaufmann, Waltham, 2012
6. Gordijn, J.: e-Business value modelling using the e³value ontology. In: Currie, W. (ed.) Value Creation from e-business models, 98–127, Elsevier, Oxford, 2004
7. Getting Started with ADAPT. http://www.symcorp.com/downloads/ADAPT_white_paper.pdf, Letzter Zugriff: 25.08.2014
8. Alter, S.: Work System Theory: Overview of Core Concepts, Extensions, and Challenges for the Future. Journal of the Association for Information Systems 14, 72–121, 2013

4.4.1.3 Kurzdarstellung Beitrag 15

Die fachlichen Überlegungen zur Verknüpfung einer analytischen Systemgestaltung mit Anforderungen von operativen Geschäftsszenarien, die Beitrag 14 angeregt hat, werden in Beitrag 15 weiterführend konsolidiert. Es erfolgt die Betrachtung eines Anforderungsmanagements für die Entwicklung von OpBI-Systemen aus einer Geschäftsmodell-, einer Geschäftsprozess- und einer IT-Systemperspektive. Beitrag 15 präsentiert die Erarbeitung eines fachlichen Ansatzes für die Modellierung von Datenbankanwendungen im Kontext der OpBI (IT-System) auf Grundlage einer Kombination der e³value-Methode (Geschäftsmodell) mit dem Work-System-Framework (Geschäftsprozess). Die gemeinsame Betrachtung von e³value und dem Work-System-Framework ermöglicht eine Verknüpfung von strategischen und prozessualen Aspekten zu Gunsten einer Analyse und Steuerung von Geschäftsprozessen. Diese Aspekte fließen in die darunterliegende OpBI-Perspektive ein, die durch ein ADAPT-Modell dargestellt wird. Dieses Modell stellt ein Instrument für eine Sammlung, Strukturierung und Analyse von Geschäftsprozessdaten zur Verfügung, um leistungsorientiert Steuerungsmaßnahmen ableiten zu können.

Die Ergebnisse von Beitrag 15 stehen methodisch in Bezug zu einer Aktionsforschung. Die Entwicklung und die Anwendung des dargestellten Modellierungsansatzes werden in vier verschiedenen Anwendungsbereichen aus dem Produktions- und Dienstleistungsumfeld demonstriert. Die Grundlage der Untersuchung sind vier Geschäftsszenarien, die in Beitrag 12 und in Beitrag 13 vorgestellt wurden. Die Aktionsforschungszyklen zeigen methodische und organisatorische Aspekte auf, um die Gestaltung von OpBI-Systemen am Geschäftsmodell eines spezifischen Unternehmens auszurichten. Im Zuge der Untersuchung kristallisieren sich unternehmensspezifische und allgemeingültige Aspekte heraus, die für eine Leistungsmessung von Geschäftsprozessen mit OpBI relevant sind. Eine gemeinsame Betrachtung der Geschäftsmodell- und der Geschäftsprozessperspektive hat sich in allen vier Anwendungsbereichen als vorteilhaft für die logische Datenmodellierung von OpBI-Systemen erwiesen.

4.4.1.4 Beitrag 15: Linking Operational Business Intelligence with Value-Based Business Requirements[15]

Introduction

Organizations measure business processes using performance indicators in terms of time, quality, or cost [1]. The maintenance of performant business processes

---

15 Hänel, T.; Felden, C.: Linking Operational Business Intelligence with Value-based Business Requirements. In: 14th IFIP Conference on e-Business, e-Services and e-Society, Delft, Oktober, 2015

has to be closely linked to business strategy so that process improvements are valuable and lead to competitive advantages [2]. Management activities of process performance are thereby associated with IT to collect and analyse data about business processes [3]. Such IT capabilities need to be correspondent and compatible to business strategy, too, to avoid missing of expected performance results [2]. One possible concept to analyse business processes is OpBI dealing with an integration of daily business data [4]. This supports business operation's managers in gaining relevant knowledge to evaluate business process performances [5]. Management actions taken in consequence of an OpBI-reliant decision making have to bring benefits to the manner of an organization creating value in its business environment. The paper's goal is therefore to investigate a linkage of OpBI with firm-specific business requirements.

The current discussion about OpBI provides no conceptual insights to consider business requirements for designing analytical systems in a particular case. For instance, analysis requirements of insurance companies differ from issues of automotive suppliers from business perspective, although technical system components can be quite similar. It is not obvious for application developers, how an OpBI system needs to be logically designed in order to maintain and improve performant business processes from a perspective of business operation's managers. A specification of OpBI systems can benefit from a value-based requirements engineering so that business value models initialize requirements for business processes and IT systems [6]. We investigate such a value-based requirements definition for OpBI systems and propose an approach to link logical design of analytical databases with firm-specific business value models. The paper contributes with a development and an application of our approach to a scientific discussion using participatory action research in context of four different organizations. This offers collaborative insights for research and practice to the discourse about business approaches so that operational management actions are beneficial for performant business processes.

Chapter 2 refines the problem of research and analyses related areas. The research method is presented in Chapter 3. Chapter 4 introduces our approach and Chapter 5 reports on its application during an action research project in four different business scenarios. Finally, a conclusion summarizes findings and further research activities.

Status quo

OpBI is understood as a decision support concept for business operation's managers to analyse business processes in favour of continuous improvements of process design and execution [4]. OpBI supports an identification of control actions based on timely relations between process performance and status of goal achievement. [5]

Problem refinement

OpBI integrates data emerging in or flowing into IT systems during operational task fulfilment [4], [5]. From a technical viewpoint, OpBI systems can be equipped with IT providing business operation's managers access to manifold sources of information and analytical options in combination with high performance data processing. The discussion about Hadoop [7], cloud computing [8], combinations of transactional and analytical databases [9], or data virtualization techniques [10] points to a variety of technical options. However, these advancements will only lead to a successful decision support, if performance analysis and action taking using an OpBI system is consistent to business goals and value creation processes. This requires a conceptual modelling of analytical requirements for OpBI systems in compliance with operational concerns of an organization. We conducted a literature review using the databases of Business Source Complete, IEEE, AIS, ACM, Emerald, and Science Direct to examine scientific publications according to MIS rankings [11]. The reviewed publications do not discuss a conceptual modelling of analytical requirements for a successful application of OpBI. A lack of discussion about conceptual modelling of operational information is evident, yet.

Related research areas

OpBI addresses performance management (PM), BI, and business process management (BPM) [12]. PM structures business strategies and translates them into goals and ratios [13]. Process PM (PPM) monitors business processes using performance indicators [14]. The PPM concept is not constrained to a specific IS support, but BPM or BI systems are discussed therein currently [1]. Monitoring business processes has a technical background coming from BPM perspective [15]. BPM systems log transactions and events for execution tracking and process modelling [16]. However, analysis of log data is limited, yet [17]. This extends especially in contexts of sophisticated processes with distributed tasks [18]. Due to an early stage of PM in the area of BPM, an integration of BI and BPM is taken into consideration [3]. From BI perspective, analysis of process data has a different focus. Business Process Intelligence supports design and redesign of an organization's processes [19]. This affects a small range of users making strategic or tactical decisions. In contrast, process-centric BI concerns an integration of BI applications into process execution [20]. This affects process performance due to accelerations and improvements in executing processes. BI provides analytical information to fulfil process-related tasks. This differs from our understanding of

OpBI in using BI techniques for analysis and control of business processes. Process-centric BI does not address a consideration of analytical information for an immediate measurement of process performance, an investigation of deviations, or a derivation of control actions.

Research method

We apply an action research method, because this has been used successfully to model business requirements and to align them with IT characteristics [6]. This is similar to our area of discourse by a conceptual modelling of OpBI systems. We extend the methodological knowledge and refer it to a participatory form of action research [21] - researchers and practitioners participate in a research process collectively. Collaboration allows a combination of modelling knowledge with practical experiences about analysing and controlling business processes. Action research supports a solution of immediate performance problems and a consolidation of conceptual knowledge on designing OpBI systems. Participatory action research has been successfully applied, too, in order to ensure that IT implementations result in business benefits [22]. Our intention is quite similar as we want to link conceptual design of OpBI systems with value-based business requirements. Therefore, we deduce a practicability of participatory action research to deliver a business contribution in consequence of an OpBI-reliant decision making. In a three-year research period, we performed an iterative and collaborative research process together with four organizations. Assumptions on designing OpBI systems were refined in cycles of diagnosis, action, evaluation, and reflective learning [21]. An approach to link value-based business models and OpBI systems emerged in consequence of our experiences. The approach builds upon the findings and a multi-perspective view on requirements engineering of Gordijn and Akkermans [6].

Linking value-based business models and OpBI systems

Our approach consists of different activities resulting in e³value modelling [6], a classification of business process requirements according to the work system framework [23] and ADAPT modelling [24]. Figure 1 classifies the elements of the approach into perspectives of a value-based requirements engineering [6].

Business model perspective	Business process perspective	OpBI system perspective
e³value	*Work system framework*	*ADAPT*
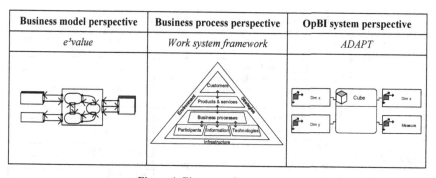		

Figure 1. Elements of our approach

An e³value model describes an exchange of value objects between business actors in a commercial network. Such a network consists for instance of an organization anywhere in a value chain with its potential customers and suppliers. Business actors with an equal value proposition can be grouped to market segments. Value objects to be exchanged in a commercial network are trading items (products, services) in consideration of economic equivalents (money). Value activities model specific performance areas, in which an organization creates or adds value to yield profits. To dig deeper in the particular mechanisms of value activities, we bridge to a consideration of business process perspective using the work system framework. Both approaches consider an internal and external view on organizations. Table 1 demonstrates the coincidence of e³value and the work system framework. A work system considers participants carrying out business processes by use of information and technology. These core elements of work system performance characterize together with general infrastructure components an insider's view on an organization's business value model. The performance output are products or services, which are objects of value exchange with customers and the value chain environment. Strategic considerations influence the insider's and the outsider's view regarding work system performance. We use elements of the work system framework and e³value to deduce requirements for an analysis and control of value activities from IT system perspective. Therefore, we use ADAPT notation to develop logical data models as measurement and structuring instrument for value activity information in operational decision contexts. The work system and e³value elements are assigned to dimensions and measures of an ADAPT model. The dimensions span a cube consisting of a set of measures having a clear reference to value objects of a business model. Relationships of dimensions and measures follow criteria of creating and exchanging values.

Table 1. Mapping of e³value and work system framework

View on organizations	Elements of e³value	Elements of work system framework
External	The whole e³value model	Strategies
	Customers, external stakeholders, partners, or suppliers modelled as market segments or actors	Environment, customers
	Value exchanges, especially value objects	Products & services
Internal	Concerning organization performing specific value activities	Infrastructure
	Value activities representing areas of performance	Business processes
		Participants
		Information
		Technologies

Action research results

We present results of an action research project that was carried out from August 2012 to February 2014 in Germany in order to develop and apply our linking approach. Four organizations participated in three subsequent cycles of action research. The considered organizations were a machine tool manufacturer, a service provider for IT and communication (ICT) products, a hydraulics engineering company, and an insurance agency. The first cycle refers to activities of interaction, application, and reflection from business model perspective and results in e³value models. The outcome of the second research cycle is represented by a work system classification. The third cycle of action research lead to ADAPT models for an OpBI database design. Illustrations of e³value and ADAPT models are presented only in context of the machine tool manufacturer due to the limited space of the paper.

Research cycle 1: Creation of value-based business models

Machine tool manufacturer

The organization modernizes gear hobbing machines. Equipment upgrades happen according to individual customer orders with negotiated budgets, period and quality requirements. Value activities (cf. Figure 2) include a deployment of new components, such as control units or milling heads. Once the transfer of a customer's machine happens, a dismantling in machine components takes place. Specific and standard parts are cleaned and listed. Employees record geometrical data and take pictures in case of incomplete drawings. Decisions about a rework or a remanufacturing depend on the machine state. Finally, execution of re-assembling happens. Disturbance variables are the individuality and the unpredictability of machines and their states. Different projects and suppliers must be coordinated in consideration of compliance with time and cost conditions.

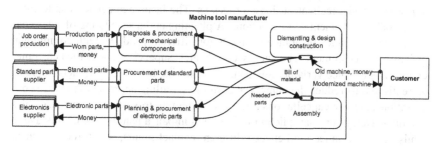

Fig. 2. e³value model of a machine tool manufacturer

ICT service provider

Logistical services are performed to distribute ICT products from different brands through different channels. Product procurement involves manufacturers or network operators. Devices are customized according to specified requirements, e.g. exchanges of electronic parts. A recovery resets returned devices to factory settings and performs functional checks. If, necessary, a partner company repairs defect devices. Final products are completed and packaged for shipment. Disturbance variables are fluctuating throughput quantities, a changing staff, heterogeneous products and fast price slumps. Especially velocity and cost efficiency are important control aspects.

Hydraulics engineering company

The organization produces hydraulic or pneumatic cylinders and job orders. The customer segment includes industrial trucks, rail vehicles, agricultural machinery, printing presses, or injection moulding machines. Manufacturing concerns activities of metal processing like milling, drilling, turning, welding, or laundry. The assembly of finished products includes functional tests, colouring, and shipment. A quality control records complaints during production and decides for rework, sorting, claim, or scrap. Disturbance variables are order withdrawals, missing materials, troubles of external manufacturers, unavailable labours, or malfunctions of e.g. automatic welders or CNC machining centres. Such disturbances lead to delays of planning cycles. Considering monthly value creation targets should overcome these uncertainties. This means that alternative outputs have to compensate adverse circumstances, if, for example, an order is cancelled.

Insurance agency

Insurance products are distributed on behalf of an insurance group. Strategic goals of the insurance group concern high premium customer portfolios, optimized trading results, and excellent business processes. The insurance agency has to fulfil these goals by efficient service actions. A planning and a scheduling of sales conversations concludes insurance contracts for different products with commercial or individual customers. The agency coordinates, supervises and settles customer claims. Disturbance variables are manifold. Expiring insurance contracts or premature dismissals reduce the number of customers. Failing approaches to agree conversation dates or cancellations counteract attempts to sustain or increase sales revenues. Delays or contradicting information impair a handling of claims due to a missing communication between different contact points, which record claims or requests.

Research cycle 2: Classification of business process characteristics

Table 2 classifies the studied organizations into the work system framework. The processes need to be dynamic with a certain variability. The business processes are deterministic and repeatable, while the performance results differ for changing situations. The tasks depend on knowledge and experience of employees executing, guiding, and instructing operational activities. The information refers to reference inputs, control indicators, resources, products, or stakeholders.

Table 2. Classification of case studies into work system framework

	Insurance Agency	Hydraulics engineer	Machine tool manufacturer	ICT service provider
Processes and activities	Consulting, claim settlement, sales conversations	Manufacturing, quality control, assembly	Dismantling, cleaning, rework, assembly	Customization, recovery, shipment
Participants	Senior manager, back office, representatives, call centre agents	Engineers, assemblers, operators, supervisors	Project teams with assemblers, engineers, project leader	Shop floor and temporary staff, supervisors and unit manager
Information	Customer records, availability and history, cross selling ratio, claims, expense ratios, premium targets and incomes, contracts	Time data, design drawings, bill of materials, defect reports, article data, consumption rates, target/ actual quantities, expense ratios, added value	Time data, design drawings, geometrical data, bill of materials, orders, delivery dates, quality indications, budged limits	Time data, expense ratios, target quantities, delivery dates, article master data, consumption rates, actual quantities, defective products
Technologies	Platform to prepare and manage proposals, policies issues, portfolios and accountings	ERP, Product data management, Machine data acquisition, Time keeping	ERP, Product data management, Time keeping, Project management system,	ERP, Warehouse management system, Machine data acquisition, Time keeping

	Insurance Agency	Hydraulics engineer	Machine tool manufacturer	ICT service provider
Infrastructure	Office equipment with interfaces to the insurance group, four employees	Office and production equipment, 100 employees, staff involvement	Office and production equipment, 70 employees, project hierarchies	Office and logistics equipment, 1,500 employees, flat hierarchies
Strategies	Increase of shareholder values, high premium customers	High quality, flexibility and velocity, reliability to customers	Specialization, focus on customer, undercutting of original prices	Diversification of sales, service and repair, high quality at low costs
Environment	Insurance group, financial markets, changing commercial and legal conditions, regional sales area	Supplier relations, high competitive pressure, growing international market	Supplier relations, high competitive pressure, deadline and cost pressure, international market	Supplier and partner relations, international market, varying order situations, fast slumps
Customers	Individual and business clients	Machine building companies	Metal processing companies	Retailers and resellers
Products and services	Insurance products, financial services	Hydraulic cylinder, job orders	Gear hobbing machines	ICT products

Information technologies mentioned in Table 2 refer to ERP, product data management, warehouse management, or collaborative portal solutions. Availability of data collection techniques is important. The infrastructure includes a low to medium specialized technical equipment. Human resources are specialists and executive staff organized in problem-oriented communication hierarchies. Customer relations are business-to-business and business-to-customer. The organizations offer specialized products or services in different price segments with a medium to high complexity. They have heterogeneous configurations and consist of sophisticated features. Their environment is characterized by competitive pressure and changing conditions in regional and international distribution areas. External factors concern behaviour of suppliers, partners, or associated companies. Strategies of the studied organizations include specialization, diversification, quality excellence, flexibility, velocity, and customer orientation.

Research cycle 3: Logical application design of OpBI systems

Machine tool manufacturer

The OpBI system supports budgeting and scheduling of modernization projects. Data gathering happens manually due to heterogeneity of working activities. A tracking system records corresponding working times. The database design (cf. Figure 3) points out expenses for performing value activities on different levels of detail. Planning and management of project workflows happen simultaneously. Current states of a machine, incurred costs, spent working times, and delivery progress of needed assemblies are demonstrated.

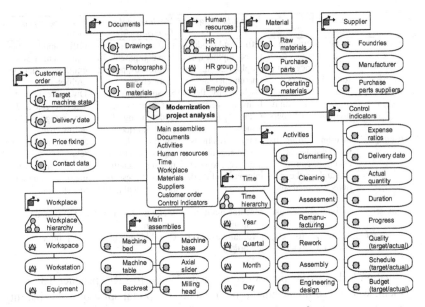

Figure 3. ADAPT model of a machine tool manufacturer

A comparison of actual performances to target indicators enables staff to intervene in case of deviations. Procurement combines supplier information with required rework orders and the quality of finished parts. This rating of providers eases a selection for similar constructed parts. Restored machine features of individual overhaul projects become comparable so that cost estimations are more confident.

ICT Service provider

The OpBI system evaluates cost transparency and efficiency to react fast and flexibly on changing order quantities. Affected IT systems are an ERP and a warehouse management system. Thereby, data collection occurs with scanners, light barriers, and a machine time tracking. The designed OpBI database provides a basis to derive management actions for an adjustment of order cycles according to product groups. The consequence is a coordination of logistical cost and product-specific price slumps. The data model facilitates a combination of production batches with similar or equal features to improve processing times. Faced by staff changes, performance targets are determined according to human resource groups. These targets depend on product groups and periods of employment. The calculation of product-specific delivery times leads to higher planning reliability as consequence of specifiable agreements for repair services in context of an outsourced repair service.

Hydraulics engineering company

The OpBI system determines a value added of manufacturing activities and cost ratios of quality issues. The underlying IT system refers to an ERP system with integrated data acquisition. Terminals collect production data using card readers and barcode scanners. A quality assurance tool collects internal quality complaints. The logical designed database supports an incremental accretion measurement of components and products during manufacturing and assembly. This ensures a constant review of value creation targets. Differences will lead to immediate decisions. A consideration of expenses to create specific features improves employment of resources, materials, and technologies. Constructors get information to determine prices for new products or add-ons during the design phase based on needed product features. Quality assurance derives actions by cost-by-cause principles using different process perspectives. The logical model enables a calculation of expenses for rework, sorting, or scrap for internal quality complaints.

Insurance agency

The OpBI system combines information of more than 1,800 customers with allocated service tasks. A platform for proposal preparation, policy issues, portfolio management, and accounting supports semi-standardized information records. Sales representatives or office employees enter this information manually. The OpBI's data model considers reasons for unsuccessful approaches to agree conversations. For example, holidays or shift work lead often to calls at inconvenient customer situations. The scheduling is managed according to reachability of customers, now, and appointments are located in nearby sales regions to reduce travel cost. The data model supports a customer-specific control of claim handling to achieve a well-founded settlement. This depends on extent of loss or damage, underlying insurance contracts, and customer behaviour. The agency monitors deadlines for claim review to accelerate handling times. It is measurable whether a customer has already reported claim information and how far such reports coincide. A comparison of monthly premiums with a number of contracts per customer leads to a prioritization of claims or a consideration of goodwill. This is beneficial to decide about win-back actions in notice management, too.

Lessons learned

The action research cycles demonstrate methodological and organizational issues to design OpBI database systems based on value-based business requirements. This delivers insights on measuring and evaluating performance of business processes in four business scenarios. The conjoint reflection of business models, business processes, and IT systems has proven to be advantageous. Valuable results were achieved in all four organizational settings despite of different situational characteristics. Figure 4 repeats the relation between the perspectives of our approach.

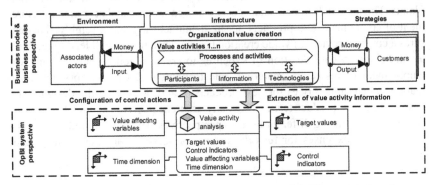

Figure 4. Relation of business model, business process, and OpBI system perspective

Joined elements of e³value and work systems link an organization's strategy with maintenance of performant business processes. The association to OpBI is represented at the bottom of Figure 4. ADAPT models are instruments to collect, elaborate, and analyse data about business processes and build the basis to configure management actions. An important aspect learned from our research is the context-sensitive enrichment of these common descriptive perspectives (cf. Table 3).

Table 3. Firm-specific and common aspects of our results

Firm-specific aspects	Common aspects
• Business contexts and strategies	• Methodological building blocks
• Business process descriptions	• Action research cycles
• Performance management situations	• Collaboration of research and practice
• OpBI database designs	• Business process orientation
• Management control actions	• Use of operational IT systems

The linkage of OpBI with firm-specific business requirements is irreducible complex by observational research methods, because it is necessary to involve situated and practical knowledge resulting from collaboration activities between researchers and practitioners. Participatory action research enables such a reference to practical contexts. Implications concerning a performance management of business processes depend thereby always on specific organizations. However, our conceptual findings allow a broader consensus on modelling OpBI systems, although they are not object of a rigorous generalization. Especially the work system framework helped us to learn about common aspects like operational IT systems and repeatable business processes.

Conclusion

OpBI will support the management of performant business processes, if the analytical concerns are in concurrence to business requirements of an organization. The paper's contribution enhances a discussion about conceptual aspects of linking OpBI systems design with value-based business requirements. We developed and applied a management approach in coherent action research cycles to provide a conceptual basis for designing OpBI systems from business perspective.

The paper's arguments shift the discussion about operational decision making from technical aspects to a consideration of business strategies. Such a view on information systems is in line with contributions about the impact of IT on business process performance [2]. The novel conceptual approach of value modelling, work system analysis, and analytical design is relevant for application developers and business operation's managers. This supports a definition and an evaluation of requirements for operational decision making in an organization's business context. Gained conceptual and practical experience from our action research project refers to four different business scenarios. The collaboration of researchers and practitioners has produced a valid conceptual approach and meaningful outcomes in practical contexts. One learning effect is that consideration of collaborative efforts leads to firm-specific implications and to reproducible conceptual insights.

This paper builds its evidence on action research so that its findings and implications have a qualitative nature. The investigated organizations represent typical scenarios of manufacturing and service provision. This indicates certain resilience of the applied action research method and is intercessional for a confident replication logic in additional business scenarios. Therefore, upcoming research activities should further consolidate conceptual considerations about the integration of analytical concerns with business value perspectives. This allows taking charge of changing analytical technologies and digital opportunities based on a given business logic or value constellation.

References

1. Blasini, J.: Critical Success Factors Of Process Performance Management Systems: Results Of An Empirical Research. In: 21st European Conference on Information Systems, Utrecht, paper 158, 1–12 (2013)
2. Trkman, P.: The critical success factors of business process management. International Journal of Information Management 30, 125–134 (2010)
3. Vukšić, V.B., Bach, M.P., Popovič, A.: Supporting performance management with business process management and business intelligence: A case analysis of integration and orchestration. International Journal of Information Management 33, 613–619 (2013)

4. Davis, J., Imhoff, C., White, C.: Operational Business Intelligence: The State of the Art. Beye NETWORK Research, Boulder (2009)
5. Hänel, T., Felden, C.: Towards a Stability of Process-Oriented Decision Support Concepts Using the Example of Operational Business Intelligence. In: Pre-ICIS BI Congress 3: Driving Innovation through Big Data Analytics, Orlando (2012)
6. Gordijn, J., Akkermans, H.: Value Based Requirements Engineering: Exploring Innovative e-Commerce Ideas. Requirements Engineering Journal 8, 114–134 (2002)
7. McAfee, A., Brynjolfsson, E.: Big Data: The Management Revolution. Harvard Business Review 90, 60–66 (2012)
8. Juan-Verdejo, A., Baars, H.: Decision support for partially moving applications to the cloud: the example of business intelligence. In: International Workshop on Hot Topics in Cloud Services, New York, 35–42 (2012)
9. Plattner, H.: A Common Database Approach for OLTP and OLAP Using an In-Memory Column Database. In: ACM SIGMOD International Conference on Management of data, Providence, 1–2 (2009)
10. Van der Lans, R.: Data Virtualization for Business Intelligence Systems: Revolutionizing Data Integration for Data Warehouses. Morgan Kaufmann, Waltham (2012)
11. MIS Journal Rankings, http://aisnet.org/?JournalRankings
12. Cunningham, D.: Aligning Business Intelligence with Business Processes. What Works 20, 50–51 (2005)
13. Otley, D.: Performance Management: A Framework for Management Control Systems Research. Management Accounting Research 10, 363–382 (1999)
14. Kueng, P., Krahn, A.: Building a Process Performance Measurement System: some early experiences. Journal of Scientific & Industrial Research 58, 149–159 (1999)
15. Janiesch, C., Matzner, M., Müller, O.: Beyond process monitoring: a proof-of-concept of event-driven business activity management. Business Process Management Journal 18, 625–643 (2012)
16. van der Aalst, W.M.P.: Process Mining: Discovery, Conformance and Enhancement of Business Processes. Springer Publishing Company, Berlin (2011)
17. Kang, B., Kim, D., Kang, S.H.: Periodic performance prediction for realtime business process monitoring. Industrial Management and Data Systems 112, 4–23 (2012)
18. Cheung, M., Hidders, J.: Round-trip iterative business process modelling between BPA and BPMS tools. Business Process Management Journal 17, 461–494 (2011)
19. Felden, C., Chamoni P., Linden, M.: From Process Execution towards a Business Process Intelligence. In: 13th International Conference on Business Information Systems, Berlin, 195–206 (2010)
20. Bucher, T., Gericke, A., Sigg, S.: Process-centric business intelligence. Business Process Management Journal 15, 408–429 (2009)
21. Baskerville, R.L.: Investigating Information Systems with Action Research. Communications of AIS 2, 1–32 (1999)
22. Breu, K., Peppard, J.: The Participatory Paradigm for Applied Information Systems Research. In: 9th European Conference on Information Systems, Bled, 243–252 (2001)
23. Alter, S.: Work System Theory: Overview of Core Concepts, Extensions, and Challenges for the Future. Journal of the Association for Information Systems 14, 72–121 (2013)
24. Getting Started with ADAPT, http://www.symcorp.com/downloads/ADAPT_white_paper.pdf

4.4.2 Prototypische Umsetzung

Eine prototypische Umsetzung der OpBI im Kontext der Analyse und Steuerung von Geschäftsprozessen ist im Anwendungsgebiet der Umformtechnik erfolgt. Dazu werden nachfolgend die Entwicklung und die Evaluation eines CASE-basierten Prototyps dargestellt. Dies bildet den Abschluss im Gang der vorliegenden Forschungsarbeit.

4.4.2.1 Kurzdarstellung Beitrag 16

Beitrag 16 betrachtet ein Framework für eine Analyse und Steuerung von Produktionsprozessen. Diese Rahmenstruktur für eine praktische Umsetzung der OpBI besteht aus verschiedenen Komponenten für eine Bereitstellung, Analyse und Präsentation von Produktionsdaten. Die Datenbereitstellungskomponente setzt an den Ergebnissen von Beitrag 14 und Beitrag 15 an. Ausgehend von einer multidimensionalen Datenmodellierung mit ADAPT werden die Phasen der Modellimplementierung und der Datentransformation diskutiert. Auf dieser Basis ermöglicht die Datenbereitstellung eine Zusammenführung von Produktionsdaten im Hinblick auf die Gestaltung und den Betrieb von Fertigungsprozessen. Die Analyse- und Präsentationskomponente berücksichtigt darauf aufbauend die Weiterverarbeitung der Daten mithilfe von BI-Werkzeugen. In diesem Kontext werden der Zugriff auf die bereitgestellten Produktionsdaten, die Definition von Berichtsobjekten, die Berichtserzeugung, das Festlegen der Präsentationsarten und die Bereitstellung der Analyseergebnisse thematisiert.

Die fallstudienbasierte Evaluation des Frameworks beruht auf Daten eines Warmwalzprozesses. Vor dem fachlichen Hintergrund des Walzens von Stahldrähten werden die Phasen des OpBI-Frameworks erfolgreich durchlaufen. In einer anschließenden Diskussion wird die Nützlichkeit von OpBI im Evaluationskontext betrachtet. Dazu werden Kriterien der Informationsqualität, die in Beitrag 5 und in Beitrag 6 theoretisch untersucht wurden, auf den Produktionskontext übertragen. Neben der Nutzendarstellung von OpBI, erfolgt auch eine Aufwandsbetrachtung für die Integration von Produktionsdaten. Kern-aspekte sind die Datenmodellierung, die Modellimplementierung, die Datentransformation sowie die Berichtserzeugung. Dabei kristallisiert sich eine Wiederverwendbarkeit und Adaptierbarkeit der instanziierten Integrationsartefakte heraus. Zusammenfassend resultieren aus der prototypischen Umsetzung der OpBI im Produktionskontext folgende Gesichtspunkte:

- Umsetzungsspezifische Erkenntnisse im Rahmen von OpBI-Anwendungen,
- Aufwand und Nutzen einer automatisierten Produktionsdatenintegration,
- Nützlichkeit von multidimensionalen Datenstrukturen für eine produktionsspezifische Entscheidungsunterstützung (siehe Beitrag 5 und Beitrag 6),
- Erweiterung der Diskussion um entscheidungsunterstützende Funktionalitäten von industriegetriebenen Themen durch Anwendung von Methoden und Werkzeugen aus dem Bereich der analytischen Informationssysteme (siehe Beitrag 4).

Beitrag 16 erbringt einen Nachweis für die Praxistauglichkeit des entwickelten OpBI-Frameworks. Dies erfolgt im Rahmen der Evaluation unter Verwendung der

Daten eines Warmwalzprozesses. Abschließend wird in Beitrag 16 auf die Nütz-lichkeit weiterer Umsetzungsbeispiele hingewiesen, um eine höhere Generalisier-barkeit zu erzielen.

4.4.2.2 Beitrag 16: Applying Operational Business Intelligence in Production Environments[16]

Introduction

Manufacturing companies use IT systems to execute, record, model, or control pro-duction processes [1]. Common examples are automation systems, tools for product development, or operational execution systems [2]. Moreover, manufacturing man-agers need intelligent and integrated decision support systems that provide infor-mation from different viewpoints of production processes systematically [3]. In or-der to gain such benefits from using information systems in production, data from different sources (e.g. automation systems) have to be collected, harmonized and integrated [4]. However, dynamic and networked process structures challenge or-ganizations in integrating data from IT systems used in production environments [5]. Integration approaches come along with a huge amount of manual work and lack in standardized and reusable methods [3]. Consequently, the analysis of pro-duction data is time-consuming and happens in different subsystems, which do not share information for a decision making automatically [4]. In order to address these challenges in integrating and analyzing production data, manufacturing companies have the opportunity to consider IT concepts from an analytical information sys-tems' perspective. Recently, literature studies discuss OpBI as a beneficial strategy to generate decision-relevant information out of production data, which stem from different IT systems [6]. However, this discussion deals rather with a common ap-plicability of OpBI in production environments [7, 8], than with implementations of certain methods and tools for an automated acquisition, consolidation, and anal-ysis of production data. Thus, there is no evidence that the concept of OpBI actually works in practice. Efforts, benefits and obstacles of integrating and analyzing pro-duction data automatically remain fuzzy in a particular application scenario. The paper's goal is therefore to investigate an actual implementation of OpBI in a cer-tain production environment.

There are currently no studies that deal with an automated integration and anal-ysis of production data in a standardized and reusable way. Discussions about Smart Manufacturing [9, 10], Manufacturing Intelligence [11], or Industry 4.0 [12] de-mand admittedly a data-driven decision support in production environments, but they do not elaborate on tangible tools and methods in order to prepare and analyze data of production processes adequately. To support such activities, we apply de-sign science research to develop an OpBI framework that joins capabilities like data

---

16 Hänel, T.; Felden C.: Applying Operational Business Intelligence in Production Environments. In: 25th International Conference on Information Systems Development, Katowice, August 2016.

234

modelling, data transformation or data manipulation for an integrated analysis and control of production processes. The evaluation happens during a framework application in context of integrating data from a rod and wire rolling process. Analytical tools and methods are used to demonstrate the functional reliability of OpBI in an industry-driven use case. Finally, process engineers perform an assessment of the OpBI application in comparison to the traditional approach of analyzing rod and wire rolling data. To the best of our knowledge, this paper is the first contribution that discusses efforts, benefits and obstacles in integrating and analyzing real-world production data by use of established tools and methods from analytical information systems' perspective, yet. We document practical knowledge about an actual implementation of OpBI in a production environment, so that practitioners and researchers gain a standardized guideline to design an automated data-driven management support for production-specific decisions.

The paper is structured as follows: Chapter 2 discusses the status quo of OpBI and its application in production environments. The paper uses phases of design science research presented in Chapter 3. Chapter 4 introduces our framework and Chapter 5 demonstrates its evaluation using an example process of forming industry. A discussion of results follows in Chapter 6. Finally, Chapter 7 concludes the paper's implications and highlights further research perspectives.

Status Quo

OpBI supports a decision making of business operation managers [13]. The concept refers to analytical IT system capabilities that collect, integrate, and present business relevant information in a decision-oriented way [14]. This allows an analysis of process performances to identify control actions for a continuous improvement of process design and execution [15]. The dashed line in Figure 1 marks the decision background of OpBI.

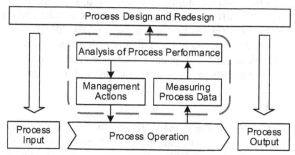

Figure 1. Classification of OpBI

Problem Refinement

Production environments open a broad potential application area for OpBI [15]. Manufacturing companies collect a lot of data about products, manufacturing processes or quality issues. Furthermore, automation systems, sensor technologies or computing devices make large amounts of data available. [4] The demand for a pervasive and ubiquitous usage of data in production environments is even increased by future-oriented smart factory initiatives [16]. A tracking of products through plants and working stations represents an exemplary scenario for data usage in a smart factory. In that context, production cockpits [17] are able to visualize throughput times, upcoming bottlenecks, material consumptions, or overall efficiencies.

An important qualification for such capabilities in a smart factory is an accurate, fast and automated integration of underlying production data [16]. OpBI offers standardized tools and methods in this context, which form a basis to take production-specific decisions, e.g. an allocation of new work to idle capacities. It has to be noted that such decisions cannot be easily reversed, if continuous workloads require a steady processing of production orders. Wrong decisions increase risks of defective products and lead to additional efforts for a correct task fulfilment. To avoid such inconvenient situations, the OpBI's activities to consolidate and harmonize production data have to ensure that decision makers are well provided with high-quality information. A seizure of quality in terms accessing and representing information can be guided by the following requirements [18]:

- Concise representation requires compactness and precision of information to avoid overwhelming and unnecessary information.
- Consistent representation requires a coherent and invariant format of information.
- Interpretability requires usage of appropriate units, definitions or labels.
- Understandability requires unambiguously and comprehensible information.
- Ease of operation requires easy manipulations of information.

A compliance of information quality in context of an automated integration and analysis of production data has not been investigated, yet. Literature studies theorize generally a positive effect of analytical IT approaches like OpBI on aspects of information quality, i.e. decision time and accuracy [19, 20]. However, a usability of OpBI concerning the abovementioned quality criteria has not been confirmed in empirical investigations [20]. The paper investigates therefore the effect of OpBI usage on information quality aspects in production environments.

Related Research

The relevance of integrating and analyzing production data becomes evident by decision support functionalities of industry-driven approaches. For example, Manufacturing Execution Systems (MES) collect, process, and present data in order to coordinate production processes [21]. Furthermore, Advanced Process Control (APC) characterizes an analysis of process data in semiconductor industries. APC solutions encompass modules to conduct operation inspections, error classifications or efficiency calculations. Statistical methods can be used to monitor equipment, or technical processes. [22] The term Manufacturing Intelligence (MI) belongs to the discussion about an extraction of information out of production data for decision support purposes, too [11]. MI focusses on a pervasive usage of data integration techniques to enable a problem-oriented information supply for decision makers [23]. This includes several aspects of analyzing production processes like for example pattern detection, real-time monitoring, or simulations [24]. Considering need for networked production data within and across manufacturing processes, the catchphrase of Smart Manufacturing asks for an intensification of MI in industrial organizations [9]. This is reasoned by observations, that existing IT solutions in production environments entail only single process improvements with insufficient opportunities for decision support [10].

All of the industry-driven concepts pursue control functions in production environments based on a comprehensive usage of data. However, these concepts do not discuss standardized and reusable approaches for automated data integration and analysis. A proper handling of production data concerning aspects of data modelling, model implementations, data transformations or automated report generation is commonly ignored. OpBI is able to fill this gap with tools and methods for an automated data integration and analysis. This finding arises from a literature review across the databases of Business Source Complete, IEEE, AIS, ACM, Emerald, and Science Direct. We used these literature sources to assess research contributions on OpBI in production environments according to MIS journal rankings [25]. In result of the literature review, application of OpBI is subject of different case studies and conceptual papers. The literature addresses for example the ability of OpBI to improve the analysis and reporting functionalities of MES as part of a company-wide decision architecture [8, 26]. OpBI enables furthermore a consideration of heterogeneous data from technical and economic perspectives [7]. Underlying data integration connects logistical and product-oriented IT systems, so that OpBI is able to support multidimensional views on flexibility requirements of production processes [6]. Looking for actual implementations of OpBI in production environments, the literature contains no knowledge about data integration methods or tools to apply OpBI in practice, yet.

Research Design

Our research follows principles of design science research (DSR) [27]. We refer to five phases of DSR in order to develop and to evaluate an OpBI framework for production-specific decision support (cf. Figure 2).

Figure 2. Phases of DSR according to[28]

The first phase aims to raise awareness for the given problem domain and results in a proposal. This is followed by suggesting a tentative design. In context of our research, the first two phases are carried out in the paper's introduction and in Chapter 2. We discussed a need for an automated data integration to support decisions in production environments and suggest an application of OpBI techniques within this problem area. Subsequently, an OpBI framework will be developed and evaluated in the course of this paper.

Development of the OpBI Framework

Figure 3 illustrates the schematic overview of our framework. We build up on framework requirements stemming from a specific process design and operation. First, there is a need for layout data regarding process equipment (e.g. machines, measuring points and instruments) and in terms of measurement parameters. Second, operational data from different process runs are required. This concerns for example planned input and output data for each process step, machine settings, or measured values. Therefore, it has to be ensured that a measurement of operational data happens actually. Examples for an IT support are sensor systems, process data acquisition tools or control stations.

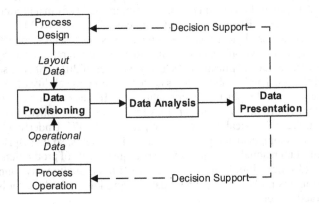

Figure 3. Design of the OpBI Framework

Both, layout and operational data flow into the data provisioning component of our OpBI framework. The component's output is a multidimensional structured database that is populated with measured values of process operation. Subsequently, a data analysis component generates analysis results that will be finally visualized to users by the data presentation component. The dashed line indicates a decision support for process design and operation based on achieved analysis results.

Data Provisioning

The data provisioning component encompasses activities from data modelling right up to data storage (cf. Figure 4).

Figure 4. Activities of data provisioning

At first, a data modelling concerns a semantic conceptualization of a multidimensional database. Content of the data model is thereby derived from process design and operation. This includes process hierarchies with subprocesses, phases, monitoring points, and determinants. Measurement parameters and process runs span further dimensions. In addition to these process-related aspects, time-related dimensions need to be modelled, too. After creating the data model, it has to be implemented in a database management system. Dimensions are transferred to database tables consisting of keys and content columns. A data type has to be defined for each column. The database tables store either descriptive dimensions or facts. The dimension tables are populated with meta-information from process design. Fact tables are populated subsequently to data model implementation during an ETL process (Extract, Transform, and Load). Thereby, measured values collected for example by a process data acquisition system need to be organized according to the implemented data model structure. In order to do so, measured values from process operation must be harmonized to data types of fact tables during a data preprocessing. The data are cleaned up and enriched by additional calculations. The second aspect of the ETL process refers to a categorization of process actions. Logical-related activities are filtered based on specified criteria and assigned to a unique identifier. This is especially relevant, if one process station handles different activities or if parallel work occurs. The final step of the ETL process stores preprocessed and categorized data in implemented fact tables of a database management system.

Data Analysis and Presentation

The data analysis component executes queries on multidimensional structured process data. This is carried out by a BI or analytics tool in order to generate certain analysis results. An analytical platform provides an interface to different users interested in a basic reporting, an interactive data discovery or a complex ad hoc report generation. Necessary objects to create reports are also defined in the analytical component. This requires e.g. filter or aggregation functionalities. Analysis results are finally presented and communicated for decision support purposes. Grids and graphs can be used exclusively as well as combined in dashboards or management cockpits. Figure 5 summarizes the activities for data analysis and presentation.

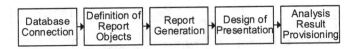

Figure 5. Activities of data analysis and presentation

Framework Evaluation

We use production data from a rod and wire rolling process in order to evaluate our OpBI framework. The underlying process setting and the evaluation of framework components is presented in the following. We have used different IT tools and methods for data acquisition, data provisioning and data analysis (cf. Figure 6).

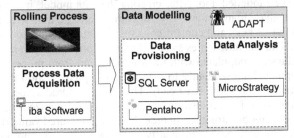

Figure 6. Evaluation Process

Rolling Process and Data Acquisition

The background of our evaluation is a hot rolling process. In this context, rolling behavior of different steel grades needs to be analyzed. The process is carried out on a semi-continuous rolling train. This plant produces round wire of eight millimeter diameter out of steel billets with a 45 millimeter edge length. Therefore, materials run through nine stations over a distance of more than 46 meters. The rolling train is divided in a roughing mill and a final rolling pass (cf. Figure 7).

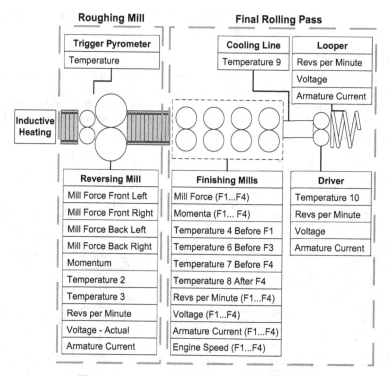

Roughing Mill

Trigger Pyrometer
Temperature

Final Rolling Pass

Cooling Line	Looper
Temperature 9	Revs per Minute
	Voltage
	Armature Current

Inductive Heating

Reversing Mill
Mill Force Front Left
Mill Force Front Right
Mill Force Back Left
Mill Force Back Right
Momentum
Temperature 2
Temperature 3
Revs per Minute
Voltage - Actual
Armature Current

Finishing Mills
Mill Force (F1...F4)
Momenta (F1... F4)
Temperature 4 Before F1
Temperature 6 Before F3
Temperature 7 Before F4
Temperature 8 After F4
Revs per Minute (F1...F4)
Voltage (F1...F4)
Armature Current (F1...F4)
Engine Speed (F1...F4)

Driver
Temperature 10
Revs per Minute
Voltage
Armature Current

Figure 7. Schema of the Rod and Wire Rolling Process

Preliminary material is heated to 1,150 degree Celsius before it flows into the roughing mill with two reversing rollers. Different rolling calibers decrement a steel billet's initial dimensions to a diameter of around twelve millimeters. Thereby, two workers use pliers to push the material in the roughing mill and to pull it out again. After each pass, a button is pressed in order to change the rolling direction. The intermediate products go subsequently through the final rolling pass consisting of four finishing mills, a cooling line, a wire driver, and a looper. The finishing mills are assembled in a so called H-V-H-V arrangement (horizontal, vertical). This allows an alternating height and width reduction of wire. There is a cooling line with three water pipes after the last finishing mill. The wire is cooled down to a temperature of 800 to 900 degrees Celsius, and then looped by a laying unit.

A process run consists of eleven roughing mill phases and four finishing mill phases. Before each run, machines are configured according to technical parameters of a rolling schedule. This includes the determination of rolling gaps and rolling speed. Process stability is checked in a control station during a process run. Mill forces, temperatures, momenta, and electrical parameters are measured by use of a process data acquisition software of iba. This company is specialized on automation systems and has implemented different measuring points (e.g. dynamometer or pyrometer) on the rolling train that are networked to the control station.

Data Provisioning

We carried out activities of data modeling and transformation for data provisioning purposes. In context of data modelling, we refer to Application Design for Analytical Processing Technologies (ADAPT). This allows us a modelling of dimensions, hierarchies and analysis cubes by predefined shapes. The semantic data model for the rod and wire rolling process is represented in Figure 8.

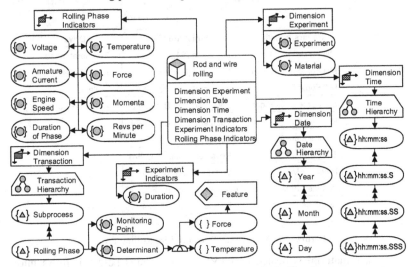

Figure 8. ADAPT Model of the Rod and Wire Rolling Process

Each rolling pass is related to an experiment, which is conducted on the rolling train. A particular material is thereby formed to predefined dimensions. This is expressed by the experiment's dimension in the ADAPT model. Experiments are conducted on a certain date. The experiment duration is between one and two and a half minutes. Acquisition of measurement data happens in a cycle of two milliseconds. Therefore, the dimensions time and date provide certain hierarchy levels in order to aggregate time and date information. The transaction dimension represents the process design. The rod and wire rolling process consists of two subprocesses with several rolling phases. Measured forces or temperatures determine the rolling phases. There are overlappings of rolling phases due to continuity of the finishing train. This happens if more than one monitoring point records measurement data at the same time. For this reason, two indicator dimensions are used in the data model. The rolling phase indicators consider parallel measurement, while the experiment indicator dimension describes the actual experiment duration. We implemented the ADAPT model in a SQL Server database. Figure 9 illustrates the corresponding galaxy schema consisting of four dimension tables and two fact tables.

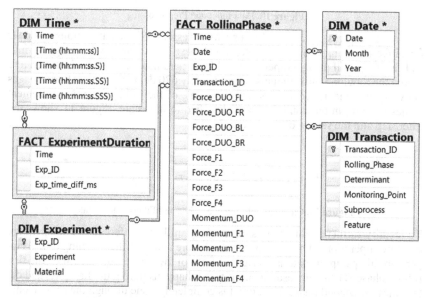

Figure 9. Galaxy Schema Implemented in MS SQL Server

The *DIM Date* table contains data for the year of 2015. *DIM Transaction* considers 33 rolling phases with three different determinants. There are 14 monitoring points, two subprocesses and 15 features. The table *DIM Experiment* contains 26 experiments and two different steel grades. Time data encompass timestamps of a 24 hour day from second level to millisecond level.

In order to populate the fact tables of the galaxy schema, we created data transformations in Pentaho Data Integration. The measurement values recorded by iba process data acquisition are exported to text files and imported into Pentaho. The data have a string format at the beginning of the ETL process. First, we cut these strings to a desired length and changed labels of measurement parameters according to their definition in the fact tables. In a next step, we replaced cryptic values and added a column for an experiment ID so that we were able to reference fact tables with the *DIM Experiment* table in our database. Figure 10 illustrates the part of the ETL process for the mentioned aspects.

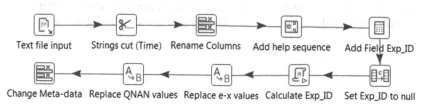

Figure 10. Data Input and Preprocessing

In further progress, a variety of steps was necessary to calculate a transaction ID for different rolling phases. We determined these IDs separately for roughing mill and finishing mill using temperature and force parameters. The initial temperature before the roughing mill amounts approximately 670 degrees Celsius. Force ranges between zero and 15 kilonewton in initial state of the rolling train. Measurement values meeting initial conditions are classified to idle state. Figure 11 shows the filter step and the setting of the transaction ID.

Calculate Force DUO   Add reference   Calculate delta   Add Operation_ID   Filter idle   Operation_ID = 0   Transaction_ID = 0

Figure 11. Calculating Reference Points and Filtering Idle State

To identify further rolling phases of roughing mill, we differentiated temperature and force operations. There is a pyrometer before and after the roughing mill. Temperature jumps up, if material is right in front of the roller. This identifies the first rolling phase. Then, a measurement of forces happens during the first pass and determines the second phase. If material is completely gone through the rollers, only values at the output pyrometer differ from initial state. This identifies the third rolling phase. However, these conditions are valid for different rolling phases, because several passes happen on the roughing mill. Therefore, we added a sequence and calculated the transaction ID based on changing operations as illustrated in Figure 12.

Figure 12 represents calculation of the transaction ID for the roughing mill. In case of final rolling pass, identification was easier due to continuity of this rolling train part. We filtered phases according to different monitoring points. So, ten rolling phases were derived, which overlap each other. We built also a dataset without overlappings in order to trace the complete final rolling pass. Next to transaction ID and experiment ID, a date column was determined, too. We used a calculation to remove the time part from imported timestamps. Furthermore, measurement intervals are calculated. This allows to determine durations of each rolling phase and experiments. In result, our ETL implementation encompasses five transformation processes using table output function of Pentaho. We run four ETL processes to transfer the transformed measurement data to 13 temporary fact tables and integrated them later to one phase-related fact table in the SQL server database. The experiment-related fact table was populated by a separate transformation.

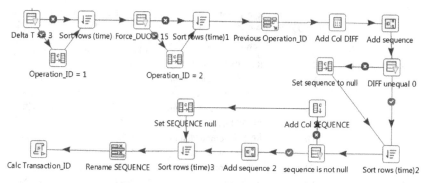

Figure 12. Identification of rolling phases

Data Analysis

The data analysis was performed on the analytical platform of MicroStrategy. We created several reports that are presented via a web interface for example in report documents or analysis dashboards in context of basic reporting. In addition, the development environment provides extensive possibilities to investigate the data according to various aspects.

MicroStrategy uses a meta-data database and our implemented rolling database connected via ODBC to the analytical platform. In order to generate reports, we built first attributes and metrics within the tool environment. Attributes and metrics are placed on grid or graph templates and enable also creation of additional report objects, e.g. filter or consolidations. Definitions of report objects are represented by meta-data. If a process is run, an analytical engine generates SQL statements in order to query the rolling database. Figure 13 illustrates an example report.

Subprocess	Rolling Phase	Experiment Material Feature	Experiment 15 100Cr6 Duration of Phase	Ratio Duration Phase to Experiment
Roughing mill	DF1	K02/001 Sw. oval	622	0.41%
	DF2	K05/001 rotund 36 mm	704	0.47%
	DF3	K02/001 Sw. oval	484	0.32%
	DF4	K05/002 rotund 27 mm	634	0.42%
	DF5	K03/001 oval	816	0.54%
	DF6	K05/003 rotund 20 mm	1,056	0.70%
	DF7	K03/001 oval	1,408	0.94%
	DF8	K05/004 rotund 15 mm	1,876	1.25%
	DF9	K03/002 oval	2,274	1.51%
	DF10	K05/002 rotund 12 mm	2,780	1.85%
	Total		**12,654**	**8.42%**
Final rolling pass	F1	K3/50 B	406	0.27%
	F2	K9/24 A	404	0.27%
	F3	K3/21 A	402	0.27%
	F4	K9/23 B	388	0.26%
	Total		**1,600**	**1.06%**

Figure 13. Example report– relation of phase durations to experiment duration

Discussion

The OpBI framework introduced in Chapter 4 has been evaluated in context of a rod and wire rolling process. We demonstrated that integration of rolling data is feasible from a technical point of view and leads to consistent results from functional perspective. Our framework has been discussed with engineers responsible for rod and wire rolling in order to make a comparison to traditional analysis. Therefore, we use information quality requirements presented in the problem refinement of the paper.

In a nutshell, using our OpBI framework improves analysis capabilities of users conducting experiments on the rolling train in favor of a profound analysis of a steel's rolling behavior. This encompasses for example faster analyses in an automated way or the possibility to calculate indicators on a different level of detail. The traditional approach was related to spreadsheet software (e.g. MS Excel) and an analysis add-on of the process data acquisition software. In particular, the engineers pointed out that analysis results were generated in a time-consuming, manual, and error-prone process. A detailed comparison of the framework approach and the traditional approach follows in Table 1.

Table 1. OpBI-Framework compared to the Traditional approach

	Traditional Approach	OpBI-Framework
Concise Representation & Consistent Representation	Two-dimensional presentation of measurement parameters and values Experiment-related presentation Manual and unstandardized reports Presentation by simple graphs or spreadsheet programs	Multidimensional presentation of descriptive information, measurement parameters and values Use of hierarchies Process-related presentation Automated and standardized reports Various presentation options (reports, documents, dashboards)
Interpretability & Understandability	Difficulties to consider external or additional parameters Static analysis perspectives	Different levels of detail Opportunity of add data perspectives or parameters Flexible analysis perspectives
Ease of Operation	Limited data manipulation options Time-consuming aggregations and calculations	Flexible options for data manipulation (drilling, pivoting, filtering, sorting) Simple aggregations and calculations

Table 1 indicates a positive effect of OpBI on information quality compared to the traditional approach of analyzing the rod and wire rolling process. The engineers mentioned in terms of consistent representation:

> *The OpBI system presents the rolling process consistently from functional and technical viewpoints.*

Concerning consistent representation, the importance to explain and predict measurement values like temperatures or forces has been pointed out. An engineer said in that context:

> *We have often complex issues in which we need to describe the effect of various influencing factors on a specific measurement parameter. Thereby, the OpBI system allows us to keep track of interactions between materials and rolling measures in different functional areas of the rolling train.*

The opinion in terms of interpretability and understandability was two-minded. Major improvements are expected in context of analyzing experiments conducted on the rolling train. Improved representation has been associated with a better interpretation and understanding of analysis issues. However, the engineers emphasize the importance and the need of expert knowledge, so that they see only an indirect effect of the OpBI system in this context. Moreover, the relevance of our framework approach for interpretations of workers operating a machine has been discussed. A technical assistant mentioned:

> *Each run on the rolling train lasts less than two minutes. So, there is no time for interpretations during an experiment.*

In this context, the OpBI system cannot bring an advantage compared to the previous approach. Changes on working behavior will still concern subsequent experiments. In order to identify such changes, the ease of operation of the OpBI system was commended by the engineers:

> Using the traditional approach provides us values always on the minimum level of detail. So it is difficult to determine average values for process phases at the flick of a switch without the OpBI system.

The discussion with engineers reveals direct and indirect relationships between criteria of information quality introduced in Chapter 2 (See Problem Refinement) and usability of OpBI. This circumstance is illustrated in Figure 14. OpBI improves directly a concise and consistent representation of information generated from production data. A direct effect also exists in context of manipulating data during analysis activities (ease of operation). Understandability and interpretability are indirectly improved by a better representation and ease of operation. However, both quality criteria depend also from analytical skills and experiences of end users. Following literature about information success e.g. [29], we are able to confirm a relationship between information quality and the usability of OpBI in production environments.

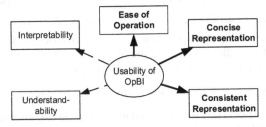

Figure 14. Relationship between Information Quality Criteria and OpBI

Illustrated usability and gained benefits from OpBI depend on main efforts in context of data modelling, database implementation, transformation processes, and report generation. However, these activities have to be performed only once and can be adapted in case of changed situations. Created report objects are reusable for new report definitions. It has to be noted that the implemented data model is only valid for a specific process configuration. Adaptations are required in case of e.g. new monitoring points or process stations. Implementations of new database models and transformation processes will be necessary, if the rolling train is retooled to another configuration (e.g. hot-rolled strip).

Next to comprehensive analysis opportunities, the framework is beneficial to identify and carry out control actions. This concerns material characteristics in dependence of measured values. It is for example possible to determine hold times in order to reach a specific temperature. An interesting decision area is the roughing mill in context of the rod and wire rolling process. Due to interaction of humans and machine, there are various potential relationships as for example the reversing time on a material's temperature profile. Furthermore, decisions can be made about usefulness of monitoring points and measurement parameters in a given process configuration. The framework and its analytical tools builds upon a process data acquisition software. Such tracking systems to control process stability are not replaced. However, analysis opportunities of our proposed OpBI solution allow process engineers to link measurement values with input parameters of machine controls dynamically. This makes a parameter setting in a given context more precise than a merely experience-based approach.

The application of OpBI in the given context requires tools that integrate and analyze production data. In order to evaluate our framework components, we used specific data integration and analysis tools. The framework application is however independent from the presented tool selection and can be done by comparable BI tools, too. Nevertheless, a new acquisition of software solutions or an extension of already existing analytical environments is required. This forces system developers to examine design and execution data in order gain a comprehensive understanding of the underlying process. Consistency of analysis results should be scrutinized by experts during each OpBI project. This ensures a coherent and accurate information base to analyze a material's behavior on the rolling train and to derive actions for decision support. Gained experiences need to be documented for future projects.

Conclusion

OpBI is able to automate integration and analysis of production data in favor of a multidimensional decision support, if specific efforts in context of data provisioning and data analysis are managed. The paper's contribution takes an implementation of OpBI functionalities into account in order to improve analysis capabilities of decision makers in production environments. In this context, we designed and evaluated a framework that guides actual applications of OpBI to integrate production data automatically. Central components of our proposed solution are modelling of multidimensional data structures as well as deployment of corresponding data transformation processes. These data processing activities enable an annotation of stationary recorded and machine-located measurement values with descriptive information of a certain process design. The multidimensional structured production data form a basis for subsequent analyses and a production-specific decision making.

The paper demonstrates an OpBI-driven framework that allows a flexible design of analysis dimensions to assess process-related measurement values in the overall context of a production process. Considering opportunities for decision support in production environments, a feasibility of OpBI becomes evident. The paper demonstrates a new application field to research and study OpBI. This enhances recent discussions about topics like Smart Manufacturing or Industry 4.0 with novel methods and tools coming from an analytical information systems perspective. The proposed framework and its evaluation in a real-world context introduce new knowledge and experiences regarding OpBI implementations in production environments. Practitioners and researchers gain insights about data integration approaches, so that they are able to extract valuable information from production data recorded for example by process automation systems. Thereby, the present investigation addresses cost in terms of data management or software tools in context of an OpBI-driven integration and analysis of production data.

The framework evaluation with data from a rod and wire rolling process provides a valid proof of concept. This is however only one example and embodies a gambit for an application of OpBI in order to automate integration and analysis of data from production processes. Further evaluations should be part of subsequent research activities, so that the paper's findings can be consolidated. Thereby, comparisons of different application scenarios will lead to a generalizability of our OpBI-driven approach and to conceptual improvements. Moreover, upcoming technologies in smart factories will lead to new sources of generating production data. Their usage for decision making opens a broad field of research for an automated data integration and analysis. The feasibility of existing tools and methods from OpBI perspective has to be permanently evaluated against their usability in future smart factories. This provides a promising field for further research in order to study and to apply adaptations and advancements of the presented data integration approach.

References

1. S. Bharadwaj, A. Bharadwaj, and E. Bendoly, "The Performance Effects of Complementarities Between Information Systems, Marketing, Manufacturing, and Supply Chain Processes," Information Systems Research vol. 18, pp. 437-453, 2007.
2. M.P. Groover, Automation, Production Systems, and Computer-Integrated Manufacturing, 3rd ed, Upper Saddle River: Prentice Hall Press, 2008.
3. D. Delen and D.B. Pratt, "An integrated and intelligent DSS for manufacturing systems," Expert Systems with Applications vol. 30, pp. 325-336, 2006.
4. L.B. Kassner and B. Mitschang, "MaXCept – Decision Support in Exception Handling through Unstructured Data Integration in the Production Context. An Integral Part of the Smart Factory," 48th Hawaii International Conference on System Sciences, Kauai, 2015.
5. S. Nahavandi, D. Creighton, V.T. Le, M. Johnstone, and J. Zhang, "Future Integrated Factories: A System of Systems Engineering Perspective," in Integrated Systems: Innovations and Applications, M. Fathi, Ed. Cham: Springer, 2015, pp. 147-161.
6. T.Hänel and C. Felden, "Operational Business Intelligence Meets Manufacturing," 19th Americas Conference on Information Systems, Chicago, 2013.
7. H. Lasi, "Industrial intelligence - a BI based approach to enhance manufacturing engineering in industrial companies," 8th CIRP conference on intelligent computation in manufacturing engineering, Gulf of Naples, 2012.
8. M. Koch, H. Lasi, H. Baars, and H.-G. Kemper, "Manufacturing Execution Systems and Business Intelligence for Production Environments," 16th Americas Conference on Information Systems, Lima, 2010.
9. J. Davis, T. Edgar, J. Porter, J. Bernaden, and M. Sarlie, "Smart manufacturing, manufacturing intelligence and demand-dynamic performance," Computers and Chemical Engineering, vol. 47, pp. 145-156, 2012.
10. Brodsky, M. Krishnamoorthy, D.A. Menascé, G. Shao, and S. Rachuri, "Toward Smart Manufacturing Using Decision Analytics," IEEE International Conference on Big Data, Washington DC, 2014.
11. C.-F. Chien, Y.-J. Chen, C.-Y. Hsu, "A novel approach to hedge and compensate the critical dimension variation of the developed-and-etched circuit patterns for yield enhancement in semiconductor manufacturing," Computers & Operations Research vol. 53, pp. 309-318, 2015.

12. J. Lee, B. Bagheri, and H.-A. Kao, "A Cyber-Physical Systems architecture for Industry 4.0-based manufacturing systems," Manufacturing Letters vol. 3, pp. 18-23, 2015.
13. J. Davis, C. Imhoff, and C. White, Operational Business Intelligence: The State of the Art, Boulder; Beye NETWORK Research, 2009.
14. W.W. Eckerson, Best Practices in Operational BI: Converging Analytical and Operational Processes, Renton: TDWI Best Practices Report, 2007.
15. T. Hänel and C. Felden, "Towards a Stability of Process-Oriented Decision Support Concepts Using the Example of Operational Business Intelligence," Pre-ICIS BI Congress 3: Driving Innovation through Big Data Analytics, Orlando, 2012.
16. Zuehlke, D. "Smart Factory – Towards a factory-of things," Annual Reviews in Control, vol. 34, pp. 129-138, 2010.
17. V. Vasyutynskyy, C. Hengstler, J. McCarthy, K.G. Brennan, D. Nadoveza, A. Dennert, "Layered architecture for production and logistics cockpits," 17th IEEE Conference on Emerging Technologies & Factory Automation (ETFA), Krakow, 2012.
18. Y.W. Lee, D.M. Strong, B.K. Kahn, and R.Y. Wang, "AIMQ: A Methodology for Information Quality Assessment," Information and Management, vol. 40, pp. 133-146, 2002.
19. D. Vujošević, I. Kovačević, M. Suknović, and N. Lalić, "A Comparison of the Usability of Performing Ad hoc Querying on Dimensionally Modeled Data Versus Operationally Modeled Data," Decision Support Systems, vol. 54, pp. 185-197, 2012.
20. T. Hänel, and M. Schulz, "Is There Still A Need For Multidimensional Data Models?" 22nd European Conference on Information Systems, Tel Aviv, 2014.
21. B. Saenz de Ugarte, A. Artiba, and R. Pellerin, "Manufacturing execution system – a literature review," Production Planning and Control, vol. 20, pp. 525-539, 2009.
22. C. Yugma, J. Blue, S. Dauzere-Peres, and P. Vialletelle, "Integration of Scheduling and Advanced Process Control in Semiconductor Manufacturing: Review and Outlook," IEEE International Conference on Automation Science and Engineering, Taipei, 2014.
23. J. Cooley and J. Petrusich, "Delivering optimal real-time manufacturing intelligence," 2013 Proceedings of PICMET '13: Technology Management for Emerging Technologies, San Jose, 2013, pp. 1658-1668.
24. C.-J. Kuo, C.-F. Chien, and J.-D. Chen, "Manufacturing Intelligence to Exploit the Value of Production and Tool Data to Reduce Cycle Time," IEEE Transactions on Automation Science and Engineering, vol. 8, pp. 103-111, 2011.
25. MIS Journal Rankings, URL: http://aisnet.org/?JournalRankings
26. T. Hänel and C. Felden, "Limits or Integration? Manufacturing Execution Systems and Operational Business Intelligence," 17th Amercias Conference on Informations Systems, Detroit, 2011.
27. S. Gregor and A.R. Hevner, "Positioning and Presenting Design Science Research for Maximum Impact," MIS Quarterly, vol. 37, pp. 337-355, 2013.
28. V.Vaishnavi and W. Kuechler, "Design Science Research in Information Systems," January 20, 2004; last updated: November 15, 2015, URL: http://www.desrist.org/design-research-in-information-systems/
29. P.B. Seddon, "A Respecification and Extension of the DeLone and McLean Model of IS Success. Information Systems Research," vol. 8, pp. 240-253, 1997.

5 Diskussion der Forschungsergebnisse

Die Diskussion der Forschungsergebnisse zeigt den Gesamtzusammenhang der Forschungsbeiträge auf, um die Vollständigkeit der Themenbearbeitung inhaltlich nachzuvollziehen. Im Anschluss daran erfolgt eine Generalisierung der Erkenntnisse und abschließend geht die Diskussion auf die Erreichung der Forschungsziele ein.

5.1 Gesamtzusammenhang der Forschungsbeiträge

Der Gang der Arbeit hat 16 Forschungsbeiträge dargestellt, die zur Erreichung der Forschungsziele der Arbeit publiziert wurden oder sich im Publikationsprozess befinden. Tabelle 4 fasst die Kernergebnisse dieser Beiträge inhaltlich zusammen und ordnet sie den Aspekten des Gesamtbeitrags der Forschungsarbeit (siehe Abschnitt 2.2, S. 31) zu.

Tabelle 4. Kernergebnisse der Forschungsbeiträge

Inhaltlicher Aspekt	Beitrag	Kernergebnis
Themenbegründung der OpBI	1	Trendanalyse der wissenschaftlichen Literatur hinsichtlich eines vermehrten Einsatzes von Technologien, Konzepten und Werkzeugen der BI für operative Entscheidungsaufgaben
Begriffliche Abgrenzung der OpBI	2	Beschreibung und Abgrenzung des OpBI-Konzepts durch Kernaspekte, Treiber, potentielle Anwendungsfelder und Umsetzungsaspekte
	3	Beschreibung und Abgrenzung des OpBI-Konzepts durch kausale Determinanten für eine integrierte Informationsverarbeitung im Rahmen der Analyse und Steuerung von Geschäftsprozessen
	4	Positionsbestimmung von OpBI für eine produktionsspezifische Entscheidungsunterstützung im Kontext des Entwicklungstands von IT-Systemen in Produktionsumgebungen und Industrie 4.0
Anwendbarkeit der OpBI als Mensch-Aufgabe-Technik-System	5, 6	Nützlichkeit multidimensionaler Datenmodelle zur Absicherung qualitativ hochwertiger Analyseergebnisse und Entscheidungen von Anwendern, die nicht mit BI-Werkzeugen vertraut sind
	7, 8	Ergänzungspotential von MES und OpBI im Kontext einer produktionsspezifischen Entscheidungsunterstützung
	9, 10	Konzeption einer Integrationsplattform zur Bereitstellung von MES- und OpBI-Funktionalitäten
	11, 12, 13	Demonstration der Vorteilhaftigkeit und der Anwendbarkeit von OpBI im Produktions- und Dienstleistungsumfeld

Inhaltlicher Aspekt	Beitrag	Kernergebnis
Gestaltungsempfeh-lung für OpBI-Systeme	14, 15	Entwicklung und Evaluation einer fachlichen Konzeption zur Verknüpfung von OpBI-Datenmodellen mit prozessorientierten Geschäftsmodellen
	16	Entwicklung und Evaluation eines Frameworks zur Analyse und Steuerung von Produktionsprozessen

Die in Tabelle 4 aufgeführten Kernergebnisse der Forschungsbeiträge sind nicht losgelöst voneinander zu betrachten. Bereits im Gang der Arbeit wurde auf Bezugspunkte und Zusammenhänge zwischen den einzelnen Beiträgen hingewiesen. Aus diesem Grund stellt Abbildung 11 einen Gesamtzusammenhang zwischen den Forschungsbeiträgen her.

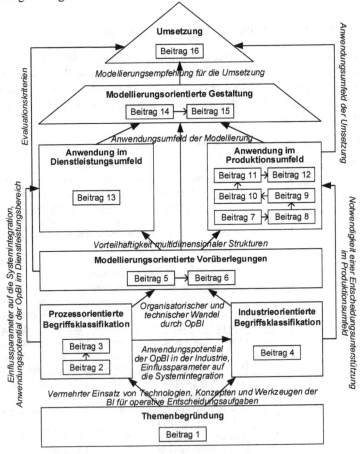

Abbildung 11. Zusammenwirken der Architekturelemente im Gang der Arbeit

Die Darstellung des Zusammenhangs der Forschungsbeiträge erfolgt unter Verwendung der Allegorie des Hauses, die zu Beginn von Kapitel 4 dargestellt wurde. Durch Pfeile mit ausgefüllten Spitzen sind die Zusammenhänge zwischen den Architekturelementen dargestellt. Umfasst ein Architekturelement mehr als einen Forschungsbeitrag, besteht ein sequentieller Zusammenhang zwischen den Beiträgen. Dies ist durch Pfeile mit einer offenen Spitze verdeutlicht. Aus der Analyse von Abbildung 11 geht hervor, dass die Ergebnisse der Forschungsbeiträge von der Themenbegründung bis zur prototypischen Umsetzung aufeinander aufbauen. Es liegt eine inhaltlich geschlossene Themenbearbeitung vor. Alle inhaltlichen Aspekte des Gesamtbeitrags der Forschungsarbeit (siehe Abschnitt 2.2, S. 31) werden von den Forschungsbeiträgen berücksichtigt.

5.2 Generalisierung der Erkenntnisse

Die Generalisierung der Erkenntnisse zielt auf eine Verallgemeinerung von Aussagen hinsichtlich der OpBI im Kontext der Analyse und Steuerung von Geschäftsprozessen ab. Die Grundlage einer Generalisierbarkeit bilden die Methoden der Forschungsbeiträge, die Tabelle 5 zusammenfasst. Eine komprimierte Methodenbeschreibung ist in Abschnitt 3.3 (S. 42) erfolgt. Detaillierte Auseinandersetzungen und Begründungen hinsichtlich der Methodenauswahl können den jeweiligen Beiträgen entnommen werden.

Tabelle 5. Verwendete Methoden der Forschungsbeiträge

Inhaltlicher Aspekt	Beitrag	Methode	Paradigma	Formali-sie-runggrad
Themenbegründung der OpBI	1	Literatur-Review & Quantitative Querschnittsanalyse	Verhaltenswissenschaftlich	Qualitativ & Quantitativ
Begriffliche Abgrenzung der OpBI	2	Problemzentriertes Interview	Verhaltenswissenschaftlich	Qualitativ
	3	Argumentativ-deduktive Analyse & Quantitative Querschnittsanalyse	Konstruktiv & Verhaltenswissenschaftlich	Qualitativ & Quantitativ
	4	Argumentativ-deduktive Analyse	Verhaltenswissenschaftlich	Qualitativ
Anwendbarkeit der OpBI als Mensch-Aufgabe-Technik-System	5, 6	Laborexperiment	Verhaltenswissenschaftlich	Quantitativ
	7, 8	Literatur-Review	Verhaltenswissenschaftlich	Qualitativ
	9, 10	Argumentativ-deduktive Analyse	Konstruktiv	Qualitativ
	11, 12, 13	Fallstudie	Verhaltenswissenschaftlich	Qualitativ
Gestaltungsempfehlung für OpBI-Systeme	14, 15	Aktionsforschung	Konstruktiv	Qualitativ
	16	Prototyping & Fallstudie	Konstruktiv & Verhaltenswissenschaftlich	Qualitativ

Die Möglichkeiten einer Erkenntnisgeneralisierung werden nachfolgend vor dem Hintergrund der in Tabelle 5 dargestellten Methoden diskutiert. Die logische Klammer für die Überprüfung einer Generalisierbarkeit bilden die inhaltlichen Aspekte des Gesamtbeitrags der Forschungsarbeit (vgl. Abschnitt 2.2, S. 31).

- Die Themenbegründung der OpBI (siehe Beitrag 1) beruht methodisch auf einer Analyse von 1057 Literaturbeiträgen, die anhand von qualitativen Merkmalen operativen oder strategischen Aufgabengebieten zugeordnet wurden. In diesen Kategorien sind quantitative Querschnittsanalysen nach funktionalen und inhaltlichen Gesichtspunkten erfolgt. Die Themenbegründung der OpBI basiert auf einer explizierten Literaturauswahl mit einem selektiven Umfang (vgl. Fettke 2006). Die Zielgruppe der Literaturanalyse sind Praktiker und Forscher, die auf BI spezialisiert sind. Es wurden Publikationen berücksichtigt, die die Kriterien eines weiten BI-Verständnisses (vgl. Gluchowski et al. 2008) erfüllen konnten. In diesem Zusammenhang ist auf die Definition von Hugh Watson zu verweisen, der eine Sammlung, Verarbeitung und Analyse von Daten zum Zweck der Entscheidungsunterstützung betont (Watson 2009).
  - o Die qualitative Kategorisierung der Forschungsbeiträge ist durch eine zweiköpfige Forschergruppe erfolgt. Ausschlaggebend dafür waren Informationsbedürfnisse für strategische und operative Managementaufgaben, die aus der Literatur abgeleitet werden konnten. Eine Generalisierbarkeit dieser Einordnung ist nicht in vollem Umfang gegeben. Die Anforderungen an eine intersubjektive Überprüfbarkeit können jedoch erfüllt werden.
  - o Die quantitative Betrachtung in den beiden Kategorien (strategisch/ opera-tiv) erfolgt zunächst nach Branchen und nach funktionalen Gesichtspunkten. Anhand von deskriptiven Statistiken werden die Kategorien anteilsmäßig gegenübergestellt und chronologisch über einen Zeitraum von 1958 bis 2013 dargestellt. Die anschließende Inhaltsanalyse der untersuchten Beiträge basiert auf Algorithmen des Text Mining. Im Rahmen der quantitativen Betrachtung ist eine Erkenntnisgeneralisierung unter Berücksichtigung des weiten BI-Verständnisses möglich. Es ist zu beachten, dass nur Beiträge untersucht wurden, die vor dem 31.03.2013 publiziert wurden.
- Die Begriffsklassifikation der OpBI bezieht sich auf die Methoden des problemzentrierten Interviews, der argumentativ deduktiven Analyse und der quantitativen Querschnittsanalyse.
  - o In einem ersten Schritt ist eine qualitative Auswertung von 14 Expertengesprächen erfolgt. In diesem Stadium lag der Untersuchungsfokus auf einer Exploration von Kernaspekten, Treibern, potentiellen Anwendungsfeldern und möglichen Imple-

mentierungsproblemen (siehe Beitrag 2). Dies bildet den Ausgangspunkt und spannt die Betrachtungsperspektiven für die Begriffsklassifikation auf. Eine Generalisierung dieser Erkenntnisse kann einer kritischen Überprüfung jedoch aufgrund der geringen Fallzahl nicht standhalten.

o Die explorierten Kernaspekte der OpBI werden in der weiteren Betrachtung einer argumentativ-deduktiven Analyse unterzogen, um einen theoretischen Bezugsrahmen für die Integrationsaspekte einer OpBI zu konstruieren (siehe Beitrag 3). Eine empirische Überprüfung der theoretischen Überlegungen erfolgte im Rahmen einer quantitativen Querschnittsanalyse von 109 prozessorientierten Unternehmen. Die Ergebnisse dieser Untersuchung unterstützen eine Generalisierung im Rahmen der Begriffsklassifikation von OpBI.

o Eine zusätzliche Absicherung erfährt die Generalisierbarkeit der Begriffsklassifikation durch eine argumentativ-deduktive Analyse (siehe Beitrag 4). Es erfolgt eine weiterführende Auseinandersetzung mit dem Einsatz von OpBI in Produktionsumgebungen. Diese konnten im Rahmen der Expertengespräche von Beitrag 2 als ein potentielles Anwendungsgebiet der OpBI identifiziert werden. Beitrag 4 trifft auf dieser Grundlage deduktionsgeleitete Aussagen hinsichtlich des Status Quo der OpBI in Produktionsumgebungen und der Einordnung der OpBI in die Industrie 4.0. Die Erkenntnisse sind genereller Natur und können auf spezifische Einzelfälle übertragen werden. Derartige Einzelfälle betreffen eine Anwendung von OpBI im Produktionsumfeld, die im weiteren Forschungsverlauf Gegenstand der Untersuchungen ist.

• Die Anwendbarkeit der OpBI als Mensch-Aufgabe-Technik-System wird mithilfe der Methoden Laborexperiment, Literatur-Review, argumentativ-deduktive Analyse und Fallstudie untersucht. Die Untersuchung der OpBI aus Anwendungssicht ist in Bezug auf die angewendeten Methoden am breitesten in der Forschungsarbeit abgesichert.

o Das Fundament für die Anwendbarkeit der OpBI im Produktions- und Dienstleistungsumfeld wurde durch ein Laborexperiment gelegt (siehe Beitrag 5 und Beitrag 6). Die Ergebnisse dieser Untersuchung betreffen die Forschungsfelder der analytischen Informationssystemgestaltung und der Informationsqualität aus theoretischer Sicht. Die Experimentbedingungen legen den Rahmen für eine Generalisierbarkeit fest. Das Experiment vergleicht den Einfluss transaktionaler, flacher und multidimensionaler Datenmodelle auf die Informationsqualität von analytischen Werkzeugen. Die Teilnehmer waren 93 Studenten ohne

Erfahrung im Umgang mit BI-Analysen. Das User Interface der Experimentumgebung ist herstellerunabhängig und verfügt über typische Funktionen von BI-Werkzeugen.

o   Die Untersuchung der Anwendbarkeit der OpBI im Produktionsumfeld basiert zunächst auf der Methode des Literatur-Reviews. Es liegen zwei explizierte Literaturanalysen vor, denen als Selektionskriterium eine gemeinsame Betrachtung von OpBI und MES zugrunde liegt (siehe Beitrag 7 und Beitrag 8). Es besteht die Möglichkeit einer Erkenntnisgeneralisierung zum 31.12.2010 im Bereich der Forschungsgebiete MES und BI. Aufbauend auf diesen Erkenntnissen wird unter Verwendung der argumentativ-deduktiven Analyse eine Integrationsplattform für OpBI- und MES-Funktionalitäten konzipiert (siehe Beitrag 9 und Beitrag 10). Dabei steht die Vorteilhaftigkeit einer modularen Systemgestaltung mithilfe von Web Services im Mittelpunkt der Betrachtung. Die Erkenntnisse sind im Zusammenhang einer produktionsspezifischen Entscheidungsunterstützung generalisierbar. Dies ist jedoch auf Überlegungen im Rahmen der Bereitstellung einer technischen Informationsinfrastruktur begrenzt. Die Anwendbarkeit der OpBI im Produktionsumfeld wird abschließend durch Fallstudien betrachtet. Die Untersuchungen fokussieren auf die Unterstützung fallspezifischer Flexibilitätsanforderungen durch OpBI in drei verschiedenen Industrieunternehmen (siehe Beitrag 11 und Beitrag 12). Eine Erkenntnisgeneralisierung anhand von Fallstudien ist dabei mit Schwierigkeiten verbunden. Nach Yin (2009) erlaubt die vorliegende Fallanzahl von drei Fällen jedoch die Vorhersage ähnlicher Ergebnisse:

o   Die Anwendbarkeit der OpBI im Dienstleistungsumfeld wird im Rahmen der kundenspezifischen Leistungserbringung einer Versicherungsagentur dargestellt (siehe Beitrag 13). In diesem Zusammenhang erfolgt die Untersuchung durch eine Einzelfallstudie, die eine typische und weitverbreitete Art der Dienstleistung betrachtet. Es sind zwei verschiedene Analyseszenarien einer Versicherungsagentur (Schadenfallbearbeitung und Neukundenakquise) in die Untersuchung eingebettet. Eine Generalisierung ist im Vergleich zu den Fallstudien im Produktionsumfeld im vorliegenden Fall noch schwieriger. Einzelfallstudien mit typisierendem Charakter haben nur informative Aussagekraft (Yin 2009).

•   Die Gestaltungsempfehlungen für OpBI-Systeme basieren auf einer Aktionsforschung und einem fallstudienbasierten Prototyp.

○ Zunächst wird ein fachliches Modellierungskonzept entwickelt und evaluiert. Es steht eine Verknüpfung von Geschäftsmodellen und Geschäftsprozessen im Vordergrund der Betrachtung, um Datenmodelle für OpBI-Systeme zu modellieren. Der Untersuchung liegt die Methode der Aktionsforschung zugrunde, die von einer Zusammenarbeit von Forschern und Praktikern gekennzeichnet ist. In drei aufeinanderfolgenden Forschungszyklen werden vier verschiedene Geschäftsszenarien betrachtet. Eine Erkenntnisgeneralisierung ist nur sehr eingeschränkt möglich. Die verschiedenen Szenarien erlauben lediglich die Identifikation von Ähnlichkeiten zwischen den Forschungsergebnissen. Dabei sind jedoch immer Einzelfallbedingungen zu beachten. Durch die fortwährende Kommunikation von Forschern und Praktikern im Verlauf der Aktionsforschung ist jedoch eine intersubjektive Überprüfbarkeit der Forschungsergebnisse gewährleistet.

○ Die abschließende Untersuchung zur tatsächlichen Implementierung von OpBI-Systemen erfolgt aus methodischer Sicht durch einen fallstudienbasierten Prototyp. Die Prototypgestaltung resultiert aus der Anwendung einer Design-Science-Systematik. Es wird zunächst ein Framework für eine Analyse und Steuerung von Produktionsprozessen konzipiert. Zu Evaluationszwecken erfolgt eine fallstudienbasierte Umsetzung der Konzeption mithilfe von BI-spezifischen Methoden und CASE-Werkzeugen. Das Framework erfüllt die Voraussetzungen für eine Wiederholbarkeit in verschiedenen Anwendungsszenarien. Es beschreibt herstellerunabhängig die notwendigen Tätigkeiten für eine automatisierte Integration und Analyse von Produktionsdaten. Die Implementierung ist jedoch immer an die Bedingungen eines Einzelfalls gebunden, sodass eine Generalisierbarkeit nicht vorliegt.

Die Diskussion zeigt, dass eine Abhängigkeit zwischen der Erkenntnisgeneralisierung und der jeweiligen Methodik der Forschungsbeiträge besteht. In diesem Zusammenhang ist die Generalisierbarkeit der Erkenntnisse im Rahmen der Forschungsarbeit unterschiedlich stark ausgeprägt. In Tabelle 6 erfolgt vor diesem Hintergrund eine überblicksartige Zusammenfassung.

Tabelle 6. Zusammenfassung der Erkenntnisgeneralisierung

Inhaltlicher Aspekt	Beitrag	Methode	Kernergebnis → Generalisierbarkeit
Themenbegründung der OpBI	1	Literatur-Review & Quantitative Querschnittsanalyse	Literaturüberblick zu Forschungsbeiträgen, die operative und strategische BI-Aufgabengebiete diskutieren → generalisierbar im Themengebiet der BI
Begriffliche Abgrenzung der OpBI	2	Problemzentriertes Interview	Praxisgeleiteter Überblick zu Kernaspekten, Treibern, potentiellen Anwendungsfeldern, und Umsetzungsproblemen der OpBI → nicht generalisierbar im Themengebiet der BI; explorative Erkenntnis
	3	Argumentativ-deduktive Analyse & Quantitative Querschnittsanalyse	Kausale Determinanten für eine integrierte Informationsverarbeitung im Rahmen der Analyse und Steuerung von Geschäftsprozessen → generalisierbar hinsichtlich der Kernaspekte der OpBI
	4	Argumentativ-deduktive Analyse	Positionsbestimmung von OpBI für eine produktionsspezifische Entscheidungsunterstützung im Kontext des Entwicklungsstands von IT-Systemen in Produktionsumgebungen und Industrie 4.0 → generalisierbar hinsichtlich der Anwendung von OpBI im Produktionsumfeld
Anwendbarkeit der OpBI als Mensch-Aufgabe-Technik-System	5, 6	Laborexperiment	Nützlichkeit multidimensionaler Datenmodelle zur Absicherung qualitativ hochwertiger Analyseergebnisse und Entscheidungen von Anwendern, die nicht mit BI-Werkzeugen vertraut sind → generalisierbar im Rahmen der Experimentbedingungen
	7, 8	Literatur-Review	Ergänzungspotential von MES und OpBI im Kontext einer produktionsspezifischen Entscheidungsunterstützung → generalisierbar im Rahmen einer gemeinsamen Betrachtung von MES und OpBI
	9, 10	Argumentativ-deduktive Analyse	Konzeption einer Integrationsplattform zur Bereitstellung von MES- und OpBI-Funktionalitäten → generalisierbar im Rahmen der Bereitstellung einer technischen Informationsinfrastruktur
	11, 12, 13	Fallstudie	Demonstration der Vorteilhaftigkeit und der Anwendbarkeit von OpBI im Produktions- und Dienstleistungsumfeld → nicht generalisierbar im Rahmen der Anwendbarkeit; vergleichende oder informative Erkenntnis

Inhaltlicher Aspekt	Beitrag	Methode	Kernergebnis → Generalisierbarkeit
Gestaltungsempfehlung für OpBI-Systeme	14, 15	Aktionsforschung	Entwicklung und Evaluation einer fachlichen Konzeption zur Verknüpfung von OpBI-Datenmodellen mit prozessorientierten Geschäftsmodellen → nicht generalisierbar im Rahmen der Gestaltung; vergleichende Erkenntnis
	16	Prototyping & Fallstudie	Entwicklung und Evaluation eines Frameworks zur Analyse und Steuerung von Produktionsprozessen → nicht generalisierbar im Rahmen der Gestaltung; einzelfallbasierte Erkenntnis

Aus Tabelle 6 wird ersichtlich, dass für die Themenbegründung und für die Begriffsklassifikation der OpBI generalisierbare Erkenntnisse vorliegen. Im Rahmen der Anwendbarkeitsuntersuchung von OpBI als Mensch-Aufgabe-Technik-System wechselt der Fokus von einer bedingten Generalisierbarkeit hin zu einzelfallabhängigen Ergebnissen. Die abschließenden Gestaltungsempfehlungen für OpBI-Systeme basieren auf wiederholbaren Konzeptionen, die an den Bedingungen von konkreten Anwendungsszenarien auszurichten sind. Demzufolge bauen die Erkenntnisse der Arbeit auf einem generalisierbaren Fundament im Kontext eines weiten BI-Verständnisses auf. Dieses allgemeingültige Wissen ist bei der Betrachtung einzelner Anwendungen und der Gestaltung von OpBI-Systemen fallspezifisch zu konfigurieren. Der Trend von einer Generalisierbarkeit hin zu einer Anwendungsorientierung der OpBI im Kontext der Analyse und Steuerung von Geschäftsprozessen wird abschließend in Abbildung 12 grafisch dargestellt.

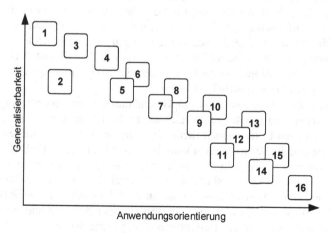

Abbildung 12. Generalisierbarkeit der Forschungsbeiträge

5.3 Diskussion der Zielerreichung

Die Diskussion der Zielerreichung klärt die Bedeutung der erreichten Forschungsergebnisse in Bezug auf die Forschungsziele der Arbeit (siehe Abschnitt 3.2, S.
40). Hinsichtlich des Erkenntnisziels ist zunächst zu beurteilen, inwieweit ein IS-
spezifisches Verständnis von OpBI im Kontext der Analyse und Steuerung von
Geschäftsprozessen geschaffen werden konnte. Im Gang der Arbeit wird dies
durch die Themenbegründung, die begriffliche Abgrenzung und die Anwendbarkeitsuntersuchung von OpBI als Mensch-Aufgabe-Technik-System adressiert. Die
Erkenntnisgewinnung erfolgte durch 13 Forschungsbeiträge, sodass die analytische Zielerreichung auf breiter Basis durch publikationsrelevante Inhalte abgesichert ist.

Im Rahmen der Verständnisproblematik konnte die Notwendigkeit einer Betrachtung nachgewiesen und eine begriffliche Klarheit von OpBI im Kontext der
Analyse und Steuerung von Geschäftsprozessen geschaffen werden. Die Erkenntnisse tragen aufgrund der hohen Generalisierbarkeit zu einem Sprachkonsens hinsichtlich OpBI bei. Dieser erlaubt eine Abgrenzung zu den Themen der BPI und
des BPM sowie zu Ansätzen einer produktionsspezifischen Entscheidungsunterstützung. Darauf aufbauend adressiert die erkenntniszielgeleitete Untersuchung
eine Anwendbarkeit der OpBI als Mensch-Aufgabe-Technik-System. Im Hinblick
auf die Gestaltungsbereiche eines Informationssystems zeigt sich, dass OpBI sowohl im Dienstleistungsbereich als auch im Produktionsumfeld angewendet werden kann. Die Anwendbarkeit ist in diesem Zusammenhang jedoch an Bedingungen gekoppelt, die durch das Zusammenwirken von Mensch und IT sowie durch
das Aufgabengebiet einer OpBI determiniert sind:

- Die Untersuchung der Gestaltungsbereiche Mensch und IT im Kontext
  der OpBI ist durch einen organisatorischen und technischen Wandel im
  BI-Umfeld motiviert. Aufgrund der damit einhergehenden Erweiterung
  des Aufgabenspektrums von BI liegt der Betrachtungsfokus auf der Be-
  dienbarkeit von analytischen Werkzeugen für Endanwender auf Anfän-
  gerniveau. Es wird nachgewiesen, dass ein Zugriff von Analysten auf
  multidimensional modellierte Daten die Informationsqualität von Ad-
  hoc-Analysen positiv beeinflusst.

- Die Aufgabengebiete einer OpBI sind durch einen Bedarf an organisatorischer Flexibilität gekennzeichnet. In die Leistungserbringung der betrachteten Unternehmen fließen Informationen aus verschiedenen Quellen ein, die bedarfsgerecht kombiniert werden müssen. OpBI-Funktionalitäten lassen sich in diesem Zusammenhang nur anwenden, sofern IT-
  Systeme vorhanden sind, die auf täglicher Basis operative Daten erzeu-
  gen. Unter diesen Voraussetzungen wird die Fähigkeit von OpBI zur Integration von verschiedenen Informationsperspektiven und zur Automation einer operativen Berichterzeugung nachgewiesen.

Das im Rahmen des Sprachkonsenses geschaffene Wissen spannt gemeinsam mit den dargestellten Kriterien zur Anwendbarkeit der OpBI als Mensch-Aufgabe-Technik-System die Verständnisdimensionen im Rahmen des Erkenntnisziels auf. Es zeigt sich, dass die Anwendung der OpBI an den Erfordernissen von Realweltprozessen auszurichten ist. Dabei ist eine Berücksichtigung von Endanwenderfähigkeiten und Aufgabenspezifika sicherzustellen.

Aufbauend auf den erkenntniszielbezogenen Ergebnissen wird im Folgenden die aktionale Zielerreichung der Arbeit bewertet. Dies erfolgt durch eine Beurteilung von IS-spezifischen Gestaltungsperspektiven für eine OpBI-getriebene Analyse und Steuerung von Geschäftsprozessen, die im Forschungsverlauf entstanden sind. In diesem Zusammenhang hat sich der Gang der Arbeit mit der Modellierung (siehe 4.4.1, S. 213) und der IT-technischen Umsetzung (siehe 4.4.2, S. 232) von analytischen Anwendungssystemen für OpBI auseinandergesetzt. Dies wurde anhand von drei Forschungsbeiträgen dokumentiert. Gestaltungsempfehlungen im Rahmen der OpBI sind im Rahmen der vorliegenden Forschungsarbeit immer vor dem Hintergrund spezifischer Anwendungsgebiete zu betrachten. Die aktionalen Erkenntnisse erlauben demzufolge keine generalisierbare Auseinandersetzung mit der Gestaltung von OpBI-Systemen, sondern fokussieren auf die Konstruktion einer Modellierungskonzeption und eines Implementierungsframeworks. Beide Artefakte wurden jedoch in praktischen Anwendungsszenarien erfolgreich validiert.

Die Qualität der aktionalen Erkenntnisse ist neuartig im Kontext einer Analyse und Steuerung von Geschäftsprozessen. Es liegt eine klare Abgrenzung der OpBI zu Konzepten des BPM und industriegetriebenen Ansätzen vor, die derartige Artefakte für eine analytische Systemgestaltung nicht bereitstellen. Diese Artefakte sind vor der Herausforderung entstanden, leistungsfähige Geschäftsprozesse zu etablieren, die stetig an sich verändernde Rahmenbedingungen angepasst werden müssen. Die Modellierungskonzeption begegnet dieser Herausforderung mit einer Anforderungsspezifikation, bei der die betriebswirtschaftliche Motivation eines Unternehmens mit der Datenbankmodellierung im Rahmen der OpBI verknüpft wird. Veränderungen aus Perspektive des Geschäftsmodells und der Geschäftsprozesse können bei der modellierungsspezifischen Systemgestaltung Berücksichtigung finden. Hinsichtlich der Umsetzung von OpBI-Systemen sind Aufwand und Nutzen einer Integration von Prozessdaten am Beispiel einer praktischen Anwendung im Produktionsumfeld dokumentiert. Abbildung 13 stellt die Zielerreichung im Forschungsverlauf der Arbeit zusammenfassend dar, um den Umfang und die inhaltlichen Ausprägungen der Themenbearbeitung nachzuvollziehen. Dabei wird auf die zu Beginn von Kapitel 4 eingeführte Allegorie des Hauses Bezug genommen.

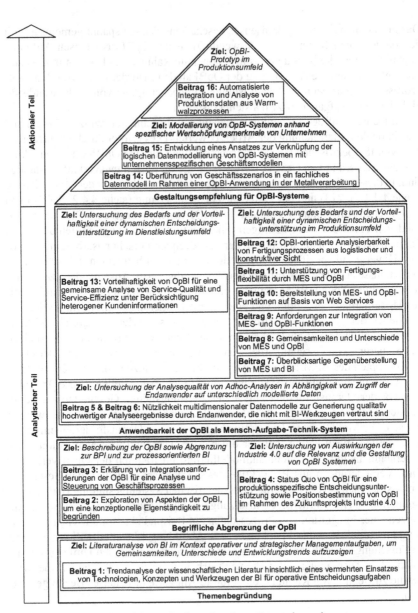

Abbildung 13. Zielerreichung in den einzelnen Bausteinen des Forschungsverlaufs

Das Haus, das den Gang der Arbeit widerspiegelt, charakterisiert mit vier Bauelementen die inhaltlichen Aspekte des Gesamtbeitrags der Forschungsarbeit. Innerhalb dieser Bauelemente sind übergeordnete Zielstellungen als einzelne Bausteine aufgeführt. Darin repräsentieren die Rechtecke den thematischen Fokus der Forschungsbeiträge im Hinblick auf die übergeordnete Zielstellung. Aus Abbildung 13 geht hervor, dass die Forschungsergebnisse sehr stark auf den Einsatz von OpBI im Produktionsumfeld fokussieren. Dies äußert sich initial in der begrifflichen Abgrenzung von OpBI, in der industriespezifische Themen Gegenstand einer eigenständigen Auseinandersetzung sind. Im Rahmen der Anwendbarkeitsuntersuchung wurden im Produktionskontext sowohl konzeptionelle als auch anwendungsspezifische Betrachtungen vorgenommen. Ebenso ist die prototypische Umsetzung vor dem Hintergrund der Fertigung von Warmwalzprodukten entstanden. Damit ist die Zielerreichung im Vergleich zwischen einem Dienstleistungs- und einem Produktionskontext unterschiedlich stark ausgeprägt. Hinsichtlich der Gestaltungsempfehlung ist zu konstatieren, dass die Forschungsbeiträge eine Bereitstellung der Modellierungskonzeption und des CASE-basierten Prototyps in den Vordergrund stellen. Eine langfristige Bewährung sowie eine verhaltenswissenschaftliche Beurteilung dieser Artefakte ist nicht Gegenstand der Forschungsergebnisse.

6 Fazit und Ausblick

OpBI-Systeme unterstützen eine Analyse und Steuerung von Geschäftsprozessen. Dies ist mit einer Nutzung von Technologien, Methoden und Werkzeugen analytischer Informationssysteme im Aufgabengebiet des Geschäftsprozessmanagements verbunden. Unternehmen werden dadurch in die Lage versetzt, Geschäftsprozesse flexibel zu halten und kontinuierlich an veränderte Rahmenbedingungen anzupassen. Vor diesem Hintergrund wurde OpBI in der vorliegenden Arbeit zunächst im Spannungsfeld der Entscheidungsunterstützung und des Geschäftsprozessmanagements dargestellt. Es zeigte sich, dass ein mangelhaftes Verständnis hinsichtlich der begrifflichen Abgrenzung und der anwendungsorientierten Umsetzung von OpBI im Kontext der Analyse und Steuerung von Geschäftsprozessen bestand. Aus diesem Grund wurde im weiteren Verlauf der Arbeit ein Forschungsrahmen aufgestellt, um ein Begriffsverständnis und Gestaltungsperspektiven für OpBI aus IS-spezifischer Sicht zu schaffen. Die Entwicklung der zugehörigen Forschungsergebnisse erfolgte durch die Publikation von erkenntnisrelevanten Inhalten. Darauf verweisend wurde in der Arbeit der Gesamtzusammenhang der Forschungsergebnisse dokumentiert und diese unter den Aspekten der Vollständigkeit, Generalisierbarkeit und Zielerreichung diskutiert.

Das Resultat der Forschungsarbeit ist eine OpBI-spezifische Wissensbasis für eine IT-basierte Analyse und Steuerung von Geschäftsprozessen. Dieses Wissen kann zweckgebunden für konkrete Datenmodellierungs- und Datenintegrationsvorhaben in praktischen Anwendungsszenarien herangezogen werden. Um zu diesem Resultat zu gelangen erfolgte in der Arbeit eine Präzision des Begriffsverständnisses der OpBI. Dazu wurden eine Themenbegründung, eine Begriffsklassifikation und eine Anwendbarkeitsuntersuchung der OpBI als Mensch-Aufgabe-Technik-System erarbeitet. Die Themenbegründung diente als Einstieg in den Forschungsverlauf. Es hat sich gezeigt, dass die Anwendungsfelder der BI branchenübergreifend im Zeitverlauf immer operativer geworden sind. Die Themenbegründung war ein geeignetes Mittel, um die thematische Unschärfe zu charakterisieren, die mit der Diskussion von BI zum Zweck der operativen Managementunterstützung einherging. Nach der Identifikation dieses Mangels an konzeptioneller Klarheit konnte im Rahmen der Begriffsklassifikation ein allgemeingültiges Verständnis der OpBI im Kontext der Analyse und Steuerung von Geschäftsprozessen geschaffen werden. Dies umfasst eine Abgrenzung zu den Konzepten der BPI und der prozessorientierten BI, die ebenso wie OpBI eine Nutzung von analytischen Informationssystemen im Geschäftsprozessmanagement adressieren. Im Zuge dieser Untersuchungen kristallisierte sich heraus, dass Produktionsumgebungen ein weitreichendes Potential für praxisbezogene Anwendungen der OpBI bieten. Damit ging jedoch erneut die Notwendigkeit einer begrifflichen Abgrenzung einher, weil auch aus einer industriegetriebenen Perspektive IT-Systeme mit entscheidungsunterstützenden Funktionen diskutiert werden. Durch eine Positionsbestimmung der OpBI im Rahmen der Industrie 4.0 konnte dieser Klärungsbedarf für aktuelle und zukünftige industriegetriebene Systementwürfe adressiert werden.

Die Themenbegründung und die Begriffsklassifikation bilden das theoretische Fundament für Anwendungen einer OpBI im Kontext der Analyse und Steuerung von Geschäftsprozessen. Die Anwendbarkeitsuntersuchung hat sich als eine sinnvolle Vorgehensweise erwiesen, um ein Bild über spätere OpBI-Anwendungsfälle zu bekommen. Es konnten neben praxisnahen Erkenntnissen zum Aufgabengebiet der OpBI auch Aussagen zum Entscheidungsverhalten zukünftiger Endanwender getroffen werden. Dabei ist die Anwendbarkeitsuntersuchung nicht als eigenständige Untersuchung aufzufassen, sondern sie bildet vielmehr das Bindeglied zwischen der theoretischen und der gestaltungsorientierten Auseinandersetzung mit einer OpBI im Kontext der Analyse und Steuerung von Geschäftsprozessen. Anwendungsbezogene Kenntnisse sind von Bedeutung, um die vielfältigen Möglichkeiten der analytischen Systemgestaltung auf konkrete Einzelfälle zu übertragen.

Für eine Bestimmung der Anforderungen an ein OpBI-System hat es sich als vorteilhaft herausgestellt, im jeweiligen Anwendungsfall die Wertschöpfungsprozesse zu beschreiben und die Informationsflüsse darzustellen. Insbesondere im Kontext der modellierungsorientierten Gestaltung ist die Wichtigkeit einer fachkonzeptionellen Auseinandersetzung mit OpBI-Systemen hervorgetreten. Durch eine Ausrichtung der Systemmodellierung an den operativen Geschäftsanforderungen eines Unternehmens lässt sich der Einsatz von analyseorientierten Technologien unter den Gesichtspunkten der Effizienz und der Effektivität optimieren. Die CASE-basierte Umsetzung der OpBI hat gezeigt, dass die Integration und die Transformation von Prozessdaten durch etablierte Technologien und Werkzeuge aus dem Umfeld der BI leistbar ist. Der Mehrwert dieser Herangehensweise besteht in der Automatisierung einer Integration und Analyse von Produktionsdaten zum Zweck einer multidimensionalen Entscheidungsunterstützung. Es ist hervorzuheben, dass die Implementierung der Analysewerkzeuge im Gegensatz zu anderen Untersuchungen vor dem Hintergrund realer Produktionsdaten erfolgt ist. Trotz der Einzelfallabhängigkeit wird damit die Praxistauglichkeit des Implementierungsansatzes für eine OpBI-getriebene Analyse und Steuerung von Produktionsprozessen als bestätigt angesehen. Aufgrund der allgemeingültigen Darstellung des Frameworks ist ebenso eine Übertragbarkeit auf andere Anwendungsszenarien möglich. Die vorgestellte Lösung stellt dabei einen Werkzeugkasten für spezifische Fragestellungen im Kontext einer Analyse und Steuerung von Geschäftsprozessen dar. Aus den Perspektiven der Datenmodellierung und der Datenintegration werden schwerpunktbezogene Analysen betrachtet, die die Grundlage für operative Eingriffe in das Prozessgeschehen bilden. Vor dem Hintergrund der Validität ist jedoch immer eine Verifizierung der Analyseergebnisse anzustreben, um fehlerhafte Entscheidungen zu vermeiden. Eine vollständige Automatisierung der Entscheidungsfindung im Sinne eines menschunabhängigen Regelkreises ist nicht erstrebenswert. Das Zusammenwirken von Mensch und IT repräsentiert den grundlegenden Charakter für die Anwendbarkeitsuntersuchung und die Gestaltung einer OpBI im Kontext der Analyse und Steuerung von Geschäftsprozessen.

Abschließend ist festzuhalten, dass die Integration von Daten zum Zweck der Analyse und Steuerung von Geschäftsprozessen mit dieser Arbeit thematisch nicht abgeschlossen werden kann. Hinsichtlich der Weiterentwicklung der vorgestellten Modellierungskonzeption und des Implementierungsframeworks sind weitere Anwendungsfälle zur Erprobung erstrebenswert. In diesem Zusammenhang bieten sich z. B. Untersuchungen für eine Einbettung der schwerpunktbezogenen Analysen in ein Gesamtsystem an. Dies betrifft neben technischen Aspekten ebenso organisatorische Handlungsempfehlungen für eine ganzheitliche Entscheidungsunterstützung. In der Literatur wird insbesondere in der Diskussion zum Thema Industrie 4.0 darauf hingewiesen, dass in den kommenden Jahren technische und organisatorische Veränderungen in der IT-Landschaft der Unternehmen zu erwarten sind. Dies betrifft neben dem produzierenden Gewerbe ebenso vor- und nachgelagerte Dienstleistungen. In diesem Spannungsfeld verbleibt ein vielversprechendes Potential für die Weiterentwicklung von entscheidungsunterstützenden Systementwürfen im Kontext der Analyse und Steuerung von Geschäftsprozessen wie OpBI.

LITERATURVERZEICHNIS[17]

Allweyer, T.: Geschäftsprozessmanagement – Strategie, Entwurf, Implementierung, Controlling, 5. Nachdruck, Herdecke, Bochum, W3L, 2012.

Arnett, S.: Operational BI – Where the Business and Customer Meet, in Business Intelligence Journal, 14, 2009, 8–12.

BARC: BI Survey 2014 – Unternehmen setzen auf Self-Service Business Intelligence, Oktober 2014, abrufbar unter: http://barc.de/news/bi-survey-2014-unternehmen-setzen-auf-self-service-business-intelligence, letzter Zugriff am 08.06.2015.

Baskerville, R.L.: Investigating Information Systems with Action Research, in: Communications of AIS, 2, 1999, 1–32.

Becker, J.; Kahn, D.: Der Prozess im Fokus, in: Becker, J.; Kugeler, M.; Rosemann, M. (Hrsg.): Prozessmanagement – Ein Leitfaden zur prozessorientierten Organisationsgestaltung, 5. Auflage, Berlin u. a., Springer, 2005, 3–16.

Becker, J.; Holter, R.; Knackstedt, R.; Niehaves, B.: Forschungsmethodische Positionierung in der Wirtschaftsinformatik – epistemologische, ontologische und linguistische Leitfragen, in: Becker, J.; Grob, H.L.; Klein, S.; Kuchen, H.; Müller-Funk, U.; Vossen, G. (Hrsg.): Arbeitsberichte des Instituts für Wirtschaftsinformatik, Münster, 2003, 1–39.

Blasini, J.: Critical Success Factors Of Process Performance Management Systems: Results Of An Empirical Research, in: 21st European Conference on Information Systems, Utrecht, 2013, paper 158, 1–12.

Blickle, T.; Hess, H.; Klueckmann, J.; Lees, M.; Williams, B.: Process Intelligence for Dummies, Indianapolis, Wiley, 2010.

Brunner, F.J.: Japanische Erfolgskonzepte: KAIZEN, KVP, Lean Production Management, Total Productive Maintenance Shopfloor Management, Toyota Production System, GD³ - Lean Development, 3. Auflage, München, Wien, Hanser, 2014.

Bucher, T.; Dinter, B.: Anwendungsfälle der Nutzung analytischer Informationen im operativen Kontext, in: Bichler, M.; Hess, T.; Krcmar, H.; Lechner, U.; Matthes, F.; Picot, A.; Speitkamp, B.; Wolf, P. (Hrsg.): Multikonferenz Wirtschaftsinformatik 2008, Berlin, GITO, 2008, 167–179.

Bucher T.; Winter R.: Project types of business process management, in: Business Process Management Journal, 15, 2009, 548–568.

Bucher, T.; Gericke, A.; Sigg, S.: Process-centric business intelligence, in: Business Process Management Journal, 15, 2009, 408–429.

Casati, F.; Dayal, U.; Sayal, M.; Shan, M.-C.: Business Process Intelligence, Palo Alto, HP Laboratories, 2002.

Castellanos, M.; Alves de Medeiros A.K.; Mendling, J.; Weber, B.; Weijters, A.J.M.M.: Business Process Intelligence, in: Cardoso, J.; van der Aalst, W. (Hrsg.): Handbook of research on business process modeling, Hershey, London, IGI Global, 2009, 456–480.

Chamoni, P.; Gluchowski, P.: Analytische Informationssysteme – Einordnung und Überblick, in: Chamoni, P.; Gluchowski, P. (Hrsg.): Analytische Informationssysteme – Business Intelligence-Technologien und -Anwendungen, 4. Auflage, Heidelberg u. a., Springer, 2010, 3–36.

---

17 Das Literaturverzeichnis umfasst nur Quellen, die zusätzlich zu den eingebetteten Forschungsbeiträgen im Text genutzt werden. Die Beiträge selbst verfügen über eigene Literaturverzeichnisse.

Chien, C.-F.; Chen, Y.-J.; Peng, J.-T.: Manufacturing intelligence for semiconductor demand forecast based on technology diffusion and product life cycle, in: International Journal of Production Economics, 128, 2010, 496–509.

Codd E.F.; Codd S.B.; Salley C.T.: Providing OLAP to User-Analysts: An IT Mandate, Ann Arbor, Codd & Associates, 1993.

Cooley, J.; Petrusich, J.: Delivering optimal real-time manufacturing intelligence, in: Proceedings of PICMET '13: Technology Management in the IT-Driven Services, San Jose, 2013, 1658–1668.

Cooper, H.: Synthesizing Research: A Guide for Literature Reviews, 3. Auflage, Thousand Oaks, SAGE, 1998.

Cunningham, D.: Aligning Business Intelligence with Business Processes, in: What Works, 20, 2005, 50–51.

Davenport, T.H.: Process innovation – reengineering work through information technol Harvard Business School Press, 1993.

Davenport, T.H.; Beers, M.C.: Managing Information about Processes, in: Journal of Management Information Systems, 12, 1995, 57–80.

Davis, J.; Edgar, T.; Porter, J.; Bernaden, J.; Sarlie, M.: Smart manufacturing, manufacturing intelligence and demand-dynamic performance, in: Computers and Chemical Engineering, 47, 2012, 145–156.

Davis, J.; Imhoff, C.; White, C.: Operational Business Intelligence: The State of the Art, Boulder, Beye NETWORK Research, 2009.

Davis, J.R.: Right-Time Business Intelligence: Optimizing the Business Decision Cycle, Boulder, Beye NETWORK Research, 2006.

Davis, J.R.: Using Operational Business Intelligence for Intra-Day Analysis and Decision Making, Boulder, Beye NETWORK Research, 2007.

Davis, J.R.; Imhoff, C.; White, C: Operational Business Intelligence: The State of the Art, Boulder, Beye NETWORK Research, 2009.

DIN EN ISO 9000: Qualitätsmanagementsysteme – Grundlagen und Begriffe, Berlin, DIN Deutsches Institut für Normung e.V., 2005.

Dumas, M.; Rosa, M.L.; Mendling, J.; Reijers, H.: Fundamentals of Business Process Management, Heidelberg u. a., Springer, 2013.

Eckerson, W.W.: Best Practices in Operational BI: Converging Analytical and Operational Processes, Renton, TDWI, 2007.

Eschweiler, M.; Evanschitzky, H.; Woistschläger, D.: Laborexperiment. in: Baumgarth, C.; Eisend, M.; Evanschitzky, H. (Hrsg.): Empirische Mastertechniken der Marketing- und Managementforschung, Wiesbaden, Gabler, 2009, 361–388.

Felden, C.: Personalisierung der Informationsversorgung in Unternehmen, Wiesbaden, DUV, 2006.

Felden, C.; Chamoni P.; Linden, M.: From Process Execution towards a Business Process Intelligence, in: 13th International Conference on Business Information Systems, Berlin, 2010, 195–206.

Ferguson, M.: Getting Started With Operational BI, 2008, abrufbar unter: http://www.beyenetwork.be/print/8399, letzter Zugriff am 05.06.2015.

Fettke, P.: State-of-the-Art des State-of-the-art – Eine Untersuchung der Forschungsmethode 'Review' innerhalb der Wirtschaftsinformatik, in: Wirtschaftsinformatik, 4, 2006, 257–266.

Frank, U.: Ein Vorschlag zur Konfiguration von Forschungsmethoden in der Wirtschaftsinformatik, in: Lehner, F.; Zelewski, S. (Hrsg.): Wissenschaftstheoretische Fundierung und wissenschaftliche Orientierung der Wirtschaftsinformatik, Berlin, GITO, 2007, 155–184.

Gaitanidis, M.; Scholz, R.; Vrohlings, A.; Raster, M.: Prozeßmanagement – Konzepte, Umsetzungen und Erfahrungen des Reengineering, München, Wien, Hanser, 1994.

Gluchowski, P.; Gabriel, R.; Dittmar, C.: Management Support Systeme und Business Intelligence – Computergestützte Informationssysteme für Fach- und Führungskräfte, 2. Auflage, Berlin, Heidelberg, Springer, 2008.

Gluchowski, P.; Kemper, H.-G.; Seufert, A.: Innovative Prozesssteuerung, in: BI-Spektrum, 4, 2009, 8–12.

Grigori, D.; Casati, F.; Castellanos, M.; Dayal, U.M.; Sayal, M.; Shan, M.-C.: Business Process Intelligence, in: Computers in Industry, 53, 2004, 321–343.

Grothe, M.; Gentsch, T.: Business Intelligence: Aus Informationen Wettbewerbsvorteile gewinnen, München, Addison-Wesley, 2000.

Hackathorn, R.: The BI Watch: Real-Time to Real-Value, in: DM Review, 14, 2004, 1–4.

Hall, C.: Business Process Intelligence, in: Business Process Trends, 2, 2004, 1–11.

Hammer, M.: What is Business Process Management?, in: vom Brocke, J.; Rosemann, M. (Hrsg.): Handbook on Business Process Management 1 – Introduction, Methods, and Information Systems, 2. Auflage, Heidelberg u. a., 2015, 3–16.

Hammer, M.; Champy, J.: Business Reengineering – Die Radikalkur für das Unternehmen, 6. Auflage, Frankfurt/Main, New York, Campus, 1996.

Han, J.; Kamber, M.: Data Mining: Concepts and Techniques, 3. Auflage, Waltham, Morgan Kaufmann, 2012.

Hansen, H.R; Neumann, G.: Wirtschaftsinformatik 1 – Grundlagen und Anwendungen, 10. Auflage, Stuttgart, Lucius & Lucius, 2009.

Harmon P.: Business Process Change: A Business Process Management Guide for Managers and Process Professionals, 3. Auflage, Boston, Morgan Kaufmann, 2014.

Heinrich, L.J.; Heinzl, A.; Riedl, R.: Wirtschaftsinformatik – Einführung und Grundlegung, 4. überarbeitete und erweiterte Auflage, Berlin u. a., Springer, 2011.

Henschen, D.: 2014 Analytics, BI, and Information Management Survey, InformationWeek Reports, November 2013.

IDS Scheer: Was ist Process Intelligence?, Saarbrücken, 2007.

Imai, M.: Kaizen: Der Schlüssel zum Erfolg der Japaner im Wettbewerb, München, Langen Müller Herbig, 1992.

Inmon, W.H. Building the Data Warehouse, 4. Auflage, Indianapolis, Wiley, 2005.

Jaeger, U.; Reinecke, S.: Das Expertengespräch als zentrale Form einer qualitativen Befragung, in: Baumgarth, C.; Eisend, M.; Evanschitzky, H. (Hrsg.): Empirische Mastertechniken der Marketing- und Managementforschung, Wiesbaden, Gabler, 2009, 29–76.

Jost, W.; Scheer, A.-W.: Geschäftsprozessmanagement: Kernaufgabe einer jeden Unternehmensorganisation, in: Scheer, A.-W.; Jost, W. (Hrsg.): ARIS in der Praxis – Gestaltung, Implementierung und Optimierung von Prozessen, Berlin u. a., Springer, 2002, 33–44.

Kagermann, H.; Wahlster, W.; Helbig, J.: Umsetzungsempfehlungen für das Zukunftsprojekt Industrie 4.0, Frankfurt am Main, acatech, 2013.

Kamlah, W.; Lorenzen, P.: Logische Propädeutik – Vorschule des vernünftigen Redens, 3. Auflage, Stuttgart, Weimar, Metzler, 1996.

Kang, B.; Kim, D.; Kang, S.H.: Periodic performance prediction for realtime business process monitoring, in: Industrial Management and Data Systems, 112, 2012, 4–23.

Kimball, R.; Ross, M.: The Data Warehouse Toolkit: The Complete Guide to Dimensional Modeling, 2. Auflage, New York, Wiley, 2002.

Koch, S.: Einführung in das Management von Geschäftsprozessen – Six Sigma, Kaizen und TQM, Heidelberg u. a., Springer, 2011.

Kornmeier, M.: Wissenschaftstheorie und wissenschaftliches Arbeiten, Heidelberg, Physica-Verlag, 2007.

Kostka, C.; Kostka, S.: Der Kontinuierliche Verbesserungsprozess: Methoden des KVP, 6. Auflage, München, Hanser, 2013.

Kronz, A.: Management von Prozesskennzahlen im Rahmen der ARIS-Methodik, in: Scheer, A.-W.; Jost, W.; Heß, H.; Kronz, A. (Hrsg.): Corporate Performance Management – ARIS in der Praxis, Berlin u. a., Springer, 2005, 31–44.

Kruppke, H.; Bauer, T.: Keine Business Intelligence ohne Process Intelligence, in: Scheer, A.-W.; Jost, W.; Heß, H.; Kronz, A. (Hrsg.): Corporate Performance Management – ARIS in der Praxis, Berlin u. a., Springer, 2005, 77–98.

Kuo, C.-J.; Chien, C.-F.; Chen, J.-D.: Manufacturing Intelligence to Exploit the Value of Production and Tool Data to Reduce Cycle Time, in: IEEE Transactions on Automation Science and Engineering, 8, 2011, 103–111.

Lassmann, W. (Hrsg.): Wirtschaftsinformatik – Nachschlagewerk für Studium und Praxis, Wiesbaden, Gabler, 2006.

Laudon, K.C.; Laudon, J.P.; Schoder, D.: Wirtschaftsinformatik – Eine Einführung, 2. Auflage, München, Pearson, 2010.

Linden, M.; Felden, C.; Chamoni, P.: Dimensions of Business Process Intelligence, in: zur Muehlen, M.; Su, J. (Hrsg.): BPM 2010 Workshops – LNBIP 66, Berlin, Heidelberg, Springer, 2011, 208–213.

Markus, M.L.; Tanis, C.; van Fenema, P.C.: Enterprise resource planning: multisite ERP implementations, in: Communications of the ACM, 43, 2000, 42–46.

Neumann, S.; Probst, C.; Wernsmann, C.: Kontinuierliches Prozessmanagement, in: Becker, J.; Kugeler, M.; Rosemann, M. (Hrsg.): Prozessmanagement – Ein Leitfaden zur prozessorientierten Organisationsgestaltung, 5. Auflage, Berlin u. a., Springer, 2005, 299–329.

Nunamaker, J.F.; Chen, M.; Purdin, T.D.M.: Systems Development in Information Systems Research, in: Journal of Management Information Systems, 7, 1991, 89–106.

Ortner, E.: Konsequenzen einer konstruktivistischen Grundsatzposition für die Forschung in der Wirtschaftsinformatik, in: Schütte, R.; Siedentopf, J.; Zelewski, S. (Hrsg.): Wirtschaftsinformatik und Wissenschaftstheorie – Grundpositionen und Theoriekerne, Arbeitsbericht Nr. 4, Universität Essen, Institut für Produktion und Industrielles Informationsmanagement, 1999, 31–42.

Popper, K.: Three Worlds – The Tanner Lecture on Human Values, in: Michigan Quarterly, 2, 1978, 140–167.

Popper, K: Logik der Forschung, 10. Auflage, Tübingen, Mohr, 1994.

Porter, M.E.: Competitive Advantage: Creating and Sustaining Superior Performance, New York, First Free Press, 1985.

Porter, M.E.; Millar, V.E.: How information gives you competitive advantage, in: Harvard Business Review, 63, 1985, 149–160.

Poser, H.: Wissenschaftstheorie – Eine philosophische Einführung, Stuttgart, Reclam, 2001.

Reijers, H.A.; van Wijk, S.; Mutschler, B.; Leurs, M.: BPM in practice: who is doing what?, in: Business Process Management – Lecture Notes in Computer Science, 6336, 2010, 45–60.

Riege, C.; Saat, J.; Bucher, T.: Systematisierung von Evaluationsmethoden in der gestaltungsorientierten Wirtschaftsinformatik, in: Becker, J.; Krcmar, H.; Niehaves, B. (Hrsg.): Wissenschaftstheorie und gestaltungsorientierte Wirtschaftsinformatik, Dordrecht u. a., Physica, 2009, 69–86.

Russom, P.: Operational Data Warehousing – The integration of Operational Applications and Data Warehouses, Renton, TDWI, 2010.

Russom, P.; Stodder, D.; Halper, F.: Real-Time Data, BI, and Analytics – Accelerating Business to Leverage Customer Relations, Competitiveness, and Insights, Renton, TDWI, 2014.

Scheer, A.-W.; Adam, O.; Erbach, F.: Next Generation Business Process Management, in: Scheer, A.-W.; Jost, W.; Wagner, K. (Hrsg.): Von Prozessmodellen zu lauffähigen Anwendungen – ARIS in der Praxis, Berlin u. a., Springer, 2005, 1–16.

Schnell, R.; Hill, P. B.; Esser, E.: Methoden der empirischen Sozialforschung, 9. aktualisierte Auflage, München, Oldenbourg, 2011.

Schrödl, H.: Business Intelligence mit Microsoft SQL Server 2005 – BI-Projekte erfolgreich umsetzen, München, Wien, Hanser, 2006.

Seidlmeier, H.: Prozessmodellierung mit ARIS® – Eine beispielorientierte Einführung für Studium und Praxis, Braunschweig, Wiesbaden, Vieweg, 2002.

Seiffert, H.: Einführung in die Wissenschaftstheorie 1 – Sprachanalyse - Deduktion - Induktion in den Natur- und Sozialwissenschaften, 12. Auflage, München, Beck, 1996.

Seiffert, H.: Einführung in die Wissenschaftstheorie 4 – Wörterbuch der wissenschaftstheoretischen Terminologie, München, Beck, 1997.

Sen, A.; Sinha, A.P.: A Comparison of Data Warehousing Methodologies, in: Communications of the ACM, 48, 2005, 79–84.

Sesselmann, H.J.; Schmelzer, W.: Geschäftsprozessmanagement in der Praxis – Kunden zufrieden stellen, Produktivität steigern, Wert erhöhen, 6. Auflage, München, Hanser, 2008.

Simon, H.A.: The New Science of Management Decision, New York, Harper and Row, 1960.

Thiel, K.; Meyer, H.; Fuchs, F.: MES - Grundlage der Produktion von morgen – Effektive Wertschöpfung durch die Einführung von Manufacturing Execution Systems, München, Oldenbourg Industrieverlag, 2008.

Töpfer, A.: Six Sigma als Projektmanagement für höhere Kundenzufriedenheit und bessere Unternehmensergebnisse, in: Töpfer, A. (Hrsg.): Six Sigma – Konzeption und Erfolgsbeispiele für praktizierte Null-Fehler-Qualität, 4. Auflage, Berlin u. a., Springer, 2007, 45–99.

Töpfer, A.; Günther, S.: Steigerung des Unternehmenswertes durch Null-Fehler-Qualität als strategisches Ziel: Überblick und Einordnung der Beiträge, in: Töpfer, A. (Hrsg.): Six Sigma – Konzeption und Erfolgsbeispiele für praktizierte Null-Fehler-Qualität, 4. Auflage, Berlin u. a., Springer, 2007. 3–40.

Toutenburg, H.; Knöfel, P.: Six Sigma – Methoden und Statistik für die Praxis, 2. Auflage, Berlin, Heidelberg, Springer, 2009.

van der Aalst, W.M.P.; van Hee K.M.: Workflow Management: Models, Methods, and Systems, Cambridge, MIT Press, 2002.

van der Aalst, W.M.P.: Process Mining: Discovery, Conformance and Enhancement of Business Processes, Berlin, Springer, 2011.

von Humboldt, W.: Über die Verschiedenheit des menschlichen Sprachbaus und ihren Einfluss auf die geistige Entwicklung des Menschengeschlechts, Berlin, 1836.

Vukšić, V.B.; Bach, M.P.; Popovič, A.: Supporting performance management with business process management and business intelligence: A case analysis of integration and orchestration, in: International Journal of Information Management, 33, 2013, 613–619.

Watson, H.J.: Tutorial Business Intelligence - Past, Present, and Future, in: Communications of the Association for Information Systems, 25, 2009, 487–510.

White, C.: Now is the Right Time for Real-Time BI, in: DM Review, 14, 2004, 47–54.

White, C.: The Next Generation of Business Intelligence: Operational BI, in: DM Review, 15, 2005, 34–37.

White, C.: The Next Generation of Business Intelligence: Operational BI, Ashland, BI Research, 2006.

Wilde, T.; Hess, T.: Forschungsmethoden der Wirtschaftsinformatik – Eine empirische Untersuchung, in: Wirtschaftsinformatik, 29, 2007, 280–287.

Yin, R.: Case Study Research Design and Methods, 4. Auflage, London, SAGE, 2009.

Yugma, C.; Blue, J.; Dauzere-Peres, S.; Vialletelle, P.: Integration of Scheduling and Advanced Process Control in Semiconductor Manufacturing: Review and Outlook, in: Journal of Scheduling, 18, 2015, 195–205.

Zairi, M.: Business process management: a boundaryless approach to modern competitiveness, in: Business Process Management Journal, 3, 1997, 64–80.

Zehe, M.; Streit, S.; Haneke, U.: Architektur eines Manufacturing-Intelligence-Systems – Produktionsabläufe stets im Blick, in: BI-Spektrum, 8, 2013, 28–32.